973.4 v.4 89904
Ada

ADAMS
THE WRITINGS OF SAMUEL ADAMS
60.00 SET

Date Due

THE WRITINGS

OF

SAMUEL ADAMS

VOLUME IV.

1778–1802

THE WRITINGS

OF

SAMUEL ADAMS

COLLECTED AND EDITED

BY

HARRY ALONZO CUSHING

VOLUME IV

1778–1802

1968
OCTAGON BOOKS, INC.
New York

Originally published in 1908 by G. P. Putnam's Sons

Reprinted 1968
by special arrangement with G. P. Putnam's Sons

OCTAGON BOOKS, INC.
175 FIFTH AVENUE
NEW YORK, N. Y. 10010

89904

LIBRARY OF CONGRESS CATALOG CARD NUMBER: 68-24196

Printed in U.S.A. by
NOBLE OFFSET PRINTERS, INC.
NEW YORK 3, N. Y.

CONTENTS OF VOLUME IV.

1778.

                                                                            PAGE

To Richard Henry Lee, January 1st   .   .   .   I
    Military Affairs—European Politics—Articles of Confedera-
    tion—Army Supplies.

To ———, January 10th   6
    New Haven Conference—Legislation on Trade—Baron
    Steuben.

To Archibald Campbell, January 14th . . .   9
    Exchange of Prisoners.

To Horatio Gates, January 14th 10
    Introducing Baron Steuben—Captain Olivier.

Vote of Town of Boston, January 21st . . . 11
    Articles of Confederation.

To John Burgoyne, February 6th . . . 12
    Declining a Conference.

To Daniel Roberdeau, February 9th . . . 12
    The Work of Congress.

To Arthur Lee, March 12th 14
    Complaints of French Volunteers.

To Jonathan Trumbull, March 19th . . . 15
    Defence of Hudson River.

To James Lovell, March 27th 16
    Postal Service—Military Academy—Exchange of Prisoners—
    Case of John Amory.

To Francis Lightfoot Lee 19
    Illness—Conditions in Boston—Military Affairs.

To Richard Henry Lee, April 20th . . . 21
    Action of France—Attitude of England.

  PAGE

To Mrs. Adams, May 5th   24
    Journey from Boston.

To the Earl of Carlisle and others   25
    Address of "An American."

To Baron Steuben, June 3rd   39
    Action of Congress.

To John Adams, June 21st   39
    The English Commissioners—Arrivals from France—Arthur
    Lee.

To Mrs. Adams, July 9th   41
    Signing of Articles of Confederation.

To James Warren, July   41
    Cases of Manley and McNeil—Appointment of Naval Officers.

To James Warren, July   45
    Office-holders — The British Commissioners — Arrival of
    French Squadron.

To Samuel Phillips Savage, August 11th . . .   49
    Return of Hancock.

To Peter Thacher, August 11th   50
    The British Commissioners—Activity of Quakers.

To James Warren, September 1st   52
    Cases of Manley and McNeil—Personal Critics—The Rhode
    Island Expedition.

To James Bowdoin, September 3rd   54
    Conduct of John Temple.

To Hannah Adams, September 8th   56
    Illness of Wife.

To John Bradford, September 8th   57
    Conduct of McNeil.

To James Warren, September 12th   58
    Case and Conduct of Manley—The Rhode Island Expedition.

To Samuel Phillips Savage, September 14th . .   61
    The Rhode Island Expedition—Activity of Tories.

To ——, September 21st   63
    Appointment of Auctioneers—Attitude of Manley—Public
    Criticism of French Admiral.

PAGE

To Mrs. Adams, September 28th 65
Death of Friends—Family Affairs.

To William Cooper, September 30th . . . 66
Assistance in Exchange of Son.

To Samuel Phillips Savage, October 6th . . . 67
Extravagance in Boston.

To James Warren, October 11th 68
Conduct of Arthur Lee—Opinion of Silas Deane—Affairs of
Du Coudray—Public Criticisms of Deane.

To James Warren, October 14th 72
Attacks on Arthur Lee—Berkenhout.

To Jonathan Trumbull, October 16th . . . 74
Death of Son.

To Timothy Matlack, October 16th 75
Proposed Manifesto of General Clinton.

To James Warren, October 17th 75
Attitude of Politicians to Tories.

To Mrs. Adams, October 20th 77
Personal Enemies in Boston.

To John Adams, October 25th 79
Military Affairs—Relations with France—The Rhode Island
Expedition—Naval Movements.

To Arthur Lee, October 26th 82
Comments on Correspondence.

To ——, October 26th 83
Falsehoods of Enemies.

To the Public, October 30th 84
Manifesto of the Continental Congress.

To Samuel Phillips Savage, November 1st . . 86
Share of New England in Securing Independence—Personal
Relations.

To James Warren, November 3rd 88
Work of Congress—Foreign Relations—Proposed Resignation.

Thanksgiving Proclamation, November 3rd . . 91
Resolution of Continental Congress.

PAGE

To Samuel Phillips Savage, November 10th . . 92
State of Society and Politics in Boston.

To Jeremiah Powell, December 1st 93
Use of Appropriation—Re-election to Congress.

To Mrs. Adams, December 13th 95
Relations with John Temple—Personal Critics—Deane and
Lee.

To the Council of Massachusetts, December 15th . 98
Enclosing Declaration of French Minister.

To James Bowdoin, December 19th 99
Conduct of John Temple.

To John Winthrop, December 21st 101
Conduct of John Temple.

To Samuel Cooper, December 25th 104
Conduct of John Temple—Deane and Lee—Proposed Resignation.

To Charles Chauncy, December 25th . . . 108
Conduct of John Temple—Gates and Heath.

1779.

To Samuel Cooper, January 3rd 111
Deane and Arthur Lee.

To James Warren, January 6th 113
Silas Deane—William Lee—Arthur Lee.

To Samuel Cooper, January 6th 115
American Representatives in France.

To Samuel Cooper, January 19th 118
Negotiations with France—Diplomatic Appointments.

To Jonathan Trumbull, February 6th . . . 120
Naval Affairs.

To John Winthrop, February 6th 121
Depreciated Currency.

To Samuel Allyne Otis, February 10th . . . 122
Recommending Richard Checkley.

PAGE

To James Warren, February 12th 123
Confidential Correspondents—Public Manners and Principles.

To the Board of War, February 16th . . . 125
Action of Governor Clinton on Flour Shipments.

To Samuel Cooper, February 21st 126
Monopoly of Trade and Land—Course of England.

To Mrs. Adams, March 7th 128
Proposed Resignation as Secretary—Personal Jealousies—News from France.

To John Adams, March 9th 131
Personal Reflections.

To Benjamin Austin, March 9th 132
Opinion of Deane and Arthur Lee.

To Mrs. Adams, March 23rd 137
Purpose to Resign as Secretary and as Delegate—Attitude of Countrymen.

To James Warren, March 23rd, 24th . . . 139
Purpose to Resign—Personal Critics—Arthur Lee.

To James Lovell, March 26th 142
Case of Otis and Henley.

To James Lovell, March 27th 143
Application of Medical Officers.

To James Lovell, March 30th 144
John Paul Jones — Retention of Prize Money — The " Alliance."

To the Council of Massachusetts, April 1st . . 145
Want of Bread—Journals of Congress.

To John Pitts, April 27th 147
Comments on Political Affairs.

To Samuel Cooper, April 29th 148
Proper Attitude toward England—Canada and Nova Scotia.

To George Washington, May 26th 150
The Marine Committee—State of the Navy.

To Benjamin Hawes, July 10th 151
Movement of Troops.

  PAGE

To the Navy Board, July 12th 152
    Movement of Ships.

To Jonathan Trumbull, July 13th   152
    Hostilities in Connecticut.

To Horatio Gates, July 14th   153
    Hostilities in Connecticut.

To the Navy Board, July 14th 154
    Penobscot Expedition.

To Meshech Weare, July 28th 155
    Investigation of Seizure.

To Arthur Lee, August 1st   155
    Enemies of Lee.

To Solomon Lovell, August 6th   158
    Military Affairs.

To the Council of Massachusetts, August 10th .   . 158
    Aid for Penobscot Expedition.

To the Council of Massachusetts, August 11th .   . 159
    Movement of Troops.

To Solomon Lovell, August 14th   160
    Movement of Troops.

To John Frost, August 17th   161
    The Penobscot Expedition.

To ——, August 17th   161
    The Penobscot Expedition.

To Henry Jackson, August 21st   162
    The Penobscot Expedition.

To Horatio Gates, August 22nd   163
    Failure on the Penobscot—Campaign Preparations—Luzerne.

To George Washington, October 12th   .   .   . 165
    Raising of Troops.

To the Navy Board, October 19th   166
    Lack of Fuel—Protection of Coast.

To Elbridge Gerry and James Lovell, December   . 167
    Subscription for Children of Joseph Warren.

To Elbridge Gerry, December 20th 168
    Appointment to Convention.

PAGE

To Elbridge Gerry and James Lovell, December 20th   169
    Education of Children of Joseph Warren.

Subscription for Benefit of Children of Joseph Warren   171

To the House of Representatives of Massachusetts,
    December 23rd   173
    Resolution of Council on Absentees.

1780.

To the Governor of Rhode Island, January 5th . .   174
    Exclusion of Secret Enemies.

To John Adams, January 13th   176
    Work of the Legislature—Military Affairs—Constitutional
    Convention—Delegates in Congress.

To John Morin Scott, February 17th   .   .   .   179
    Condition of Public Records.

To James Lovell, March 5th   180
    Political Details.

To the Legislature of Massachusetts, March 9th .   182
    Petition for Permission to Purchase Property of Absentees.

To John Adams, March 15th   182
    The Massachusetts Constitution.

To James Lovell, March 25th   183
    The Vermont Controversy—Work of Congress—The Penob-
    scot Expedition—The Eastern Territory—Need of Consulate in
    France.

To John Adams, May   187
    Work of the Legislature—The New Constitution.

Article Signed "Vindex," June 12th   .   .   .   188
    Origin of the Contest—Character of the Army—Duty of the
    People.

To James Bowdoin, June 20th   191
    Defence of Connecticut.

To John Fellows, June 20th   192
    Control of Hudson River—Military Plans.

To Robert Howe, June 20th   194
    Movement of Massachusetts Troops.

PAGE

To John Fellows, June 21st 195
Plans for Defence of Hudson River.

To Robert Howe, June 21st 196
The Defence of Hudson River.

To La Fayette, June 197
Assistance of France—Military Preparations in Massachusetts
—The Coming Election.

To John Adams, July 10th 199
The Massachusetts Constitution—The French Fleet.

To Hannah Adams, August 17th 200
Paternal Advice.

To James Bowdoin, August 22nd 201
French Opinion of Massachusetts Troops — The Vermont
Controversy—The New Constitution.

To John Lowell, September 15th 203
The Vermont Controversy—Condition of the Army.

To Mrs. Adams, September 19th 206
Sacrifice in Public Service—The Southern Campaign.

To James Warren, October 6th 207
The Massachusetts Election—Reflections on Congress.

To Mrs. Adams, October 10th 209
Visit of Arthur Lee to Boston—Election of Hancock—Treason of Arnold.

To Mrs. Adams, October 17th 211
Opinion of Arthur Lee—Election of Hancock.

To James Warren, October 24th 212
Public Service and Proper Government.

To Richard Henry Lee, October 31st . . . 215
The Campaign in Virginia—Opinion of Arthur Lee.

To Samuel Cooper, November 7th 216
Visit of Arthur Lee to Boston—Legislation for the Army—
The Southern Campaign.

To Mrs. Adams, November 11th, 13th . . . 219
Robbery of the Mail—The Massachusetts Election.

To James Warren, November 20th . . . 221
Activity of Personal Enemies—Local Politics.

To Thomas Wells, November 22nd 223
Advice on Married Life.

PAGE

To Mrs. Adams, November 24th   225
Reflections on Results of Public Service.

To Elbridge Gerry, November 27th   227
Proposed Retirement of Adams—Necessity for Public Service
of Gerry—Character of Massachusetts Government.

To John Adams, December 17th   230
Military Activities—Treason of Arnold—Diplomatic Appointments—The Massachusetts Constitution.

To John Adams, December 20th   234
Conditions in the South—Need of a Navy.

To John Scollay, December 30th   236
Support of Warren's Children—The New Government of
Massachusetts—Character of the Population.

1781.

To Richard Henry Lee, January 15th .   .   .   239
Opinion of Arthur Lee—Recurrence to First Principles.

To John Pitts, January 17th   241
Office-seeking.

To James Warren, February 1st   242
Effect of Foreign Influence.

To Mrs. Adams, February 1st   244
Relations with Dr. Cooper—Relations with Hancock.

To Mrs. Adams, March 15th   248
Desire to Return Home—Situation of Son.

Article, Unsigned, April 2nd   250
Character of Government—The Massachusetts Election.

To Caleb Davis, April 3rd   253
Admission of Belligerent Subjects—Affairs at Boston.

Article, Unsigned, April 16th   255
The Massachusetts Election—The Duty of Citizens.

To Samuel Cooper, April 23d   258
Political Details—Attacks of Rivington.

To Thomas McKean, August 29th   260
Return of John Laurens—Peace and the Fishery—Executive
Appointments.

                                                              PAGE
To Thomas McKean, September 19th   .   .   .   262
    Recommending Major Brown—Need of Strong Navy.

To Horatio Gates, October 11th   .   .   .   263
    Proposed Court of Inquiry—The Southern Campaign.

To William Heath, November 21st   264
    Relations of Canada and Vermont.

To Selectmen of Other Towns, December 14th   .   265
    Letter of Boston on the Fishery—Instructions to Repre-
    sentatives.

To John Adams, December 18th   .   .   .   267
    Local Politics.

To John Adams, December 19th   .   .   .   268
    Proposed Revision of Statutes—Education—Public Manners
    —Action of Boston on the Fishery.

                        1782.

To Alexander McDougall, May 13th   .   .   .   271
    Purpose of Patriots.

To John Lowell, May 15th   272
    Legislative Procedure—Election of Representatives.

To John Lowell, June 4th   274
    Controversy with Governor as to Legislative Procedure.

To Arthur Lee, November 21st   275
    Petition of William Burgess.

To Arthur Lee, December 2nd   277
    Affairs in Canada.

                        1783.

To Arthur Lee, February 10th   277
    Case of Landais—The Fishery.

To the Selectmen of Boston, March 10th   .   .   280
    Election as Moderator.

To Arthur Lee, April 21st   281
    Political Fictions—Journals of Congress.

PAGE

To Benjamin Lincoln, May 1st 282
Case of John Allan—Recommendations.

To Horatio Gates, May 2nd 284
Case of John Allan—The Saratoga Campaign.

To Elbridge Gerry, September 9th 285
Committee of Correspondence—Relation of Congress to the
People.

To John Adams, November 4th 287
Need of Public Jealousy—Foreign Influences—Negotiation
with Holland.

1784.

To John Adams, February 4th 291
Commending Appleton.

To Elbridge Gerry, February 25th 292
Work of the Committee of Correspondence—Financial Legislation—Case of Gridley.

To John Adams, April 16th 294
Action on Treaty—Treatment of Aliens—Need of Commercial Treaty—Danger of Popular Conventions—The Cincinnati.

To John Adams, April 17th 297
Cases of Noyes and Dashwood.

To Elbridge Gerry, April 19th 298
The Cincinnati—Gerry's Proposed Retirement.

To Elbridge Gerry, April 23rd 301
The Court of Appeals—The Cincinnati—Foreign Influence.

To Noah Webster, April 30th 304
Commutation of Pay of Officers—Popular Committees and
Constitutional Government.

To John Adams, June 20th 307
Personal Greeting.

To John Adams, December 2nd 307
Case of Dashwood.

To Richard Henry Lee, December 23rd . . . 309
Conditions in Congress—Effects of Peace—Foreign Relations
—National Policy—Attitude of England.

PAGE

1785.

To Richard Henry Lee, March 24th 313
The Six Nations—Case of John Allan.

To Richard Henry Lee, April 14th 314
Introducing Macauley Graham.

To John Adams, July 2nd 315
Conditions of Trade—Massachusetts Election.

To John Adams, August 16th 316
Case of Captain Stanhope.

To Richard Henry Lee, December 17th . . . 318
Case of Captain Landais.

1786.

To John Adams, April 13th 320
William Gordon—Relations with England.

To John Adams, July 21st 322
Political Liberty and National Faith—The Tories.

1787.

To Richard Henry Lee, December 3rd . . . 323
The National Constitution.

1789.

To Richard Henry Lee, April 22nd 326
Powers of Congress—Commending Leonard Jarvis.

To the Legislature of Massachusetts, May 27th . 327
Accepting Election as Lieutenant-Governor.

To Richard Henry Lee, July 14th 329
The State Governments—Political Applications.

To Elbridge Gerry, August 22nd 330
Congressional Control of Lighthouses — Constitutional
Amendments.

  PAGE

To Richard Henry Lee, August 24th   .   .   .   333
   Nature of the Constitution—Importance of Amendments.

To Richard Henry Lee, August 29th   .   .   .   335
   Power of Removal—Relations with Washington—The Eastern Boundary.

1790.

To the Legislature of Massachusetts, May 28th   .   338
   Accepting Election as Lieutenant-Governor.

To John Adams, September 2nd   339
   Application of Captain Lyde.

To John Adams, October 4th   340
   Political Reflections.

To John Adams, November 25th   344
   Nature of the Constitution—The American Legislatures—
   Succession in Office—Effects and Nature of Good Government
   —Universal Education and Liberty.

1794.

To the Legislature of Massachusetts, January 17th   .   353
   Death of Governor Hancock—The Federal Constitution—
   The Massachusetts Constitution—Essential Principles of Gov-
   ernment—Public Education.

Proclamation, February 19th   360
   Appointing Day of Thanksgiving.

To the Legislature of Massachusetts, May 31st .   .   363
   General Election—European War—Object of the Constitution.

To the Legislature of Massachusetts, June 4th .   .   366
   Use of Castle Island.

Proclamation, November 3rd   368
   Appointing Day of Thanksgiving.

PAGE

1795.

To the Legislature of Massachusetts, January 16th . 369
  Object of Frequent Sessions—Purity of Elections—European
  Affairs — Fortifications — Pennsylvania Insurrection — Amend-
  ment of State Constitution.

To Jeremy Belknap, March 30th 374
  Action of Continental Congress with Reference to Captain
  Cook.

To the Legislature of Massachusetts, June 3rd . . 375
  Re-election as Governor—Duty of Public Officers—Justifica-
  tion of Colonial Settlers—Foreign Relations—Public Education
  —Amendment of State Constitution—The Judicial System—
  Public Credit.

To the Public, July 4th 382
  Address at Laying of Corner-stone of State House.

Proclamation, October 14th 383
  Appointing Day of Thanksgiving.

1796.

To the Legislature of Massachusetts, January 19th . 386
  Agriculture, Commerce, and Manufactures—The National
  and State Constitutions—Treaty-making Power—The Treaty
  with England.

To the Legislature of Massachusetts, May 31st . 391
  Duty to the Union—Duty of the Legislators.

Proclamation, October 6th 393
  Appointing Day of Thanksgiving.

To the Legislature of Massachusetts, November 17th 396
  Choice of Presidential Electors.

To the Senate of Massachusetts, November 23rd . 397
  Vacancies in Electoral College.

To the Legislature of Massachusetts, November 24th 398
  Vacancies in Electoral College.

PAGE

1797.

To the Legislature of Massachusetts, January 27th . 399
Retirement of Washington—General Elections—Public Education—The Militia—Determination to Retire from Public Life.

Proclamation, March 20th 405
Appointing Day of Thanksgiving.

To John Adams, April 17th 408
Introducing Mr. Wyllys.

1801.

To Thomas Jefferson, April 24th 408
Congratulations on Election—Political Comments.

To Thomas Jefferson, November 18th . . . 411
Congratulations on Peace.

1802.

To Thomas Paine, November 30th 412
Defence of Infidelity—Effect of Proposed Age of Reason.

THE WRITINGS OF

SAMUEL ADAMS.

TO RICHARD HENRY LEE.

[MS., Samuel Adams Papers, Lenox Library.]

Boston Jany 1 1778

My dear Sir

I had the Pleasure of receiving your Letter dated at York the 23^d of Novr last, which mentions your having before written to me by a young Gent^n Capt Romane who was to pass through this Place in his Return to France. That Letter has not yet come to Hand. I shall regard all your Recommendations with the utmost Respect.

Our military Affairs in the middle Department are in such a Situation as to afford us too much Reason to be chagrind. We have indeed sufferd no shameful Defeats, but a promising Campaign has however ended ingloriously. To what are we to attribute it? I believe to a miserable Set of General Officers. I mean to make some Exceptions. For the Sake of our Country, my dear Friend, let me ask, Is our

Army perpetually to be an unanimated one ; because
there is not Fortitude enough to remove those bad
Men. I remember the Factions in Carthage which
prevented her making herself the Mistress of the
World. We may avoid Factions and yet rid our
Army of idle cowardly or drunken officers. How was
Victory snatchd out of our Hands at German Town !
Was not this owing to the same Cause ? And Why
was only one General officer dischargd ? Was it
because there were just Grounds to suspect only
one ? is there not Reason to fear that our Commander in Chief may one day suffer in his own
Character by Means of these worthless Creatures ?
May he not suffer under the Reputation of an unfortunate Commander, than which I think he cannot
suffer a greater Evil. It is difficult to seperate from
the Minds of the People the Idea of unfortunate
from that of the Want of some necessary soldierly
Quality. At best the unfortunate General has Pity
only as the Reward of his Services ; and how soon
does Pity degenerate into Contempt. Cicero if I
mistake not some where tells us, that when a General
is fortunate it matters not whether it is ascribd to his
being a Favorite of the Immortal Gods, or to certain
good Qualities in him which others are incapable of
observing. His Soldiers will encounter every Danger
under his Conduct. His Enemies will be confounded
at his Approach. His Country will revere him. The
Reverse is equally just. As therefore we regard the
Reputation of the Com^{dr} in Chief of our Armies,
which is of the greatest Importance to our Affairs,
let us promote this Winter a strict Scrutiny into the

Causes of this unfortunate Campaign. Our Affairs
are far from wearing a desperate Aspect. Our Successes at the Northward must give us Reputation
abroad ; and Reputation is a Kind of real Strength.
That our Men are brave, Brandy Wine & Germantown can witness. Let us then give them officers
worthy of them, and Heaven will prosper our righteous
Cause. There is indeed one thing which to me appears threatning. It is absolutely necessary that the
Commissarial Departm^t should be restored to a better
State, or the Army will soon suffer. This my dear
Sir requires your speedy Return to Congress. Did
the Army suffer or was it in Danger of suffering
before the Alterations in that Department the last
Summer, why then should we not put it upon its old
Footing & prevail upon the former Commissary, who
is the fittest Man I know, to act again in that office.[1]

I have been favord with a Letter from Dr Lee
since his Return to Paris from Berlin.[2] The Powers
of Europe I perceive, are too timid, or too intent
upon enslaving others, to espouse the Cause of Liberty in America. No Matter, my Friend. We shall
not be obligd to them ; and they will hereafter be
more sensible of our Importance when they find that
we have struggled thro our Difficulties without them.
We shall do greater Honor to our Selves and our
Cause ; and those Liberties for which we pay so dear
a Price will be more justly & more highly valued by
our selves and our Posterity. France, in my Opinion,
misses the Sight of her true Interest in delaying to

[1] *Cf.*, vol. iii., page 317.
[2] Wharton, *Revolutionary Diplomatic Correspondence*, vol. i., p. 517.

take a decisive Part.   She runs a great Risque ; for
if Britain should be so politick as to recognize our
Independence which she sees us determind at all
Hazzards to maintain, and should propose to us a
Treaty of Alliance offensive & defensive, would not
the flattering Expectations of France be cut off ?   I
mention this, not because I expect or wish for it.
But should such Recognition & such Proposals be
made the next Spring, which may happen, would
France have any Reason to fault America for acceed-
ing to it ?   We are independent.   The Nations of
Europe may acknowledge it when they dare to do it.
We have Fortitude enough to maintain it.   This is
our Business.   The Nations may reap honest Advantages from it.   If they have not Wisdom enough to
discern in Season, they will regret their own Blind-
ness hereafter.   We will dispose our Favors as we
please.

The Letter from Congress to the Assembly of this
State, inclosing the Articles of Confederation, came
to Hand the Day of its Adjournment, which is to a
shorter Day than was intended that the weighty
Matters recommended might be considerd with all
possible Speed.   The Assembly will meet on the 7th
Instant.   It will be difficult for the Members to prevail upon themselves to make a new Law after having
been necessitated so late to repeal one framed for the
same purpose.   A Com^t however I am inclind to
think will be appointed to meet those of the other
States mentiond in the recommendation.   The Articles
of Confederation seem to be well liked.   I suppose
you will have the Sense of this Assembly soon.

I am much pleasd with a spirited Act lately made by your Assembly for the Supply of our Troops and the beneficial Effects it has had. I am not in much Pain about Cloathing for this year. A large Quantity has been lately brought here by the Agent of the Clothier General—Part of which has been made & I suppose by this time arrivd at Camp. The Taylors and others are busily employd. Every Method should nevertheless be tryed for further Supplys. A Superabundance will not be amiss. Laws in other States similar to yours will eventually facilitate this Part of our Work.

I understand that our Army is gone or going into Winter Quarters at the Distance of 18 Miles from Philadelphia. Why could not Barracks have been as well erected near enough to have . . . . the Enemy all the Winter. Our Army was within three or four miles of them the whole Winter when they were in this Town. I hope the Campaign will be opend by us very early the next Spring.

I should have written to you before this time, but on my Arrival here I found the Gen¹ Assembly sitting, unluckily for me as it engagd me in publick Business; and I have been obligd to spend a Fortnight in the Country.

Adieu my friend & believe me to be affectionately,
Your,

TO ————.

[MS., Samuel Adams Papers, Lenox Library.]

BOSTON Jany 10 1778

MY DEAR SIR/

The General Assembly of this State having sat the greatest part of the Time since I arrivd here & the Council constantly has prevented my writing so often to my Friends, and when I have wrote, so fully as I have an Inclination to do. The Assembly is now sitting, and have made Choice of Mr Cushing Mr Pain and a Country Gentleman[1] whose Name I do not now recollect, to join Committees of other States at New Haven agreable to a late Recommendation of Congress. But having been obligd so lately to repeal an Act of a similar Nature to that which is now proposd, I am doubtful whether they will be prevaild upon to pass a new one. It will however have its due Consideration if the joynt Com^tes should propose such a Measure. I expect every Day to have the Articles of Confederation brot forward, and have good Reason to think it will be agreed to, even those parts which it may be wishd had been different, for the Sake of that Union which is so necessary for the Support of the great Cause.

The Resolutions of Congress recommending passing a Law similar to that lately passed in Virginia &^c were yesterday read at the Council Board. I had the Opp^ty of hearing them read once, so that I cannot yet form my Judgment of them. Indeed I think it is easy to see the Necessity of such a Law as that of

---

[1] Elisha Porter of Hadley.

Virginia, but whether it would be practicable to put
into Execution a Law prohibiting the Sale of Goods
without Licence requires Consideration for Nothing
more betrays the Weakness of Government than to
make Laws wch cannot be executed.   I am sensible it
is nearly of as much Importance to suppress the
Monopolizers as to provide for our Army, but the
blow must be levelled at them only.   If the Popular
Indignation can once be raisd to a suitable Pitch as I
think it can it will become dangerous for them to
withhold their Goods or demand an exorbitant Price
for them and the Evil will be cured.   I think every
Step should be taken for the Downfall of such
Wretches, and shall be ready to joyn in any Measure
within Doors or without which shall be well adapted
to this Effect.

It is the general Observation of those who are in
the way of observing that the sinking our State bills
for Notes & thereby lessening the Quantity in Circulation & the Taxes we have laid has already reduced
the price of Goods.

This was mentioned to me by M^r S A Otis with
whom I have just dined.

I have written to Bro Gerry by the Baron De
Steuben whom I strongly recommend to the Notice
of my worthy Colleagues & others.   Mr Gerry will
shew you my Letter, which makes it needless for me
to add further than that from the recommendatory
Letters of Dr Franklin & other papers wch I have
seen & the Conversation I have had with the Baron,
I really esteem him a modest candid & sensible
Gent^n.   The D^r says he is spoken highly of to

him by two of the best Judges of military merit in
France, tho he is not him self a Frenchman but a
Prussian.

Since I last wrote to you I am favord with yours of
27 Dec[r] inclosing among other papers Copy of a Letter from your Correspondent in Holland. Before you
knew the Contents I bolted out your Letter in the
presense & hearing of Madam & other good Ladies. I
cannot promise you that Mischief is not done. I am
endeavoring (and M[r] Gerry will say it is just like
him) to turn the torrent toward Braintree ; for I really
think my Namesake is full as suspectable as I am. I
thank M[rs] Clymer for her good opinion of me, and I
can assure her, the Hint you gave me of this in your
Letter to me was very timely & is likely to make
Matters easy with me.

I might have dated this Letter at the Council
table where I am writing in Haste.

My best Regards to all who love our Country in
Sincerity. Col[o] Chase tells me your Son behaves
well & that he is very clever.

Your Family is well provided for as I am informd.
You will never I am perswaded think your self under
an obligation to baulk your publick Sentiments from
an Idea of Gratitude to private Friends. *Sat Verbum.*
I may explain my self more fully in another Letter.
Adieu my friend.   Burn this.

TO ARCHIBALD CAMPBELL.[1]

[MS., Samuel Adams Papers, Lenox Library.]

BOSTON Jany 14 1778

SIR

Your Letter of the 10th Instant came to my hand on the 12, and I should instantly have returnd an Answer upon an Affair, in the Dispatch of which you must feel yourself so nearly interrested, had an opportunity presented.

Col° Allens Exchange, it is probable, may not so easily be negotiated as that of Col° Webb ; But this Gentleman has been much longer in Captivity than the other.   And although I have no personal Acquaintance with him, yet I am well assured that he is a brave Soldier.   Such a Character, you, Sir, must esteem ; and this is also the Character of Col° Webb. I have not been insensible of the Obstruction which may have hitherto prevented the Exchange of Col° Allen, and the true Source of it.   If private or partial Motives have prevaild in the Mind of any Gentleman in New York, to the Prejudice of a Man of distinguishd Merit, I can only observe, that it is totally inconsistent with those pure Principles, which you will allow me to say, have, and I trust ever will actuate Americans in the present Contest.   You will excuse my saying any more *to you* on so delicate a Point.

I sincerely wish the Release of every man in Captivity ; and shall for my own part be well pleasd with your availing your self of an Exchange with either

---

[1] An officer in the English army.

of the above mentiond Gentlemen, if it may be consistent with the Sentiments of Congress.

My first Concern is for the Honor & Safety of my Country. Having premised this, I can readily subscribe with due Respect,

Y^r very hbl Servt,

TO HORATIO GATES.

[MS., Samuel Adams Papers, Lenox Library.]

BOSTON Jany 14 1778

DEAR SIR

Yesterday I took the Liberty of writing to you by the Baron De Steuben a Native of Prussia who I doubt not will deliver the Letter into your Hand. He will previously wait on Genl Washington to whom he has Letters of warm Recommendation from the Commissioners of America in France. He has also Letters to Mr President Laurens and other Members of Congress from gentlemen of Note in that Country. He offers his Services to America as a Volunteer; wishing to give no Offence by interfering in Command. He appears to me to be a modest, candid & sensible Gentleman; and, I have Reason to think, from the Letters I have seen, he has great military Merit. Of this you will be able to form a decisive Judgment.

There is a certain Canadian Officer, by the Name of Laurens Olivier, a Captain, whose Character and warm Attachment to our Cause while he was an Inhab^t of Canada, my Friend Mr Thos Walker a

Gent[n] well known to M[r] Gerry, speaks highly of. This Officer will make known certain Difficulties he is under to you.   I am told he is a deserving Man ; Such a Character I may with Confidence recommend to your patronage.   You may rely upon it I will never willingly trouble my self or you with persons of a different sort.

I am &[c],

VOTE OF TOWN OF BOSTON.

[MS., Boston City Clerk's Office ; the text, with variations, is in *Boston Record Commissioners' Report*, vol. xviii., p. 298.]

[January 21, 1778.]

The Articles of Confederation and perpetual Union between the several States now represented in the Continental Congress, having been laid before this Town, were distinctly and repeatedly read and maturely considerd, Whereupon ; Resolvd, as the opinion of this Town, that the said Articles appear to be well adapted to cement the Union of the said States, to confirm their mutual Friendship, establish their Freedom and Independence, and promote their general Welfare : And the Representatives of the Town are hereby instructed, to give their Votes in the General Assembly, that the Delegates of this State may be authorizd to ratify the said Articles of Confederation in order that the same may become conclusive.

TO JOHN BURGOYNE.[1]

[MS., Public Record Office, London; a draft is in the Samuel Adams Papers, Lenox Library.]

BOSTON Febry 6th, 1778.

SIR

I should not have failed yesterday to have returned an Answer to your Letter, which was brought to me the preceding Evening, had it not been for the violence of a Disorder which had seized me near a Week before. That Disorder still continues to afflict me much, and prevents my seeing any one but my physician, or doing any business even of the most trifling Nature.

Under such Circumstances, you will excuse me if I decline to engage with you in Conversation, upon a subject in which you think the general Cause of Humanity and possibly the essential Interests of both our Countries are concerned.

I have the Honor to be
Sir
Your most humble Serv[t]

TO DANIEL ROBERDEAU.[2]

[MS., Samuel Adams Papers, Lenox Library.]

Feb 9 1778

SIR

I have not been unmindful of the favor you did me in writing to me some time ago. My not having returnd an Answer has been owing, I do assure you,

---

[1] Lieutenant General in the English army.
[2] *Cf., Appleton's Cyclopaedia of American Biography.*

altogether to many Avocations, and at last to a bodily
disorder by which I have been confind to my House
and great part of the time upon my bed for near a
fortnight. I am now about my Room and gladly
take the Opportunity to drop from my Pen an Expression of the honest Friendship which I feel for
your self and your agreable Connections.

I find by the Letters I receive from Mr Lovell
who is kind enough to write to me often, that Congress is reduced to a small Number present. This
has not been unusual in the Winter Season. But
you have a great Deal of Business and that of the
arduous Kind. It would be a strong Inducement to
me to leave domestick Enjoym^t, that I might take as
great a Share of the Burthen with you as my Shoulders
would bear. It is no Satisfaction to me, you may
rely upon it, to be able to plead the Want of Health
sufficient to go through so long a Journey at this
rigorous Season. My Brother Gerry can recollect
with how much pleasure the few who were at Baltimore passed through the Fatigues of Business the
last Winter, when our Affairs wore a more gloomy
Aspect than they have ever yet done. We did it
with Alacrity, because there was a Spirit of Union
which leads to wise & happy Decisions. I hope the
same Spirit now prevails and that Measures are taking
to collect & support an Army and to introduce Œconomy & Discipline among officers of Rank as well as
private Soldiers, so as by Gods Blessing to insure us
a successful Campaign. Your Resolution respecting
Burgoyne I think must have nettled him. I have
long with Pain suspected a perfidious Design. This

Resolution must have crossd it. It will cause much
Speculation in Europe. No Matter. The Powers
there seem more inclind to speculate than to espouse
the Rights of Man. Let them speculate. Our Business is to secure America against the Arts & the
Arms of a treacherous Enemy. The former we have
more to apprehend from than the latter.

Please to pay my due Regard to your Sisters &
Family in which M^{rs} A desires to be joynd & be
assured that I am

Y^r unfeigned friend

TO ARTHUR LEE.

[MS., Samuel Adams Papers, Lenox Library.]

Boston March 12th 1778

My dear Friend

This Letter will be deliverd to you by Captn Romanet a young French Gentleman Nephew to General Grobouval Commander of the french Artillery.
He is a modest well behaved youth, and is one of Monsr
du Coudrays Corps many of whom I suppose are returnd to France dissatisfied with the Determination of
Congress against ratifying Mr Dean's Compact. The
Necessity of doing this was disagreable to the Members, but it could not have been otherwise, without
causing a great Uneasiness in our Army at a very
critical Juncture. I hope no ill Consequences will result to our Country and Cause from the Complaints
of these Gentlemen. Mr Romanet ingenuously acknowledges to me that M^r Du Coudrays Disappointment appears to him to have been necessary, and

possibly his Connections in France may give Weight
to his opinion.

I have been favord with your acceptable Letter of
the 31 July from Paris. From your not having noticed
several Letters which I have written to you, I suspect
they have miscarried. I know not that they would have
servd any other good Purpose, than to have shown
how desirous I was of reviving a Correspondence
which heretofore . . . . .

TO JONATHAN TRUMBULL.

[MS., Massachusetts Archives ; a text is in W. V. Wells, *Life of Samuel Adams*,
vol. iii., pp. 7, 8,]

STATE OF MASSACHUSETTS BAY   BOSTON Mar 19 1778

SIR/

I am to acquaint your Excellency in the Name & by
order of the Council of this State, that your Letter of
the 16th Instant directed to the President, relative to
the Defence of Hudsons River has been receivd & read
at that Board. The General Assembly is now under
a short Adjournment, and the Council are not authorizd in their Executive Capacity & seperate from the
House of Repts to order any Part of the Militia
of this State beyond its Limits. The Assembly will
meet on the first Day of the next Month. Your Excellencys Letter, together with another receivd this
Day from Govr Clinton upon the same Subject, will
then be laid before that Body ; and altho the Government of this State are now under the Necessity of
keeping up more than fifteen hundred of the Militia
to guard the Troops of Convention & for other

extraordinary Service in and about the Town of Boston, yet there can be no Doubt but a due Attention will be given to so interesting & important a Concern as the Defence of Hudsons river.

I have the Honor to be with the most cordial Esteem
                    Y^r Excys most Humble Servt

TO JAMES LOVELL.

[MS., Samuel Adams Papers, Lenox Library.]

BOSTON March 27 1778

MY DEAR SIR

You cannot imagine how much I feel my self obligd to you for writing to me frequently. Your Letters however do not come to me in regular Order. How is it that I did not receive those of the 10th & 16th of Feby by the Post till yesterday? I am affraid there is some Deficiency in the Post office Department; but as I would fain hope our Friend Mr Hastings is not in Fault, I will beg you in his Behalf, to move to the Post Master General for an Addition to his Salary, for he assures me he cannot live upon what he now receives.

I am very sorry your Letter of the 10th did not come in Season, for I should have gladly interrested my self for so valueable a Citizen as Mr Leach at the late annual Meeting. I have long wishd that for the Reputation as well as substantial Advantage of this Town a military Academy was instituted. When I was in Philadelphia more than two years ago I mentiond the Importance I conceivd it to be of, in Letters to my Friends here. At least we might set up

a publick School for military Mathematicks, and I
know of no one better qualified for an Instructor
than Mr Leach.   I wish he had mentiond it to me.
Perhaps he may have had *Promises* of Attention to
him from some other Person upon whom he relies.
I will consult with such Men of Influence in the
Town as I am acquainted with, and will not be wanting in Endeavors to improve your Hints for the
mutual Benefit of the Publick & Mr Leach.

I am pleasd to observe in your Letter of 28 Feb^y
that Mr Burgoyne seems to be alterd in his Ideas of
Congress.   The Gentleman to whom you request me
to communicate the Contents of that Letter,   I am
not in the least acquainted with, but shall comply
with your Request whenever I shall find an opportunity of doing it.

I fear from what you mention in your Letter of
the 7th of March that *the Expectations of the People*
with Regard to Ty. & Independence will be baulkd.
If they are, the Cause in my opinion will be injurd &
the Confidence of the People in those who have the
Mannagement of our Affairs *civil* & *military* lessend,
which I should be very sorry to see.   In the same
Letter you tell me that Lt Col^o Anstruthers Request
to seek his own Release on Condition of his getting
Col^o Allens is granted.   I now inclose a Letter which
I had mislayed & omitted to send, relating to Lt Col^o
Campbells who I wish might be exchanged for Friend
Ethan.[1]

I do not wonder that you have been mortified upon

---

[1] Allen. *Cf.* page 9.

the Delay of a certain Affair to which you refer in
your Letter of the 10th Instant.   I wrote you the
Opinion of this Town respecting that Affair above a
Month ago.   I shall only observe that in my opinion,
every one who is intrusted with the Affairs of the
Publick does not feel so sensibly for its Reputation
as I think you do.   I have inclosd the Instructions
of the General Assembly to their Delegates in Congress upon the Confederation, and when I shall have
the pleasure of seeing you I may perhaps give you
the Causes why that important Matter was not determind sooner.   I immediately after reading your last
mentiond Letter communicated to the Council that
part of it which relates to the Propriety & Necessity
of making regular Returns of what is done here in
Consequence of the Recommendations of Congress ;
and a Committee of that Board is now looking over
the Journals & Papers for that Purpose.   In the
same Letter you mention your having receivd a Letter from Mr John Amory, with his Request that you
w^d put a memorial into Congress for him.   In what
Manner could Congress interpose for him if you
should comply with his Request?   His Residence in
this State was deemd by the Genl Assembly to be
dangerous to the State.   Will Congress order or
recommend that He should reside in it notwithstanding ?   " He was surprizd into an Oath of Allegiance ! "
He said upon his Examination here that he was *not*
compelled to take the Oath.   He did not recollect
the Form or Tenor of the Oath he had taken—but
desired to live peaceably in his Native town but could
not in Conscience take up Arms against the British

King.   I will desire Mr Appleton to write to you on the Subject.

TO FRANCIS LIGHTFOOT LEE.

[MS., Samuel Adams Papers, Lenox Library.]

[BOSTON, ——, 1778.]

MY DEAR SIR

It was much longer than the usual time before your very acceptable Letter of the 22 Decr came to my hand.   I receivd it as a singular Favor and felt the more thankful for it, because I knew that hardly anything could induce you to write a Letter but the urgent Affairs of our Country or the powerful feelings of private Friendship.   I should have written you an Answer sooner but the peevish nominal Saint who scrap'd an Acquaintance with me at Baltimore the last Winter, has followd me even to this place.   I think he is the most impertinent & troublesome Visitant I ever had.   I am so thoroughly disgusted at the Creature that I have taken every Method that could be devisd to prevent my being ever plagud with him again.   He seems at length to be about leaving me & he may depend upon it I shall deny all his Visits for the future.

The Spirit of Avarice, I am sorry to be obligd to say it, prevails too much in this Town; but it rages only among the few, because perhaps, the few only are concernd at present in trade.   The old substantial Merchants have generally laid aside trade & left it to Strangers or those who from nothing have raisd fortunes by privateering.   The Body of this Community

suffer proportionably as much as the great continental
Publick.   It must be confessd that the Charges of
Trade are enormous, and it is natural for men when
they have at great Risque & Expence imported Com-
modities which are wanted by every body, if they
must receive in payment for them what is valued by
no body, to demand as much of it as they please,
especially if it is growing daily into less Repute.
This you know has been the Case.   There is but one
effectual Remedy; & that is to lessen the Quantity
of circulating paper Money.   This is now doing here.
Our Assembly have laid on a very heavy Tax, & are
determind to repeat it again and again.   Besides which
they have called in a large Quantity of their bills, for
which they have issued Notes pay^ble with Interest.   The
Effects are already felt & the prices of Goods have
been for some time past gradually sinking.

You tell me we have a great many men now inlisted
& that you hope Means will be found to collect them.
I joyn with you in these hopes, and that we may
keep them together when they are collected and make
a good Use of them.   Howe I understand has fortified
himself by a Line of Redoubts from River to River.
Has he more than 13 or 14 [sic] Men in America?   If
not why should we wait till he is reinforced before we
make an Enterprize somewhere.

Your Resolution to stop the Embarkation here I
fancy has nettled Burgoyne.   He has since been
soliciting Interviews with A & B & wishes for
private Conversations upon a Matter in which " he
thinks the General Cause of Humanity and possibly
the essential Interests of both our Countries are con-

cernd."[1]   He has not prevaild upon A to comply with
his Request ; for more Reasons than one which I
think must be obvious upon a short Review of our
History.   The Resolutions of Congress will afford
Matter of Speculation for the Politicians in Europe.
But must they not all acknowledge that Burgoyne
himself had made it necessary ?   After a solemn Declaration made to the very Officer with whom he had
enterd into the Convention that it was broken on our
Part, Does he, if he believes his own Declaration
hold him self bound by it on his part ?   Would
he not, if sufferd to go to Sea, most probably carry a
Reinforcement to Gen[l] Howe & laugh at us for puting
it in his Power ?

I have twenty things to say to you, but my ill state
of Health prevents my adding more than that I am,
with sincere Regards to M[rs] Lee in which M[rs] A very
cordially joyns

Y[r] affection[e]

TO RICHARD HENRY LEE.

[MS., American Philosophical Society.]

BOSTON April 20 1778

My Dear Sir——

I most heartily congratulate you on the happy and
important News from Europe which will be conveyd
to Congress by M[r] Dean the Brother of our late
Commissioner who will be so kind as to deliver you
this Letter.   France has acted with Magnanimity ;

---

[1] Cf. page 12.

while Britain continues to discover that Meanness and Poverty of Spirit, which renders her still more than ever contemptible in the Eyes of all sensible People. The Moderation of France is such as becomes a great and powerful Nation. Britain forgetfull of her former Character, sinks into Baseness in the Extreme. The one is generously holding out the Arm of Protection to a People most cruelly oppressd while the other is practicing the Arts of Treachery and Deceit to subjugate and enslave them. This is a Contrast which an ancient Britain would have blushd to have had predicted to him. It is a true Contrast, and we will blush for them.

Commissioners we are again told are coming out to treat with us. This is what we had Reason to expect. Her only Design is to amuse us & thereby to retard our operations, till she can land her utmost Force in America. We see plainly what Part we are to take; to be before hand of her; and by an early Stroke to give her a mortal Wound. If we delay our vigorous Exertions till the Commissioners arrive, the People abroad may, many of them will be amusd with the flattering Prospect of Peace, and will think it strange if we do not consent to a Cessation of Arms till propositions can be made and digested. This carries with it an Air of Plausibility; but from the Moment we are brought into the Snare, we may tremble for the Consequence. As there [are] every where awful Tories enough, to distract the Minds of the People, would it not be wise for the Congress by a Publication of their own to set this important Intelligence in a clear Light before them, and fix in their

Minds the first Impressions in favor of Truth? For I do assure you, it begins to be whisperd by the Tories & as soon as they dare to do it they will speak aloud, that this is but a french Finesse and that Britain is the only real Friend of America. Should not the People be informd with the Authority of Congress that Britain persists in claiming a Right to tax them and that the new or intended Act of Parliament, expressly declares her Intention to be only a Suspension of the Exercise of the Right till she shall please again to exercise it? that is till she shall have lulled them into a State of Security. That her Commissioners are not to be vested with full Powers to finish any Treatys, nor even to promise a Ratification of them. This will be left in great Uncertainty, till it shall be considerd in Parliament. They are allowed, as one of our Friends expresses it, to proclaim a Cessation of Hostilities, and revoke their Proclamation, as soon as in Confidence of it our Militia are allowd to go home. They may suspend the Operation of prohibitory Acts of Trade; and take off that Suspension where our Merchants in Consequence of it shall have been inducd to send their Ships to Sea. In short they may do every thing that may tend to distract and divide us, but Nothing that can afford us Security. The British Court have Nothing in View but to divide by Means of their Commissioners. Of this they entertain sanguine Expectations; for I am well assured, that they say they have *certain Advice*, that they have a large Party in Congress, *almost a Majority*, who are for returning to their Dependency! This cannot be true—D^r

Franklin in a Letter of the 2ᵈ of March informs me that America at present stands in the highest Light of Esteem thro' out Europe, and he adds, A Return to Dependence on England would sink her into Eternal Contempt.

Be pleasd to present my due Regards to all Friends, and acquaint my worthy Colleagues that Mʳ Deans great Haste prevents my writing to them. I intend to set out on my Journy to York Town next Week where I hope for the Pleasure of seeing you. In the mean time be assured that I am

Your affectionate,

I thank you for your
Favor of Mar 1ˢᵗ which
I recᵈ three days ago—

TO MRS. ADAMS.

[MS., Samuel Adams Papers, Lenox Library.]

PALMER 84 Miles from Boston
May 5ᵗʰ 1778

MY DEAR BETSY

I wrote to you by my kind Host Mʳ Greenleafe. Yesterday I left his House and slept the last Night at Colº Henshawˢ. He and his Lady treated me with great Hospitality & Friendship. This day I dined at Brookfield with Mʳ Ward a Minister in that Town. He married Miss Coleman Mʳ Pembertons Niece. I am much obligd to them for their kind Treatment of me. I made them promise to visit you when they go to Boston. This Afternoon I met my Son on the Road. I was sorry I could not have the

Pleasure of conversing with him. I parted with him with great Regret. May Heaven bless him! Tell him I shall never think him too old to hearken to the Advice of his Father. Indeed I never had Reason to complain of him on that Account. He has hitherto made me a glad Father. This implys that I esteem him a wise Son. I have been the more sparing of Advice to him because I have thought he did not need it; but in these critical Times when *Principles* & *Manners* as well as the *Liberties of his Country* are in Danger he has need to be on his Guard. My Children cannot imagine how much Comfort I have in believing they are virtuous. I am not willing to admit of a Fear that they will ever deprive me of this Comfort. My warm Affections are due to my Family and Friends. Adieu my dear Betsy.

Your affectionate,

"AN AMERICAN" TO THE EARL OF CARLISLE AND OTHERS.

[W. V. Wells,[1] *Life of Samuel Adams*, vol. iii., pp. 18–26; printed in the *Massachusetts Spy*, July 16, 1778.]

To the Earl of Carlisle, Lord Viscount Howe, Sir William Howe (*or, in his absence*, Sir Henry Clinton), William Eden, *and* George Johnstone.

Trusty and well-beloved servants of your sacred master, in whom he is well pleased.

As you are sent to America for the express purpose of treating with anybody and anything, you will pardon an address from one who disdains to flatter those whom he loves. Should you therefore deign to read

---

[1] Also attributed to Adams in *The Remembrancer*, 1778, p. 306.

this address, your chaste ears will not be offended
with the language of adulation,—a language you
despise.

I have seen your most elegant and most excellent
letter "to his Excellency, Henry Laurens, the President, and other members of the Congress." As that
body have thought your propositions unworthy their
particular regard, it may be some satisfaction to your
curiosity, and tend to appease the offended spirit of
negotiation, if one out of the many individuals on
this great continent should speak to you the sentiments of America,—sentiments which your own good
sense hath doubtless suggested, and which are repeated only to convince you that, notwithstanding
the narrow ground of private information on which
we stand in this distant region, still a knowledge of
our own rights, and attention to our own interests,
and a sacred respect for the dignity of human nature,
have given us to understand the true principles which
ought, and which therefore shall, sway our conduct.

You begin with the amiable expressions of humanity, the earnest desire of tranquillity and peace. A
better introduction to Americans could not be devised.
For the sake of the latter, we once laid our liberties
at the feet of your Prince, and even your armies have
not eradicated the former from our bosoms.

You tell us you have powers unprecedented in the
annals of your history. And England, unhappy England, will remember with deep contrition that these
powers have been rendered of no avail by a conduct
unprecedented in the annals of mankind. Had your
royal master condescended to listen to the prayer of

millions, he had not thus have sent you. Had moderation swayed what we were proud to call "*mother country*," her full-blown *dignity* would not have broken down under her.

You tell us that all "parties may draw some degree of consolation, and even auspicious hope, from recollection." We wish this most sincerely for the sake of *all parties.* America, in the moment of subjugation, would have been consoled by conscious virtue, and her hope was, and is, in the justice of her cause and the justice of the Almighty. These are sources of hope and of consolation which neither time nor chance can alter or take away.

You mention "the mutual benefits and consideration of evils that may naturally contribute to determine our resolutions." As to the former, you know too well that we could derive no benefit from a union with you, nor will I, by deducing the reasons to evince this, put an insult upon your understandings. As to the latter, it were to be wished you had preserved a line of conduct equal to the delicacy of your feelings. You could not but know that men who sincerely love freedom disdain the consideration of all evils necessary to attain it. Had not your own hearts borne testimony to this truth, you might have learned it from the *annals of your own history;* for in those annals instances of this kind at least are not *unprecedented.* But should those instances be insufficient, we pray you to read the unconquered mind of America.

That the acts of Parliament you transmitted were passed *with singular unanimity*, we pretend not to doubt. You will pardon me, gentlemen, for observing that the reasons of that unanimity are strongly marked in the report of a committee of Congress agreed to on the 22d of April last, and referred to in a late letter from Congress to Lord Viscount Howe and Sir Henry Clinton.

You tell us you are willing "to consent to a cessation of hostilities both by sea and land." It is difficult for rude Americans to determine whether you are serious in this proposition or whether you mean to jest with their simplicity. Upon a supposition, however, that you have too much magnanimity to divert yourselves on an occasion of so much importance to America, and, perhaps, not very trivial in the eyes of those who sent you, permit me to assure you, on the sacred word of a gentleman, that if you shall transport your troops to England, where before long your Prince will certainly want their assistance, we shall never follow them thither. We are not so romantically fond of fighting, neither have we such regard for the city of London, as to commence a crusade for the possession of that holy land. Thus you may be certain hostilities will cease by land. It would be doing singular injustice to your national character to suppose you are desirous of a like cessation by sea. The course of the war, and the very flourishing state of your commerce, notwithstanding our weak efforts to interrupt it, daily show that you can exclude us from the sea,—*the sea, your kingdom !*

You offer "to restore free intercourse, to revive mutual affection, and renew the common benefits of naturalization." Whenever your countrymen shall be

taught wisdom by experience, and learn from past misfortunes to pursue their true interests in the future
we shall readily admit every intercourse which is necessary for the purposes of commerce and usual between
different nations. To revive *mutual* affection is utterly
impossible. We freely forgive you, but it is not in
nature that you should forgive us. You have injured
us too much. We might, on this occasion, give you
some instances of singular barbarity committed, as well
by the forces of his Britannic Majesty as by those of
his generous and faithful allies, the Senecas, Onon-
dagas, and Tuscaroras. But we will not offend a
courtly ear by the recital of those disgusting scenes.
Besides this, it might give pain to that humanity which
hath, as you observe, prompted your overtures, to
dwell upon the splendid victories obtained by a
licentious soldiery over unarmed men in defenceless
villages, their wanton devastations, their deliberate
murders, or to inspect those scenes of carnage painted
by the wild excesses of savage rage. These amiable
traits of national conduct cannot but revive in our
bosoms that partial affection we once felt for everything which bore the name of Englishman. As to the
common benefits of naturalization, it is a matter we
conceive to be of the most sovereign indifference. A
few of our wealthy citizens may hereafter visit England and Rome to see the ruins of those august
temples in which the goddess of Liberty was once
adored. These will hardly claim naturalization in
either of those places as a *benefit*. On the other hand,
such of your subjects as shall be driven by the iron
hand of Oppression to seek for refuge among those

whom they now persecute will certainly be admitted
to *the benefits of naturalization*. We labor to rear
an asylum for mankind, and regret that circumstances
will not permit you, gentlemen, to contribute to a
design so very agreeable to your several tempers and
dispositions.

But further, your Excellencies say, " We will concur to extend every freedom to trade that our respective interests can require." Unfortunately, there is
a little difference in these interests which you might
not have found it very easy to reconcile, had the
Congress been disposed to risk their heads by listening to terms which I have the honor to assure you
are treated with ineffable contempt by every honest
Whig in America. The difference I allude to is, that
it is your interest to monopolize our commerce, and
it is our interest to trade with all the world. There
is, indeed, a method of cutting this Gordian knot
which, perhaps, no statesman is acute enough to un-
tie. By reserving to the Parliament of Great Britain
the right of determining what our respective interests
require, they might extend the freedom of trade, or
circumscribe it at their pleasure, for what they might
call our *respective interests*. But I trust it would not
be for our *mutual satisfaction*. Your " earnest desire
to stop the effusion of blood and the calamities of
war " will therefore lead you, on maturer reflection,
to reprobate a plan teeming with discord, and which,
in the space of twenty years, would produce another
wild expedition across the Atlantic, and in a few
years more some such commission as that " with
which his Majesty hath been pleased to honor you."

We cannot but admire the generosity of soul which
prompts you " to agree that no military force shall be
kept up in the different States of North America
without the consent of the General Congress or particular Assemblies." The only grateful return we
can make for this exemplary condescension is, to
assure your Excellencies, and, on behalf of my countrymen, I do most solemnly promise and assure you,
that no military force shall be kept up in the different
States of North America without the consent of the
General Congress and that of the Legislatures of
those States. You will, therefore, cause the forces
of your royal master to be removed; for I can venture to assure you that the Congress have not consented, and probably will not consent, that they be
kept up.

You have also made the unsolicited offer of con-
curring "in measures calculated to discharge the
debts of America, and to raise the credit and value of
the paper circulation." If your Excellencies mean by
this to apply for offices in the department of our
finance, I am to assure you (which I do with " perfect
respect") that it will be necessary to procure very
ample recommendations. For, as the English have
not yet pursued measures to discharge their own debt
and raise the credit and value of their own paper circulation, but, on the contrary, are in a fair way to
increase the one and absolutely destroy the other,
you will instantly perceive that financiers from that
nation would present themselves with the most
awkward grace imaginable.

You propose to us a device to "perpetuate our

union." It might not be amiss previously to establish this union, which may be done by your acceptance of the treaty of peace and commerce tendered to you by Congress. And such treaty I can venture to say would continue as long as your ministers could prevail upon themselves not to violate the faith of nations.

You offer, to use your language, the inaccuracy of which, considering the importance of the subject, is not to be wondered at, or at least may be excused, "in short, to establish the powers of the respective Legislatures in each particular State, to settle its revenue, its civil and military establishment, and to exercise a perfect freedom of legislation and internal government, so that the British States throughout North America, acting with us in peace and war, under one common sovereign, may have the irrevocable enjoyment of every privilege that is short of a total separation of interests, or consistent with that total union of force on which the safety of our common religion and liberty depends." Let me assure you, gentlemen, that the power of the respective Legislatures in each particular State is most fully established, and on the most solid foundations. It is established on the perfect freedom of legislation and a vigorous administration of internal government. As to the settlement of the revenue and the civil and military establishment, these are the work of the day, for which the several Legislatures are fully competent. I have also the pleasure to congratulate your Excellencies that the country for the settlement of whose government, revenue, administration, and the

like, you have exposed yourselves to the fatigues and
hazards of a disagreeable voyage and more disagreeable negotiation, hath abundant resources wherewith
to defend her liberties now, and pour forth the rich
stream of revenue hereafter. As the States of North
America mean to possess the *irrevocable* enjoyment
of their privileges, it is absolutely necessary for them
to decline all connection with a Parliament who, even
in the laws under which you act, reserve in express
terms the power of *revoking* every proposition which
you may agree to. We have a due sense of the kind
offer you make to grant us a share in your sovereign ;
but really, gentlemen, we have not the least inclination to accept of it. He may suit you extremely
well, but he is not to our taste. You are solicitous
to prevent a total separation of interests ; and this,
after all, seems to be the gist of the business. To
make you as easy as possible on this subject, I have
to observe, that it may, and probably will, in some instances, be our interest to assist you, and then we
certainly shall. Where this is not the case, your
Excellencies have doubtless too much good sense as
well as good nature to require it. We cannot perceive that our liberty does in the least depend upon
any union of force with you ; for we find that after
you have exercised your force against us for upwards
of three years, we are now upon the point of establishing our liberties in direct opposition to it. Neither
can we conceive that, after the experiment you have
made, any nation in Europe will embark in so unpromising a scheme as the subjugation of America.
It is not necessary that everybody should play the

Quixote. One is enough to entertain a generation
at least. Your Excellencies will, I hope, excuse me
when I differ from you as to our having a religion in
common with you ; the religion of America is the
religion of all mankind. Any person may worship in
the manner he thinks most agreeable to the Deity ;
and if he behaves as a good citizen, no one concerns
himself as to his faith or adorations, neither have we
the least solicitude to exalt any one sect or profession
above another.

I am extremely sorry to find in your letter some
sentences which reflect upon the character of his
most Christian Majesty. It certainly is not kind, or
consistent with the principles of philanthropy you
profess, to traduce a gentleman's character, without
affording him an opportunity of defending himself ;
and that, too, a near neighbor, and not long since an
intimate brother, who besides hath lately given you
the most solid additional proofs of his pacific disposition, and with an unparalleled sincerity which would
do honor to other princes, declared to your Court,
unasked, the nature and effect of a treaty he had just
entered into with these States. Neither is it quite according to the rules of politeness to use such terms
in addressing yourselves to Congress, when you well
knew that he was their good and faithful ally. It is
indeed true, as you justly observe, that he hath at
times been at enmity with his Britannic Majesty, by
which we suffered some inconveniences ; but these
flowed rather from our connection with you than any
ill-will towards us ; at the same time it is a solemn
truth, worthy of your serious attention, that you did

not commence the present war,—a war in which we
have suffered infinitely more than by any former
contest, a fierce, a bloody, I am sorry to add, an unpro-
voked and cruel war,—that you did not commence this, I say, because of any connection between us and our present ally ; but, on the contrary,
as soon as you perceived that the treaty was in
agitation, proposed terms of peace to us in consequence of what you have been pleased to de-
nominate an insidious interposition. How, then,
does the account stand between us ? America,
being at peace with the world, was formerly drawn
into a war with France in consequence of her
union with Great Britain. At present, America being
engaged in a war with Great Britain, will probably
obtain the most honorable terms of peace in consequence of her friendly connection with France. For
the truth of these positions, I appeal, gentlemen, to
your own knowledge. I know it is very hard for you
to part with what you have accustomed yourselves
from your earliest infancy to call your Colonies. I
pity your situation, and therefore I excuse the little
aberrations from truth which your letter contains. At
the same time it is possible that you may have been
misinformed. For I will not suppose that your letter
was intended to delude the people of these States.
Such unmanly, disingenuous artifices have of late been
exerted with so little effect, that prudence, if not
probity, would prevent a repetition. To undeceive
you, therefore, I take the liberty of assuring your Excellencies, from the very best intelligence, that what
you call "the present form of the French offers to

America," in other words, the treaties of alliance and
commerce between his most Christian Majesty and
these States, were not made in consequence of any
plans of accommodation concerted in Great Britain,
nor with a view to prolong this destructive war. If
you consider that these treaties were actually concluded before the draft of the bills under which you
act was sent to America, and that much time must
necessarily have been consumed in adjusting compacts of such intricacy and importance, and further,
if you consider the early notification of this treaty by
the Court of France, and the assurance given that
America had reserved a right of admitting even you
to a similar treaty, you must be convinced of the
truth of my assertions. The fact is, that when the
British minister perceived that we were treating with
the greatest prince in Europe, he applied himself immediately to counteract the effect of these negotiations. And this leads me, with infinite regret, to
make some observations which may possibly be by
you considered in an offensive point of view.

It seems to me, gentlemen, there is something
(excuse the word) *disingenuous* in your procedure. I
put the supposition that Congress had acceded to
your propositions, and then I ask two questions :—
Had you full power from your commission to make
these propositions ? Possibly you did not think it
worth your while to consider your commission, but
we Americans are apt to compare things together
and to reason. The second question I ask is, What
security could you give that the British Parliament
would ratify your compacts ? You can give no such

security ; and therefore we should, after forfeiting
our reputation as a people, after you had filched
from us our good name, and persuaded us to give to
the common enemy of man the precious jewel of our
liberties,—after all this, I say, we should have been
at the mercy of a Parliament which, to say no more
of it, has not treated us with too great tenderness.
It is quite needless to add that, even if that Parliament had ratified the conditions you proposed, still
poor America was to lie at the mercy of any future
Parliament, or to appeal to the sword, which certainly is not the most pleasant business men can be
engaged in.

For your use I subjoin the following creed of every
good American :—I believe that in every kingdom,
state, or empire there must be, from the necessity of
the thing, one supreme legislative power, with authority to bind every part in all cases the proper object
of human laws.   I believe that to be bound by laws
to which he does not consent by himself, or by his
representative, is the direct definition of a slave.   I
do therefore believe that a dependence on Great
Britain, however the same may be limited or qualified,
is utterly inconsistent with every idea of liberty, for the
defence of which I have solemnly pledged my life
and fortune to my countrymen ; and this engagement
I will sacredly adhere to so long as I shall live. Amen.

Now, if you will take the poor advice of one who is
really a friend to England and Englishmen, and who
hath even some Scotch blood in his veins,—away
with your fleets and your armies, acknowledge the
independence of America ; and as ambassadors, and

not commissioners, solicit a treaty of peace, amity, commerce, and alliance with the rising States of this Western world. Your nation totters on the brink of a stupendous precipice, and even delay will ruin her.

You have told Congress, "if, after the time that may be necessary to consider this communication and transmit your answer, the horrors and devastations of war should continue, we call God and the world to witness that the evils which must follow are not to be imputed to Great Britain." I wish you had spared your protestation. Matters of this kind may appear to you in a trivial light, as mere ornamental flowers of rhetoric, but they are serious things, registered in the high chancery of Heaven. Remember the awful abuse of words like those by General Burgoyne, and remember his fate. There is One above us who will take exemplary vengeance for every insult upon His majesty. You know that the cause of America is just. You know that she contends for that freedom to which all men are entitled,—that she contends against oppression, rapine, and more than savage barbarity. The blood of the innocent is upon your hands, and all the waters of the ocean will not wash it away. We again make our solemn appeal to the God of heaven to decide between you and us. And we pray that, in the doubtful scale of battle, we may be successful as we have justice on our side, and that the merciful Saviour of the world may forgive our oppressors.

I am, my Lords and Gentlemen, the friend of human nature, and one who glories in the title of

An American.

TO BARON STEUBEN.

[MS., Emmet Collection, Lenox Library.]

YORK TOWN June 3ᵈ 1778

SIR/

I very gratefully acknowledge the Receipt of your Favor of the 28ᵗʰ of May by Mʳ Ternant, as well as another which was deliverd to me in Boston. It affords me great Satisfaction to find that Congress, sensible of your Merit, have put it in your Power to do eminent Service to our Country in the Army, and that your Services are so acceptable there. This is the Fulfillment of my earnest Wishes when I had the Pleasure of conversing with you in Boston. May Heaven prosper you. Mʳ Ternants Haste prevents my adding more than that I am with very cordial Esteem

Your affectionate

very humble servᵗ

TO JOHN ADAMS.

[MS., Adams Papers, Quincy.]

YORK TOWN June 21 1778

MY DEAR SIR

Although we are exceedingly pressd with publick Business at this Juncture I cannot omit the Opportunity that now offers of writing to you. The general Scituation of Affairs, and the particular Transactions between the British Commissioners and the Congress will be transmited to you by this Conveyance, by the Committee for foreign Affairs. Since I

last came to this Place from Boston, several Gentlemen have arrivd here from France viz Mr Simeon
Dean, Mr Carmichael, Mr Stephenson, & Mr Holker.
Mr Carmichael comes strongly recommend[ed] by D^r
Franklin & Mr Silas Dean ; but Dr Lee in his Letter
gives Reasons why he cannot place a Confidence in
him. From a long Correspondence with Dr Lee, I
conceive so great an Opinion of his Candor as well
as inflexible Integrity & Attachment to our Country,
that I cannot entertain a Doubt that he would suffer
partial Considerations to operate in his Mind to the
Prejudice of any Man. Such a Difference of Sentiments concerning a Gentleman who I imagine must
be of some Consequence, could not take Place without at least apparently good Grounds ; and it may
produce such Effects on this Side of the Water as
may prove uncomfortable to us if not injurious to
our Cause. Would it not then be doing some Service, to exercise your Prudence in endeavoring to
investigate the real Grounds of it, in doing which
possibly some things may open to View of Importance and at present not thought of.

Dr Lee is a Gentleman of a fair and generous
Mind. I wish therefore that you would freely converse with him upon this Subject if you think you
can do it with Propriety ; and let him know that
I have lately receivd many Letters from him, which
I have duly attended to and would have acknowledgd
to him by this Opportunity, if I had Leisure.

By the last Accounts I have had from Braintree
your Lady & Family were in Health, though anxiously wishing to hear of your safe Arrival.

I shall write to you as often as I can & shall esteem
my self happy in receiving your Favors.
    I remain very affectionately
            Your Friend,

TO MRS. ADAMS.

[MS., Samuel Adams Papers, Lenox Library.]

PHILAD^e July 9 1778

MY DEAR BETSY

Mr Mc Lean the Bearer of this Letter arrivd in
this City yesterday, and tells me he saw you on the
Day he left Boston, and that you were then in Health.
He now returns in so great Haste as to afford me
Time only to let you know that I still enjoy that inestimable Blessing. I now write at the Table in Congress, having just put my Hand to the Confederation
with my Colleagues & the Delegates of seven
other States. North Carolina and Georgia whose
Members are absent have acceded to the Confederation. M^r H has just obtaind the Leave of Absence
and is going home on Account of his ill State of
Health & the Circumstances of his Family. He tells
me his Wife is dangerously ill.
                    Adieu my dear,

TO JAMES WARREN.

[MS., Samuel Adams Papers, Lenox Library.]

PHILAD^e July — 1778

MY DEAR SIR

Capt Manley[1] has obligd me with your favor of

-----

[1] Recently of the Ship *Hancock*. The record of his court martial was laid
before the Continental Congress on August 5, and ordered to be referred to
the Marine Committee for filing among its papers.

the 5th. He and McNeil are both here with different Views. The one to obtain another Ship, and the other to get the Sentence of the Court Martial by which he is censurd & broke, reversd. Perhaps both may be disappointed. I have receivd a Number of Letters by both. One from you. To this I shall pay a very particular Regard, because I am well satisfied you never suffer Prejudices to divert your Attention from the great object—the publick Good. " Manly is a blunt, honest and *I believe* brave officer.' I observe your Caution ; and I admire it because I think it is a proof of your Integrity. Manlys Bravery is an Article of your Beliefe. His Bluntness & Honesty, of Certainty. I have not yet lookd into the Papers ; but I recollect, when they were read in Congress, to have heard the Want of Experience imputed to him, and some thing that had the Appearance of blameing him for not giving out any Signals for the Direction of the Ships under his Command. This it must be ownd, strongly implys the Want if not the total Absense of Discretion. Now I would ask my Friend, whether the Character of a blunt & honest officer entitles him to the Command of one of our Capital Ships if he is "deficient in point of Experience & Discretion." The Characteristick of a Sailor is the blunt honest Tar. They carry this Character to an inimitable Height. But surely every honest blunt or even brave Tar is not fit for Command in our Navy. I some times fear there was an Error in the beginning. Thus much for Manly. " His Address (viz Mc Neils) is insinuating. His Assurance great. He may tell you fine Storys " &c.

How contemptible does he appear. I should think
he had taken a Lesson from Hutchinsons political
Book, if I had not Reason to believe that he used to
despise him most heartily. But I advert to a Letter
from another of my Friends to whose upright opinions I have always given Weight; there I find " He
is *open* & *sincere.*" Synonimous Terms with blunt &
honest. " His Temper is naturally *warm* which he
has sometimes indulgd in speaking his Mind freely
of Persons in office "--This you know has always
been deemd an unpardonable Sin, and I am affraid
it always will be. To be sure it always will be so
deemd by that Kind of Men *in office* who meet with
none to hinder them from persisting in the most expensive Blunders but the *open sincere* and *warm*
Friends of our Country. I am warrented in supposing
this Character belongs to Capt Mᶜ Neil, because my
worthy Correspondent in whose Veracity & Judgment
I have before told you I place a Confidence, has
affirmd to me, that he knows his Sufferings for our
glorious Cause. Has not Mᶜ Neil struck upon this
Rock ? It is possible he has. Says my friendly Correspondent " We all know his Zeal & Sufferings for our
glorious Cause." Such a Character commands my
Friendship ; but it has no Consideration in the present
Appeal. Has he had a fair Trial ? I pay a proper
Regard to the Decisions of a Court martial, & shall
not give my Vote for altering them in any Instance
but when Error Fraud or partiality shall appear plainly
to my own Satisfaction.

Our Navy officers must not expect to pick & chuse
for themselves. They ought to be content with the

Appointments given to them. It is true Appointments should be made with more Discretion than I think they can be by any Men at three or four hundred Miles Distance. For this Reason I moved that they should be made by the Navy Board, which obtain in a certain Degree as you have seen or will see by a Letter from the Marine Committee. Had this been the Case before Olney would have remaind in the Resistance & Bush must have waited for another. If the Queen of France is a better Vessel it will turn out not to the Disadvantage of Olney. While we have more officers in Commission than Ships, there must be Disappointments, Envy, & Suspicions (oftentimes unreasonable) of each other. This is the Make of Man, and we may as well think of stopping the Tide as altering it. The Appointment of Landais affords an ample Subject for the Observations of Speculatists and the Resentment of Navy officers. I think he is, as you observe an ingenuous & well behaved Man, and if he is an able & experiencd officer, as we are assured he is by those whose Duty it is to give us the best Intelligence, it is a pity that two very good Lieutenants sh^d have the Ship & the Service on that account. I hope others may be found to fill their places. "It is an opinion that I was Landais' chief Patron." On this occasion you discover your self, as you are disposd to do on every occasion, partial in my favor. If I was in any Degree instrumental in promoting Capt Landais, it was because I really thought he would be of eminent Use to our Navy. And I question whether it would not have been thought a well judgd Appointment, if there had not been a

fanciful Predilection in favor of Another. Even the
Name of the Ship may have given Disgust to some
Men. I hope when Manly is provided with such a Ship
as will please him the Difficulties or Obstructions in the
Way of getting the Alliance manned will be removd.
I am very sure your Exertions will not be wanting to
promote the Service.

Adieu,

TO JAMES WARREN.

[MS., Samuel Adams Papers, Lenox Library.]

Philad^a July 1778

My dear Sir/
   It is but seldom I can find Leisure to write a long Letter. You must excuse me if I give you my Thoughts
as I am able to recollect and adjust them into any
Order. I find ――― to be an excellent Member of
Congress. He is a thorough and zealous Republican, and an able Supporter of the publick Liberty.
I am satisfied it would be for the great Benefit of our
Country, if you and he were to form an intimate Connection with each other. This I am very desirous of,
because I have no Idea of your being long secluded
from the publick Councils. He will go home shortly.
   I have not yet answerd your Letters of the 26th
and 28th of June. I am in Pain about the Ship in
your Harbour. Her Owners neglect to put her into
Repair, and I fear a great Number of her Officers
and Crew for Want of Skill or Experience will be at
a Loss what to do with her if she meets with a Storm.
What a Pity is it, that an honest old Pilot has

lately been dischargd, who used to steer successfully through Rocks & Quick sands! And that he should suffer this hard Usage, only because, unknown to him one who was a hearty Well wisher to the Voyage, and was anxious that Capacity & Merit might always govern Promotions, had venturd to declare him the fittest Man to take the Command. Ambition, or rather Vanity, and Avarice—an insatiable Thirst for Places and Preferment, without Ability or Intention to fulfil the Duties of them, tends to the Ruin of any Country, and if not eradicated, will soon effect it. It would be the Glory of this Age, to find Men having no ruling Passion but the Love of their Country, and ready to render her the most arduous and important Services with the Hope of no other Reward in this Life than the Esteem of their virtuous Fellow Citizens. But this, some tell us, is expecting more than it is in the Power of human Nature to give. Be it as it may. There are some Men to whom the publick Confidence most certainly ought to be refused. I mean those who in perilous Times have never dared to avow the publick Sentiments.

Last Saturday[1] Congress rec^d another Letter from the British Commissioners. You have it inclosd with a short Resolution[2] in Consequence of it. This shuts the Door until they will be pleased to open it. Governor Johnstone has acted so base a part as to hint the offer of Bribes not only to the President but every other Member of Congress, as you will see by

[1] July 18; the letter was dated July 11.

[2] " That no answer be given to the letter of the 11th instant from the British commissioners."

the Inclosd Letter to Mr R. Morris.   By this he has
in my opinion forfeited the Character of an honest
Man & justly exposd himself to Contempt.   I hope
some Strictures will be made in the Newspapers on
this as well as the disrespectful & even insolent Language in the Commissioners Letter, not so proper to
be noticed by Congress.   I am assured that a Bribe
of 10,000 Guineas has been offerd to a Gentleman
of Station & Character here.   He refusd it as you
might suppose with suitable Resentment, telling the
Lady who negociated this dirty Business, that the
British King was not rich enough to purchase him.

   M^r D[1] of whom I may perhaps hereafter have much
to say to you is arrivd with the Sieur Gerard.   I
have long ago formed my opinion of the American
Commissioner & have not yet alterd it.   That of the
french Minister is, a sensible prudent Man, not wanting in political Finesse & therefore not to be listned
to too implicitly.   The french Squadron lies off Sandy
Hook.   I have inclosd the Names & Rates of the
ships together with the Spanish Ships in N York as
deliverd to us by a Prisoner lately escaped from
thence.   Their Force bears no proportion to each
other.   The Question in my Mind is whether the
french Admiral will risque his large Ships to be workd,
as they must be in an Engagement, in the Narrows
—the Width of the Channel is   and its Depth at
low Water   .   I am told that this is a favorite
Expedition of Count d'Estaign himself, proposd by

---

[1] Silas Deane; Congress on July 11 was notified by him of his arrival on the
Languedoc.

him & not M^r D, to the french Court, and that his
Reputation as a Politician as well as an Admiral is at
Stake. From the Character I have rec^d of him, I
make no Doubt he will answer the highest reasonable
Expectations of the King his Master and of America. M^r D^s political Friends, some of whom I suppose are in Boston, are disposd to give him great
Eclat on Account of the Aid afforded us in sending
this Squadron. His interest with the french Ministry is represented as very forceable in procuring it
and the Newspapers mention the favors conferd on
him even by the King himself. The Truth as I conceive it is, the total overthrow of Burgoyns Army
was an Event which it was thought would produce
Overtures from Britain, and France was apprehensive
of our listening to Terms & compromising Matters.
Hence it was, more than from any other Cause or
the Interest of any Individual that a Treaty was
facilitated & agreed to and to secure us in their Alliance & support us in sending this Squadron, and the
Purpose of M Gerards Mission. We are informd
that Eleven Sail of Merchantmen & a Frigate have
fallen into his Hands.

I have declind answering your Letter of the 26 of
June till I could assure you that the Sum you wishd
for was granted for the Use of your Department. I
now have the Pleasure of informing you that it will
be orderd as soon as it arrives from York Town. It
is every hour expected. The Marine Committee
have agreed that the Navy Board shall appoint
Commanders for Vessels of War under Twenty
Guns.

TO SAMUEL PHILLIPS SAVAGE.

[MS., Samuel Adams Papers, Lenox Library.]

PHILAD Augt 11 –78

MY DEAR FRIEND

I yesterday had the pleasure of receiving your favor by the post, covering the News papers and a Letter, as you emphatically express it, " from one of my closest Friends"; for all which I thank you most heartily.

You ask me what occasiond the very sudden return of Mr H.———[1]. I answer in his own Word to me, His own Want of Health & the dangerous Illness of his Lady. You say he arrivd quite unexpected—you must surely be mistaken; for he publickly said he had Leave of Absence from his Constituents. You add, various are the Conjectures for the true Cause. It is the Lot of a great Man to have every Movement he makes critically scanned, and the strangest Constructions are oftentimes put upon those parts of his Conduct which may be most easily explaind. You have so many Twistings in your Typography and my Eyes are grown so dim with Age that I cannot well discover whether you inform me that his Friends say the *Air* or *Airs* of Philadelphia *doth* not suit him; though I must conclude the former from your usual Correctness in Grammar, for there is an evident false Concord in admitting the latter. Pray let me know whether the News Papers have not done him Injustice in announcing that he made his Entrance into Boston on Sunday. I should think they had; for a well bred Man will carefully avoid counteracting the *vulgar Prejudices* or injuring the Feelings of the People where he may happen to be.

---

[1] Hancock; *cf.* page 41.

I congratulate you on the present happy Appearance
of our publick Affairs, & joyn with you in Praying that
Heaven may still prosper them.

I shall take it as a favor if you will deliver the inclosd Manuscript, without suffering a Copy to be
taken, to Mrs A. I told her, I would send it to her as
being not an unfit Subject for female Inspection &
Criticism.

I am very affectionately,

Yours,

TO PETER THACHER.[1]

[MS., Samuel Adams Papers, Lenox Library.]

PHILAD Augt 11 –78

MY DEAR SIR

I am quite ashamd that I have not yet acknowledgd
the two Letters which I have had the Pleasure of receiving from you since I left Boston ; you will excuse
me when I tell you, I have many Letters, which are
daily accumulating, unanswerd, and very little Leisure.
This by the Way, must convince you how unfit a Person I am even if I were otherwise qualified, to undertake the important Task you require of me in your last.
While I am giving you the true Reason of my Silence,
I hope it will not prevent your writing to me by every
opportunity. Herein you will lay me under great
obligations.

By the late Publications, you have seen, and doubtless have made your own Comments on the epistolary

---

[1] A clergyman, of Malden, Mass.

Correspondence between the British Commissioners
& Congress.   The short Resolution on their last Letter, has put an End to it.   Last Week the Minister
from France had an Audience in Congress.   The
Manner of conducting this Ceremony, together with
a Letter from his most Christian Majesty and the
Speeches of the Minister and the President are publishd in the inclosd News Paper.   I have had several
opportunitys of seeing him at his own House, and a
few days ago he made a Visit to the Delegates of the
Massachusetts who live together.   He is easy and
polite in his Manners and converses freely without
much Ceremony.

Nothing can equal the barefaced Falshood of the
Quakers & Tories in this City, unless perhaps their
Folly, in giving out that M. Gerard does not come in
the Character of a publick Minister, but only to obtain Pay for the Stores we have receivd from that
Country.   These Quakers are in general a sly artful People, not altogether destitute, as I conceive, of
worldly Views in their religious Profession.   They
carefully educate their Children in their own contracted
Opinions and Manners, and I dare say they have in
their Hearts as perfect a System of Uniformity of
Worship in their Way, and are busily employd about
spiritual Domination as ever Laud himself was, but
having upon professed Principles renouncd the Use
of the carnal Weapon, they cannot consistently practice the too common Method made use of in former
times, of dragooning Men into sound Beliefe.   One
might submit to their own inward Feelings, whether
they do not now & then secretly wish for fire from

Heaven in support of their Cause, in order to bring them upon a footing with those whose *Consciences dictate* the kindling fires on Earth for the pious Purpose of convincing Gainsayers, and who keep the Sword in their Hands to enforce it. He who in the Spirit of the Apostle professes to wish Peace to all those who love the Lord Jesus Christ in Sincerity, must discover an unmortified Pride & a Want of Christian Charity to destroy the peace of others who profess to have that sincere Affection to the Common Master, because they differ from him in Matters of mere opinion. But the Post is just going. I must therefore conclude with assuring you that I am affectionately,

Yours,

TO JAMES WARREN.

[MS., Samuel Adams Papers, Lenox Library.]

PHILAD Sept 1 –78

MY DEAR SIR

After having been disappointed several Weeks I am at length favord with your very acceptable Letter of the 18 of August. You have formerly hinted to me your Apprehension that I m^t think your Letters came to me too frequently. I could not then suppose you to be in Earnest; but your Silence from the 17 July to the Date of your last, which you own to be many Days, is a very serious Comment, & obliges me in a formal Manner to assure you, that you cannot gratify me more than by writing to me often.

My Enemies in Boston are exceedingly mistaken

if they think I have condescended to become a Party
Man in their unimportant Disputes about Manly &
McNeil,[1] Neither of whom, in my opinion have derived
any Honor from the Decisions of the late Courts
martial. I wonder how Manly can attribute his Disappointment to me. At my Request he called to see
me. I found him to be one of those Men who stand
in Need of Advice & gave him the best I could. I
told him what Questions would probably be asked
him that he might prepare to answer them. In short
I said every thing to him as a Friend which was
proper for me to say. Perhaps I was too candid to
be thought a Friend. I intended to have been present
at the Committee, but was unavoidably hinderd. He
did not call on me a second time. McNeil is still
here. He has called on me twice or thrice. I know
not in what part of the City he lives. His Friends &
his Enemies may be assured that I will give my Voice
on the Subject Matter of his Petition according to
my best Skill & Judgment. In this I expect to be
justified by those to whose good opinion alone I pay
the least Regard—the candid & impartial.

I heartily despise those small Dealers in Politicks
who are propagating idle Stories to injure me. *Little
Insects will be for ever playing about the glimmering
Light of a farthing Candle.* It is out of their Power
to disturb the peace of my Mind. You took too
much Pains, my dear Friend, to stop their Clamor,
when you read a Paragraph in my Letter which was
designd for your Perusal & not theirs. I am however
obligd to you for your kind Intention.

---

[1] *Cf.* pages, 41, 57, 59, 63.

Your Letter informs me that M^r H is gone on the
Expedition to Rhode Island.[1] This is also announcd
in the Boston News papers, which, to do them Justice
I must observe, never fail to notice all the Movements of a *Great* Man. I am anxious to know the
Event of this Expedition. But I am called off &
must leave you abruptly. Adieu. I must write you
again very soon.

Be so good as to let M^rs know that I am well.

TO JAMES BOWDOIN.

[*Collections* of Massachusetts Historical Society, 6th ser., vol. ix., pp. 423–425.]

[PHILADELPHIA, Septr 3, 1778.]

DEAR SIR,—A few days ago I received a letter
from your son in law Mr Temple dated New York,
August 23^d, requesting me by the first opportunity to
inform you of his & Mrs Temple's arrival there, &
that, for particular reasons he should be exceedingly
happy if your affairs would permit you to meet them
at Philadelphia, or as near it as might be convenient
to you. He requested this of me, because excepting
that letter & another to Mr President Laurens, he had
not written a line since his arrival at N. Y., & he had
still weighty reasons for declining it. He also desired
me to cause it to be made as convenient as might be
(at his expence) for Mrs Temple & her little boy, who
had not been well since their arrival, to get to Philadelphia. His baggage which is both heavy & bulkey,
he intended to get transported in a Flag, if any should

---

[1] See page 60.

be suffered to pass, to Boston, or some port as near
it as might be, & hoped to see me soon in this city.
His letter to the President was read in Congress.   It
was short and contained little more than to sollicit
leave to come to Philad^a to pay his respects to Congress.   This was refus'd upon the idea that he might
be a secret emissary from the British Court.   I think
it is best for him that his request is not granted; for
the jealousy of the people at large would, I believe,
render his residence here very uncomfortable.   A certain Doctor Burkenhout, who came from London in
the same packett with M^r T——, is now in prison in
this city, committed by the authority of this State,
under the same suspicion.   I took occasion to inform
Congress from my own knowledge of Mr Temple,
that although he had been formerly an officer of the
Crown of Great Britain, and in the Customs,[1] yet he
had constantly given great offence to his brother
Commissioners & other friends of that government,
particularly Bernard & Hutchinson, by his attachment to those who espoused the liberties of America ;
that he went to England seven years ago, where, I
understood, he had since lived the greater part of the
time, entirely out of favor at Court & in private life ;
and that I had reason to think his connexions in
Boston had long expected his return to spend his
days there.   Congress afterwards ordered the Secretary to inform Mr Temple, that if it was his intention
to reside in any one of the United States, the same
should be signified by him to the State in which he
intends to reside, & the approbation of that State

---

[1] *Cf.* Vol. I., page 316.

obtaind before a passport could be granted to him. Thus the matter stands in all its particulars, a view of which I thought it proper you should be acquainted with. I wish Mr Temple had turned his attention first to Boston. It is probable he will now do it, and that you will receive a letter from him.

I am with the greatest sincerity,

Your affectionate friend, and humble servant,

TO HANNAH ADAMS.[1]

[MS., Samuel Adams Papers, Lenox Library ; the text is in W. V. Wells, *Life of Samuel Adams*, vol. iii., p. 53.]

PHILADELPHIA Sept 8th 1778

MY DEAR DAUGHTER

Your very dutiful and obliging Letter of the 28th of August came to my Hand yesterday and brought me the afflicting News of your Mothers Illness. When you tell me "the Doctor thinks she is on the mending Hand," and "he hopes she will be cleverly in a Day or two," I am apt to conclude her Disorder had not much abated when you wrote. I know "she is exceedingly loth to give me the least Pain," and therefore I suspect she has dictated to you to make the best of it to me. "She begs of me not to make myself very anxious for her." This is a Request which it is impossible for me to comply with. I shall be very uneasy till I hear again from you. I pray God she may recover her Health and long continue a rich Blessing to you and me. I am satisfied "you do all that lies in your Power for so excellent a Mother."

---

[1] Later the wife of Thomas Wells.

You are under great Obligations to her, and I am
sure you are of a grateful Disposition. I hope her
Life will be spared and that you will have the Opportunity of presenting to her my warmest Respects. I
rejoyce to hear that your late Disorder was so gentle
and that you have got over it. I commend you my
dear, to the Care and Protection of the Almighty.
That He may reward your filial Piety is the ardent
Prayer of

Your very affectionate Father,

TO JOHN BRADFORD.

[MS., Samuel Adams Papers, Lenox Library.]

PHILAD^E Sept 8th 1778

My dear Sir

I have lately had the pleasure of receiving two
Letters from you, one by Capt Manly and the other
by yesterdays Post. The latter makes mention of
some Notice you had receivd "from a warm Friend
to you & me" that "Cap Mc Niel was making Mis-
representations at Philad^e to your Disadvantage." I
have a particular Reason for my Curiosity in wishing
to know who this Friend is. If I had that Knowledge I might perhaps see Grounds of Suspicion that
the Design was far different from that of giving you
a friendly Hint. I assure you I have heard Nothing
here to your Disadvantage. If Capt McNiel is the
Person I am to understand to be your Enemy, I will
tell you that he has called on me not more than twice
or thrice, since he arrivd here, and that he has not
mentiond your Name to me nor any thing relating to

your Department, nor indeed any thing that would tend to bring you to my Thoughts. I know not in what Part of the City he lives. I suppose he is preparing to meet the Marine Committee to whom his Petition is referrd. When it may be proper for me to give my Opinion, I intend to do it, with Freedom & Impartiality, not feeling my self interrested in the Party Disputes which I perceive there are in Boston between two Men, neither of whom in my opinion has derivd much Honor from the Decisions of the Courts Martial respecting them. If I shall hear any thing said to your Prejudice here you may depend on my letting you know it ; being determind if possible to prevent your suffering an Injury which one of your Friends at least thinks he has in being stabbd in the dark. I intend to write you more fully of these Matters at another Time. At present I can only add a Request that you w^d be so kind as to deliver the inclosd Letter to my Daughter and forward the other which is from my Servant to his Friends in Milton. My dear M^{rs} A, I am informd is very unwell.

I am with the most friendly Regard to your Family,

very affectionately,

Yours,

————

TO JAMES WARREN.

[MS., Samuel Adams Papers, Lenox Library.]

PHILAD^e Sept 12 1778

MY DEAR SIR

Your obliging Letter of the 25 of Augt by the

Post came duly to my hand. As you again mention
Cap Manly, I will speak of him to you with Candor.
I never saw him but once, viz last Spring in Boston,
till he came to this City. I had preconceivd an
opinion of his Bravery, in speaking of which you tell
me "no Caution ought to be used," though I have
never yet been pointed to a single Instance of it. I
confess his Appearance in Boston did not strike me
most agreably. He was in the Midst of a Crowd,
who were shouting his Entrance into the Town ; and
like some of his Superiors, he seemd to be intoxi-
cated with popular Applause. I had other Apprehensions, but I give you my most charitable
Thoughts. I retaind however an opinion of him ; for
I concluded, that *Huzza for the brave M,* would
be a sufficient Inducement to him to lay a Pop
Gun Schooner alongside the Eagle, if good Fortune
should throw her in his Way. You think "his Judgment and Abilities would not be equal to others in
the Direction of more Ships than one." Here lies
the Difficulty. Consider his Rank in our little Navy
& judge how soon the Time may perhaps *must* come
when he may have the Command of more Ships, if
you give him the Command of one. Having said
this to you & to no one else, though I have heard
the same thing mentiond by others, *you* will not conclude that I am here deeply engagd in a Party
against him. Some I know will, or will pretend to
form this Conclusion, not from real Regard to the
Merit of M., the Honor of our Navy or the great
Cause we are engagd in, but from a different Motive
and very inferior to either.

I am glad that Landais "rises in your Esteem"—
that "other Captains are convincd he is Master of
his Business which with his agreable Manners & Disposition forcd Conviction of the Judiciousness of his
Appointment." I fancy now that I shall soon be
dischargd the shameful Imputation of having been
"his chiefe Patron here." I have a particular Reason
now to urge that every possible Exertion may be
made to get his and all the other Ships manned.
Last Evening a Letter from Governor Trumbull was
read in the Committee, strongly recommending a
Captain for the Ships at Norwich, who, added to
great Qualifications, can readily get Men for her.
I mentioned Manly as having the Character of a
brave and very popular officer, and read those Parts
of your last Letter to me which related to him. I
am convincd that he need not impute his being
overlookd to any other Cause than the Decree of the
Court Martial which acquitted him *with Honor*.

The Rhode Island Expedition is at Length finishd.
Our Cause is not dishonord though we did not succeed to our Wishes. Congress has approvd the
Retreat—thankd Gen¹ Sullivan & his brave Troops
and applauded the patriotick Exertions of New England. Major Gen¹ Hancock was unluckily at Boston
& missed the Laurel! In my opinion it is in a great
Degree impolitick at this Juncture to suffer an Odium
to be cast on the Count D'Estaing. If there should
be a Disposition to do it I am perswaded Men of
Discretion & Influence will check it. The Tories
will try their utmost to discredit our new Alliance.
And he who not long ago expressd his Opinion that

"a Connection with France will ruin America" will
not fail to promote a Jealousy if he can thereby
establish his Popularity.   Such a Man should be critically watchd on this Occasion.   Adieu my Friend.

TO SAMUEL PHILLIPS SAVAGE.

[MS., Samuel Adams Papers, Lenox Library; a portion of the text is printed in
W. V. Wells, *Life of Samuel Adams*, vol. iii., p. 40.]

PHIL^E Sept 14—78

D^R S^R

I rec^d your favor of the 3^d with the News papers inclosd.   I note well the Contents.   Our Boston Papers
never fail to mark all the Movements of Great Men &
to give Honor where Honor is due.   The *spirited
Exertions* of our Major Generals to be sure ought
properly to be noticed.   Some of them have had the
good Fortune never to be out of the Way of making
a Figure, while others are wisely following the unpopular Steps of Fabius or Count Daun.   The Marquis
La Fayette every one acknowledges, made surprizing
Dispatch in going to Boston and returning to R I ;
but he was sadly mortified in not being present in the
Action on that Island.   He did all that Man c^d do
Impossibilities are not to be expected.   But he arrivd
in Season to take a distinguishd Share in the well
timed & well conducted Retreat.   In *Him* we indeed
see an Instance of a young Nobleman "of Rank &
fortune foregoing the pleasures of Enjoyment of domestick Life and exposing himself to the Hardships
and Dangers of a Camp," not in *his own* but a foreign
Country, "in the glorious Cause of freedom."

Congress requested the President to write to him

& in their Name acknowledge his Zeal & spirited Services on this Occasion by which he has given a fresh proof of his Attachment to our Common Cause. I am sorry to hear there is a Disposition in some persons in Boston to cast an odium on the french Admiral for his leaving Rhode Island. In my Opinion it is at this Juncture impolitick in the Extreme. Even if his Conduct was thought to be blameworthy Prudence I think would dictate Silence to us. Men of Discretion and Influence will surely by all means check such a Disposition.

The Tories will try their utmost to discredit our new Alliance. You know how much depends upon our cultivating mutual Confidence. It is not in the Power of undisguisd Tories to hurt our Cause. Injudicious tho honest Whigs may & too often do injure it. Those whose chief aim is to establish a Popularity in order to obtain the Emoluments of places or the Breath of Applause will think they may serve *themselves* by declaiming on this Subject, or prompting others to do it; and they will not fail doing it though they essentially wound their Country.

If there be any of my virtuous & *publick* spirited fellow Citizens who pay the least Regard to my opinions I wish they would particularly regard what I say on this Occasion.

I have written in haste and must break off abruptly.

TO ————.

[MS., Samuel Adams Papers, Lenox Library.]

PHILAD^E Sept 21, 1778

MY DEAR SIR/

I beg you not to impute my omitting hitherto to
acknowledge your Favor of the 4th of July to Negli-
gence. I have frequently thought of its Contents ;
and although I was not able to obtain what you
wishd for, I think you will not doubt my Sincerity
when I assure you that whenever it shall be in my
Power to render you substantial Service I shall do it
with the utmost Cheerfulness. It is the Opinion of
Gentlemen here that the Appointments of Auctioneers
to make Sale of such Prize goods as fall to the Share
of the Continent should be made by the Authority
of the particular States where such Goods may be
forfeited.

Your Letter was deliverd to me by Capt Manly.
I am informd by some of my Boston Friends that he
speaks of me with a Degree of Bitterness, supposing
that I prevented his having another Ship. This
gives me not the least Disquietude. He may have
been taught to believe it, by Persons who care but
little for him and less for the Honor of our Navy or
the great Cause we are contending for. Neither he
nor his Friends could be at a loss for the true Cause
of his Disappointment, if they would advert to the
Judgment of the Court Martial which acquitted him
with Honor. What a strange Inconsistency was there
in that Court, in recommending Cap Manly for another Ship, and at the same Time holding up so great
a Deficiency in his Conduct as the neglecting to prepare Signals for a Fleet under his Direction, and in

general his Want of Experience. This was said by
many ; and it ought to be satisfactory to Cap Manly,
that though I clearly saw the Justice of the Remark, I
was silent. In this, it is possible, I was not altogether
blameless. I have never felt my self disposd to take
a Side in the Disputes which I understand have run
high between Partizans of Manly & McNiel. I think
Neither of them can derive much Honor from the
Decisions of their respective Courts Martial. I wish
for the Credit of our Country that both had behavd
more to the Satisfaction of the Publick. One of
them is still here. I suppose he is preparing to meet
the Committee to whom his Petition is referrd. When
it may be proper for me to speak my Mind his Friends
& his Enemies may be assured I shall do it with
Candor & Freedom. In doing this I expect to be
justified, by sensible & honest Men. If I stand fair
with them, *you well know*, how unsolicitous I am
whether others are pleasd or not.

There is another Matter of greater Consequence
which I wish to mention to you. I am informd there
are Persons in Boston disposd to make a popular
Clamor against the french Admiral for leaving Rhode
Island. I cannot help remonstrating to my Friends
against it as in a great Degree impolitick. Even if it
should be thought he had taken a wrong step, it is
our Wisdom at this Juncture to forbear criminating
him. The Tories will try their utmost to discredit
our new Alliance. They cannot succeed but by
making injudicious Whigs their Instruments. There
are two things from which I am more apprehensive
than I am from the joynt Efforts of all our Enemies,

viz the intemperate and misplacd Zeal of our honest
Friends, and an insatiable Desire in others who are
called Friends to establish a Popularity in order
to obtain the Splendor or Emoluments of Places,
or that vanity of vanities the Breath of Applause.
Adieu my Friend,

TO MRS. ADAMS.

[MS., Samuel Adams Papers, Lenox Library.]

PHILAD[E] Sept 28 1778

MY DEAR BETSY

Your Letter of the 16th which I just now receivd, is
like cool Water to a thirsty Soul. It gives me in-
expressible Pleasure to have it under your own Hand,
that you are in the Way of Recovery from a dangerous Disorder. I earnestly pray God to restore
you to perfect Health ; and let me intreat you, my
Dear, to be very careful of your self.

I exceedingly regret the Loss which the Town has
sustaind by the Death of D[r] Eliot & D[r] Greenleafe.
In Times so degenerate as these are, it is much to be
lamented that Men of such Exemplary Piety and
Virtue are taken away. I hope the Depravity of
Manners is not so great as to exclude all Hopes of
Childrens rising up and serving God and their Country in the Room of their Fathers. May Heaven
grant us a Time of Reformation !

I think you have done well in putting your Servant
Boy Job an Apprentice to a Sail Maker. I hope you
will injoyn it on him to let you see him often, that
you may give him your Advice, and tell him it is my
Desire that he would attend to it. I love the Boy,

and am still of opinion, that if he is properly mannagd
he will make a good Citizen.

Remember me to my Daughter, Sister Polly and
the rest of my Family & Friends, and accept of the
best Wishes of

your most affectionate,

Write to me by every opportunity.

TO WILLIAM COOPER.

[MS., Samuel Adams Papers, Lenox Library.]

PHILAD^E Sept 30 1778

MY DEAR SIR

I have the pleasure of committing this Letter to the
Care of your youngest Son who having been unfortunately taken in the Brig Resistance, was sufferd
to come to this City to be exchangd for the Purser
of the British Ship Mermaid who is now in N York
on his Parole. This Exchange I effected without
Delay ; and procured from the Navy Board here an
Advance of fifty Dollars, for which he is to account
with the Eastern Navy Board in the settlement of his
Wages. I apprehended this Sum would not be sufficient to discharge the Expence of his Board in this
very expensive place & carry him through his Journey
& therefore I advancd him forty Dollars more, taking his Draft upon you which you will please to repay
to Mrs Adams in Boston.

I introducd your Son to your old Friend the President who receivd him with great Courtesy. Upon
my hinting to the President that if he had publick
Letters to send to Boston, this young Gentleman
would take good Care of them, and it would be

the Means of providing him with an Horse for his
Journey, he very politely told me he should be glad
[to] serve him in that Way, He as well as Monsr
Girard having Letters which m^t be as well sent by
him as by any other Person. I assure you it is not
Flattery to tell you that I am exceedingly pleasd with
your Son. His modest Assurance is very engaging. If his Life is spared and his Morals well fixed,
I think he will make an excellent Citizen. That
the Children of N England may rise and serve God
& their Country in the Room of their Fathers is the
most ardent Prayer of

your cordial Friend,

TO SAMUEL PHILLIPS SAVAGE.

[MS., Samuel Adams Papers, Lenox Library.]

Philad^E Oct 6-78.

My dear Sir

I receivd your favor of the 23^d of Septr by yesterdays Post. You tell me that Boston is become a new
City, and explain your self by mentioning the exceed
ing Gayety of Appearance there. I would fain hope this
is confind to Strangers. Luxury & Extravagance
are in my opinion totally destructive of those Virtues
which are necessary for the Preservation of the Liberty and Happiness of the People. Is it true that
the Review of the Boston Militia was closd with an
expensive Entertainment? If it was, and the Example is followed by the Country, I hope I shall be
excusd when I venture to pledge myself, that the
Militia of that State will never be put on such a Footing as to become formidable to its Enemies. I am

told that such a Practice is contrary to the Letter of the Militia Act. I trust then I was misinformd when I was told that it was countenanced by those who of all Men ought to pay the most sacred Regard to the Law. Are we arrivd to such a Pitch of Levity & Dissipation as that the Idea of feasting shall extinguish every Spark of publick Virtue, and frustrate the Design of the most noble and useful Institution. I hope not. Shall we not again see that Sobriety of Manners, that Temperance, Frugality, Fortitude and other manly Virtues wch were once the Glory and Strength of my much lov'd native Town. Heaven grant it speedily!

Adieu.

TO JAMES WARREN.

[MS., Samuel Adams Papers, Lenox Library.]

PHILA^d 11 Octob^r 1778

MY DEAR SIR

In the inclosd Newspaper you will see certain Queries calculated to impress on the Minds of the people the Idea of Dr Lee's having held a criminal Correspondence with a Person known to be at the same time in the Service & under the Direction of the British Ministry. I hope it will not be in the Power of this Querist to do essential Injury to so eminent a Patriot; who took the earliest & most decisive Part in opposition to the Measures of the British Court, and whose invariable Attachment to the Liberties of our Country never was, and I think cannot be justly suspected. Yet it may be necessary to guard against it;

for I plainly though silently saw when I was last in
Boston a Malevolent Disposition towards Dr Lee, in
a certain Gentleman, who, till he is better known, will
have a great Influence in the Massachusetts State.
The Instance you may recollect, as you was knowing
to it in the Time of it. I then supposd it to proceed
from his having strongly attachd himself, and for a
Length of Time to a Circle of Men, and imbibd their
Prejudices, who are far remote from the Connections
of Dr Lee, and who differ widely from them in the
Adoption of publick Measures regarding either Politicks or Morals.

You may remember that some time ago, in a Letter[1] I informd you that I had much to say to you
about M^r D ; of whom I had long formd my Opinion
& had not seen Reason to alter it. I have hitherto
said Nothing to you about him ; because I knew it
would lead me to Subjects of great Delicacy, which,
if exposd to the Enemy, as they would be if my Letter should fall into their Hands, might disgrace, or
otherwise be prejudicial to our publick Affairs. This
Caution prevents my communicating to you many
things of which I wish to unburthen my Mind.

M^r D was originally taken up by a secret Committee of Congress appointed to procure from France
the necessary Supplys for carrying on the War. By
them he was sent to that Country in the Character of
a mere Merchant. About that Time another Committee was appointed, whose Business it was to form
a Correspondence abroad, and particularly to feel the
political Pulse of France in Hopes of forming a Con-

---

[1] *Cf.* page 47.

nection with that powerful Nation. This Committee also took up M^r D ; and he carried Letters from D^r F to some Men of Eminence, which might enable him in some Measure to penetrate into the Disposition of the Court of France towards America. With these Views M^r D was sent to France. He was to be Agent to the secret Com^e of Commerce. To the secret Com^e of Correspondence he was to be the Inquisitive Man or Intelligencer. He had no political Powers whatever ; and yet he sent us over, Majors, Colonels, Brigadiers & Majors General in Abundance & more than we knew what to do with, of his own creating, till at length M^r Du Coudray arrivd with the Commission (or an Agreement signd by M^r D in behalf of the United States, that he should have one) of a Major General, with the Command of our Artillery ; together with his Suite of about 70 Gentlemen of different Ranks. All this was done, as I said before without any Authority. Congress was exceedingly embarrassd ; being loth to discredit their Commissioner (for before the Arrival of M Du Coudray he was commissiond joyntly with Mess Franklin & Lee) I say being loth to discredit him by disannulling the Convention, and at the same Time judging it dishonorable as well as unsafe for America to ratify it. This however was agreed to in a Com^e of the whole House. Not having the records before me, I do not recollect whether it was confirmd in the House ; but Du Coudray soon after died, his Suite or most of them returnd with Gratifications & M^r D was recalled. After which he was directed to return speedily and give an Acco^t of the State of our Affairs in Europe.

This has given an Occasion to his Friends to hide the
true Reason of his being recalled, & to hold up in the
News Papers an ostensible one, supposing it to be
more for his Reputation.

Our Affairs even in France wore a gloomy Aspect
during the last year until the News of our Army at
the Northward being completely victorious. This
was the decisive Language which commanded our
Success in the Cabinet of France. To this we are
indebted for the Acknowledgm^t of our Independence,
the Treaty and the french Fleet. M^r D is compli-
mented with having procurd this Fleet, and his "spirited Exertions" like those of other *Great* Men have
been puffd off in the News Papers. Unthinking Men
may be amusd with a Golden Snuff Box &^{c}. After
all they are mere Things of Course, especially in the
Honey Moon of National Matrimony.

Since Mr D^s Return as well as before, there have
been Suggestions of his Misconduct in France; and
among other things, of his Misapplication of publick
Money. I cannot say whether these Suggestions are
well grounded or not. Congress is devoting every
Hour to an Enquiry into the Grounds of them which
can be spared from an Attention to other great Affairs, particularly the Finances. The Conduct of an
honest Man will bear the strictest Scrutiny. If the
Friends of M^r D have any Suspicions of his being
tardy, I am inclind to think they will be more apprehensive of a Detection from the Vigilance & Integrity of Dr Lee than any thing else. On such
occasions it is not unusual for the most unblemished of
Characters & sometimes the Lives of the best of them

to be sacrificd in order to prevent "Transactions dark & mysterious" from being brot into open Light.

I have written this Letter in Confidence & shall continue the Subject when I can find Leisure. Adieu.

TO JAMES WARREN.

[MS., Samuel Adams Papers, Lenox Library.]

PHILAD^e Oct 14 — 78

MY DEAR SIR

In my last I inclosd a News paper containing certain Queries calculated, as I conceive, to blast the Reputation of a truly virtuous Man.

I must inform you that Dr Lee & Dr Berkenhout, mentiond by the Querist, were formerly fellow Students at Edinburgh; and as both were esteemed learned in their Profession, it is not improbable that on that Account they kept up their Acquaintance while both continued in Great Britain. Dr Lee you know was requested by Congress to go over to France, where he was made a joynt Commissioner with Messrs Franklin & Dean. It is possible that a Correspondence might afterwards have been carried on between them; but from the Knowledge I have of Dr Lee, I will venture to pledge my self it was not a criminal one, as the Querist would seem to insinuate, and if Dr Berkenhout was in the Service & under the Direction of the British Ministry, which by the Way is but base Suspicion here, it was utterly unknown to Dr Lee. It is doubtful whether any Correspondence was held between these two Gentlemen.

I am rather inclind to think it is a Creature of the Querists own Fancy, or an artful Suggestion thrown out to the Publick to serve the Cause of our Enemies. America sho^d beware how she suffers the Character of one of the most able & vigilant Sup porters of her Rights to be injurd by Questions designd to impute Slander, without any Reasons offerd why such Questions should be made. It is the old Game of mischievous Men to strike at the Characters of the good and the great, in order to lessen the Weight of their Example & Influence. Such Patriots as Lord Russell & Algernon Sydney of the last Age, have of late been falsly & audaciously chargd by a Scotch Tool of the most nefarious Court, with having receivd Bribes from the National Enemy ; and it is not strange that a Gentleman whom the leading Whigs of America have always placd so high in their List of Patriots, who has renderd the most laborious & important Services to our Country in England France & other Parts of Europe, who so often & so seasonably developd the secret Intrigues & Practices of wicked Men & who at this time stands high in the Esteem & Confidence of the Congress, & in addition to this, when it is considerd that there are too many disaffected & insidious Men still lurking among us, it is by no Means a strange Thing that Dr Lee is also chargd with a criminal Correspondence with the Enemy, without even the Shadow of Reason.

The Post who has been retarded by violent Rains is just arrivd & brings me your obliging fav^r of 30 Sept. It contains very interesting Matters which shall have

my Attention at a more leisure Hour than the
present.

Adieu,

TO JONATHAN TRUMBULL.

[MS., Samuel Adams Papers, Lenox Library.]

PHILAD Oct 16 — 78

SIR

I had the Honor of receiving your Excy^s Letter
of the 5th Instant,[1] and sincerely condole with you on
the heavy Loss your Family and the publick sustain
by the Death of your eldest Son. His Services in
my opinion merited great Consideration, and it now
behoves the Publick to render the Settlement of his
Affairs as easy to his surviving Friends as possible.
I have communicated the Contents of your Letter to
my Colleagues & the other Members of Congress, &
you may be assuredSir that we shall interrest ourselves in obtaining with all possible Speed the Attention & Decision of Congress on the Matters set forth
in your Representation.

Mr Sherman was so obliging as to give me the
perusal of your Letter to him, and I am happy that
Congress as a Body concurs with you in the Sentiment therein containd; having passd a Resolution
by a great Majority expressing their Sense that true
Religion & good Morals are the only solid Foundations of publick Liberty and Happiness. . . . . . .
I am Sir with the most cordial Esteem & Respect
Y^r Excy^s most obed^t hbl serv^t

---

[1] Printed in *Collections* of Massachusetts Historical Society, 7th ser., vol. ii.,
p. 276.

TO TIMOTHY MATLACK.

[*Pennsylvania Archives*, 1st ser., vol. vii., p. 14.]

PHILAD^A, Octob^r 16, 1778.

SIR,

I am informd that General Clinton designs to send to the Governor or Assembly of each of the United States, Copies of an insulting Paper, called a Manifesto or Proclamation, calculated to promote a Rebellion, and that the one intended for this State is to be sent by Water up the Delaware. And as it appears to be the Design of the Enemy, as far as it may be in their power, further to pursue their barbarous practice of laying waste our Sea Ports, and that they would be particularly gratified by an opportunity of destroying this City; would it not be proper that one or two of your Gallies should be ordered to watch for them in the River, that they may seize their Vessel & bring the Men up, *blindfold*, to be confined & dealt with according to the Laws of Nature and Nations. You will excuse this Hint, and be assured that I am,

Your very humble Servt,

TO JAMES WARREN.

[MS., Samuel Adams Papers, Lenox Library.]

PHILAD Oct 17 1778

MY DEAR SIR

If I was to tell you that I wonder much at the Conduct of some of our Politicians it might discover my own Folly; for it is said a wise Man wonders at Nothing. Be it so. I am curious to know who made the Motion for the Admission of Gray, Gardiner & Jemmy Anderson? Which of the B[oston] Mem-

bers supported the Motion? Are the Galleries of
the House open? Do the People know that such a
Motion was made? A Motion so alarming to an old
Whig? Or are they so incessantly eager in the Pursuit of Pleasure or of Gain as to be totally thoughtless
of their Country? I hope not. Gracious Heaven!
Defend us from Vanity Folly & the inordinate Love
of Money. Your News Papers are silent upon every
Subject of Importance but the Description of a Feast,
or the Eclat of some Great Man. Your able Patriot is
wholly employd in spirited Exertions of the Military
Kind, or surely he w^d have pourd forth all his Elo-
quence against so detestable a Motion.—" The Motion did not obtain." I rejoyce in this; But Do you
do Justice [to] the House by so faint an Expression?
I hope they rejected it with every Mark of Contempt
& Indignation. Do the Gentlemen who made &
supported this Motion know, that even in this Quaker
Country, they are trying & condemning & I suppose
will hang some of their considerable Men for Crimes
not inferior to those of Gray & Gardiner. Jemmy
Anderson I have forgot. I suppose he is a little Man
& a Scotchman. It is the opinion of the People in
this Country, that a Galloway could not atone for his
publick Crimes with the Sacrifice of an hundred
Lives. A Galloway, a Gray, a Gardiner! Examine
them & say which is the greatest Criminal. Confisca-
tion you tell me labors—" it labors very hard"! I
have heard objections made to it, not in this Country,
but in my own. But I thought those objections were
made by interested Men. Shall those Traiters who
first conspired the Ruin of our Liberties; Those who

basely forsook their Country in her Distress & sought
Protection from the Enemy when they thought them
in the Plenitude of Power—who have been ever since
stimulating & doing all in their Power to aid and
comfort them while they have been exerting their
utmost to enslave & ruin us. Shall these Wretches
have their Estates reservd for them & restored at the
Conclusion of this glorious Struggle in which some
of the richest Blood of America has been spilled, for
the sake of a few who may have Money in England
& for this Reason have maintaind a dastardly and
criminal Neutrality? It cannot be. I venturd
to speak my Mind in a Place where I could claim no
Right to speak. I spoke with Leave which I should
have disdaind to have done, had I not felt the Importance of the Subject to our Country. I will tell you my
Opinion. If you do not act a decisive Part—If you
suffer those Traiters to return & enjoy their Estates,
the World will say, you have no Sense of publick
Injury & have lost your understanding.

Adieu my dear Friend,

TO MRS. ADAMS.

[MS., Samuel Adams Papers, Lenox Library.]

PHILADELPHIA Octob 20th –78

MY DEAR BETSY

A few days ago Mr Brown, a publick Messenger
carried a Letter from me to you, which I hope you
will receive before this reaches you. I feel a Pleasure
when I sit down to write to you and omit no opportunity. My Boston Friends tell me with great Solicitude that I have Enemies there. I thank them for

their Concern for me, and tell them I knew it before. The Man who acts an honest Part in publick Life, must often counteract the Passions Inclinations or Humours of weak and wicked Men and this must create him Enemies. I am therefore not disappointed or mortified. I flatter my self that no virtuous Man who knows me will or can be my Enemy; because I think he can have no Suspicion of my Integrity. But they say my Enemies "are plotting against me." Neither does this discompose me, for what else can I expect from such kind of Men. If they mean to make me uneasy they miss their Aim; for I am happy and it is not in *their* Power to disturb my Peace. They add, The Design is to get me recalled from this Service. I am in no Pain about such an Event; for I know there are many who can serve our Country here with greater Capacity (though none more honestly). The sooner therefore another is elected in my Room the better. I shall the sooner retire to the sweet Enjoyment of domestick Life. This, you can witness, I have often wishd for; and I trust that all gracious Providence has spared *your* precious Life through a dangerous Illness, to heighten the Pleasures of my Retirement. If my Enemies are governd by Malice or Envy, I could not wish them a severer Punishment than their own Feelings. But, my Dear, I thank God, I have many Friends. *You* know them. Remember me to them all as you have opportunity. I could say many more things to you, but I am called off. My Love to my Daughter & Sister Polly and the rest of our Family and Connections. Adieu. Your most affectionate,

TO JOHN ADAMS.

[MS., Adams Papers, Quincy.]

PHILAD^a Octob 25, 1778

My dear Sir/

Your Favor of the 24th of May did not reach my hand till yesterday. The Gentleman who brought it, Mr Archer, tells me he had a Passage of Eleven Weeks. I will show him the Respect due to the Character you give him, & properly regard such future Recommendations as may come from you.

I suppose you have been fully & officially informd of the State of our military Affairs since the Enemy evacuated this City and met with a Drubbing at Monmouth. And as publick Letters will doubtless be forwarded by this Conveyance, it is needless for me to give you a particular Detail of what has happend since. By those Letters you will be informd that Dr Franklin is appointed Minister Plenipotentiary at Versailes. It is not yet determind how you will be disposd of ; but as Congress entertain great Expectations from your Services, you may depend upon Employment being allotted for you somewhere. The critical Situation of the Powers of Europe in general, renders it somewhat difficult for us to determine, to which of them to make our Addresses at present. Every Cabinet I suppose is busily engagd in making the necessary Arrangements and preparing for the opening of a Campaign, if War should take Place. In this Case, I should think France must be our Pole Star, while it continues, and our Connections must be formd with hers. In the mean time however, Holland, whose Policy is always to be at Peace, may be open for a Negociation; and in my opinion, we ought to take the earliest opportunity to tempt her.

The two main Armies at & near New York have been quiet since the Enemy retreated to that City. We have made another Expedition against Rhode Island. Our Arms were not disgracd, though we did not succeed to our Wishes. Gen¹ S behavd as usual with Bravery; but some will have it that there is a Mixture of Imprudence in every thing he does. He promisd himself to share with Gates in the Glory of Victory, and as an officer of Spirit, no doubt he felt vexed with the Disappointment; but he was too sanguine in my Opinion when he expected that the Count D Estaing would remain there, in the Circumstances which he was thrown into by a violent Storm he met with when in Pursuit of Lord Howe. This unforeseen & unavoidable Accident left him too much inferior to the British Squadron to run the Risque with any Degree of Prudence. It was a Misfortune which we all regret, but must bear. Knowing the high Temper of the People of my native Town, I immediately upon hearing it, wrote to some of the principal Men to prevent Blame being cast on the Count for leaving Rhode Island; a Disposition which I apprehended the artful Tories (for such there are even there) would encourage with a View of discrediting our new and happy Alliance, in the Minds of injudicious Whigs. I am happy to be informd that the Count and his Officers, and indeed every french Gentleman is treated there with the highest Marks of Respect and Friendship.

For some Weeks past there have been Reports here

that the Enemies Troops at N York were about to embark, as they gave out on a grand Expedition, and we are now assured that Sixteen Sail of the Line and about one hundred and fifty Transports put to Sea on Tuesday the 20th Ins^t. Various are the Conjectures of their Destination. Whether to Boston, South Carolina or the West Indies, a few Days will decide. The Count D Estaing has sufficiently securd his Ships in Case of an Attack on them ; and if they land their Troops with Intent to march them to Boston, it is my opinion they will repent of their Expedition. It appears to me most probable that the Troops are bound to the West Indies, and that the Ships of War, after having convoyd them to a certain Latitude will return for the Protection of the Garrisons which I suppose are to be left at Newport and New York. The Enemy will be loth to quit the small Portion of Land they possess within the United States, for though they must despair of subduing us by Arms, it will be necessary for them to oblige us to continue the Expence of large Armies in order to nonplus us in the Art of financiering. This may be a Method of carrying on the Contest, the most puzzling to us ; but I trust we shall disappoint them.

The Marquiss De la Fayette whose extraordinary Merit is fully known to you, does me the Honor of taking the Care of this Letter, and will deliver it to you.

I am, my dear Sir, with the greatest Sincerity
                                        your affectionate,

TO ARTHUR LEE.

[MS., Lenox Library; a draft is in the Samuel Adams Papers, Lenox Library.]

PHILADELPHIA Octob 26 –78

My DEAR SIR

Your several Letters dated as in the Margin,[1] with the Inclosures came to my Hand. And although I have not hitherto acknowledgd to you the Receipt of them, I assure you I have been and am still improving the Intelligence you have given me, to the best of my Power, for the Advantage of this Country. From our former Correspondence you have known my Sentiments. I have not alterd them in a single Point, either with Regard to the great Cause we are engagd in or to you who have been an early, vigilant & active Supporter of it. While you honor me with your confidential Letters, I feel and will freely express to you my Obligation. To have answerd them severally would have led me to Subjects of great Delicacy, and the Miscarriage of my Letters might have provd detrimental to our important Affairs. It was needless for me to run this Risque for the sake of writing; for I presume you have been made fully acquainted with the State of our publick Affairs by the Committee, and as I have constantly communicated to your Brother R. H. the Contents of your Letters to me, it was sufficient on that Score, for him only to write, *for he thinks as I do.*

The Marquiss De la Fayette, who does me the Honor to take this Letter, is this Moment going, which

---

[1] 1777 : July 31, October 4, November 11, December 18, December 19; 1778 : January 2, January 9, February 8, February 16, March 1, April 1, April 16.

leaves me Time only to add that I am and will be your
Friend, because I know you love our Country and
Mankind.

I beg you to write to me by every Opportunity.
Adieu my dear Sir,

TO ———————.

[MS., Lenox Library.]

PHILAD Oct 26 –78

Mr Duncan yesterday brought me your very affectionate Letter of the   Instant.   I rejoyce that you
have recoverd your usual State of Health and that my
Family enjoy that invalueable Blessing.

Is it possible that M could make & propagate so
barefaced a Story as you mention?   Are you not misinformd? I lose every Sentiment of Regard for him as
a Man of Truth.   I have heard that my Enmity to
G. W. was objected ag^t me on a late Occasion.   I did
not wonder that those who believd it were displeasd
with me.   My very worthy Friend & colleague M^r D
satisfied the Minds of those who meant well and explaind some things relating to M^r ——— which were
new & surprising to them.   I console myself that those
who try to injure me (I must not call them Enemies)
are obligd to fabricate malicious Falshoods for their
purpose.

Tell my Friend M S. that I will answer his Letter
the next post.   In the mean time ask him whether a
Christian is bound to confide in the Man who has
attempted seven times (though in vain) to ruin him.
Adieu.

MANIFESTO OF THE CONTINENTAL CONGRESS.

October 30, 1778.

[W. V. Wells, *Life of Samuel Adams*,[1] vol. iii., pp. 46, 47.]

The United States having been driven to hostilities by the oppressive and tyrannous measures of Great Britain, having been compelled to commit the essential rights of men to the decision of arms, and having been at length forced to shake off a yoke which had grown too burdensome to bear, they declared themselves free and independent.

Confiding in the justice of their cause; confiding in Him who disposes of human events; although weak and unprovided, they set the power of their enemies at defiance.

In this confidence they have continued through the various fortunes of three bloody campaigns, unawed by the power, unsubdued by the barbarity of their foes. Their virtuous citizens have borne without repining the loss of many things which make life desirable. Their brave troops have patiently endured the hardships and dangers of a situation fruitful in both beyond former example.

The Congress, considering themselves bound to love their enemies as children of that Being who is equally the Father of all, and desirous, since they could not prevent, at least to alleviate the calamities of war, have studied to spare those who were in arms against them, and to lighten the chains of captivity.

The conduct of those serving under the King of Great Britain hath, with some few exceptions, been

---

[1] Also attributed to Adams by Niles, *Principles and Acts*, pp. 476, 477.

diametrically opposite. They have laid waste the
open country, burned the defenceless villages, and
butchered the citizens of America.

Their prisons have been the slaughter-houses of
her soldiers, their ships of her seamen, and the
severest injuries have been aggravated by the grossest
insults.

Foiled in their vain attempts to subjugate the
unconquerable spirit of freedom, they have meanly
assailed the representatives of America with bribes,
with deceit, and the servility of adulation. They
have made a mock of religion by impious appeals to
God, whilst in the violation of His sacred command.
They have made a mock even of reason itself, by
endeavoring to prove that the liberty and happiness
of America could safely be intrusted to those who
have sold their own, unawed by the sense of virtue or
of shame.

Treated with the contempt which such conduct
deserved, they have applied to individuals. They
have solicited them to break the bonds of allegiance
and imbue their souls with the blackest crimes. But
fearing that none could be found through these
United States equal to the wickedness of their purpose, to influence weak minds they have threatened
more wide devastation.

While the shadow of hope remained that our enemies could be taught by our example to respect those
laws which are held sacred among civilized nations,
and to comply with the dictates of a religion which
they pretend, in common with us, to believe and
revere, they have been left to the influence of that

religion and that example.   But since their incorrigible dispositions cannot be touched by kindness and compassion, it becomes our duty by other means to vindicate the rights of humanity.

We, therefore, the Congress of the United States of America, do solemnly declare and proclaim that if our enemies presume to execute their threats, or persist in their present career of barbarity, we will take such exemplary vengeance as shall deter others from a like conduct.   We appeal to the God who searcheth the hearts of men for the rectitude of our intentions ; and in his holy presence declare that, as we are not moved by any light or hasty suggestions of anger or revenge, so through every possible change of fortune we will adhere to this our determination.

Done in Congress by unanimous consent, the thirtieth day of October, one thousand seven hundred and seventy-eight.

TO SAMUEL PHILLIPS SAVAGE.

[W. V. Wells, *Life of Samuel Adams*, vol. iii., pp. 56, 57 ; a draft is in the Samuel Adams Papers, Lenox Library.]

PHILADELPHIA, Nov. 1, 1778.

MY DEAR SIR,—

I duly received your favor of October—by the last post, and should have immediately answered it, had I not been that day exceedingly engaged.   I do not keep copies of all my letters,—they are trifles.   You were mistaken in supposing that I ascribed the independence of America to New England *only*.   I never was so assuming as to think so.   My words are, that

America is obliged to New England, and this is an
acknowledged truth. It is the opinion of others, as
well as myself, that the principles and manners of New
England, from time to time, led to that great event.
I pray God she may ever maintain those principles
which, in my opinion, are essentially necessary to
support and perpetuate her liberty. You may see my
sentiments of the patriotism of other States in a letter
I lately wrote to Mrs. Adams (if it is in being), in
which I relate a conversation which passed between
Monsieur ———— and myself. But enough of this.
I love my country. My fears concerning her are that
she will ruin herself by *idolatry.*

A part of your letter, you tell me, is confidential.
I always keep the secrets of my friends when I can do
it honestly, though I confess I do not like to be en-
cumbered with them. In this instance I will be your
confidant. But let me ask you, can a difference between Mr. ———— and me, either real or imaginary,
be of any consequence to the world? I think not.
Tories, you say, triumph. They may make sport of
it; but indeed, my friend, it is too unimportant a
matter for a sensible Whig to weep and break his
heart about. I am desirous of making you easy; and
I do assure you that, so far from brooding in my heart
an unfriendly disposition towards that man, I seldom
think of him, unless I happen to take up a Boston
newspaper or hear his name mentioned in chit-chat
conversation. You call upon me by all that is sacred
to forgive him. Do you think *he* has injured *me ?* If
he has, should he not ask for forgiveness? No man
ever found me inexorable. I do not wish him to ask

me to forgive him ; this would be too humiliating. If
he is conscious of having done or designed me an
injury, let him do so no more, and I will promise to
forgive and forget him too; or, I would add, to do
him all the service in my power. But this is needless ;
it is not in my power to serve him. *He* is above it.

If you wish to know the foundation of this wonderful collision, ask my friend J. W., or another, whom
you properly call my closest friend. To them I have
related the trifling tale, and they can repeat it to you.

The precepts and examples you refer me to I shall
always reverence most highly.

I am, with unfeigned sincerity,

Your obliged and affectionate friend,

TO JAMES WARREN.

[MS., Samuel Adams Papers, Lenox Library.]

PHILAD^A Novr 3 1778

MY DEAR SIR

In your last you ask me what we are doing ? Many
Things indeed. And if you will suppose some things
to be done well, I will frankly confess to you that in
my opinion others might have been done better. I
think we do as well as we can considering the Pile of
Business every Morning laid on our table. In order
that the Affairs of the Treasury may be better attended than they possibly can be by Members of
Congress who are obliged to give their Attendance
in the House we have establishd a new Board to consist of a Treasurer Comptroller Auditor & two Chambers of Acco^ts of three each. These officers are all

chosen from without Doors. We are taking Measures
for the Appretiation of the Currency. Every Adept
in financiering is busily employd and I hope we shall
before long agree in an effectual Plan. We have appointed Dr F. Minister Plenipo. at Versailes & written a Letter of Credence to our good & great Ally.
The Situation of the general Affairs of Europe render
it somewhat difficult to determine to which of the
other Powers at present to make our Court. Every
Cabinet will, I suppose, this winter be deeply engagd in making Arrangements and preparing for
the opening a Campaign in Case of a general War
which it is more than probable will happen. Our
Friend A L is in Spain. Our other Friend J A will
be employd somewhere. France must be our Pole
Star & our Connection must be formd with hers.
Holland whose Policy is always to be at Peace may
be open to Negociation & the sooner we tempt her
the better. Spain must joyn with France. But she
is dilatory. I wish she would recollect how much she
was injured by it the last War, when she sufferd the
common Enemy to beat France & her self in Detail.
The Spirit of Chatham is indeed extinguishd in
Britain. His decisive Mind might have dictated the
Seizure of their Float at Sea. Perhaps it is well
the Great Man is no more. The Millions are safely
arrivd & the Tone of Neutrality at Madrid is become
languid. A formidable Fleet lies equip'd in Cadiz
which operating with that of France at this Juncture
might give a fatal Blow to the boasted Sovereignty
of Britain on the Ocean. The Count D' Estaings
Squadron I suppose will go to the West Indies. If

so, must not the British follow with a great Part of their Troops, if they mean to keep Possession of their own Islands. They may leave Garrisons at N York & Newport, with a View of obliging us still to maintain a great Army, in hopes we shall be undone by Expences while they despair of subduing us by the Power of their Army. We must have a respectable Army in the Spring to put a good face on our Negociations or to fight. I hope we shall secure to the United States, Canada Nova Scotia & *the Fishery* by our Arms or by Treaty. Florida too is a tempting object in the South. Perhaps if you should show this Letter to some Folks, it may be thought to confirm an opinion from whence an objection was drawn against me on a late occasion "that I was averse to Reconciliation." We shall never be on a solid Footing till G B cedes to us what Nature designs we sh[ould] have or we wrest it from her.

The Marine Committee have obtain a Warrant for 150,000 Dollars for your Department which will be forwarded speedily. Congress has increasd your Salaries to 3000 Dollars p Annum. I had this in View when I intreated you in my last, not to resign your Seat. Nothing would reconcile me to this but your having one here. I am determind to make Room for you by a Resignation next Spring. I flatter my self I can yet be in some Degree useful to my Country in a narrow Sphere. I wish for Retirement & covet Leisure as a Miser does money.

Adieu,

RESOLUTION OF THE CONTINENTAL CONGRESS.

November 3, 1778.

[MS., Papers of the Continental Congress.]

It having pleased Almighty God through the Course of the present year, to bestow great & manifold Mercies on the People of these United States; And it being the indispensible Duty of all Men gratefully to acknowledge their obligations to Him for Benefits receivd.

Resolvd, That it be and hereby is recommended to the legislative or executive Authority of each of the said States, to appoint Wednesday the 30th day of December next to be observd as a Day of publick Thanksgiving and Praise. That all the People may with united Hearts on that Day express a just Sense of His unmerited Favors:—Particularly in that it hath pleased Him, by His over ruling Providence to support us in a just and necessary War for the Defence of our Rights and Liberties;—By affording us seasonable Supplys for our Armies—by disposing the Heart of a powerful Monarch to enter into Alliance with us and aid our Cause—by defeating the Councils and evil Designs of our Enemies, and giving us Victory over their Troops—and by the Continuance of that Union among these States, which by his Blessing, will be their future Strength & Glory.

And it is further recommended, that together with devout Thanksgivings may be joined a penitent Confession of our Sins, and humble Supplication for Pardon through the Merits of our Savior. So that under the Smiles of Heaven, our publick Councils

may be directed—our Arms by Land and Sea pros-
perd—our Liberty and Independence secur'd—our
Schools & Seminaries of Learning flourish—our
Trade be revivd—our Husbandry and Manufactures
increasd, and the Hearts of all impressd with undis-
sembled Piety, with Benevolence, and Zeal for the
publick Good.

And it is also recommended that Recreations un-
suitable to the Purpose of such a Solemnity may be
on that Day—

TO SAMUEL PHILLIPS SAVAGE.

[MS., Samuel Adams Papers, Lenox Library.]

PHILAD Novr 10th 1778

MY GOOD OLD FRIEND

I am at present in great Haste ; but as a Supple-
ment to my last I will ask you, *Who* among the Sons
of America ought to enforce the Example of the
illustrious young Foreigner ? *Who* is substituting
other Means of Dissipation in my native Town in
Lieu of Theatrical Entertainments &c &c ? *Who*
has mixed the Grave and the Vain, the Whigs and
the Tories in Scenes of Amusement totally incompat-
ible with the present serious Times ? Who among
the Grave and Who among the Whigs, I mean such
Whigs as have a feeling for their distressd Country
and the Multitudes of distressd Individuals in it,
are present at such Entertainm^ts ? Is there a Man
among them to whom our Country has entrusted her
Independence, her Virtue, her Liberty ? What can

be the Views and Designs of such a Man, but to establish a Popularity by forming a Coalition of Parties and confounding the Distinction between Whigs and Tories, Virtue & Vice? When I was last in Boston, I seizd an Opportunity to advise my Fellow Citizens to beware of their popular Men—to penetrate their Views and Designs. There was comparatively no great Danger from a great Man set over them by the British Tyrant. When the People set up a Great Man of their own, their Jealousy is asleep, & they are in Danger of a *Master*. I have no personal Prejudices or Attachments. Many things I have to say to you if I had Leisure.

My due Regards to your Lady, to M^r S and his Family.

Adieu,

P. S.—I am not inattentive to what you said in my last relating to my Friend Mrs M. I will endeavor to serve her in the Instance she mentions, but she must not depend upon Success.

TO JEREMIAH POWELL.[1]

[MS., Samuel Adams Papers, Lenox Library ; a text is in *Historical Magazine*, 1st ser., vol ii., pp. 196, 197.]

PHILADELPHIA Decr 1, 1778

Sir/

I did myself the Honor a few Days ago, of Joyning with my Colleagues in an Answer to your Letter to

---

[1] President of the Council of Massachusetts.

us of the fifth of November last, so far as it related to the Distribution of a Quantity of Flour purchasd on Account of the State of Massachusetts Bay. I beg Leave to refer you to our Letter, which will be forwarded by this opportunity. The five hundred Dollars therein mentiond as receivd by me, were carried to the Credit of the State in my Account settled the last Winter. Since my Arrival here in July, I have availd my self of the Practice of the Delegates of every State, by applying to Congress for a Warrant on their Treasury for a Sum of Money to pay the extravagant, though necessary Expence of living. I purpose to repeat this Application, as there may be occasion for it, until I shall be directed differently or to the Contrary; and shall credit the Sums so receivd in my next Account.

I am informd that the General Assembly have been pleased to appoint me one of their Delegates in Congress for the year 1779. This repeated Mark of Confidence in me is indeed flattering. The Duties of the Department are arduous and pressing. I will never decline the Service of our Country; but my Health requires Relaxation, and at this Period of my Life my Inclination would lead me to wish to be employd in a more limitted Sphere. I will nevertheless continue to act in Congress to the utmost of my Ability in Pursuance of the Powers and Instructions with which I am honord, in hopes, that as the Month of April will complete another full Year of my Residence here, I shall then be relievd by one of my absent Colleagues or some other Gentleman, and permitted to return to my Family.

I am with every Sentiment of Duty & Regard to
the General Assembly,
            Sir
        Your Honors
            most obedient
                & very humble servant,

TO MRS. ADAMS.

[MS., Samuel Adams Papers, Lenox Library ; a portion of the text is in W. V.
    Wells, *Life of Samuel Adams*, vol. iii., pp. 57, 58.]

PHILADELPHIA Decr 13 1778

MY DEAR BETSY,

Captn. Johnson will deliver you this Letter, which
incloses a Publication in the last Tuesdays Paper.
You will easily guess which of the Massachusetts
Delegates it is intended for. The Design of it is to
represent Mr Temple as a British Emissary and that
Delegate as listening to his Proposals of Accommodation with Great Britain, and thus to beget a Suspicion
of him in the Mind of the Minister of France, with
whom he has the Honor of being on friendly Terms.
That Delegate has been so used to the low Arts of
Tories in his own Country, as to have learnd long ago
to treat them, wherever he sees them, with ineffable
Contempt. He does not think it worth his while to
satisfy the Curiosity of the Writer, but he can assure
his Friends, that he had never called on M^r T but
once and that was to show him the way to Mr President Laurens' House, to whom he had Letters to
deliver, one of which was from the Council of Massa-
chusets Bay. As a Delegate from that State, he
could do no less than show such a Piece of Civility

to M^r T, and he is determind, notwithstanding the
apparently friendly Hint, to treat him as he thinks
proper.   Indeed he has been told by a *real* Friend,
that there are Persons *in Pay* to watch his Words and
Actions.   He thankd his Friend, and told him that
such kind of Intimations were not new to him.   It might
be well or ill grounded, & he was perfectly indifferent
about it.   He had a private Conversation a few Days
ago with Monsieur ————, in which the Subject of
the Hint beforementiond was brought up.   That Per-
sonage was pleasd to say, that he well knew the Character of the Delegate before his Arrival in America,
and that there was no Reason to doubt of his Attachment to the joynt Interest of France & America—
that he had sufficient Proofs of it to prevent any ill
Impressions being made on his own Mind ; with other
Expressions of Friendship & Confidence. ———— ————
Between our selves, I can not say I am not embarrassd with Mr T^s Arrival here ; He is highly recommended, and I believe him to be an honest American.
But the Time & Manner of his leaving England fix a
Suspicion in the Minds of well disposd Men, which
cannot easily be removd ; and his Residence at the
Court of America, if I might so express it, gives bad
Men a Sort of Occasion, to say that Congress, not-
withstanding all they have publickly given out, are
secretly treating with the Ministers of Great Britain
through their Emissaries in America, than which
Nothing can be more contrary to Truth.   I do not
care therefore how soon M^r T thinks of returning to
New England.
    It is diverting enough to hear the different Lan-

guage held forth concerning me, by a kind of Men whom I despise beyond Expression. In New England they say I am averse to an Accommodation with Great Britain, and make that an Exception against me. In Philadelphia I am chargd, indirectly at least, with a frequent Exchange of Visits with the Companion of Berkenhout, Lord Lindsay, Governor Johnston & the Son of Lord Bute, with a View of secretly bringing about an Accommodation with that King and Nation which I have solemnly abjurd. What is there which Malice joynd with a small Share of Wit will not suggest! I am not apt to conceal my Sentiments. They are far from being problematical. They are well known here & at Boston; and I can trust my Consistency in the Judgment of every honest and sensible Man that is acquainted with me. The Censure of Fools or Knaves is Applause.

Mʳ Silas Dean has lately publishd a Paper here filled with Insinuations and Assertions without any Evidence to support them, against Dʳ Lee. I have long ago formd my Opinion of both those Gentlemen, and have never yet seen Reason to alter it. I have sent the Paper to my Friend General Warren. I wish you would invite him to a Dish of Tea, and desire him to let you see it and my Letter which inclosd it. You may read this Letter to him and other Confidential Friends, but dont let it go out of your own Hands.

I never was in better Spirits than at present.—My Love to my Daughter, Sister Polly & the Rest of our Family & Friends. Adieu my dear Betsy,

Your very affectionate,

I forgot to tell you that last Friday Mʳ President

Laurens having dischargd the Duties of his Station for more than one year with Fidelity & to the Acceptance of the Members, resignd the Chair, and John Jay Esqr a Delegate from New York was chosen in his Room. To this Gentleman I chearfully gave my Vote.

Mrs Clark and her Sister Miss Daily in whose house the Massachusetts Delegates are agreably scituated present their respectful Compliments to you.

TO THE COUNCIL OF MASSACHUSETTS.

[W. V. Wells, *Life of Samuel Adams*, vol. iii., p. 59; a draft is in the Samuel Adams Papers, Lenox Library.]

MARINE COMMITTEE, PHILADELPHIA, December 15, 1778.

SIR,—

Pursuant to the direction of Congress and the request of the Minister Plenipotentiary of France, I have the honor of transmitting to the Council of Massachusetts Bay a declaration under the hand and seal of that Minister, promising a reward to every vessel that shall take or destroy a vessel of the enemy loaded with masts or spars, and destined to the ports of Halifax, Newport, or New York. It is the particular desire of the Minister that this declaration may be addressed to that Honorable Board, to the end that the same may be made known in such a manner as their wisdom shall direct.

I am, sir, your most obedient and very humble servant,[1]

---

[1] Signed by Adams as chairman of the Marine Committee of the Continental Congress.

TO JAMES BOWDOIN.

[MS., Samuel Adams Papers, Lenox Library.]

PHILAD⁵ Decʳ 19ᵗʰ 1778

MY DEAR SIR

Mʳ Temple[1] was so obliging as to deliver me your Letter of the —— of November. The Day after his Arrival in this City, I offerd him my Service and introduc'd him to Mʳ President Laurens, to whom he had Letters of high Recommendation, and among others from the Council of Massachusetts Bay. The President read these Letters publickly in Congress. I did not fail to communicate the Contents of those which I was honord with to individual Members. But the Time of his leaving England, his coming in a Packet, the Company which came with him, and the greater Indulgencies granted to him in New York than had been allowd to others fixed a suspicion of him in the Minds of well disposd Persons which could not be removd. Those of a different Character took Occasion to insinuate that whatever Congress might give out publickly to the Contrary, they were secretly listening to Terms of Accommodation offerd by the British Ministers through their Emissaries in America. The Minister Plenipotentiary of France could not but be attentive to these Suggestions. In a private Conversation with him at his House the other Day, when no one was present with us, Mʳ Temples Name was mentiond. He said he knew not his personal Character—he understood that he was well recommended, but as he was under

---

[1] *Cf.* page 54.

the violent Suspicions of the People here, his Residence so near the Congress might make improper
Impressions on the Minds of Persons abroad. It
may reasonably be supposd that he is determind to
merit the Character at his own Court, of a vigilant &
faithful Minister. Mr Dean who appears to be inimical to my truly patriotick Friend A Lee Esqr has endeavord to raise the like Suspicions of him that he
has a predilection for the Court of London because
he showed Civilities to his Friend Ld Shelburne in
France. Such is the force of prejudice in the Minds
of some Men or their total Want of political Understanding. I was my self, pointedly, though not
by Name, called upon in a publick Newspaper, to
be cautious of making too frequent Exchanges of
Visits with J T Esqr. You know much I have been
used to despise Publications of this Kind & I despise
them still. But in the present Instance I confess I
was embarrassd, being under the Necessity of violating my own Inclination to pay all due Respect to a
Gentleman, whose personal Merit I had formerly
been acquainted with, and who was so honorably
mentiond by some of my most virtuous & dignified
fellow Citizens, or on the other hand of prejudicing
the Character which as a publick Man I ought to
maintain in the Minds of Congress, of the Minister
of France and of the People. I have done Mr Temple the most substantial Acts of Friendship in my
Power, though I could not have the Pleasure of so
much Conversation with him as I wishd & intended
to have. He leaves this City suddenly. I am inclind
to believe that the President of this State as well as

the Chief Justice, with both of whom I have this day had the pleasure of dining, are satisfied in the Uprightness of Mr Temples Intentions. Having given you a candid State of things, I conclude with assuring you that I am with every Sentiment of Regard,

Your affectionate Friend

& very humble Servant,

TO JOHN WINTHROP.

[MS., Samuel Adams Papers, Lenox Library.]

PHILAD Decr 21 1778

MY DEAR SIR

Your obliging Letter of the [9th] of November was deliverd to me by Mr Temple immediately after his Arrival here. I must candidly confess that when the Gentleman informd me by his Letter dated in New York, of his Intention then to pay a Visit to this City, I was disagreably impressd with it, and interrested my self, as far as I could do it with Decency, to prevent it. A certain Dr Berkenhout was here at that Time. He had formerly been a fellow Student with Dr Lee in Edinburgh ; and although he brought no Letters from him, he made an Advantage of the old Connection, and addressd himself to Richard Henry Lee Esqr, the Doctors Brother & a Member of Congress, who from the Beginning of our Contest has been exceedingly obnoxious to our Enemies from his firm & invariable Attachment to our Cause. Dr Berkenhout was put into Prison by the Authority of this State on Suspicion, and afterwards dischargd for Want of Evidence against him. Perhaps he sufferd the more, from a certain Set of Men for valueing himself on Col° Lee; and the Col° himself has since sufferd the Reproach of an angry Writer and disappointed Man, for shewing Civility to a Person who was once acquainted with his Brother. So true is the Observation I have somewhere met with, that a Man hardly ever speaks with another, but sooner or later he finds that he has receivd Good or Harm from it.

Had Mʳ Temple arrivd at that Juncture, I do verily believe he would have shared the Fate of Berkenhout. And the Testimonials he has since brought with him, added to the warm Recommendations of some of my most virtuous and honorable Fellow Citizens have not been sufficient to obtain for him a welcome Reception. The Time & Manner of his leaving England, the Company he came with and the favorable Treatment he met with in New York, were judgd to be Grounds of Suspicion which more than balanced the Recommendations of his Friends & Countrymen, who, though acknowledgd to be very respectable, it was supposd, might possibly be partial in their Judgments of him. His Connections in Boston, & the Character he had sustaind there before he left that Place, it was said, made him the fittest Instrument to carry into Effect the Purposes of the British Ministers. The honest and zealous Whigs clamord against him because they imagind him to be a British Emissary; and the artful Tories, who would cordially receive such a Character into the Bosom of their Councils, if they could be sure of keeping him among themselves, joynd in the Clamor, either because they believd him to be a true American, or, if they judged him to be a

Spy, as they pretended, they did not chuse to trust
him in the Hands of those who might possibly draw
from him the Secrets of his Employers and detect
him. The Tories appeard to be the most acute Politicians, as in my Opinion, I am sorry to say it,
they too often are. Thus M^r T has had the Misfortune
to be spoken ill of both by the Friends and Enemies of
the Publick. A very grievous Misfortune, when the
People scrutinize and decide upon Characters with
Candor & Moderation, which perhaps does not take
Place at all Times in any Country.

I have shown Mr Temple the most substantial Acts
of Friendship in my Power ; yet I must own to you I
have been somewhat embarassd. A Delegate of the
Massachusetts Bay who has been heard to say that
" Jealousy is the best Security of publick Liberty,"
has been called upon in a publick News Paper " to
be cautious of too frequently exchanging Visits with
J T Esqr who is suspected to be a Spy " &^{c}. I have
no Reason to think it was a friendly Caution ; but
rather that it was designd to bring an odious Suspicion on the Delegate himself. But though he feels
a Contempt of such Kind of Publications, he has
learnd that it is Wisdom to receive Instruction even
from an Enemy. I have said that Jealousy is the
best Security of publick Liberty. I have expressd
my Fears that America is too unsuspecting long to
preserve Republican Liberty. I do not suspect M^r
Temple ; but I have been under the Necessity of
violating my own Inclination to pay every kind of
Respect due to that Gentleman, or risque the *consistent* Character which a Delegate of that State

ought to support in the Opinion of Congress, of the
Minister of France and the People of America.   I
have converst with that Minister on this Occasion ;
and I have Reason to think we concur in opinion,
that however pure the Views & Intentions of any
Gentleman may be, yet if a Suspicion generally prevails that he is secretly employd by the British Court
his continuing to reside near the Congress may make
improper Impressions on the Minds of our Friends
abroad.   Mr Temple left this City yesterday.

I congratulate you my dear Sir on our Countrys
having thus far sustaind the glorious Conflict.   Our
Independence, I think, is secured.   Whether America
shall long preserve her Freedom or not, will depend
on her Virtue.

I cannot conclude this tedious Epistle without
expressing an ardent Wish for the full Recovery of
your Health and bespeaking another & another of
your Favors.

I am with most respectful Compliments to your
Lady & Family,

Your very affectionate Friend
& humble Servt,

TO SAMUEL COOPER.

[MS., Samuel Adams Papers, Lenox Library.]

PHILADELPHIA Decr 25 1778

MY DEAR SIR

I have receivd your Favors of the 7th & 20th of
November, the former of which was deliverd to me
by the Honble Mr Temple.   That Gentleman is intitled

to my Esteem from the opinion I entertain of his
personal Merit, and from your Recommendations and
those of some others of my virtuous Fellow Citizens.
I have done him every Act of Friendship in my
Power; but Circumstances, of which he is not un-
apprized, have prevented my having so much Conversation with him as I could have wishd for. The Time
and Manner of his leaving England, the Company he
came with, the favor granted him at New York of
writing a Letter to Mr President Laurens requesting
Permission to pay his Respects to Congress, and
another to myself, neither of which, it was presumd,
could have passd without the Inspection of General
Clinton, nor sufferd by him to pass unless they had
been adapted to his Views—These were made the
Grounds of Suspicion of him then; and they were
afterwards judgd sufficient to overbalance the Letters
he brought from his Friends & Countrymen, respectable as they were acknowledgd to be by all, who
might be supposd possibly to have judgd partially in
his Favor. I am sorry our Friend has been thus unfortunate because I believe his Motives in coming
here were pure; and yet we must allow those, who
never were acquainted with him to give all that
Weight to Circumstances which in other Instances we
m^t our selves be inclind to think reasonable. I am
satisfied there is a Design among them to leave no
Method untried to raise a popular Clamor against
those who took an early active Part & have continued
consistent in Support of the Liberties of America.
They are at this time endeavoring to stimulate a
Persecution against my patriotick Friend Dr Lee,

who from the Knowledge I have of his publick Conduct since he has been employd by Congress and a
constant political Correspondence with him for near
ten years past, I am well assured, deserves the highest
Esteem and Gratitude of these United States and
Massachusetts Bay in particular. It concerns those
who are determin'd to persevere in this glorious Contest till the Liberty and Independence of America
shall be firmly establishd to be exceedingly circumspect lest their Conduct should be misrepresented by
designing Men and misunderstood by others. An
angry Writer has lately insinuated in a publick Newspaper among other injurious things, that Arthur Lee
Esqr communicated the secret Negociations of France
& America to the British Ministers, because he showd
Civility to Lord Shelburne in Paris. Had Mr Temples
Friends appeard to be very intimate with him here,
the like Insinuation might have been thrown out, &
with a similar View, to draw an odious Suspicion on
them. Indeed such an Attempt was made as you will
observe in the inclosd Paragraph taken from Dunlaps
Paper.[1] You who know much of my Heart will easily
guess which of your Delegates the Hint was intended
for. I leave it to your Conjecture. I have openly
declared my Opinion that Jealousy is a good Security
of Publick Liberty. I have expressd my Fears that
America is too unsuspecting long to continue free.
These I know are the sentiments of Dr Lee. When
Men hold these Sentiments & honestly act up to the
Spirit of them they must necessarily become exceedingly obnoxious to those who are watching every

---

[1] *The Pennsylvania Packet.*

Opportunity to turn the good or ill Fortune of their
Country, and they care not which to their own private
Advantage.   Such Men there are in this Country, in
France & indeed in all Countries & at all times.
Some of them you & I have known. Such Men there
always have been & always will be, till human Nature
itself shall be substantially meliorated.   Whether
such a Change will ever happen and when, is more
within your Province than mine to predict or ascertain.   A Politician must take men as he finds them
and while he carefully endeavors to make their
Humours & Prejudices, their Passions & Feelings,
as well as their Reason & Understandings subservient
to his Views of publick Liberty & Happiness, he must
frequently observe among the many if he has any
Sagacity, some who having gaind the Confidence of
their Country, are sacrilegiously employing their
Talents to the Ruin of its Affairs, for their own private Emolument.   Upon such Men he stamps the
Stigma *Hic niger est*, and if he thinks them capable
of doing great Mischief to prevent it, he ventures to
hold them up to the publick Eye.   This he does at
the Risque of his own Reputation ; for it is a thousand
to one but those whose Craft he puts at Hazard, will
give him the odious Epithets of suspicious dissatisfi-
able peevish quarrelsome &ᶜ, and honest, undiscerning Men may be inducd for a time to believe them
pertinent ; but he solaces himself in a conscious Rectitude of Heart, trusting that it will sooner or later be
made manifest ; perhaps in this World, but most assur-
edly in that Day when the secret Thoughts of all Men
shall be unfolded.   I have many things to say to you

particularly of Arthur Lee & Silas Dean Esq.rs Of both these Gentlemen I long ago made up my opinion, and I have never seen Reason to alter it. But I will relieve you by putting an End to this tedious Epistle. I intend to get myself excusd from further publick Service here, and hope before long to think aloud with you & my other Confidential Friends in Boston. I do not mean however to quit the Service of our Country altogether while I am capable of rendering myself in the least Degree serviceable. I earnestly wish for more Retirement & Leisure. *Esto perpetua!* is my most ardent Prayer for this rising Republick. That will depend upon the Principles and Manners of the People. Publick Liberty will not long survive the Loss of publick Virtue. Favor me, my dear Sir, with your Letters frequently while I remain here, and be assured of the warmest Sentiments of Friendship & Esteem in the Breast of

your very affectionate,

TO CHARLES CHAUNCY.

[MS., Samuel Adams Papers, Lenox Library.]

PHILAD.Decr 25 1778

REVEREND & MUCH ESTEEMED SIR

I am greatly indebted to you for your very acceptable Letter of the 7th of Novr by Mr Temple. That Gentleman, in my Opinion took an unguarded Step on his late Arrival in New York. I mean his writing a Letter to the late President Mr Laurens requesting Permission to pay his Respects to Congress, and another Letter to myself. This excited a Suspicion

in the Minds of the true Friends of our Cause, that
what they had before seen in the English News papers,
viz that he & Dr Berkenhout were sent to America by
the British Ministry might not be without Grounds.
This Desire of paying a respectful Visit to Congress
was judgd to be a Reason merely ostensible ; and
the Time & Manner of his leaving England, the Company he came with and the Readiness with which the
British General granted him the Liberty of sending
his Letters, the Contents of which must most undoubtedly have been under his Inspection, it was said,
afforded Reason to believe his real Design was to
gain an honorable Admission into this City, & the
Confidence of Members of Congress & others thereby
the more easily to cooperate with the British Commissioners, and carry their Designs into Effect.   The
Jealousy of the People when it is properly directed or
as some chuse to call it, a prudent Caution, is in my
Opinion one of the best Securities of publick Liberty.
And we must allow them to give all that Weight to a
Train of Circumstances respecting our Friend, which
in other Instances we sh^d ourselves judge to be reasonable.   His Friends have given him high Recommendations.   But say others, his Friends may be partial
to him.   His Connections are among the warmest
Patriots.   His Testimonials come from the most
virtuous Citizens.   *They* have a good Opinion of him.
True, and this might be a strong Inducement to a
politick Minister to make Choice of *him*, & may make
him the fittest Instrument to answer his Purpose.
For my own Part I know Mr Temples former Character Conduct & Sufferings & have also a good opin-

ion of him. I have done him the most substantial
Acts of Friendship in my Power. But so deep rooted
were the Suspicions of him and so general, that I
have been under a Necessity of forbearing to visit
him so often as I otherwise should have done, lest I
might lose that consistent Character and that Confidence which it is my Duty as far as I am able, to
support, in the Minds of Congress, the Minister of
our Ally & the People of America. I have Reason
to believe that I am on Terms of Friendship with the
Sieur Gerard. In private Conversation with him, I
purposely mentiond Mr Temples Name, & I conclude
we concur in Sentiment that however upright the
Heart of any Gentleman may be yet if an Opinion
prevails among the People that he is a secret Emissary
from the Enemy, his Residence near the Congress,
might, at this Juncture especially, make improper
Impressions on the Minds of *our Friends* abroad.
Mr Temple has lately taken his Leave of this City &
I believe some Gentlemen of Character have since
conceivd a more favorable Opinion of him than they
did before.

You have my hearty Thanks for your Sermon lately
publishd which I have read with pleasure. The Evil
you therein mention is indeed alarming. Amidst the
great Variety of pressing Affairs, Congress is devoting certain Hours of every Day to investigate a radical Cure ; and I am in strong Hopes that an effectual
Plan will shortly be laid before the General Assemblies
of the several States.

When General Gates was orderd to Boston a considerable Embarkation of the Enemies Troops had

been made at N York & it was apprehended they
would attempt a Landing somewhere near that Place.
His military Abilities and Experience, his political
Principles & Attachments and the Confidence which
the Troops and People of the Eastern States had in
him, were the Considerations which inducd his being
sent thither.   Had the Enemy turnd their whole Force
that way of Course the Commander in Chief would
have followd.   General Heath has given entire Satisfaction to Congress during his Command there.
The Change took Place on the Spur of the Occasion,
and probably in the Spring a different Arrangem^t may
be made.

I am my dear Sir with the most cordial Esteem &
Affectionate,

your Friend
& very humble Servt,

TO SAMUEL COOPER.

[MS., Samuel Adams Papers, Lenox Library.]

Jany 3-79

MY DEAR SIR

I embrace the opportunity which now offers of
writing a few Lines to you.   In my last I told you I
had many things to say particularly concerning A L
& S D Esq^{rs} [1]. If I could have the Pleasure of sitting with you by a fire Side, I would more freely
open my Mind to you than I chuse to do upon
Paper, considering the Risque of its falling into
wrong hands.   One of these gentlemen, as I was

---

[1]Arthur Lee and Silas Deane.

informd in the year 74 by some who were well acquainted with him, was of a dubious political Character, and was appointed a Delegate in Congress by
a Majority of only one of the Electors; it being
thought that his own Vote turnd it in his favor.   In
75 he was again elected ; and he very early attachd
him self to Men of different Sentiments from those
which most if not all your Delegates brought with
them from your Country & strenuously maintained.
This Difference of Sentiment was said to arise from
local Attachments, but in Reality they arose from
different Principles & Views.   What M^r D^s political
Principles were if he had any I never could learn.
His Views always appeard to me commercial & interrested.   Whether I was mistaken or not Time
perhaps will soon discover.   He was very little known
in America till the year 75, if at all in Europe.

The other took an early, decided and active Part
in Support of the great Cause.   In London he had a
great Share in the open Opposition made to the
Tyranny of the British Court & their Measures
respecting America.   There he turnd his Attention
from the Practice of Physick to which he had been
regularly educated in Edinburgh, to the Study of the
Law.   This he did by the Advice of some of the
most able Advocates for the Liberties of America,
from an Opinion they had conceivd of his promising
Usefulness to that Cause in that Way.   He answerd
their Prospects.   He constantly aided your Agent
the late M^r De Berdt[1] to whom his Knowledge of
Affairs renderd his Services essential.   That his Pen

---

[1] Cf. Vol. I., page 89 et seq.

was employd for America in General, his Junius
Americanus abundantly testifies ; and that, and his
other Publications witness his Attachments to Massachusetts Bay & South Carolina in particular.   His
private Letters to his Friends are written with that
Freedom as well as Zeal which would have exposd
him to the Risque even of his Life from the Resentment of an unprincipled & nefarious Court, if any of
them by Accident or Design had fallen into their
Hands.   This I know to be true.   I must conclude
at present with giving it to you as my fix'd Opinion,
founded on particular observations, that there is a
joynt Combination of political & commercial Men to
exclude all vigilant Patriots from publick Councils &
Employments knowing that Vigilance & unimpeachd,
unsuspected Fidelity will be an effectual Bar to the
carrying such politico commercial Plans into Execution.   I will write to you again by the first good
Opportunity.   In the mean time I am with perfect
Esteem,

Y^r affectionate Friend,

TO JAMES WARREN.

[MS., Samuel Adams Papers, Lenox Library.]

PHILAD^E Jan 6 –79

MY DEAR SIR

In your last you desire to know how Matters have
operated since the Recall.   I will answer this Question
at another Time when I have more Leisure ; and at
present only say, that Mr Dean arrivd here, I think in

July, and in August he was admitted into the House, or to use his own Phrase *had an Audience*, in which, with as much Vanity as I ever saw in a Man of Sense, he assumd to himself almost the whole Merit of all the Services which had been renderd at least by Americans in France; as if he would have it to be believd that one of his Colleagues had done but little if any thing, the other worse than Nothing, himself every thing. And with as much Spleen & ill Nature he would even go out of the regular Path of Decency & Propriety to draw in Invective and diminish the Characters of the two Mr Lees & Mr Izard.[1]   In short the publication which you have seen is a Specimen of his Narrative.   I have before given you my opinion of that Performance, and shall not trouble you further upon that, than just to remark that his insinuating that M^r W L[2] still remains an Alderman of the City of London, because his Name is inserted in that List in the Court Kallendar of 78 discovers something more than Childishness and Folly.   His design seems to be at once to prejudice the Reputation of that Gentleman in the Minds of his Countrymen and to hold up the Appearance of glaring Impropriety of Conduct in Congress, in appointing the Alderman of London an American Commissioner; and that this was done through the undue Influence of family Connections; for he takes particular Care to inform his Readers, that the two Brothers in Europe have two Brothers in Congress which cannot be denied.   Neither can it

---

[1] Ralph Izard. *Cf.* Wharton, *Revolutionary Diplomatic Correspondence*, Vol. I., p. 589.
[2] William Lee. *Cf., Ibid.*, p. 586.

be denied, that they are a Family, who have been as
early, as uniform, as persevering and as able Patriots
as perhaps any in the United States. M^r A L, you
are fully sensible was most indefatigable in supporting
our Cause in England. By penetrating into the
Designs of a most unprincipled Court, he was able to
give us the most timely and important Intelligence,
which he did at the Risque of his Life; while M^r D
was, in the Opinion of some of his own Countrymen
as well as others, of a doubtful political Character.
Mr Lee continued to transmit to our Friends in
France as well as to Congress before he left England,
the most accurate Accounts of things there. Such
was the opinion entertaind by Congress of his Abilities his Integrity, his Zeal and Attachment to his
Country which indeed had been long experiencd, that
he was employd as a most useful & necessary Man.
The vigilant Eye of so consistent a Patriot, may be
formidable to a Combination of political & Commercial Men, who may be aiming to get the Trade, the
Wealth, the Power and the Government of America
into their own Hands. He must therefore be hunted
down ; and the *young* as well as the old Hounds are
all ready for the Game.

Adieu,

TO SAMUEL COOPER.

[MS., Samuel Adams Papers, Lenox Library.]

Jany 6 –79

MY DEAR SIR

I wrote to you on the 3^d Ins^t by Express and then
promisd to write again by the first good Opportunity.

The Bearer of this Letter is a young Gentleman of
your Country who is passing thro this place in his
way home.   He appears sensible, tells me he was
educated at H. College, has since studied Physick,
was taken at Sea & carried into England, was liber-
ated or made his Escape & went over to France, from
Paris he went to Dunkirk on the Encouragement of
Mr Dean & enterd Surgeon on board the Revenge
Sloop, built by order of a Com^e of Congress authorizd
thereto & at the Continental Expense, and till lately
supposd to have ever since remaind Continental Property, but now so invelopd in political Commercial
Mystery as that it cannot be ascertaind whether she
is ownd by the United States or private Persons, or
whether she is the property partly publick & private.
I will tell you more of this Matter when the Mystery
shall be unraveld if it ever is ; in the mean time remember my dear Sir what I said in my last of commercial Combinations.

In the latter End of 75 one of the Characters in my
last was left out of the Delegation of the Colony he
had represented, and a Number of his Friends gave him
a sort of Certificate or Letter of Recommendation as
they had before done to one of your Delegates,[1]
which led me to think it was their Opinion he needed
a Prop in his own Country.   Soon after, the Congress
appointed a secret Committee of Commerce, with a
View of procuring from abroad the necessary Articles
for carrying on the War.   They also appointed a
secret Committee of Correspondence.   Their Business was to form political Connections abroad & to

---

[1] *Cf.* Vol. III., p. 269.

feel the pulsations of foreign Powers & particularly France. The first of these Committees engagd M^r ―― to go to that Kingdom for the purpose of their Commission & the Corresponding Com^e took the Advantage of his intended Residence there to facilitate the salutary Purpose of their Appointment. At the same Time they wrote a Letter to M^r ―― then in England from whom the Congress had before receivd the most accurate Intelligence, requesting a Correspondence with him & pledging Secrecy & Confidence. M^r ―― arrivd in France in June 76. Thus you see we had an Intelligencer to let us know what was doing or meditating against us in England; and a political Commercial Agent who was to inform us what was doing or could be done for us in France. The one had before settled a Correspondence & formd Connections in several parts of the Continent of Europe & particularly France; the other was a perfect Stranger in every Nation in Europe, but bearing Letters to considerable Men there. The one was altogether the political Man, the other had to do with Commerce as well as politicks. The one by his Address obtaind in England such Assurances as satisfied him that France would afford such Aid to America as she could consistently, the other was better skilld in the commercial Part of his Agency than the political. The one in London in the Months of March and April discoverd that he might successfully & actually did treat with a Merchant in France of no Capital but a favorite at Court for a Supply to the Value of £200,000 sterling—the other arrivd in the Month of June following, found him

out & was somehow concernd in forwarding the
Supplys thus contracted for. I dare say you are apt
to draw this Conclusion that the one was the political
Negotiator in this Instance & the other the Commercial Agent only—yet, will you believe it, it is
positively affirmd that the one did every thing & the
other Nothing. I will explain it to you in my next.

TO SAMUEL COOPER.

[MS., Samuel Adams Papers, Lenox Library.]

Jany 19–79

My dear Sir

Inclosd is the Newspaper of this Day. Philalethes
in attempting to show that the Supplys from France
were not a Present *from that Court*, which nobody
that I know of has asserted, has abundantly proved
one thing which Common Sense has insisted on viz
that A Lee had been negociating with Mr Beaumarchais for those Supplys, before Mr Dean arrivd
there. No one I suppose would have thought of
weighing Mr Deans Merit so critically, had he appeard content with his full Share of it. But when he
takes so much Pains to represent his Colleagues as
having done Nothing, it becomes a Piece of Justice
to enquire whether they have in Reality been such
unconcernd or impotent Spectators of their Countrys
Misery and Want. Dr Franklin has the *Honor* of
being Mr Deans *venerable Friend;* Mr Lee, an insignificant or troublesome Colleague. And yet Mary
Johnsons assiduous Applications procurd the sending
a Ship loaded with Merchandise & Stores to the

Value of twenty five Thousand Pounds Sterling ; and
this Negociation was settled before Mr Deans Arrival
in France.   Mr Lee acted as the *political* Minister.
He pressd on Mr Beaumarchais "the maintaining the
War in America as the great Object." And indeed
it was so.   Mr Lee and every Man of Discernment
knew, that it was the Policy of France to consider it in
this View.   On this Consideration he succeeded, and
yet, says Mr Beaumarchais, "the Gratitude of Congress is due to the indefatigable Pains Mr Dean has
taken thro' the whole of the *Commercial* Transaction."
The Truth is, as I suppose, that Mr Dean did not
care to return without some such Letter of Recommendation ; and it was probably as easily obtaind as
the other which I mentiond in my last.   Mr Beaumarchais is a Man of Ingenuity & Wit.   Horace was
the Delight of the Court of Augustus.   A Royal
Letter & a Snuff Box, as I once told one of my
Friends, are Things of Course, especially in the
Honey Moon of National Matrimony.   A Monarch
politely compliments thro' the Minister the Ministers
Sovereign.   When the Merchant and the Courtier
unite in one Man, the Courtier is safe in imitating
his Master, and pays *his* Compliment in the Stile &
Manner of the Merchant.

Mr Deans Friends are in hopes he will be sent to
Holland as a Reward for his good Services, from
whence he may prcbably send or bring another mercantile Letter of Recommendation.   Doubtless deep
Commercial Connections may be formd there.   They
are willing M^r J A should go to Spain.   The Design
of this is to get M^r A L removd from thence.

Others are for sending M^r A to Holland leaving M^r
L in Spain, to whose Influence in that Country our
Armies are indebted for Supplys of Blanketts Shoes
and Stockins.   I am sorry to be obligd to think, that
a Monopoly of Trade, and not the Liberty of their
Country, is the sole Object of some Mens Views.
This is the Cake which they hope shortly to slice and
share among themselves.

Adieu,

TO JONATHAN TRUMBULL.

[MS., Samuel Adams Papers, Lenox Library.]

PHILAD Feb 6 –79

SIR

The Marine Com^e have done themselves the Honor
of writing to you by this Post.   The great Dammage
which has been done to the Trade at the Southward
& particularly Chessapeak Bay by the Enemies
Privateers has causd such pressing Demands for the
Aid of our Ships of War as laid us under the Necessity of ordering the Queen of france immediately on a
Cruize that Way.   This I mention as a Reason why
she could not be employd with the Confederacy &
the other Ships but her Destination will remain a
Secret.

I hope the Expedition proposd by your Excy &
agreed to by the Com^e will be performd in 2 or 3
Days, for I fear if it should be known to the Enemy,
not only the desired Event w^d be prevented but there
would be danger of our losing our Ships.

I have only time to beg the favor of your Excy to forward the inclosd by the first Opp^{ty} by the post or otherwise.

TO JOHN WINTHROP.

[MS., Samuel Adams Papers, Lenox Library.]

PHILAD^E Feb 6 1779

MY DEAR SIR

I have receivd your favor of the 21st of January. Every Body sees that the Depreciation of the Paper Currency is owing to the Floods of it which have been necessarily issued. In Addition to which a great Quantity more especially of the Emissions of 20 May 1777 & 11 April 1778 has been counterfeited. This last Consideration was sufficient Inducement to the calling out of Circulation all the Bills of those Emissions as speedily as possible. The lessening the Quantity in Circulation is the only Means of restoring the Value & Credit of the Remainder. It would therefore be a happy Event if every possessor of them would receive Loan Office Certificates for them instead of new Bills in June next but this cannot be expected. In proportion as this may be done the only effectual Means, besides that of taxing which I hope will be chearfully submitted to by the People, of remedying the great Evil will have its effect. Congress have not cried down those Emissions, as the Expression is or resolvd that the Bills should sink in the Hands of those who would not exchange them for Loan Office Certificates, as has been done in the Eastern States. This might have been too harsh a

Remedy. They have left it in the Option of the
Possessors to receive either such Certificates or new
Bills. This is the obvious Intention of their Resolutions on the Subject. The Wish of every discerning honest Man must be as obvious, viz that as many
of the Bills may sink in the Loan Offices as the
People can possibly spare, and as soon as possible.
I think therefore you have judgd right of their Views.
It would be an Act of Charity and a great Service to
the publick if those who can afford to put their Money
to Interest would ease their poorer fellow Citizens
who are possessd of those Bills, by exchanging them
for other Bills without a Discount.

I am &ᶜ,

TO SAMUEL ALLYNE OTIS.

[MS., Samuel Adams Papers, Lenox Library.]

PHILADᴱ Febʸ 10 1779

DEAR SIR

The late Mʳ Andrews before his sudden & unexpected Death had written to a young Kinsman of
mine in this place, Mʳ Richard Checkley, proposing
to him to go to Boston with a View of employing
him in his Warehouse. I know not whether Mʳ A
intended to employ him in his own separate Affairs
or in those in which he was joyntly concernd with
you for the publick. Mʳ C had not heard of his
Death till he was just about setting off on his Journey
to Boston when I informd him of it. He is a young
Man who, I am told, bears a good Character and is
used to Business. If you can employ him it will be

doing him a singular Benefit and I shall acknowledge
it as a great favor. I ask it only on this Condition,
that it may be perfectly consistent with your Views.
I am with Cordial Esteem, Sir

y^r hble Servt

TO JAMES WARREN.

[MS., Samuel Adams Papers, Lenox Library.]

PHILAD^E Feb 12 –79

MY DEAR S^R

Will you be so kind as to present my due Regards
to Mrs Warren and let her know that immediately on
my receiving her Letter for Miss Wray I deliverd it
to the Care of my worthy Friend Col° Laurens who
has since informd me that he has forwarded it in his
own Packet to South Carolina.

I have lately written several Letters to my Friend
D^r C & have informd him that you & he & M^r S are
my only confidential Correspondents in Boston. I
have other trusty Friends there, but I have not
Leisure to write to them all. I have expressd my
wish that the honest & virtuous Friends of our Country would cultivate a cordial Esteem for each other.
I am affraid there are little Jealousies among them
which prevent their uniting their Councils and Efforts
against that Inundation of Levity Vanity Luxury
Dissipation & indeed Vice of every kind which I am
informd threatens that Country which has heretofore
stood with unexampled Firmness in the Cause of
Liberty and Virtue. This Torrent must be stemmed,
and in order to do it effectually, there must be Asso-

ciations of Men of unshaken Fortitude. A general
Dissolution of Principles & Manners will more surely
overthrow the Liberties of America than the whole
Force of the Common Enemy. While the People
are virtuous they cannot be subdued; but when once
they lose their Virtue they will be ready to surrender
their Liberties to the first external or *internal* In-
vader. How necessary then is it for those who are
determind to transmit the Blessings of Liberty as a
fair Inheritance to Posterity, to associate on publick
Principles in Support of publick Virtue. I do verily
believe, and I may say it inter Nos, that the Principles
& Manners of N Eng^d, producd that Spirit which finally has establishd the Independence of America; and
Nothing but opposite Principles and Manners can
overthrow it. If you are of my Mind, and I think
you are, the Necessity of supporting the Education
of our Country must be strongly impressd on your
Mind. It gives me the greatest Concern to hear
that some of our Gentlemen in the Country begin to
think the Maintenance of Schools too great a Burden.
I wish they could hear the Encomiums that are given
to N Eng^d by some of the most sensible & publick
spirited Gentlemen in the southern States, for the
Care & Expence which have been freely borne by our
Ancestors & continued to this time for the Instruction
of youth. Virginia is duly sensible of the great Importance of Education, and, as a friend in that Country informs me, has lately adopted an effectual Plan
for that necessary Purpose. If Virtue & Knowledge
are diffusd among the People, they will never be
enslavd. This will be their great Security. Virtue

& Knowledge will forever be an even Balance for Powers & Riches. I hope our Countrymen will never depart from the Principles & Maxims which have been handed down to us from our wise forefathers. This greatly depends upon the Example of Men of Character & Influence of the present Day. This is a Subject my Heart is much set upon. But I fear I have wearied your Patience. I will conclude with my most ardent Prayer that our last Days may be our best Days and our last Works our best Works.

Adieu my dear Friend,

Pay my due Regards to your Circle in Plymouth. Are you intimate with Mr D. I mentiond him to you in a former Letter as an excellent Republican.

TO THE BOARD OF WAR AT BOSTON.

[MS., Samuel Adams Papers, Lenox Library.]

PHILAD Feb 16 1779

GENT^N

I rec^d your Let^r of 27 Jan and immediately communicated such of the Contents as relate to your Application to the Govr of N Y, to the Delegates of that State. They assured me that the Gov^{rs} refusing to grant a Permit to Mr Shepperd for the Transportation of Flour from thence must have been owing to the real & very great Scarcity of that Article there; and they desired me to satisfy you in that point, fearing that it m^t be supposd to arise from other Motives. I will consult with my Colleagues and if any Means can be used by us to ensure Success to your Application from that Quarter you may depend upon our Exertion.

I am inclined to think that Govr C, who in my Opinion is a truly good Man, is apprehensive of being imposd upon by Speculators, unless he uses great Caution; and he may perhaps not be fully apprisd of your asking under the express Authority & Commission of Massachusetts State. And yet I sh^d suppose your Letter to him would have been sufficient without authenticated Documents manifesting your Appointment. South Carolina is at so great a Distance that no Interposition of ours could avail, if it were necessary in the present Instance; but I am of Opinion there will be no Difficulty there in Case your Vessel arrives, the Embargo being over. I will write to Mess P in B & endeavor, sh^d there be any obstructions there to get them removd. A Com^e of Con have under Consideration a Letter from the Council of M B[1] on the Subject of provisions, & I am informd they are ready to make Report.

If any thing sh^d occur which will make it expedient for me to write you further I shall not omit the first Opp^{ty}. In the mean time I am &^c,

---

TO SAMUEL COOPER.

[MS., Samuel Adams Papers, Lenox Library.]

PHILAD Feb 21-79

MY DEAR SIR

By the last Post I sent to M^r W C[2] some Extracts

---

[1] Massachusetts Bay.   [2] William Cooper.

from an extraordinary Letter which I hope he has
receivd.   I think our Apprehensions are thereby
strengthned, of an intended Monopoly of all the
Trade and I may add of the richest Lands in America.   The private & publick Letters of my Friend on
the other side of the Atlantick having honestly stated
Facts and led to important Discoveries, have renderd
him an object of the hottest Resentment of interrested
Men.   I protest to you solemnly that the warm
Affection I feel for a Man whom I never saw, is
founded in a thorough Conviction of his long and
unremitted Attachment to the Interests of America
& of Mankind.   But I will leave this Subject for the
present.

   The Spring advances, and very probably some new
Overtures may soon be made, if it is only to feel the
Pulse of America.   Perhaps there may be a real
Design in the British Cabinet to propose Terms of
Accommodation.   We ought then to be previously
thoughtful of so serious and momentous a Subject.
I have Reason to think that Britain finds herself per-
plexd in the forming of Alliances and procuring
Resources to her Satisfaction.   She has repeatedly
and in vain applied to Russia first for Ships of War &
then for Troops.   Her disappointment may be owing to
the superior Policy of France, who by interesting Russia as well as her self in the Affairs of Prussia & the
Empress of Germany may have made it improper for
Russia to take any Measure which might tend to
involve Europe in War.   I am affraid if we should
be seriously engagd in negociating a Peace, there
would be an intemperate pressing from without Doors

for a speedy Conclusion, which would precipitate the Affair to our Disadvantage. It is probable that Peace may be the desireable Object in all the Courts in Europe while they are making the necessary Arrangements and preparing for War if that sh^d be the Event. If Britain should refuse to acknowledge the Independence of America a War with France & Spain w^d probably ensue and the flame would spread. In that Case, Britain might be obligd so far to withdraw her Troops from America as to leave it in our power *with the Spirit of Enterprize* to make such Acquisitions as w^d ensure a safe & lasting Peace. But if Europe shall remain quiet & Britain with the Acknowledgm^t of our Independence sh^d pro-pose Terms of Accommodation, would it be safe for America to leave Canada, Nova Scotia & Florida in her hands. I do not feel my self at a Loss to answer this Question ; but I wish to be fortified with the Sentiments of my judicious Friends. You may easily discern that I write this Letter in the utmost Hurry.   Adieu.

TO MRS. ADAMS.

[MS., Samuel Adams Papers, Lenox Library.]

PHILAD^E March 7–1779—

MY DEAR BETSY

Yesterday your obliging Letter of the 3^d of Feb-ruary was deliverd to me by Mr Hoskins. I thank you for the Concern you express for my Health, which through the Divine Favor I again enjoy as usual. The Advice you give me on this Head shall be duly regarded.

Your Wish that I would resign the Office of Secretary perfectly coincides with my own Inclination.
I never sought for that or any other Place. Indeed
I never was pleasd with it, for Reasons which you
are not unacquainted with. I am very sorry for
M^r —— that he should treat me with Unkindness.
I never gave any just occasion for it; but if he was
bid to do it, how could he disobey? I heartily forgive him, for I do verily believe it did not proceed
from the Malevolence of *his* Heart. To do him
Justice I must say he is a good naturd Man, and
would do the Duties of that office better than I
should. But if he depends upon the Interest of a
certain popular Gentleman he may be disappointed ;
for he proposd last Summer to M^r L, who mentiond
it to me with a generous Disdain. But a Change of
Place oftentimes induces a Change of Opinion, and
even a Promise made in York Town or Philadelphia,
may be forgot in the Hurry of Affairs in Boston.
I do not think Mr A. is my Enemy ; or if he is, I
am under no great Apprehensions from it. There
are others who are of much more Consideration, at
least in their own Estimation than he ; and even
these might upon certain Conditions be made my
Friends. I mean as much my Friends as they are
or can be to one another. A few flattering Speeches
to this Man, and a Promise to that, of a Vote &
Interest to keep him snug in the Possession of
Places & Emoluments would effectually secure their
gracious Smiles. But who would condescend to such
Baseness for the Friendship of any Man ? Let those
who can do this, enjoy the Fruits of it. I do not

covet them upon such Terms. I should become contemptible in my own Eyes; and *you* know that I had rather be despisd by all the World, hard as my Fate would be, than to be conscious to my self that I deservd Contempt.

I receivd a Letter a few Days ago from France dated the 7th of December, in which my patriotick Friend Arthur Lee is mentiond in Terms of the highest Confidence and Respect. I will give you the following Extracts.—"Your old Friend is a Man of *Honor* and *Integrity*"—"He has been of Opinion that the publick Money has been too freely issued here, and has often opposd it."—"Insinuations, I have been told, have been made at Court against him, that he was too friendly to the English, too much attachd to Lord Shelburne, and even that he corresponded with his Lordship and communicated Intelligence to him. This, whoever suggested it, I am perfectly confident was a cruel Calumny, and could not have made Impression, if his Colleagues had contradicted it in the Manner you and I should have done. You and I have had Opportunity to know his invariable Attachment to our Cause long before Hostilities commencd; and I have not a Colour of Ground for Suspicion that from that time to this he has deviated an Iota from the Cause of his Country, in Thought Word or Deed. When he left England, or soon after, he wrote a Letter of mere Compliment to his Lordship, a mere Card to bid him farewell, and receivd such another in Return; which he assures me are all the Letters that ever passd between them, and I have not a Doubt of the Truth of it "—" Some of the Gentlemen of Character who are now in America from this Country, particularly the —— and ——, it is to be feard, have had Prejudices insinuated into them against your old Correspondent. I am extremely sorry for this, because I think it is against a worthy Character, and because I think it will be likely to have unhappy Effects both with you and abroad."

You may show the foregoing Extracts to such of my Confidential Friends as you think proper. They are the Sentiments of one in whom they have great Confidence, and may serve to convince them that the Insinuations of Mr Dean though artfully made and designed to prejudice the Reputation of an honest Man, are groundless, and that Dr Lee, who took an early decided and active Part in this glorious Contest, continues the *consistent* Patriot.

Your Letters my dear, cannot come to me too frequently. Remember me to my Daughter, Sister Polly, Brother Tommy and other Friends, and be assured that I am

most affectionately

your

March 9th

TO JOHN ADAMS.

[MS., Samuel Adams Papers, Lenox Library.]

Mar 9 [1779]

M^r L will write you fully by this Opp^{ty}. I take up my pen chiefly to let you know that I am in the Land of the Living and bear you affectionately on my Mind. While I am in this World I am resolvd that no Vexation shall put me out of Temper if I can possibly command myself. Even old Age which is making Strides towards me shall not prevail to make me peevish. I find that an older Man than I am, can in the apparent Coolness of Mind, stabb a dreaded Rival to the Vitals. His Words are like Honey, but there is a large Mixture of Poison. You who are in the Midst of Life & Usefulness, do not expect to escape the envenomd Shaft, but you have always the Cure at hand, Moderation, Fortitude & Prudence. It matters little what becomes of an old worn out Servt in this World. He has his foot on the Grave & with Pleasure views it. But the virtuous Patriot, who is in the full Exercise of the Powers of Body & Mind, shall have my remaining feeble Voice in his Support ag^t the insidious Enemy of him & Mankind. I have said eno on this Head, & have not time to begin a new Subject. Adieu.

TO BENJAMIN AUSTIN.

[MS., Samuel Adams Papers, Lenox Library.]

PHILAD^E Mar 9—79

My dear Sir

Mr Hoskins who arrivd here a few days ago, was kind enough to deliver to me your favor of the 7th of Feb. It gave me a particular pleasure, because I was convincd that you had not totally forgot your old Friend. You see, I rank myself among your friends. How often have we chatted together by the fire side, and settled essential Points to mutual Satisfaction. Yet we have not always thought alike of Men who have conducted the noble Contest for the

Rights of our Country, which we have been & are
still engagd in. I congratulate my Countrymen on
our having thus far got through the Conflict, but we
are still engagd in it. And I repeat it, because while
too many of our Countrymen are flattering themselves
with the airy Prospect of Peace, Britain, if we may
credit our latest & best Accounts from Europe, is
preparing for a vigorous Campaign. It is prudent
for us to enquire of the Watchman *What of the
Night?* The Caution given us on another occasion
may with propriety be adapted to this. *Be ye ready ;*
lest when the Time of Danger approaches, ye be
found distracted with the eager Pursuit of Riches, or
sleeping in the delusive Lap of pleasure & Dissipation. But this is a Digression from the intended
Subject of my Letter. You ask my opinion of two
Men who have lately appeard on the publick Stage ;
and with your usual Frankness, express your own
opinion without a Doubt, that Congress will soon
convince the one of his Folly & the other of his
Weakness. But have you not misunderstood the
Characters of these Men ? Has not the first by his
artful Address conceald his Weakness from the publick Eye, while the other, by an improper Use of the
Weapons in his hands, has given Advantage to his
Adversary, and thereby discoverd his Folly. M^r
Dean had in his first Publication said so much as to
make it necessary that some other Person should say
more. Common Sense undertook the Task and producd stubborn & undeniable facts, but not contenting
himself with relating such facts only as were pertinent
to his Argument he gave occasion to the Swarms of

Writers against him to avail themselves, by diverting the Attention of his Readers from the proper Point. I will mention an Instance. After he had provd to the Satisfaction of every one, that the Cannon & Stores forwarded to America by Mr Deane, had been negociated by Mary Johnson & Beaumarchais before his Arrival in France, and consequently that the Merit of the Negociation did not belong to Mr Dean, what Necessity was there for Common Sense to mention them as *a Present?* It was nothing to his purpose; and it was too delicate a Subject for him to touch upon, or to attempt to prove if it had been true. His prudence therefore and even his Veracity was called in Question by his Adversaries, and his Authority & Influence as a Writer of facts lessend. The faithful Historian however, will hereafter unfold the secret Politicks of the present Day. The Newspaper Writings of these two Men, have drawn not only the Conduct but the Characters of others into Dispute. Had Mr Dean been only called upon explicitly to state his Charges, if he had any, against Dr Lee, I believe he would not have attempted it, and a Scrutiny of any Mans Character but his own would have been unnecessary. Although he has insinuated many things against the Doctor, & steppd aside from the Line of Propriety & Decency to bring in Invective, yet I do not recollect that he has explicitly criminated him in either, nor do I believe it is in his Power. If no one steps forward to accuse him, why should his Integrity be doubted? Why should you, my Friend, express yourself in so languid a Tone, " I cant *yet* but have a great opinion of D^r

Lee," and "rather than the Cause of America should
be betrayd I would give up the dearest Connections
I have on Earth." Has Dr Lee forfeited the good
opinion you "always had" of him? Do you doubt
his Integrity & Attachment to the Cause of America?
Has any one chargd him with Mal Conduct? Shall
the mere Insinuations & angry Reflections of a disappointed Man lessen your good opinion of one
whom you know to have been, early, decided, active,
persevering and inflexible in the Cause of America?
If this should be the prevailing Disposition, what
honest Man will be safe? The consistent Patriot,
after having endurd Fatigue & Danger for the Establishment of publick Liberty, would find himself still
in the greatest Perils among his own Countrymen.
I will say nothing decisively of Mr Dean at present;
but I would assure you of one thing, that were I connected with Dr Lee as a publick Man, and conscious
of my own Tardiness, I should think I had every
thing to apprehend, not from a peevish, fretful
Temper with which interrested Men have attempted
to stigmatize him, but from his stern Virtue and
Republican Jealousy. I may be partial to Dr Lee.
I confess I feel the strongest Obligation to him, for
the eminent Services he renderd to America when he
was in England, and to the Massachusetts Bay in
particular. I hope my Countrymen are not all ungrateful. Some of them, I have been taught to
believe are so ; otherwise the publick Character of an
old Servant would not have been aspersd, nor w^d it
have been said, as I am informd it has, that he had
been *bribd* to desert his Country. It is his honorable

Lot to have Enemies. Honorable, because he flatters
himself his Enemies are among the weak & the
wicked. I leave my own Character, under God, in
the Care of my virtuous fellow Citizens. I will contend for Dr Lees, because I am his Friend; and I am
his friend, because I have long had abundant Reason
to be convincd that he is a Friend to our Country.
I have said I may be thought partial to him. Be
pleasd then to take the Testimony of another, and
show it to his Friends and his Enemies. "Your old
friend, says one, is a Man of Honor and Integrity."
"He has been of opinion that the *publick Monies*
have been too *freely* issued here, & has often opposd
it." Let me remark here that it is no Wonder he
has exposd himself to the Resentment of a Man thro
whose hands the Chief of the money passed. "Insinuations, I have been told, have been made at Court
against your old friend that he was too friendly to
the English, too much attachd to Ld Shelburne &
even that he corresponded with his Lordship & communicated Intelligence to him. This, *whoever* suggested it, I am *perfectly confident* was a *cruel
Calumny*. You and I have had opportunity to
know his *invariable* Attachment to our Cause long
before Hostilities commencd & I have not a Color
of Ground for Suspicion that from that time to this
he has deviated from the Cause of his Country in
Thought Word or Deed."

You may tell the Friends of Virtue and Liberty,
that the Letter from which the foregoing Extracts
are taken was written to me by one in whom they
have always very justly placed great Confidence. I

could transcribe more Passages which mention D^r
Lee as "a worthy Character," the unwarrantable
Lengths to which the Animosities of interrested Men
have been carried against him, & the Inveteracy of
many Subaltern & collateral Characters but I think
I have given enough to satisfy every reasonable Man.
Adieu.

TO MRS. ADAMS.

[MS., Samuel Adams Papers, Lenox Library.]

PHILAD^A Mar 23 1779

MY DEAR BETSY

In Answer to a part of yours of the 20th of Feb.
which I overlookd, I will transcribe an Extract of a
Letter which I wrote last December to the Council
of Massachusetts State. You may show it to my
Friends & inform that I am still determind to return
to Boston in April or May—there to resign the place
I hold as Secretary and to get my self excusd from
any further Service here. No "Bribe" shall prevail
on me to desert my Country. I will still exert my
poor Abilities in her Service. But as I am satisfied
that there are others who are much more capable of
serving her in this Department than I am, I may be
allowd to say, that after near five years absense from
my Family, and in a Climate unfriendly to my Health,
I have Reason to expect I may be permitted to spend
the Remainder of my Days in my native Place and
enjoy the Pleasures of domestick Life. There, I
shall on all occasions contribute my Mite in promoting the Peace and Prosperity of my fellow Citizens.
In their Service, I began my political Race. I have

ever kept their Interest in View. It will never be in
my Power to render them much more Service; but
my best Wishes for them will be coequal with my
Life.

I do not think my Countrymen are ungrateful; but
I am affraid there is a Faction among them, consisting
of a few Men, who are under the Dominion of those
Passions which have been the Bane of Society in all
Ages—Ambition and Avarice. I wish their Number
may not increase. They are congenial Spirits with
Hutchinson and those who aimd at grasping Wealth
and Power. America, when she was wise, was jealous
of such Designs. She opposd them though they
were backd with the Wealth and Power of Great
Britain. Such Kind of Men do me great Honor as
they ever have done in being my Enemies. While
such Men exist, and I believe they ever will in this
World of Vanity, an honest Man would feel mortified
indeed, to have it said that all Men spoke well of
him. These Men hate, but I would not believe them
if they were to say, they despisd the Man whose Integrity they cannot shake. They dread, but they
cannot despise him of whom they entertain an opinion,
that he is a virtuous Citizen.—I do not covet their
Esteem. They are not among the Multitude of my
Brethren, of whom I should count it an Honor to be
accepted. The Eclat of the World is Vanity. There
is a solid Satisfaction in ones having, and being
conscious that he merits the good opinion of Men of
true Discernment and real Worth. But to have a
Name among the weak and the wicked is Shame
and Reproach. Adieu my Dear. I hope to see you

shortly, and then I will explain to you why I have written in this Strain.

TO JAMES WARREN.

[MS., Samuel Adams Papers, Lenox Library.]

PHILAD^E March 23 1779

MY DEAR SIR

I am to acknowledge the Receipt of your Favor of the 12th & 28th of Feby. The Letter you mention in the former came to hand, but I am apt to think it will have no Effect at all. There was an omission in the Navy Boards not having Notice officially of the inclosd Resolution of Congress, but I hope the Delay has not been attended with any material Inconvenience.

I do sincerely hope the General Assembly will appoint another Person to take my place here. I wrote a Letter to them last December, requesting that I might be relievd by one of my absent Colleagues or some other Gentleman, & permitted to return to my Family in the Spring. I find my Health declining, and the Air of this Country is unfriendly to it. I am therefore steadfastly determind to get my self excusd in April or May at farthest. In doing this, I shall immediately make Room for an abler Man. Such may easily be found, and, I hope, prevaild upon to come. I shall also gratify those whose Hearts are bent upon my Removal, and shall save them Abundance of Pains in *making their Interest* to effect it. These Men agree with me, if in Nothing else, in wishing most cordially for my Retirement from publick Business. Perhaps they would

chuse to have me recalled with Disgrace. I hope this
is not in their Power; though I think I could bear
even that with becoming Fortitude, for I am conscious that I do not deserve to be disgracd by my
Country, and can be happy in the Reflections of my
own Mind. The Arts they make use of are contemptible. Last year, as you observe, I was an
Enemy to General Washington. This was said, to
render me odious to the People. The Man who
fabricated the Charge did not believe it himself.
When he endeavord to make others believe it, he
attempted to injure me by imposing upon them. His
own Heart must therefore reproach him with com-
plicated Acts of Injustice, and if he has any Feeling
he must despise himself. If I indulgd the Spirit of
Revenge, could I wish for more? Now, you tell me,
their Art is, to prejudice the People against the Lees,
and propagate that I am a Friend to them. How
trifling is this? Am I accountable to the People for
my opinions of Men? If I have found from long
& intimate Acquaintance with those Gentlemen, that
they are, and have been from the Beginning of this
Contest, among the most able & zealous Defenders
of the Rights of America and Mankind, shall I not
be their Friend? I will avow my Friendship to them
in the Face of the World. As an Inhabitant of
Massachusetts Bay, I should think my self ungrateful,
not to esteem Arthur Lee most highly, for his voluntary Services to that State, in Times of her greatest
Necessity, to the Injury of his private Interest, and
at the Risque of his Life.

Adieu my Friend.

March 24—79

The Bearer of this Letter being prevented setting off by a Storm, I have had Time to transcribe the inclosd Extracts. They were written to me, as you will observe, in Confidence. I think I am warranted in communicating them to *you*, because I know the Writer has as much Confidence in your Prudence & Discretion as in mine, if not more. And I do not see how I can better use them for the purpose he intended in sending them to me, than by sending them to you. The Parts which are descriptive of the Weakness, or if you think more proper, the reserved Caution of Age, you will judge prudent to keep secret for the present. There are some of our Friends, who, having so long habituated themselves to admire the Wisdom of the Philosopher cannot easily be perswaded to believe, that in the different Character of a Politician, he may be liable to human Frailties at the Age of more than three score and ten. Those Parts which may serve to set Dʳ Lee in his true Character of an honest & diligent Servant of the publick, you will make Use of for that Purpose. For it is of equal Importance that the Fidelity of one or the Treachery of another, in the service of the publick, should be made known. A Man of inflexible Republican Virtue cannot but incur both the Dread & the Hatred of those who are—ambitious—desirous of making Fortunes—artful and enterprizing—especially if much of the publick Money has passd, unaccounted for, through their Hands. Mʳ Dean would have the World believe that Dʳ Lee is a dishonest Man & a Traitor. The Writer of these Extracts, who has had full Opportunity of enquiring, says, he is "a Man of Integrity and Honor,"—"a worthy Character"—"invariably attachd to the Cause of America." I am inclind to think, that no honest & sensible Man who is acquainted with both will hesitate to determine, which of their Opinions to rely upon, or which of them in the present Case ought to be supposd the *impartial* Judge.

Adieu.

TO JAMES LOVELL.

[MS., Samuel Adams Papers, Lenox Library.]

March 26

Mess Otis and Henley are under a Difficulty which I wish m^t have your Attention, and that you w^d consult our Brother Mr Gerry to whom they have written on the Subject. In Consequence of the most pressing Letters from the Board of War, they have lately purchasd a Quantity of Woolen Goods at 5 Months Credit, to be paid for in Currency at 75 for one provided Bills on Europe continue at 25, otherwise is that Proportion. They consulted the most judicious and publick spirited Merchants upon Change who thought it an advantageous Bargain. But the Board of War in a Letter to them say they hope & expect they have got rid of the Bargain. To insist upon this would seem hard and unjust, and to leave the Matter to be settled at a distant Time would be precarious and unsafe for them. I hope Gentlemen with you do not look upon them as that Kind of Men who seek publick Employment without any View of serving the Publick. They are Men of Honor and Reputation; and as such they expect to fullfil the Contracts they make, and they ought to be supported by their Employers.

A Prize is arrivd in Salem taken by one of our Privateers, said to have on board 1500 bls of Flour, 1400 bls of Beef and Pork, besides dry Goods.

M^{rs} A made a Visit to M^{rs} L a day or two ago & informd me that your Family were in Health. They are shortly to move into the House of S Waterhouse an Absentee.

TO JAMES LOVELL.

[MS., Samuel Adams Papers, Lenox Library.]

Mar 27

The Gent^n of the Medical Departm^t have diverse Times applied to Congress for Consideration on Acco^t of the depreciating Currency. It appears to me that they are as much intitled to it, as the officers of the Line ; for altho they may not run Risques in the fighting Way, they very probably do, equally, in the Midst of putrid Fevers &^{c}. Those of them who are the Subjects of this State, have applied to the General Assembly ; and tho ample Provision is made for officers & Soldiers, no Provision is made for them, because they are not considerd as Part of the Quota of this State. I wish you would take this Matter under your Consideration. This is the first Time I have ever interposd in behalf of that Department. I have hitherto refraind on Account of my Sons being one, whom I early cautiond not to expect any Advantage, as a Servant of the Publick from his Connection with me.

TO JAMES LOVELL.

[MS., Samuel Adams Papers, Lenox Library.]

March 30

Capt Paul Jones, it is supposd may be now in Philadelphia in Command of the Alliance. If Congress will recollect the Mannagem^t of the Cutter Revenge commanded by Cunningham, which I imagine has not been cleard up to this Day & probably never will be, they will think it *just to the Publick* and necessary that Enquiry sh^d be made, while Jones is on the Spot, concerning the Squadron lately under his Command. Whether it was fitted out at the Expence of the Publick either french or american or joyntly by both. Or whether it was a Project of private Men so artfully contrivd & conducted as that they can declare the property to be either publick or private as may best suit their Interest. Landais is esteemd here a good Commander & an honest Man. But he is left in France & cannot inform you any thing about it. And whether the Character which Jones has given to all his officers (Landais only excepted) may operate as a Bribe, may be worth your particular Vigilance. The Reputation of our Navy, to say Nothing of the Honor of Congress which ought never to be suspected, will suffer, if our Seamen, after having venturd their Lives in cruizing upon the Enemy in Europe should return to America without receiving their Prize Money, & be told [here] that no one knows, whether the Vessels into which they inlisted were publick or private Property, tho they were taught to believe in Europe they were ownd & commissiond by the United States. If [our]

Ministers or Agents abroad either with or without special Direction of Congress shall think it proper to employ our Ships of War (which has been the Case of the Alliance at least) in Expeditions or Services in Europe, ought they not to be directed, when the Service is performd, if it cannot be done conveniently before, to make known the Circumstances & Events to Congress? I am told that a Commodore Gillon has written a Letter to the late Mr President Jay concerning the attaching the American Ship of War Alliance to "an amphibious Squadron of french Cruizers, subjecting them to the Orders of Capt Paul Jones and giving Continental Commissions to a Number of french men, who were put upon Court Martials on American Citizens." And it is apprehended this Information will be withheld from Congress, because, tho intended to be laid before them, it was not expressly so desired. It is allowd that Jones has behavd with Bravery; but I think the Expedition with all its Circumstances should be the Subject of thorough & immediate Enquiry. Landais, I am informd is in Prison. He is an officer of Congress, and Congress should know, whether he is justly a . . . .

TO THE PRESIDENT OF THE COUNCIL OF MASSACHUSETTS.

[MS., Samuel Adams Papers Lenox Library.]

PHILAD Apr 1 1779

SIR

We had the Honor of receiving by the Hands of N ^1 Gorham Esqr & others a Com^e of the General

---

[1] Nathaniel Gorham, of Lunenburgh, Mass. On February 27 the House of

Court, your Letter of the 1ˢᵗ of March. Congress
had before considerd the Subject of it and come in to
Resolutions which we forwarded to you in Season.
If any thing further can be done for the Reliefe of
the Inhabitants of Massachusetts Bay from the Distress they are under for Want of Bread, the Honble
Assembly may rely upon our utmost Exertions. We
have also rec^d another Letter by Express, inclosing
a Resolution of the Assembly relating to the Necessity of ascertaining the Powers of foreign Consuls in
the American Ports. This we immediately laid before
Congress & the Matter is under the Consideration of
a Committee.

A Resolution yesterday passd, which directs that
the proceedings of Congress from the first of Jan^y
last, excepting such as require Secrecy for the present, be publishd with all Dispatch and transmitted
weekly to the Assemblys of the respective States.
This will enable us to comply with a former Instruction with Ease. The printing of the Journals preceding the Time just mentiond, will not be interrupted
by the execution of this Resolution.

We are with Sentiments of Duty & Regard to the
Genl Assembly

                    Sir

                              your most hbl Serv^{ts 1}

Representatives appropriated £500 each to Gorham and Ebenezer Wells for
their expenses while visiting the southern states as a committee of the House.

[1] Signed by Adams, Gerry, Lovell and Holten, delegates of Massachusetts in
the Continental Congress.

TO JOHN PITTS.

[MS., Samuel Adams Papers, Lenox Library.]

PHILAD April 27–79

MY DEAR SIR

I have rec^d several of your favors which I have not
yet answerd. You will not I am sure, impute it to
Inattention or Neglect. I have been often sick. I
have been fatigud with Business, whereby I am become greatly indebted to all my Friends in the Epistolary Way. Shortly I hope to see them when I
shall make a satisfactory Apology. Upon what
Foundation do they build their Hopes of Peace?
Congress, they say, have receivd great News. No
such thing. There is Nothing I know of worth your
hearing which you have not already heard. Be not
amusd by the Tales of *interrested* Politicians, Speculators & Tories. A false Hope of peace in the Time
of War does a World of Mischiefe. The latest &
best Advices I have seen mention Britain as breath-
ing Nothing but Revenge. Besides, were we to
expect serious Overtures, did a wise Nation ever
remit their Exertions at such a Juncture? I hope
America will persevere in this glorious Struggle till
she obtains what in Reason she ought to insist upon
This you will tell me is saying just Nothing at all
Very true ; and why should one speak when it is the
Time to be silent? At a proper time when I shall
have the pleasure of seeing you, I will chat with you
upon the Subject. Let me only ask you at present,
Is not the Fishery as valueable to America & more
so to old Massachusetts than the Tobacco Fields of
the middle States or the Rice Swamps of the South ?

Ask my old F^d the Hon T C^1 what he thinks of
the pious Lord Dartmouth now.   Adieu.

TO SAMUEL COOPER.

[MS., Samuel Adams Papers, Lenox Library.]

PHILAD^E April 29, 1779

My DEAR FRIEND

I have not yet acknowledgd your Favors of the
14th & 15th of March.   The Subject of the former is
of the last Importance.   I have always been of
Opinion that America would be in more Danger in
the Point of coming to an Accommodation with
Great Britain than in any Stage of the War.   Un-
practicd as we are in the Business of Treaties and
perhaps too unsuspecting of the Intrigues of Courts,
we may be led into Conventions which may put us
into a State of *Insecurity* while we are nominally independent.   The Advice which some Persons would
affect to give us not to insist upon too much, should
be receivd with the greatest Caution.   What do they
mean by it, and how far w^d they have us extend it?
If we had hearkned to such Advice in the Infancy of
this Contest, we should have submitted [to] Britain
the Right of taxing us, & humbly supplicated her to
suspend the Exercise of it.   In doing this we might
have prevented the Horrors of War, & have been her
quiet Slaves.   No Terms have yet been proposd by
Britain.   She possibly may offer them soon, and her
proposals possibly may be insidious & inadmissible.
I do believe she is at this Moment employing her

---

^{1} Thomas Cushing.

secret Emissaries to find out the Disposition of America & what would be her Ultimatum. Should not the People then speak the Language which becomes them & assure her that after so virtuous & successful a Struggle they are determind to demand enough for the Purpose of securing their own internal & external Happiness. This is the Aim of the Revolution and the Extent of the Wishes of our good & great Ally, who I dare affirm, is invariably determind not to seperate his Interest from that of America, & to support the Cause of the United States as his own. Our Happiness depends upon Independence. To be prosperous we must have an extensive Trade. This will require a respectable Navy. Our Ships must be mannd, and the Source of Seamen is the Fishery. Among those who ought to see the Importance of the Fishery, I am affraid there are some who think that in insisting upon *that* we should insist upon too much. Nova Scotia & Canada would be a great & permanent Protection to the Fishery. But these, say some, are not Parts of the United States, and what Right should *we* have to claim them? The Cession of those Territories would prevent any Views of Britain to disturb our Peace in future & cut off a Source of corrupt British Influence which issuing from them, might diffuse Mischiefe and Poison thro the States. Will not then the Possession of Nova Scotia & Canada be necessary, if we mean to make Peace upon *pacifick* Principles? If we are to have no overtures this year, and Providence blesses us with *the Spirit of Enterprize*, would it not be better for us, provided it be practicable, to wrest those Places from the Hands of the Enemy than trust to the Uncertainty of Treaty? I confess we have a Choice of Difficulties. I pray God we may surmount them all! None however reach the Pinnacle of Eminence & Glory but the virtuous & brave. Adieu my dear Sir. I hope to see & *live* with you shortly; but I shall expect another Letter from you before I leave this Place.

THE MARINE COMMITTEE OF THE CONTINENTAL CONGRESS TO GEORGE WASHINGTON.

[MS., Letter Book of the Marine Committee, Library of Congress ; a draft is in the Samuel Adams Papers, Lenox Library.]

May 26th 1779

SIR

Your Excellencys Letter to this committee of the 25th instant together with an Extract from another of the 17th instant to the President of Congress has been duely considered by the Committee.

Unfortunately the situation of our frigates is such as to afford no reason to expect that they can possibly be collected in season to execute the plan proposed. The Providence of 32 Guns and the Ranger of 18 are already ordered on a Cruize and it is supposed must be at Sea before different orders can reach them at Boston.

The Warren of 36 Guns and the Queen of France of 20 have lately returned from a Cruize and are unmanned. Although the Naval force of the enemy at New York is at present trifleing, yet as their situation in this respect is very fluctuateing they may probably be so reinforced as to render it too hazardous to risque only the Two frigates in this River viz : the Confederacy of 36 Guns & the Deane of 28 Guns the latter of which wants a great number of hands to make up her complement.

Add to this that though the force of the enemy on the water would be inferior to ours, yet might they not retire under cover of the Batteries on shore and receive effectual protection from any annoyance that could be attempted from the Guns of our small Ships. I am desired by the Committee to assure you Sir that they shall always be ready with the greatest alacrity to employ our little fleet in the execution of such plans as may be suggested to them by your Excellency when our circumstances shall be such as to render it practicable.

I am y^r Excellencys
Obe^t Servt [1]

TO BENJAMIN HAWES.

[MS., Massachusetts Archives.]

STATE OF MASS. BAY.
COUNCIL CHAMBER. July 10th 1779

SIR

The Council being informd that a Detachment of Troops destind for the Defence of the State of Rhode Island are waiting at or near the Town of Wrentham ready to march you are directed to forward them and all others in the like Circumstances within the Limits of your reg^t to the Place of their Destination with all possible Dispatch.

---

[1] Signed, "S. Adams, Chn."

TO THE NAVY BOARD AT BOSTON.

[MS., Massachusetts Archives.]

STATE OF M B. COUNCIL CHAMBER July 12 1779

To the Honble the Commissioners of the Continental Navy Board

GENTLEMEN

The Council Board having given orders that the Ships in the Service of this State and employed in the present Expedition to Penobscott proceed to Sea upon the Signal given from the Continental Frigate Warren, you are requested to give order to the Commander of the Frigate & other Ships under your Direction to proceed to place of Rendevous already agreed on.

In the Name & Behalf of the Council.[1]

TO JONATHAN TRUMBULL.

[MS., Massachusetts Archives; a portion of the text is in W. V. Wells, *Life of Samuel Adams*, vol. iii., p. 70.]

STATE OF MASS BAY COUNCIL CHAMBER July 13 1779

SIR

Your Excellencies Letter of the 11th Current was duly receivd & read in Council; in Consequence of which, orders are issued to the Brigadiers of the Counties of Hampshire & Berkshire to detach and forward on under proper officers with all possible Dispatch a Number consisting of one sixth part of

[1] Wholly in the autograph of Adams ; the original was signed by Jeremiah Powell, President of the Council, as in the case of letters printed on pages 153–155, 158, 160, 161, 162.

their Militia to such place in Connecticutt as your
Excy shall appoint & to continue in Service for the
Defence of the State of Connecticutt during the space
of one Month after their Arrival at the place appointed unless they shall be sooner dischargd.   It is
presumd that the Aid of one thousand Men at least
will be afforded by means of this order.   The Council
very sensibly feel the Distress which the State of
Connecticutt have already sufferd by the Incursions
& Depredations of a desperate & malicious Enemy,
and trust in God that the People of New England
will be always spirited to exert themselves upon every
pressing occasion for the Common Safety & that
their Exertions will be attended with the divine
Blessing.

TO HORATIO GATES.

[MS., Massachusetts Archives; a portion of the text is in W. V. Wells, *Life
of Samuel Adams*, vol. iii., pp. 70, 71.]

STATE OF MASS BAY COUNCIL CHAMBER July 14 1779

SIR

Your Letter of the 12th Instant with its Inclosure
has been receivd by the Council.   The Progress of
the Enemy into the State of Connecticutt, and the
Devastations they have already made in some of the
Towns there, require our vigorous Exertions.   Orders
have been given to forward the Troops destind for
the Defence of Rhode Island with all possible Dispatch.   And the Commanding officers of the Counties
of Hampshire and Berkshire are also directed to
detach a Number from their Militia & march them

forthwith for the Reliefe of Connecticutt, to such place as Govr Trumbull shall appoint, of which due Notice is forwarded to the Governor. Should the Enemy, direct their force to Connecticutt or any part of New Eng^d & attempt to make that the Seat of the War, this Summer, Nothing shall be wanting on the part of this Board, to defeat their Designs. In the Name & behalf of the Council I am——

Sir your most obedient

humble Servt

TO THE NAVY BOARD AT BOSTON.

[MS., Massachusetts Archives.]

STATE OF MASSACHUSETTS BAY COUNCIL CHAMBER July 14, 1779

To the Hon the Commissioners of the Continental Navy Board

GENTLEMEN

This Board being duly informd by the Board of War that the Ships & Vessels in Service of this State on the Expedition to Penobscot are ready to proceed to Sea upon the proper Signals being given from the Frigate Warren, you are requested to give the necessary order to Captain Salstonstal as soon as may be.

In the Name & Behalf of the Council

I am &c

TO MESHECH WEARE.[1]

[MS., Massachusetts Archives.]

STATE OF MASSACHUSETTS BAY COUNCIL CHAMBER July 28—1779

SIR

It having been suggested to this Board that a Vessel belonging to the subjects of his Catholick Majesty has been plunderd on the high Seas by the Captain of a Vessel from Liverpole, suspected to be Capt George Hewet of the Prize Brig Adventure lately brot into this Port—And the Board being informd that Cap Evans of Portsmouth & his Mate who arrivd here a few days ago & are since gone to that town can give Information touching the same— It is the Request of this Board that the Honorable the Council of New Hampshire will be pleasd to cause a strict Examination to be made into a Report which is of great Importance to the United States, as the aforesaid Act of Pyracy is said to have been committed under American Colours.

I am

in the name &c

TO ARTHUR LEE.

[R. H. Lee, *Life of Arthur Lee*, vol. ii., pp. 226–228, under date of August 1, 1777.]

BOSTON, Aug. 1st, 1779.

It was not till the last week that I received your favour from Nantes of the 6th of March. Our friend Mr. Lovett sent it to me from Philadelphia. I resent the treatment you have met with in America with all

---

[1] President of the Council of New Hampshire.

the feelings of friendship. Among your enemies you may depend upon it there are some of the worst kind of men. I cannot help entertaining a violent suspicion that they are the enemies of their country. I am sure that they cannot at present do a more vital injury to the great cause of America than by raising the popular jealousy and clamour against its earliest, most able, and persevering friends. This they are endeavouring to do not only with regard to you but others ; and they are masters of so much sophistry as to deceive some who, as I think, are not so wary and suspicious of *them* as they ought to be. Mr. ——— in the opinion of some of his own party, was injudicious in his publication of the 5th Dec. last. They are at least constrained to say it, whether they think so or not. It is the opinion of the best men, I know, that he has done more mischief than it will ever be in his power to atone for. I never had but one opinion of this man since the year 1774, when I first knew him, and that is, that he is commercial and interested. I believe he has for a twelvemonth past, thought it his interest to throw us into divisions and parties, and that he has been as influential in effecting it as any man in America. Interested men, men who are united in politics and commercial combinations are and must be his advocates. *Perhaps the persons whose names you mention in the last part of your letter, may be his secret but powerful supporters ;* I do not pretend to affirm it. These men most certainly, should preserve their minds free from prejudice in disputes of this kind. *They* should stand totally unconnected with any party, as they would

avoid doing injury to the joint cause of France and
America, and lessening that strong attachment and
mutual confidence between the two nations, which
every true friend and subject of both wishes may
long subsist.

Your letter to the editor of the Leyden Gazette,
written upon your seeing Mr. . . . .'s first publication, fell into my hands a fortnight ago. I published it with a few loose observations in one of our
newspapers. I have since had the pleasure of being
informed, that you have sent to congress a reply to
Deane's accusations, which has given great satisfaction to impartial men. I foresaw soon after his
arrival, that your lot would be to suffer persecution
for a while. This is frequently the portion of good
men, but they are never substantially injured by it.
Our friend and your late colleague, in his letter to
me, has mentioned you in the most honourable as
well as the most friendly terms. I should have written to him by this opportunity, but I am led by yours
to believe that my letter would not reach him. But
if he should be in France when you receive this letter,
pray mention my friendly regards to him, and let him
know that his lady and family are in health.

The young gentleman who carries this letter is
Mr. William Knox, brother to the general, and has
the character of an honest friend to the liberties of
his country; your kind notice of him as such will
oblige me.

I have many things to say to you; but the short
notice I have had of the sailing of this packet, leaves
me no time to add more than to assure you that I
am, with perfect sentiments of friendship, yours, &c.

TO SOLOMON LOVELL.[1]

[MS.,Massachusetts Archives.]

August 6th 1779

SIR/

The Council not having receivd any Intelligence of the State of the Army under your Command since your Departure from Boston, are apprehensive that it must have been unluckily intercepted. They have therefore orderd the Dispatch of an Express to you for the Purpose of being informd from you with the utmost precision of your Scituation & Circumstances, the Information to be forwarded to this Board without Delay.

There is no News of the Movements of the Enemy that may be depended upon. You are fully sensible of the Necessity of compleating the Design of this Expedition with all that *Speed* as well as prudence & Discretion which characterizes you as an officer vested with so important a Command.

TO THE PRESIDENT OF THE COUNCIL OF MASSACHUSETTS.

[MS., Massachusetts Archives; a text, with modifications, is in W. V. Wells, *Life of Samuel Adams*, vol. iii., p. 73.]

PROVIDENCE Aug[t] 10th 1779

SIR

I have the Pleasure to acquaint the Hon[ble] the Council Board, that I arrivd here last Evening, and, upon communicating their Request to Major General Gates, I found him ready, as usual, to afford every

----
[1] Brigadier General of the Suffolk County militia.

Assistance in his Power, for the Service of the great
Cause. He has orderd Col° Jackson with a Detach-
ment from his Regiment consisting of four hundred
Men, to joyn General Lovel at Penobscot. This
Core, I have Reason to believe, both Officers and
Privates, will do honor to themselves & their Coun-
try, when an Opportunity shall present. I had the
Satisfaction of seeing them on their March this Morn-
ing at Sun rise, and the Council may expect them in the
Neighborhood of Boston tomorrow Evening. In the
mean time, I hope that Transports and every Accommodation will be prepared for them that their Passage
to the Place of their Destination may not be delayd.
I shall immediately forward to Brigadier General
Godfrey the order of the Honble Board, for the de-
taching four hundred Militia to serve in Providence
in the Room of these Troops, and remain with all
Regard,

> Sir your most obedient

> > hble Servant,

TO THE PRESIDENT OF THE COUNCIL OF MASSACHUSETTS.

[MS., Massachusetts Archives; a text, with modifications, is in W. V. Wells,
Life of Samuel Adams, vol. iii., p. 73.]

> PROVIDENCE 11 Aug. 1779

SIR

General Gates writes to the Council by this Express. Col° Jackson's Regiment will have arrivd at
Boston before this Letter reaches you. I presume
they will sail under the strongest Convoy that can be
made up. Should they meet with a superior force of

the Enemy at Sea, I conceive it ought to be a point settled & indispensible that the Commanders of the Armed Vessells run the utmost Risque to give the Troops an Opportunity of making their Escape. I wrote yesterday to Gen¹ Godfrey & this morn⁸ receivd his Answer with Assurance of punctual Obedience to the orders of Council.

With Sentiments of Esteem & Respect I am

your most hbl Serv*

TO SOLOMON LOVELL.¹

[MS., Massachusetts Archives.]

Aug* 14ᵗʰ 1779

SIR

The Council have now to acquaint you that Col° Jackson's Regiment will at all events embark this Day & the Transports will sail without Delay. This Regiment we trust, under God, will be a sufficient Reinforcement to you ; and from the Ardor of your Troops, as well as from your own Bravery, Activity, Prudence & Zeal for the great Cause, we have Reason to expect speedily to hear that the Designs of the Enemy at Penobscot are defeated & their Army captivated.

In the Name of the Council

I am &ᶜ

P.S. Upon the Reception of this Letter you will

---

¹ Endorsed as "forwarded by Majʳ Braddish to Messʳˢ Sam¹ or Enoch Freeman at Falm° . Duplicate by Spy Boat."

immediately send your orders to Townsend where the Transports are to stop unless Col° Jackson shall meet your Directions at Sea.

TO JOHN FROST.[1]

[MS., Massachusetts Archives.]

State of Massachusetts Bay Council Chamber Augt 17 1779

SIR

The Council have receivd your Letter dated the 16th. It is the opinion of the Board that it would have been prudent in you to have acquainted Brig^r General Lovel with the Circumstances of the remaining Part of the Men detachd from your Brigade for the Expedition to Penobscot; and it is the Direction of the Board that you immediately on the Receipt of this Letter dispatch an Express to the General informing him of the Number of Men now ready, agreable to the Representation you have made in your Letter, and requesting him, if he shall think it necessary and proper, to forward a Vessel from Penobscot with a suitable Convoy to transport them.

TO —— ——

[MS., Samuel Adams Papers, Lenox Library.]

Boston Aug. 17, 1779

My dear Sir

I did not write by the last Post, because I was at Providence upon Business with General Gates. He,

---

[1] Brigadier General of the York County militia.

with his usual Readiness to serve the Common Cause,
has spared Col° Jacksons Reg^t to joyn our Forces at
Penobscot. They were marchd to this place with the
greatest Dispatch & have sailed with a fair Wind,
under Convoy of two Vessels of Force. It needs not
to be mentiond to you, how necessary it is to remove
the Enemy from their Lodgment there. I cannot
but hope the Business is by this Time effected; but
should any untoward Accident happen, a Regiment
of regular Troops will support our Militia, and animate that Part of the Country. Our last Accounts
from General Lovel were of the 6th Instant. There
was then no unpromising Circumstance, but the Want
of a few *disciplind* Soldiers. We had a Letter from
Mr Freeman of Falmouth, dated I think the 12th, by
which we were informd that one Pote, a fisher-
man . . . While I am writing, an Express arrives
from Penobscot with Letters of the 13th—a Reinforcement to the Enemy consisting of 1 Ship of 64 Guns
3 Frigates . . .

TO HENRY JACKSON.[1]

[MS., Massachusetts Archives.]

STATE OF MASS. BAY COUNCIL CHAMBER BOSTON Augt 21 1779

SIR

This Board have rec^d your Letter dated the 19th at
Portsmouth and are happy in your safe Arrival there
with the whole Fleet under your Command. They
approve of your Resolution to march to Falmouth,
and make no doubt but upon your Application to the

---

[1] Colonel of militia. This letter was addressed to Jackson at Portsmouth.

People of Portsmouth, or as it appears to the Council most effectual, to the Selectmen of the Towns Eastward of Portsmouth, you will be amply provided with Waggons &ᶜ for the Transportation of your Baggage Provisions & military Stores. By the time of your Arrival at Falmouth, you will probably receive Directions for your further Conduct from Brigʳ Genˡ Lovel who is authorizd, if he shall judge it necessary, to call in the Militia of the Counties of York Cumberland & Lincoln. It is expected that so spirited, experiencd and well Disciplind a Regiment as yours is, will add Vigor to the Inhabitants of that Part of the State, upon whose Attachment to the Cause of their Country great Dependence is to be had. A single Disappointment though attended with Loss should by no means be a Discouragement to us. It is hoped that a respectable Body of the Militia will be again collected, at such place as Genˡ Lovel if necessary shall think most convenient, and that by the Smiles of Heaven our Enemies in that Quarter will yet be subdued. We pray God to protect & prosper you.

TO HORATIO GATES.

[MS., Samuel Adams Papers, Lenox Library.]

BOSTON Augᵗ 22ᵈ 1779

MY DEAR SIR

Yesterday I recᵈ your favor of Fryday last by Express. By the Councils Letter which you must have receivd, you will see that Events untoward have taken place at Penobscot. Our Troops were dispersd, and I fear our Ships are burnt. Better so, however,

than to fall into the Enemies Hands.   We could not
command Success, but we have endeavord to deserve
it. Disappointments are to be expected in so arduous
a Conflict, and when they come fairly one can bear
them with Patience & Fortitude ; but when they
happen through Misconduct, they are vexatious.   I
suspect there has been bad Mannagement, but I will
not make up my Judgment till I am fully informd.
The Moment an authentick & explicit Account arrives, you shall have it from me.   I will not yet despair of Success.   Witness Tyconderoga & Saratoga.
An Instance which *you* and our Country will never
forget.   We have directed & authorizd Gen¹ Lovel
to call in the Militia & have sent him a Proclamation
to disperse thro the Eastern Counties.   Who knows
but Laurels are yet ordaind for Lovel & Jackson.   He
arrivd on fryday last with the whole Fleet under his
Command at Portsmouth, and is to march through a
good Road to Falmouth where he will probably receive Lovels orders.   The Selectmen & Committees
of the Towns are directed to provide him with Waggons to transport his Baggage Provisions & military
Stores.   I flatter myself we shall yet subdue the
Enemy at Penobscot.   To alleviate our Misfortunes,
some Ships taken from the Jamaica Fleet by the
Providence Queen of France & Ranger are arrivd at
this Harbor which added to one arrivd here a few
Days ago & another at Cape Ann makes six out of
ten which we know are taken.   The Contents of all
are fifteen or sixteen hundred hhds of Sugar, twelve
hundred hhds of Rum, Piemento, Ginger, Fish &ᶜ.
The richest of the Cargos are arrivd.   We are told

of a Vessel at Salem in thirty Days from Cadiz & Bilboa, which brings an Account of the Declaration of War in Spain against Britain. This corresponds with Accounts just rec^d from Havanna. I believe they are true.

The Chevalier de la Luzerne has honord me with several private confidential Conversations, in which I have communicated to him my Sentiments with Freedom and Candor. I have conceivd an high opinion of him and of M. Marbois, who is a Member of the Parliament of Meitz. I want him to see you & Governor Trumbull. The Chevalier has not yet determind what Route to take. Should he go thro Springfield I wish to know whether you could furnish him with an Escort to General Washingtons Head Quarters. Your Answer to this speedily will oblige me.—God bless you my dear Friend. Believe me to be sincerely yours——

TO GEORGE WASHINGTON.

[MS., Massachusetts Archives; the text, dated November 12, 1779, is in W.V. Wells, *Life of Samuel Adams*, vol. iii., pp. 71, 72.]

STATE OF MASS BAY IN COUNCIL Octr 12 1779

SIR

Your Excellencys Letter of the 4th of October to the Council of this State was duly receivd, and immediately laid before the General Assembly which fortunately happend to be then sitting. The Assembly have chearfully complid with your Requisition and accordingly orderd two thousand Men to be raisd with all possible Dispatch for the Purpose mentiond.

The Council have appointed Brig^r General Fellows
to take the Command. Inclosd is Copy of the Resolution of the General Assembly. Wishing that Success may ever attend the Arms of the United States
& their Ally, I am in the Name & Behalf of the
Council

y^r Excellencys

most obedient

& humble Servant

TO THE NAVY BOARD AT BOSTON.

[MS., Samuel Adams Papers, Lenox Library.]

BOSTON Oct 19, 1779

GENTLEMEN

Such are my Apprehensions of great Numbers of
the Inhabitants of this Town perishing in the ensuing
Winter for Want of Fuel unless Measures are taken
to guard the W,ood Coasters from the Eastward, that
I cannot satisfy myself without once more applying
to you and most earnestly requesting that the Queen
of France may be employd a short time in that Service. I have venturd to promise the People the
Service of that Ship upon the Assurance given to
me by your Hon^{bl} Board. I beg you would not think
my Design is to be troublesome to you, but you will
excuse me in pressing a Matter in which I think I
am justified, by the Rules of Justice, & Mercy to
a Community whose Constancy & Firmness as well
as Sufferings in the great Cause entitle them to the
Protection of the Continental Navy.

I am with every Sentiment of Regard

Gentⁿ y^r very hbl Servt

TO ELBRIDGE GERRY AND JAMES LOVELL.

[MS., Samuel Adams Papers, Lenox Library.]

Dec^r — 1779

GENTLEMEN

Mr Woodbury Langdon[1] did me the Honor of a Visit this Morning and deliverd to me your Letter of the 19th of November directed to Mr Hancock and myself. I cannot but feel the Sentiments of Gratitude to the Gentleman who has originated a Subscription for the Support of the Children of our very worthy deceasd Friend. I had been informd of it before; having lately seen a Letter on the Subject, in which the Name of Congress is mentiond in Terms more than "inadvertent." I am much displeasd, when I find the tender Feelings of Humanity & Benevolence towards these helpless Orphans accompanied with the Passion of Anger, and Resentment (probably misplacd) towards that Body, which their "brave Father," if living, would not fail to honor & revere. I should be very sorry, that the "various Causes" in one Paper, should be explaind by the harsh Expressions of "Ingratitude that is unparralled [sic]," in another. I have never heard that Application has been made to the Assembly of Massachusetts Bay in Behalf of these Children; and if there had been, I am at a Loss to conceive, from what good or generous Motives it was introducd into a Paper when the very Use of it must tend to expose & exclude them from the Character of "patriotick humane & generous." Nor can I readily think of a Reason, why the Monies to be collected, should not be paid into the Hands of

---

[1] Member of Congress from New Hampshire.

one of the Massachusetts Delegates, since it would
not then have conveyd the Idea in a strong Light,
that those who had been formerly among the most
intimate Acquaintance and affectionate Friends of
their "illustrious Ancestors," were totally regardless
of "what they owe to his *deserted youth.*"

I will communicate your Letter to Mr Hancock
and consult him thereon. In the mean Time be
assured that I am sincerely

Your Friend,

TO ELBRIDGE GERRY.

[J. T. Austin, *Life of Elbridge Gerry*, vol. i., pp. 310, 311.]

BOSTON, Dec. 20, 1779.

MY DEAR SIR,

Last Saturday the two houses of assembly of this
state made choice of yourself and Mr. Osgood to
represent them in the convention recommended by
the joint committees of the five eastern states to be
held at Philadelphia. As it was a doubt in the minds
of some of the members, whether so many of the
other states would send their agents as to make a
convention, it was thought prudent to leave it to the
gentlemen who represent this state in congress, to
agree upon any two of their number for that service.
But it was overruled for several reasons; one was,
that it was necessary to send one gentleman at least,
immediately from hence, because it was supposed
such an one must be better acquainted with particular
circumstances in this state, necessary to be made
known to that assembly, and which are perpetually

varying, than any gentleman could be who has been absent for any length of time. Some gentlemen were loth you should be taken off a moment from your important services in congress, but all were desirous of your assistance in the convention, in case it shall meet. Mr. Osgood will set off with all possible speed.

I am with truth and sincerity,
Your affectionate friend,

TO ELBRIDGE GERRY AND JAMES LOVELL.

[MS., Samuel Adams Papers, Lenox Library.]

BOSTON Decr 20th 1779

GENTLEMEN/

Since my last Letter to you, I have had an Opportunity of conversing with Doctor John Warren,[1] Brother of our deceasd Friend, concerning the Scituation of his Children. He tells me that the eldest Son was, as early as it could be done, put under the Care and Tuition of the Revd Mr Payson of Chelsea; a Gentleman whose Qualifications for the instructing of Youth, I need not mention *to you*. The Lad still remains with him. The eldest Daughter, a Miss of about thirteen, is with the Doctor; and he assures me, that no Gentlemans Daûter in this Town has more of the Advantage of Schools than she has at his Expence. She learns Musick, Dancing, writing & Arithmetick, and the best Needle Work that is

---

[1] Numerous bills of John Warren against the United States, for the expenses of the education of Joseph Warren, are in the Massachusetts Archives.

taught here. The Doctor, I dare say, takes good
Care of her Morals. The two younger Children, a
Boy of about seven years, and a Girl somewhat older,
are in the Family of John Scollay Esqr, under the
particular Care of his Daughter at her most earnest
Request; otherwise, I suppose, they would have been
taken Care of by their Relations at Roxbury, and
educated as reputable Farmers Children usually are.
Miss Scollay deserves the greatest Praise for her
Attention to them. She is exceedingly well qualified
for her Charge; and her Affection for their deceas'd
Father prompts her to exert her utmost to inculcate
in the Minds of these Children, those Principles which
may conduce, " to render them worthy of the Relation
they stood in " to him. General Arnold has assisted,
by generously ordering five hundred Dollars towards
their Support. This I was informd of when I was
last in Philadelphia. I called on him & thank'd him
for his Kindness to them. Whether he has done
more for them since, I cannot say. Probably he
originated the Subscription[1] you have mentiond to
me. I have omitted to tell you, that two years ago I
was in this Town and made a visit to the present
General Warren at Plymouth. His Lady was very
sollicitous that the eldest Daughter should spend that
Winter with her, and desired me to propose it to
Miss. I did so; but I could not prevail upon her.
She said, that Mrs Miller (Mr Charles Millers Lady)
at whose House she then was, did not incline to part
with her, and that it would be a Breach of good

---

[1] The text of this subscription, from an autograph copy by Adams in the
Lenox Library, is printed below, pages 171–173.

Manners, and ungrateful for her to leave Mrs Miller against her Inclination. She very prettily expressd her Obligations to both those Ladies, and thus prevented my saying any more. I am very certain it was Mrs Warrens Intention to give her Board and Education. You know the distinguishd Accomplishments of that Lady. I think it does not appear that *Betsy* has been altogether friendless and "deserted"; or that the others are in danger of "suffering irreparably on Account of their Education." Yet as I am very desirous that they should have the greatest Advantage in their Growth into Life, I shall, among other Friends, think my self much obligd to any Gentleman who, from pure and *unmixd* Motives, shall add to those which they now enjoy.

I have not yet had the Honor of an Interview with Mr Hancock, since I sent him the Letter which you wrote to us joyntly, and requested his Sentiments thereon. Adieu, my dear Friends, and believe me to be respectfully

Yours,

COPY OF A SUBSCRIPTION PROPOSD FOR THE BENEFIT OF THE CHILDREN OF THE LATE MAJOR GENERAL WARREN—DATED AT PHILADELPHIA; & INCLOSD IN A LETTER FROM E. GERRY & JAMES LOVELL TO JOHN HANCOCK & SAMUEL ADAMS.

The Honble Major General Warren who after devoting his Time & Talents for many years to his Country, gloriously fell in defending her Rights & Liberties, in the well fought Battle of Bunkers Hill, left four Orphan Children—Minors, two Sons and two Daughters—who from his Attention to the great & common Cause of these States, were left unprovided for and who on his Death found themselves without Parents, or the Means of Support.

The Honble Congress has resolvd to be at the Expence of the Education of the Elder Son ; the other Son and two Daughters remain to this Time without other Assistance than what some generous & charitable Persons have afforded them. Application has been made to the Assembly of the Massachusetts Bay & in September last to Congress on the Subject ; but the Multiplicity of Business or other Causes have hitherto prevented their obtaining any Grant in their Favor—in the mean time the Children of this patriotick Hero are suffering greatly on Account of their Education, and unless speedily relievd must suffer irreparably. Nothing more need be said on a Subject which every patriotick as well as humane and generous American must feel sensibly, on recollecting the Character and Death of their brave Father, to induce them to their Reliefe, & thereby to discharge some Part of what they owe the brave Father of these deserted youth.

Whatever Sums may be subscribd, will be receivd by the Honble the President of the Council of the State of Massachusetts Bay in Boston, & under their Direction will be applied to the Support and Education of these Children, in such a Manner as is becoming their Birth, and as will tend to render them great and good Citizens, & worthy of the Relation they stand in, to their illustrious Ancestor.

PHILADELPHIA Novr 1st 1779

We the Subscribers engage to pay the Sums affixd to our Names to the Honble William Paca Esqr [1], to be transmitted to the President & Council aforesaid. Witness our Hands.

TO THE HOUSE OF REPRESENTATIVES OF MASSACHUSETTS.

[MS., Massachusetts Archives.]

STATE OF MASSACHUSETTS BAY IN COUNCIL Decr 23^d 1779

[2] [Ordered that Genl Ward

       Mr Thos Cushing

       Mr Adams

       Mr Fisher Esqr

       Mr Pitts be

a Com^tee to wait upon the Hon^e House of Representatives with the following message]

The Council Board have taken your Message of this Day in due Consideration. It is important ; nor out of Season. It is most certainly incumbent on those who have accepted of Places of the highest Trust, to attend constantly to the Duties of their Stations. This is the just Expectation of the Publick & ought never to be dispensed with. The Board have been so sensible of the obligations they owe to their Country in this Regard, that they have frequently orderd a Call of their Members when it became necessary and previous to your Message they directed the Attendance of those who are now absent. If the Publick suffers Injury from a Want of Application to its pressing Affairs, in any others ;—Members of the

---

[1] Member of Congress from Maryland.

[2] The portion here bracketed is not in the autograph of Adams.

General Assembly, it is hoped the joynt authority of both Houses will be employd effectually to prevent it.

TO THE GOVERNOR OF RHODE ISLAND AND PROVIDENCE PLANTATIONS.

[MS., Samuel Adams Papers, Lenox Library; a text is in Massachusetts Archives, and also in W. V. Wells, *Life of Samuel Adams*, vol. iii., pp. 98, 99].

STATE OF MASSACHUSETTS BAY Jany 5th 1780

SIR

The General Assembly of this State, conceiving that great Evil may arise to the United States, from permitting Persons inimical to our Common Cause, to reside within them; And having Reason to apprehend, that certain Persons who by an Act of Government have been excluded from this State, are meditating a Design to obtain a Residence in the State of Rhode Island, have thought it necessary to address you on the Subject, and to request that you would be pleasd to communicate their Sentiments to your General Assembly.

It is, in the Opinion of this Assembly, highly criminal for a Citizen to be an indifferent Spectator of the Miseries of his Country — much more so, to desert her while struggling for her Liberty — and still more, to seek Refuge in the very Time of her Conflict in the Arms of her cruel & inveterate Enemies. It cannot then be thought strange, that those who love and reverence their Country, feel an Indignation against the Men, who have held her Safety, her Liberty & her Honor at so cheap a Rate.

The Injury which this State unavoidably sustain from the Arts of too many internal Enemies, hath

been a sufficient Caution against receiving into her
own Bosom, those who have withdrawn their Persons and their Aid in the Time of Danger & Distress; & there is less Reason for others to expect
Favor and Forgiveness, who having basely betrayed
such a Diffidence in the Wisdom and Fortitude of
their Country and the righteous Cause she is contending for, have imagind themselves more secure,
under the Power of its Invaders, and fled to them for
Protection.

It is indeed much to be regretted, that the greatest
Vigilance is insufficient to detect the most virulent
Enemies of the publick Liberty in every Instance,
and bring them to condign Punishment. This Government, however, hath taken every Measure which
Prudence dictated, to effect so necessary a Purpose.
Notorious offenders have been proscribed by the
Laws, and forbidden to return from their voluntary
and shameful Exile. Mutual Interest as well as mu-
tual Friendship most strongly remonstrate against
such Persons being permitted to reside within any of
the Sister States. While we are embarkd in the same
Cause; While we are actuated by the same Principles
and Views; While we partake of the same publick
Feeling, and are confederated for the same great
Purpose of mutual Safety and Defence; Honor and
Justice forbid us to entertain a Suspicion, that the
State of Rhode Island would afford Shelter & Pro-
tection to those, who have forfeited the Rights of
Citizens in the United States.

In the Name & Behalf of the General Assembly

I am &ᶜ,

TO JOHN ADMAS.

[MS., Samuel Adams Papers, Lenox Library.]

BOSTON Jany 13, 1780.

MY DEAR SIR

I gladly embrace the first opportunity I have had of writing to you since you left this Country. Mr Jon^n Loring Austin is the Bearer of this Letter. He is appointed by the General Assembly to negociate an Affair in Europe which will be communicated to you by a Letter written to you by the President of the Council & signd in their Name. The Measure is the favorite offspring of the House of Representatives, & was adopted by many Members of the Council. I wish it may succeed to their Expectation.

The Assembly has been sitting five or six Weeks, and it is probable will rise tomorrow. Among other things, they have passed an Act for securing to their own officers & Soldiers in the Army of the United States, a Compensation for the Depreciation of their pay. It is done in a Mode agreeable to a Committee of officers from the Army, so that there is no Doubt but the Rest of the officers & the Soldiers will be satisfied with it. Money has been sent to the Army to inlist those whose three years are expired, & who may be inclind to continue in the Service, & we are well assured that great Numbers have engagd, so that there is a good Prospect of our States Batallions being well filled. Indeed there is all imaginable Reason to expect that the General will be furnishd in the Spring with an Army better disciplined than even those which have provd their Superiority to the

Enemy in several Campaigns. The more they are
inured to actual Service, the more perfect they will
be in Discipline ; and the Courage of a Soldier in the
Time of Action, in a great Measure . . . from a confidence in his military Knowledge. What Events may
take place in the Spring we cannot certainly predict.
An Army we know will be necessary, either to fight
the Enemy, or to give Assurance & Stability to the
skillful Negociator of Peace. The Plan you mentiond
to me as having been proposd by you to Monsr ———
the last October was a twelvemonth, if it could be
fully accomplishd, might in one of the ways above
mentiond or the other, secure to us the Objects
which I know your heart is much set upon as well
as mine.   Independence is a mere Charm, [and]
unless by Arts or by Arms we secure to ourselves
those Advantages we may not have the Fortitude
to assert it as we ought, but by which alone we shall
be enabled, under God, to maintain it.   You have
the . . . , and for my self I confide both in
your Wisdom & Integrity.

You will see by the inclosd Paper that our Convention is adjournd.   The Roads thro the Country
are so blockd up by incessant & heavy Snows, that it
has been impracticable for the Members to attend.
It is proposd to keep it alive by short Adjournments
till a sufficient Number shall arrive to proceed to the
Business.   Those among us who can remember the
year 1717 say there has not been so much Snow on
the Ground since that Time.

M^r L informs me that Col° Laurens the younger
has declind going to Europe.   " The little Gentle-

man " (he will pardon me the Joke) will, if he recollects, help us to guess who will probably obtain the next Choice.

The Delegates in Congress for the last year are again chosen excepting General Ward in the Room of Mr Dana. I own it is not becoming an old Man to be mutable—and yet I am intimately acquainted with one who took his Leave of his good Friends in Philadelphia with almost as much Formality as if he was on his dying Bed soon after resolving to visit them once more. In [your] horrid Catalogue of evil Dispositions with which Age is infested we do not find Vanity. This perhaps may be common to the old & the young, tho I confess it is the more pardonable in the latter. It is difficult for a Man in years to perswade himself to believe a mortifying Truth that the Powers of his mind whether they have been greater or less, are diminishd.

Pray assure Mr Dana of my affectionate Regards, and Col° Laurens if you meet with him. I am informd he is gone or going to Europe. My old patriotick Friend M^r A L, I am perswaded is before this time on his Passage to America. But if not, let him know that the Hopes of seeing him at Philadelphia is a strong Inducement to me, otherwise against my Inclination, to visit Philadelphia once more.

A Letter from Genl Heath dated at Head Quarters Decr 21 says " the health & Spirits of the Troops are not to be parralled. The Enemy at N Y are undoubtedly embarking a large Body of Troops from 8 to 10,000—they would have saild before this Time but have been under Apprehension that the Coast

was not clear.   Their Destination is said to be to the
Southward but some say to the W. I. most probably
both."

TO JOHN MORIN SCOTT.[1]

[MS., Massachusetts Archives; a text is in W. V. Wells' *Life of Samuel Adams*,
vol. iii., pp. 146, 147.]

BOSTON Feb 17 1780

SIR

Your Letter of the 19th of Jany did not reach my
Hand till yesterday.—I am sorry to acquaint you
that the Affairs of this Government immediately previous to the Enemies taking Possession of this Town
in the year 1775, being under the Direction of Persons inimical to us, the Papers in the files of the Secretary of the Province were derangd & thrown into
such disorder, as to render it impracticable for me
immediately to comply with your Request to send you
authenticated Copies of the papers you have mentiond.   I can conceive of no Reason why you should
not be servd with Copies as you desire.   The Council have orderd the papers to be lookd up for the
Use of a Committee appointed to state our Claim.
This will be done with the greatest Despatch, and
will enable me to convince you of the Readiness with
which I am disposd to gratify you in all Cases
consistent with the Duties of my office.

In the mean time I am with great Esteem &c

_____

[1] Secretary of State of New York.

TO JAMES LOVELL.

[MS., Samuel Adams Papers, Lenox Library.]

BOSTON Mar 5 1780

MY DEAR SIR

I have receivd since I last wrote, your 21st, 25th & 28th of Jany and 8th & 16th of Feb^y, with the inclosd which I have distributed according to your Request. My Time has been spent for two Months past, partly in my sick Chamber and partly in our Convention for forming a Constitution which we finishd yesterday for the Inspection of the People. You shall have a Copy of it when it can be got thro the Press. Considering the Winter we have had and the utmost Impossibility of travelling, I am not so much surprizd at your Presidents not having receivd the Letters which have been sent from the General Assembly relating to Vermont. Mr Avery assures me that Duplicates were sent, so that I hope they have before this time got to hand. A Committee was appointed by the General Assembly to state our Right to the Land in Question, with an Intention that our Agent m^t be ready at Congress by the Time appointed, but on their representing that they should not be able to report at the last Session they were directed to do it at the next which will begin next Wednesday. I will then endeavor to get the Number of our Delegates necessary to be present in Congress reducd.

I wish you would send your Account of Time & Expences to the Assembly. Twenty fiv eDollars pr Day and Expences were allowd to me for the year 79. I inform you of this that you may judge whether the Allowance for Time & Service is raisd in Proportion to other things.

In your Letter of the 16 of Feb you mention your having inclosd to me the Day before two Letters from Gen¹ Lincoln, and your having had four sent to your Care. I have receivd only two, and them by Mr Torrey, one of them for the Generals Lady which I have forwarded by a safe hand, and the other for his Son.

"Our Newspapers are remarkeable lately for more groundless Paragraphs than most others." It is true. And there are some Men who with all other political Qualities, cannot keep a political Secret. I thought it not prudent to mention it, and did not to any one; but to my great Surprize saw it in one of the Papers. It was however a great Wonder, as I was told a paragraph of one of your own Letters was either read or explaind in a large table Circle, and so it got into the Press. The Intelligence was far from being displeasing to any of your virtuous fellow Citizens, unless to those who think your Presence in Congress indispensible.

In the Hint I gave you in one of my Letters I was far from intending you should think I meant Capt Mc Neil. I am sure he is a Man of too much Honor to write the anonimous Letter the Committee receivd.

I hope the General Assembly when they come together will turn their Attention principally to the fitting up & supplying their Quota of the Army. The Council have given Col° Blaney their best Advice and he appears to be well pleasd with the Candor & Respect they have shown him.

TO THE LEGISLATURE OF MASSACHUSETTS.

[W. V. Wells, *Life of Samuel Adams*, vol. iii., p. 136.]

To the Honorable Council and House of Representatives, in General Court assembled.

March 9, 1780.

The petition of Samuel Adams of Boston humbly shows:—

That when the British troops were in possession of the town of Boston, in 1775, he suffered the loss of the greatest and most valuable part of his household furniture, and has since been indulged with the use of sundry articles belonging to certain absentees until the General Assembly should be pleased to otherwise order them to be disposed of.

Your petitioner prays the Honorable Court that he may be permitted to avail himself of the purchase of the said furniture at the prices that may be set upon them by good and discreet men.

And as in duty bound, he shall pray, &c.

TO JOHN ADAMS.

[MS., Adams Papers, Quincy.]

BOSTON March 15 1780

MY DEAR SIR/

The immediate Departure of Mr Appleton who takes the Charge of this Letter, prevents my saying to you more than a very few Words. Col^o Niles informd me yesterday that your Lady & Family were well when he saw them on Saturday last. Our General Assembly began a Session the last Week. They are intent on filling up their Quota of the Army. The

Convention is adjournd till the first Wednesday in June next.[1] The Fabrick is not materially injurd. It is proposd that the People should state their Objections if they have any, and that the Convention shᵈ adapt it to the General Sentiments & give it the Sanction—a New Convention to be called, if two thirds of the people shall think it expedient in the year 95 to make Alterations as Experience may dictate. Mʳ Appleton is the Son of our Friend the Loan Officer. I think he will not dishonor his Country abroad.

My Regards to Dʳ F— Mʳ D— Colᵒ L if you see him & all Friends—Adieu my dear Friend.

TO JAMES LOVELL.

[MS., Samuel Adams Papers, Lenox Library.]

Boston Mar 25 1780

My dear Sir

Your Favor of the 9ᵗʰ was deliverd to me by Mʳ Brailes . . . . one day this Week & the Day following that of the 28 of Feb by the Post.—"New York presses Congress hard upon the Resolution, in Regard to Vermont." &c. Our Assembly in their first Letter to Congress on the Subject, expressd a Doubt whether they should be ready by the Time appointed. They immediately appointed a Comᵉ to state their Claim, consisting of three Gentlemen, two of whom viz Mʳ Bowdoin & Mʳ Lowell are not Members. The great Business of the Con-

---

[1] Its address to the public is printed in W. V. Wells, *Life of Samuel Adams*, vol. iii., pp. 90–96.

vention of which all the Com^e were Members inter-
vened. Their Report however is expected in a very
few Days. I wish this Matter could be settled to the
Satisfaction of all. If there was Reason to expect
that all *would* be satisfied with a Decision of Congress,
I should think the sooner it is done the better. But
the Grant People, you say, now refuse. It may be
a Question then whether it w^d be best to attempt a
Settlement in the Time of War, and especially at a
Juncture of it, when the only Object of all should be
to prosecute it with their utmost united Force and
Vigor. Nothing however but the Multiplicity of most
pressing Affairs, has prevented this State being ready
hitherto. They are in Earnest to support their Claim.
They were discontented with the Decision in 1739,
and I think afterwards directed their Agent Mr Bollan
to manifest it to the King in Council. I will examine the Letters of that Day & make this certain to
you. Ethan Allen was in this Towne last Winter,
and returnd disgusted on his being informd that we
were determined to support our Claim.

The Resolutions of Congress, a Sketch of which you
sent to me, came to the Council by the same Conveyance. The Assembly being sitting, they were laid
before them. Every practicable Measure is taking
to promote the great Business of recruiting the Army
& every other Essential to a *vigorous Campaign*. I
have noticed the honest Intention of ——— without
feeling any Jealousy on the Occasion. It is always
my Endeavor to render the recommendations of Congress *most* respectable; tho I perceive, that the artful Writers in some of the Philadelphia Papers affect

to hold up a Contrast between the present & the "illustrious Congress of '74"—I may be supposd [to] be impartial, having had the Honor of being a Member from the Beginning; and I do verily believe that in point of Understanding, Wisdom, Integrity, and Diligence in Affairs they are as respectable now as they were then. It is the Wish of Tories and Britons to make them appear little in the Eye of the World. Under God they have done Wonders. By an affectionate Union of the Members with each other, by their joynt & unwearied application to the publick Business, by Vigilance Zeal and an inflexible Independence of Spirit they will continue reverd by the Friends and dreaded by the Enemies of our Country.

I thank you for the Intelligence you inclosd, and have made a prudent Use of it, by communicating it to some of the leading members of the Assembly who are my confidential Friends. To others I have given it in my own way as Articles of my political Creed, and I think to good Effect. What do you think of Penobscott? The late Expedition,[1] tho it turnd out very unfortunate, was perhaps as great an Exertion as has been made by any State since the War began. Our State must *demand* a reimbursement. It is more than probable that if we had succeeded we sh^d have had the Charge paid *with thanks*. And we sh^d have richly deserved it. Britain I doubt not considers that an important Post and so will . . . . if she regards her Navy.

You know that by our Charter the Crown reservd the Masts. Another Circumstance I will . . . . remind

---

[1] *Cf.* Pages 154, 158 *et seq.*

you of, that part of our Eastern Country was held by
the Crown & the People of the Province as it were in
joynt Tenancy. He could not originate the Sale of
any Part of it, nor could they complete the sale without his Confirmation. Will it not be her Policy to
keep Possession of that part of our Territory till
Terms of Peace are proposd, that she may take
occasion to say she is in Possession of her own. And
will it not then be somewhat difficult for Mediator to
find Arguments against her holding it? Should not
Congress assist us in endeavoring to recover possession? We want Ships. If a french Squadron should
again visit these Seas it is natural for a Massachusetts
Man to wish, that they should make Hallifax their
capital object. Probably America w^d think it for
her Interest if she . . . . that the Masts & the Fishing
Ground must be the great Security of their Independence & Prosperity? We must have the reach of our
arms or we shall never be able even to defend ourselves . . . .

I declare to you I shall not feel perfectly easy till
those two provinces are annexed to the United States
as Nature seems to have designd, and the unmolested
Right to the Fishery is secured to us.

I believe my letter is become tedious to you. I will
conclude with mentioning that several Persons have
hinted to me the Necessity of establishing an American Consul in France. If it should be thought expedient to propose it to Congress & they should
judge it proper, Mr Perez Moulton[1] (whom you
know) desires me to inform the Mass Delegates that

---

[1] *Cf.* Vol. III., p. 293.

he intends residing in that Country a few years &
would gladly accept of that appointment.

TO JOHN ADAMS.

[MS., Samuel Adams Papers, Lenox Library.]

[May, 1780.]

My dear Sir

The Son of our worthy Friend General Warren takes
the Care of this Letter.   I need to say Nothing to
recommend him to your Patronage and Advice.   The
Marquis La Fayette who tarried here a few Days ago
did me the Honor to deliver me your Favor of————.
The other to which you refer me is not come to
Hand.   I enclose you several Acts of the General
Assembly passed the last Session, besides which another passed granting to the Subjects of France
within this State equal Privileges with those granted
to the Subjects of the United States in France agreable to the Treaty and another for instituting a
Society for promoting Arts & Sciences.   The Sud-
deness of Mr Warrens Departure prevents my sending the two last by him.   I also inclose the Form of
the Constitution as revisd & alterd by the Convention
and recommended to the People.   The Town of
Boston have been in Meeting three Days, upon this
important Affair.   It is this moment finishd.   The
Town have unanimously agreed to the Constitution
with a few Alterations (I think for the better) except
the third Article.   They have proposd that in the
16th Article of the Declaration of Rights provision be
made for the Liberty of Speech as well as the Press,
in both Cases to respect publick Men in their publick
Conduct.   In the Proviso under the 7 Article Chap. 2

they have added to the Exception, so far as may be
necessary for the Defence of a neighboring State in-
vaded or threatned with immediate Invasion. In the
7 Art. Chap. 6. the Words "upon the most urgent
& pressing Occasions" are proposd to be expungd
and the Words "of War, Invasion or rebellion de-
clard by the Legislature to exist" to be inserted in
their Stead. And the Time is limitted to *Six* instead
of 12 Months. The Religious Article was considerd
by itself, and occasiond much but candid Debate.
The Town have proposd a new Draft of the Article
which I have not by me. If Mr Warren does not call
on me too early tomorrow I will transcribe it. The
Convention is adjournd to the 7th of June to receive
& act upon the Returns of the People agreably to the
Resolution of Convention inserted in the last pages
of the inclosd, to which this Town has agreed. The
short Notice I have had of this opportunity & my
being obligd to attend the Town Meeting has prevented my writing so largely as I could have wishd.
Please to present my affectionate Regards to M^r
Dana & let him know that I receivd his Letter by
the Marquis, & that Attention will be given to his request for certain papers of Importance. I shall set
off for Philad^e in a few Days. Adieu my dear Sir.

I wrote you by Mr J. L. Austin who I hope is arrivd.

ARTICLE SIGNED "VINDEX."

[*Boston Gazette*, June 12, 1780.]

Messieurs Edes,

*An old Correspondent begs room for a few Words in
your next.*

Formerly this great contest was carried on upon

paper. The conspirators against the rights and
liberties of our country left no art untried, to induce
the people to submit to their unrighteous claims.
But they were circumvented by our watchful patriots.
They were, if I may use the expression, out-reasoned
by some, and laughed off the stage by others ; and
we will never forget those steadfast and persevering
friends, who forever prov'd themselves incapable of
being brib'd by the soft whispers of flattery, or awed
by foul-mouthed calumny and the threats of power.
Afterwards the contest became more serious and important. The people of this country were not driven
to take up arms, they did it *voluntarily* in defence of
their liberty. They properly considered themselves
as called by GOD, and warranted by HIM, to encounter every hazard in the common cause of *Man*.
We have had for several years past a well-appointed
Army.—An Army of which both Officers and Privates
are daily increasing in discipline—An Army inferior
perhaps to none at this time on the face of the earth
and headed by a COMMANDER, who feels the
Rights of the Citizens in his own breast, and experience has taught us, *he* knows full well how to
defend them.—May Heaven inspire that Army yet
more and more with Military Virtues, and teach their
hands to war and their fingers to fight ! May every
citizen in the army and in the country, have a proper
sense of the DEITY upon his mind, and an impression of that declaration recorded in the Bible, " Him
that honoreth me I will honor, but he that despiseth
me shall be lightly esteemed."—" God helpeth those
who help themselves," says an eminent writer. Per-

haps the sentiment is better expressed in holy writ, where, when we are bid to work out our own salvation, we are told that " It is GOD who worketh in us." It seems to be the Divine Constitution, that success shall generally crown virtuous exertions. We have seen this verified throughout this glorious Struggle. The Military skill and prowess of our Army have kept us from being overwhelmed by our powerful enemies; and the political exertions of the CON-GRESS have, by the smiles of Heaven, obtained for us an Alliance with the most illustrious Nation in Europe; and the warmest wishes of other Powers. Our affairs appear to be approaching to a *great crisis*. As momentary visits did not entirely fulfill the purpose of our generous ALLY, we may daily expect from him a naval and land force, designed to co-operate with our own troops; and by a longer stay on the coasts of this continent, to give the United States the opportunity of employing all their resources to the greatest advantage. CONGRESS has called upon the several States to make ready for this great crisis, and the *several States* have seconded the call of *Congress*. The PEOPLE, the PEOPLE must, under GOD, give energy to this all important call, and enable the combined Forces *at once* to put an end to the War. If the PEOPLE *NOW* exert themselves, *one* struggle more, by the blessing of Heaven, will rid us of all our Enemies. The Expectations at VER-SAILLES from this joint effort are even sanguine— CONGRESS is impatient to answer their just expectation—The eyes of EUROPE are upon us, anxiously waiting for the great event. Our GEN-

ERAL, with his officers and army, are filled with ardor and generous ambition to signalize their valour in the SALVATION of our country—SUPERIOR BEINGS would look down with the utmost astonishment, if we should let this GOLDEN OPPORTUNITY slip—It cannot be. Our young men, ambitious of laurels, will, at such a time, fly to their arms with the speed of the wind, and ALL will be engaged in furnishing them with necessary supplies, so shall this very campaign be DECISIVE and GLORIOUS. *This* State began the noble contest ; we will *honor ourselves* by our utmost exertions to put a glorious end to it : we will contend with our sister States in *nothing*, but who shall have the greatest share of honor in this last and crowning effort— Be assured, my dear countrymen, the liberty, the happiness of America, and its consequence in the eyes of the world, depend upon our PRESENT activity and spirit—We will not be wanting to ourselves, and the LORD do that which seemeth to him right.

VINDEX.

TO JAMES BOWDOIN.

[MS., Massachusetts Archives ; a draft is in the Samuel Adams Papers, Lenox Library, and the text is in W. V. Wells, *Life of Samuel Adams*, vol. iii., p. 102.]

HARTFORD June 20 1780

SIR

We have the Honor of transmitting to you the Copy of a Letter from General Washington to Governor Trumbull. The Contents are of so pressing Importance, that we thought it our indispensible Duty, without Delay, to forward an Express to Brigadier General Fellows, of the County of Berkshire, with a Letter the Copy of which we also inclose ; and to inform Major General Howe who commanded West Point, of the Measures we have taken.

Although we have acted on this urgent Occasion, *without Authority*, yet we flatter our selves, that in Consideration of the very critical Situation of the Army, our Proceeding thus far will meet with the Approbation of the General Assembly.

We are with the greatest Respect & Esteem
Sir your most obed^t & very humble Serv^ts [1]

TO JOHN FELLOWS.[2]

[MS., Samuel Adams Papers, Lenox Library.]

HARTFORD June 20 1780

SIR

The inclosd Copy of a Letter from his Excy Genl Washington to His Excy Governor Trumbull will show the Danger we are in of losing the Defence of the North River & of having the Communication cut off between the Eastern & Southern States, unless an immediate Supply of Men & Provisions is sent to Major General Howe who commands the Fortifications at the Highlands. Measures will be adopted without Delay by the State of Connecticutt

---

[1] Signed also by Elbridge Gerry, as were the succeeding four letters.
[2] Brigadier General in the continental army.

for this Purpose ; and as we have accidentally met at this place (one of us on his Journey to & the other from Congress) we think it our Duty, in behalf of the Executive Authority of the State of Massachusetts Bay, who cannot be notified of this Affair in Season, to urge you as you regard the Interest & Wellfare of your Country, immediately to put your Brigade under marching orders to repair to West Point, on the Application of Major General Howe, with Provisions sufficient to subsist them. As the Garrison is in great Want of Supplies, we think it advisable on this urgent occasion, and indeed indispensibly necessary that you should forthwith take all the Provisions in your County, that will not be wanting for the Consumption of its Inhabitants, & give Receipts for the same payable at an early Period & at the Current Prices, & that you should impress as many Waggons (if they cannot otherwise be procured) as will be requisite for the Transportation of the Provisions to the Highlands.

We submit it to your Consideration, whether it will not be expedient to notify the State of Vermont, & the Commanding Officer in the County of Hampshire to hold their Militia in Readiness to march at the shortest Notice, & to collect a sufficient Quantity of Provisions for their Subsistence. Your own Experience, & knowledge of the Importance of that Post, render it needless for us to press you to procure the most expeditious & vigorous Exertions for its Support ; nor need we describe the deplorable Situation in which his Excellency Gen¹ Washington & the brave Army under his Command would be involvd,

should a successfull Attack be made on the Post
mentiond.

We shall immediately transmit to the Government
of the State of Massachusetts a Copy of this Intelligence & of our Application to you, & remain with
Esteem

Sir your most obed^t & very hbl Serv^{ts},

TO ROBERT HOWE.[1]

[MS., Samuel Adams Papers, Lenox Library.]

HARTFORD June 20 1780

SIR

Being accidentally present in this Town, when his
Excy Genl Washingtons Letter of the 18th was receivd by Governor Trumbull, the Contents of which
he was pleasd to communicate to us, we judgd it
necessary to write a Letter to Brig^r General Fellows
of the County of Berkshire in the State of Massachusetts Bay, a Copy of which is inclosd.   We indeed
have no Authority, from the State we have the Honor
to represent in Congress, to take this Measure, but
we considerd the Circumstances of Affairs too pressing
to admit of Delay.   We shall dispatch an Express to
the Government of Massachusetts with the Intelligence receivd, and wish you to acquaint the Commander in Chiefe of the Measure we have taken.

We are &^{c}

---

[1] Major general in the continental army.

TO JOHN FELLOWS.

[MS., Samuel Adams Papers, Lenox Library.]

HARTFORD June 21 1780

SIR

We wrote to you yesterday, & inclosd Copy of a Letter of the 18ᵗʰ Instant from his Excy General Washington to his Excy Govʳ Trumbull, mentioning the Arrival of a Fleet at the Hook & the Probability of its containing Sir H. Clinton with his Army, and of his immediately attacking our Post at the High-lands; since which we have certain Intelligence that the Fleet was on the 19ᵗʰ at ———— Point, within twenty Miles of our Fortifications, and we have no Doubt that by this Time the Army have debarkd & commencd their Operations. We therefore think it necessary that you should forthwith march your Men to the Reliefe of the Garrison, & take with you a sufficient Quantity of Provisions to subsist your Brigade on the March to the Highlands & fourteen Days after they shall have arrivd, with as much more as can be obtaind for the Use of the Garrison. It will answer but little Purpose to march your Men without Supplys. We have great Reliance on that Zeal & Patriotism which has so often distinguishd the County of Berkshire in this great Contest ; but should it so happen that Waggons cannot otherwise be procured, we hope you will not hesitate a Moment to take them wherever they may be found, on Cer-tificates payable at an early Period, agreable to our former Recommendation. The Militia of the Western Counties, will upon this Plan be put into immediate

Motion, & we think it advisable for you to send Expresses to the State of Vermont & the County of Hampshire, urging the Necessity of their marching their Militia with Provisions for the Reliefe of the Garrison in the Manner mentiond.

We remain &ᶜ,

TO ROBERT HOWE.

[MS., Samuel Adams Papers, Lenox Library.]

HARTFORD 21 June 1780

SIR

We wrote to you yesterday. Having this Morning receivd intelligence of the Movement of the Enemy up the River, we have sent another Express to Brigʳ Genˡ Fellows, urging him immediately to march to your Reliefe with his Brigade of Militia with Provisions to subsist them on their Way to & 14 Days after they shall arrive at West Point. We have also advisd him to throw into the Garrison all the Provisions that can be procured, & to send Expresses to Vermont & the County of Hampshire in the State of Mass. Bay, urging the Necessity of their marching their Militia with Provisions for the Reliefe of the Garrison in the Manner mentiond. But it may be nevertheless necessary, if you think it a proper Measure, to send an Express to General Fellows for expediting this Business. The most vigorous Measures are making by this State & we have no Doubt but they will be effectual.

We are &ᶜ,

TO THE MARQUIS DE LA FAYETTE.

[MS., Samuel Adams Papers, Lenox Library.]

BOSTON June 1780

MY DEAR MARQUISE

Yesterday your very obliging Letter of the 30 of
May was brought to me by Mons Guinard. The
Succour coming from France will be so seasonable
and important, that if America is not wanting to her
self, she will have it in her Power, by the Blessing
of Heaven, to gratify the utmost of her Wishes.
His most Christian Majestys Expectation from us
must needs be great, and Gratitude to so generous an
Ally, as well as a due Attention to our own Safety,
Interest & Honor, lay us under the strongest Obligations to be in Readiness to cooperate with the greatest
Advantage.   I have long been fully sensible of your
most cordial & zealous Attachment to our great Cause;
and to your personal Representations to his Majesty,
in Addition to the Benevolence of his Royal Heart, I
will take the Liberty to attribute his Design to afford
us such Aid and for so long a Time as may put it in
our Power to employ all our Resources against the
Enemy.   It fortunately happend that the General
Assembly of this State was sitting when the Letter &
Inclosures from the Committee of Congress came to
the President of the Council.   They were immediately
laid before the Assembly, & I have the Pleasure to
assure you that the filling our Battalions by an immediate Draft furnishing the Army with Provisions and
every other Measure for the fulfilling the just Expectations of your Sovereign & of Congress on this most

important Occasion are the Objects of their closest
Attention. I had for several Months past been flattering my self with the Prospect of this Aid. It
strongly impressd my Mind from some Circumstances
which took place when you was at Philadelphia the
last year. But far from Certainty I could only express to some confidential Friends here, a distant
Hope, tho, as I conceivd, not without some good Effect.
At least it servd to enliven our Spirits and animate
us for so great a Crisis. If it were possible for one
to be forgetful of our all important Cause for a Moment, my particular Friendship *for you* would be a
prevailing Inducement with me, to make my utmost
feeble Exertions to prevent your Disappointment after
the great Pains you have taken to serve us. I have
Endeavord, & shall continue those Endeavors while I
stay here, to brighten the dark Side of the Picture
which your Imagination has painted in one part of
your Letter before me. God forbid that we should
be obligd to tell our friends when they arrive, that we
have not a sufficient Army to cooperate with them
nor provisions to feed the few Soldiers that are left.
I think I may venture to predict that this State
will comply with the Requisitions from her, to give
the utmost Respectability to our Army on so promising an Occasion. I was in the Council Chamber
when I receivd your Letter & took the Liberty of
reading some parts of it to the Members present. I
will communicate other parts of it to some leading
Members of the House of Representatives as Prudence
may dictate, particularly what you mention of the
officers Want of Cloathing.

I thank you my dear Sir for the friendly remembrance you had of the Hint I gave you when you was here. Be pleasd to pay my most respectful Compliments to the Commander in Chiefe, his Family &c. and be assured of the warm affection of your obliged friend & very hbl Servt

TO JOHN ADAMS.

[MS., Adams Papers, Quincy.]

PHILADELPHIA JULY 10 1780.

MY DEAR SIR

I wrote to you several Times when I was at Boston, and receivd your Favor by the Marquis de la Fayette. Another, to which you referrd me, has not yet come to hand. This Letter will be deliverd to you by Mr Searle, a Member of Congress for the State of Pennsylvania. He will be better able to inform you of the State of things here, than I can, who after twelve Months Absence from this City, returnd but a few days ago. The People of Massachusetts have at length agreed to the Form of a civil Constitution, in Nothing varying from a Copy which I sent to you by a Son of our Friend General Warren. This great Business was carried through with much good Humour among the People, and even in Berkshire, where some Persons led us to expect it would meet with many Obstructions. Never was a good Constitution more wanted than at this Juncture. Among other more lasting Advantages, I hope that in Consequence of it, the Part which that State must

take in the War, will be conducted with greater Attention and better Effect. Who is to be the first
Man, will be determind in September, when if our
News papers rightly inform us, the new Government
is to take Place. The Burden will fall on the Shoulders of one of two Gentlemen whom you know. May
Heaven lead the People to the wisest Choice. The
first chosen Governor may probably have it in his
Power to do more good or more Hurt than any of his
successors. The french Fleet is not yet arrivd. Perhaps their long Passage may turn out for the best.
An earlier Arrival might have found us not altogether prepared to cooperate with them to the best
Advantage. I now think we shall be ready to joyn
them. One would think the Exertion which America
might make with such Aid, would rid us of British
Barbarians. I hope this will be a vigorous and an
effective Campaign. I left Massachusetts exceedingly active in filling up their Battalions by Drafts,
besides raising 4000 Militia for the Service.

Mr Laurens arrivd here from the Southward a few
Days past. He will speedily embark for Holland to
prosecute a Business which you are not unacquainted
with. Adieu my dear Sir.

Y^r affectionate Friend

TO HANNAH ADAMS.

[MS., Samuel Adams Papers, Lenox Library; the text is in W. V. Wells, *Life
of Samuel Adams*, vol. iii., pp. 53, 54.]

Philad^E Augt 17 1780

MY DEAR HANNAH

Nothing I assure you, but Want of Leisure has

prevented my acknowledging the Receipt of your very obliging Letter of the 12ᵗʰ of July. You cannot imagine with how much Pleasure I receivd it. I have no Reason to doubt your Sincerity when you express the warmest Affection for your Mother and me, because I have had the most convincing Proof of it in the whole Course of your Life. Be equally attentive to every Relation into which all-wise Providence may lead you, and I will venture to predict for my dear Daughter, an unfailing Source of Happiness in the Reflections of her own Mind. If you carefully fulfill the various Duties of Life, from a Principle of Obedience to your heavenly Father, you shall enjoy that Peace which the World cannot give nor take away. In steadily pursuing the Path of Wisdom & Virtue I am sometimes inclind to think you have been influenced with a View of pleasing me. This is indeed endearing, and I owe you the Debt of Gratitude. But the pleasing an Earthly Parent, I am perswaded, has not been your principal Motive to be religious. If this has any Influence on your Mind, you know you cannot gratify me so much, as by seeking most earnestly, the Favor of Him who made & supports you—who will supply you with whatever his infinite Wisdom sees best for you in this World, and above all, who has given us his Son to purchase for us the Reward of Eternal Life—Adieu, and believe that I have . . .

TO JAMES BOWDOIN.

[*Proceedings* of Massachusetts Historical Society, 1st ser., vol. xii., pp. 229, 230.]

PHIL . Aug. 22, 1780.

MY DEAR SIR,—I have received your favor of the

31st of July & forwarded the letter inclosed to Mrs. Reed who resides in the country.

The Count de Rochambeau, in a letter to Congress, speaks very highly of the attention of the Government of Massachusetts, & of the appearance of the numerous Militia so seasonably forwarded when an attack was expected in Rhode Island. And the Minister of France, who on every occasion expresses his great regards for that state, mentioned the same thing to its Delegates in the most flattering terms. It is a pity that a Militia, always ready to turn out with a view of doing essential service, should be disappointed. They were so full of ardor that the Count was under a necessity of urging their return to their necessary affairs at home, with the promise of their being again called for, when Gen! Washington should judge that the circumstances of affairs should require it. We are impatient for the arrival of the 2^{d} division of the French Squadron, which we are informed by letters from Boston was spoke with near a month ago by a vessel bound to Salem. The season is advancing fast, & our troops must daily consume provision the bare transportation of which is an immense cost. I perceive that the General Assembly stands further prorogued to the 31st of this month. I am sorry that a state of our claim of territory in the New Hampshire Grant has not yet been forwarded to Congress; for although it is my wish as an individual that this uncomfortable dispute may subside till a more convenient season, yet I would not willingly be under the necessity of saying, when called upon after so long notice, that our state is not ready. It might have the appearance of a consciousness in ourselves, that our claim is not well founded.

Our new Constitution is much approved of by many gentlemen here. I understand it is soon to be in force. I do most earnestly pray that Heaven may direct the people to the choice of a wise man for their Governor, & incline him to accept of the trust.

The post is just going, which obliges me to conclude.

I am with very great respect,
Your assured friend & Very hbl^e Servt.

TO JOHN LOWELL.

[*Historical Magazine*, 1st ser., vol. i., p. 260 ; a portion of the text is in W. V. Wells, *Life of Samuel Adams*, vol. iii., pp. 106, 107 ; a draft, dated September 17, 1780, is in the Samuel Adams Papers, Lenox Library.]

PHILADELPHIA, Sept. 15, 1780.

On Tuesday last, Congress took up the disputes relating to the New Hampshire grants, agreeably to an order, which passed the 9th of June, and for want of nine states, exclusive of the three interested ones, the matter was put off till yesterday. The delegates of New Hampshire and New York, were prepared with instructions from their respective states. A letter from Mr. Chittenden and others styling themselves " The Executive Council of Vermont," was sent in by their agents now in this city, claiming the rights of sovereignty of an independent state, and refusing to submit the question of their independence to Congress, as being incompetent to judge and determine thereon. As there was no question proposed, a conversation, rather than a debate, ensued, which ended with a call for adjournment at the usual hour. This day, a letter was sent in to the president from agents in Vermont, praying that in case any question should be agitated concerning the rights and independence of their state, they might be admitted to be present and hear the debates. Another conversation was begun, which was very soon interrupted by a call of the attention of the house to the present state and circumstances of the army. I am of opinion that Congress will not easily agree in the question proper to be first put, however obvious it may seem to be. This is among a thousand other affairs with which it is the fate of Congress to be plagued to the exclusion of considerations of infinitely greater consequence, and which require immediate attention. As an individual, I wish most heartily that it could subside, as things of much greater moment generally do, till "a more convenient season." But New York presses hard for a decision, and I submit to *your judgment* whether it would not be *prudent* that the claims of Massachusetts to the lands in question should be here in *readiness*, lest a *construction* should be put *on a further delay* that a consciousness in the Assembly, of the state having no right in them is the *real* occasion of it. I mention this *to you in particular*, because I recollect how far you had gone in investigating the *title*. If you can be spared from the *Assembly*, I hope you will be appointed *to vindicate the claim.*

I just now told you that the attention of Congress was called to the army. General Washington has written several letters acquainting Congress of the distressed circumstances of the army for want of provisions and particularly meat. They have several times lately, been without provisions for three or four days. They have even plundered the neighboring villages, and what will be the consequence of such a spirit in our army if it should prevail, may be easily conceived. You are sensible that the dependence is chiefly on the Eastern States for that kind of supply. Massachusetts has indeed been more punctural than the rest. The Commissary General has told me that the very existence of the army has been in a great measure owing to the industry and care of our Committee at Springfield. Yet even *our* supplies have not been equal to expectation. 597 head of cattle have been sent from Massachusetts to the army from the first of July to the seventh of September. About 200 to the posts at the Northward and about 200 to the French army, which last are not included in the supply required as our quota. Congress have pressingly called upon New Hampshire, Massachusetts and Connecticut for 1000 head weekly, less than which will not be more than sufficient for the immediate demands of the army. Our quota is 285 as you will see by a resolution forwarded by this express. Besides which, magazines must be laid up this winter for the army the next year. Indeed, my friend, we must make the utmost exertion in the great cause. It is now 12 o'clock, and the express will set off very early in the morning. I suppose our countrymen have by this time made choice of their Senators and Magistrates. I hope heaven has directed them to a

choice that will do them honor.   I cannot help feeling anxious to know whether they have united in a man for the governor, endowed with those virtues which should be characteristic of the first magistrate. Be pleased to let my much esteemed friend, Dr. Cooper, know *that if he has written*, I have not received a line from him since I left Boston.   We suffer for want of such favors.   In hope of receiving one from you,
I remain very affectionately yours,

TO MRS. ADAMS.

[MS., Samuel Adams Papers, Lenox Library.]

PHILADELPHIA Sept 19 1780

MY DEAR BETSY

In a Letter to Mr Appleton of the 17th, I desired him to inform you that I was well.   I thank God I continue so, tho I am very sollicitous to know how it fares with you and my dear Connections in Boston. Our Friends at that Distance may be in their Graves before one may even hear of their previous Sickness. You cannot wonder then that I am in Anxiety every Moment.   Upon this Consideration alone, the publick Service so far from one's Family, must be conceivd to be a Sacrifice of no small Value.   The Man who has devoted himself to the Service of God and his Country will chearfully make every Sacrifice.   I will not fail daily to commend you to the Care and Protection of Heaven, in Hopes of seeing you the next Spring.

By a Letter of good Authority from Hillsborough in North Carolina dated the 9th of Sept[r], we are informd that Col[l] Marian of South Carolina who commanded a Body of Militia had surprisd a Party of the En- emy near Santee River escorting 150 Prisoners of the Maryland Division. He took the Party & re- lievd the Prisoners, & was on the March to Cross Creek, where General Gates had sent L[t] Col[l] Ford with proper Officers to conduct them to Hillsbro'. When they joyn, our Loss in Continentals will be small in Comparison of what was expected. Pray send the Inclosd to Captain James Shepherd. Re- member me to my Family & Friends. Adieu my dear.

My worthy Friend Arthur Lee is not yet arrivd.

TO JAMES WARREN.

[MS., Samuel Adams Papers, Lenox Library.]

PHILAD[A]. Octob [6] 1780

MY DEAR SIR

I have not yet acknowledgd your Favor of the 17th of Sept[r].

It is no Novelty to me to hear you expressing your well directed Zeal for the Safety & Welfare of our Country ; and I cannot but applaud your Jealousy of Injury to the Publick from a Misapplication of the Resolutions of Congress respecting the Admission of British Effects. A Resolution is now on the Table to guard it from the Dangers which you apprehend.

I have now before me your Letter of the 17th of

Sept^r, & I am obligd to you for the favorable Allowance you make for my having omitted to write to you lately. Without Partiality I may say, you have done me but Justice. And yet I would have written a Letter by the last post, if I could have given you any tollerable Assurance respecting your Affair with Mr B. I will continue to press the Matter till it is finishd.

Why will you upbraid me, my Friend, with the Votes of "my beloved Town," in favor of a Man, whom neither you nor I would set up for a Governor? It is true, I love the People of Boston most fervently. I have spent much of my Time in their Service, & have labord to promote their Reputation and true Interest. I confess that I feel chagrind and am disappointed at the Preference they have given. But is an honest & virtuous People incapable of Error? They acted, you will say, with their Eyes open. They knew the different Characters, Abilities & Merit of the Candidates. But, they were deceivd with false Appearances for the Moment. A due Attention to the Administration of Government will enable them to measure the Capacity of him whom they have made the object of their present Choice. That Watchfulness, & Jealousy, which I still hold to be the best Security of the publick Liberty, will guard them against future Mistakes.

I have not Time at present to write you so long a Letter as I intended. But before I conclude I must inform you, that it is hinted to us by a Friend, that Col^o Sears, who has lately been at Camp, has reported in Boston that M^r M declared there repeatedly, that

Congress consisted of a Set of Ro———s, & that he should turn his Back upon them. I wish, if M^r S heard that Declaration, he w^d certify it, that proper Notice may be taken of it. No Member of any Body of Men will answer for the Character of every Individual ; but if M^r M expressd himself in that Manner, it was false and injurious. I have heard of such Language before, coming from Persons of contemptible Characters, influencd by Men who rightly judge, that to destroy the Confidence of the People in Congress, is to wound our Cause in the most tender Part. It is the Language of Tories, which in times passd would not have been sufferd to pass unpunishd.

Adieu.

TO MRS. ADAMS.

[MS., Samuel Adams Papers, Lenox Library.]

PHILAD Oct 10 1780

MY DEAR BETSY

I had the Pleasure last Week of receiving your very affectionate Letter of the 14th of Septr by the Post. You did not expressly tell me that you was well. A material Circumstance, which you must never omit to mention. It is a great Satisfaction to me to be informd, that Mr Arthur Lee was respectfully treated by my Friends in Boston. My Friends are his, & I believe, on the same Principle. But M^r —— has not seen him. Is not M^r —— my Friend ? He professes to be such ; and I do verily believe he is as much so as he can be. Could I always adjust my Ideas of Politicks to his Views, I might perhaps insure the most flattering Expressions of his Friendship.

I expect soon to see it announcd in the Papers, that Mr Hancock is elected Governor of the Common Wealth of Massachusetts. I confess I did not foresee that Boston would have been so united as I find they were, when two such Competitors as he & Mr Bowdoin were set up. Their respective Characters, Abilities & Merit were well known to the Electors, who have therefore acted with their Eyes open. It is to be presumd, that they have been influencd to this Choice by the pure Motives of publick Affection. A due Attention to the Administration of Government, I fancy, will soon determine whether they have acted with Wisdom or not.

By the inclosd Paper you will observe, that the late Genl Arnold, after having committed the blackest Treason against his Country has thrown himself into the Arms of its Enemies. You know, that I have long had my Suspicions of this Traitor, & therefore you will not wonder that I am not so much astonishd as if any other officer had been detected. He has been gibbeted in the Streets by the Populace, anathematizd by the Clergy in the Pulpit, & his Name has with Indignation been struck out of the List of Officers by Order of Congress.[1] Remember me to my Family & Friends.

Adieu.

---

[1] A draft dated October 3, 1780, has at this point the words : " This City has for some time past been a complete Hospital, and many are still sick."

TO MRS. ADAMS.

[MS., Samuel Adams Papers, Lenox Library.]

PHIL. Oct 17-1780

My dear Betsy

Yesterday I had the pleasure of receiving your Letter of the 27 of Septr by the hand of my valueable Friend Mr Arthur Lee. As it was three weeks old I had a Right to expect another by the Post, but am disappointed. I have ever esteemd Mr Lee one of the most virtuous, active & able American Patriots. This opinion, you know, I have long entertaind of him, and therefore you justly conclude, that he meets with the most cordial Reception from *me*.

You was mistaken when you supposd that I had heard who were chosen into the highest Places under our new Constitution. We are not so well informd. I had Reason to believe that Mr Hancock would be the Governor. I am disposd to think, that my Fellow Citizens had upright Views in giving him their Suffrages. Many Circumstances have combind to make his Election appear to be politically neces- sary; and if the People, who are now blessd with so great a Privilege, will exercise that Watchfulness over Men whom they exalt to Places of Power, which their Duty & Interest should lead them to do, I flatter myself that his will prove a happy Choice. You may wonder at my saying so; but I think I am not misguided in my Judgment in this Instance. If they have now chosen a wise & virtuous Governor, a few only will be disappointed; if otherwise, Many will see their Error, and will be inducd to greater

Vigilance for the future. I am far from being an Enemy to that Gentleman, tho' he has been prevaild upon to mark me as such. I have so much Friendship for him, as to wish with all my Heart, that in the most critical Circumstances, he may distinguish between his real Friends & his flattering Enemies. Or rather between the real Friends of the Country & those who will be ready to offer the Incense of Flattery to him who is the first Man in it. This will require an accurate Knowledge of Men. I therefore again wish that he may have the most able & faithful Councellors to assist him in the Administration of Affairs. Can I say more? If, with the best Advice he is able to hold the Reins of Government with Dignity, I wish him a Continuance of the Honor. If he renders our Country secure in a flourishing Condition, I will never be so partial & unjust as to withhold my Tribute of Applause.

Adieu my dear

———

TO JAMES WARREN.

[MS., Samuel Adams Papers, Lenox Library.]

PHILADELPHIA Oct 24 1780

MY DEAR SIR

I have not yet laid aside your Letter of the 17ᵗʰ of Septʳ which is the last I have been favord with from you. It ill becomes you, my Friend, to think of retiring into private Life, who can lay your hand on your heart, and say that in your publick Conduct your have in no Instance deviated from virtuous

Principles. If ever the Time should come, when vain & aspiring Men shall possess the highest Seats in Government, our Country will stand in Need of its experiencd Patriots to prevent its Ruin. There may be more Danger of this, than some, even of our well disposd Citizens may imagine. If the People should grant their Suffrages to Men, only because they conceive them to have been Friends to the Country, without Regard to the necessary Qualifications for the Places they are to fill, the Administration of Government will become a mere Farce, and our publick Affairs will never be put on the Footing of solid Security. We should inquire into the Tempers of Men, in order to form a Judgment in what Manner the publick Trusts to be reposed in them will be executed. You remember the Character of Pisistratus. He was a Citizen of Athens, supposd to have many excellent Qualities, but he had an insatiable Lust of Pre-eminence. Solon could discover his Vanity, but the People were blinded by a false Glare of Virtues and he was their Idol. Under Pretence of his having escaped imminent Danger from a violent Faction, and the further Insecurity of his Person he artfully obtain a Guard of Soldiers, by which Means he possessd himself of the Citadel & usurpd the Government. But though he made himself Sovereign, & thus far overthrew the popular Election, the Historian tells us, " that he made no Change in the Magistracy or the Laws.—He was content that others should hold their Places according to the establishd Rules of the Constitution, so that he might continue *Archon*, independent of the

Suffrages of the People. This he effected; for though several Attempts were made, to deprive him of the Sovereignty which he had so violently obtaind, he held it till his Death & left it to his Children." Such was the Ambition of this Man, who indeed assumd the Government, and such were the Effects of it. Power is intoxicating; and Men legally vested with it, too often discover a Disposition to make an ill Use of it & an Unwillingness to part with it. How different was Pisistratus from that Roman Hero and Patriot Lucius Quinctius Cincinatus who, tho vested with the Authority of Dictator, was so moderate in his Desires of a Continuance of Power, that, having in six Weeks fulfilld the Purposes of his Appointment, he resignd the dangerous office, which he might have held till the Expiration of six Months.—When we formerly had weak and wicked Governors & Magistrates, it was our Misfortune; but for the future, while we enjoy and exercise the inestimable Right of chusing them ourselves, it will be our *Disgrace.* I hope our Countrymen will always keep a watchful Eye over the publick Conduct of those whom they exalt to Power, making at the same time every just Allowance for the Imperfections of human Nature; and I pray God we may never see Men filling the sacred Seats of Government, who are either wanting in adequate Abilities, or influencd by any Views Motives or Feelings seperate from the publick Welfare.

Adieu.

TO RICHARD HENRY LEE.

[MS., Samuel Adams Papers, Lenox Library.]

PHILADᴱ Octob 31 1780

My dear Sir

I cannot begin this Letter but by intreating you to impute my past Omission to any Cause you please excepting a Forgetfulness or willful Neglect. The making of Apologys is among Friends so formal a Business that I hardly know how to set myself about it. I am sure you will not be prevaild upon to suspect the Cordiality of my Affection for you. That I assure you would be punishing me more than I am conscious I deserve. I will frankly own to you that I am astonishd at the Reflection of four Months having elapsd since I last came to this City, without my having written to you one Letter, even to acknowledge the favor I have receivd from you. But will you my friend bury what may seem to you a Fault in oblivion upon my Promise to amend for the future.

I have more to say to you than my Leisure will at present allow. And indeed the Situation of your Country, I fear is likely to be such as to render the Conveyance of Letters precarious and a free Communication of Sentiments unsafe. Should they fall into the Enemies hands we know not what Use they will make of them—to be sure an ill use & very probably injurious to our great Cause.

I hope the People of Virginia are able to prevent the Troops that may have arrivd from taking a Post there. It will give our Enemies occasion to boast of their having subdued that populous State, in order to give an unfavorable Aspect to our Affairs, in Europe.

This, with other important Considerations, should induce you to make every possible Exertion to defeat
their Design.   I have always thought that the Intelligence contained in a Letter of Col° Campbell intercepted last Spring was genuine.   If so, the making a
Lodgment at Portsmouth is a material Part of their
Plan.

Upon conversing with your Brother Mr Arthur Lee,
I am confirmd in my own opinion that his Character
is very different from that which his Enemies gave
him two years ago.   You know I have long corresponded with him, and a Mans confidential Letters are
so sure a Criterion by which to judge of his real Disposition, that I before thought I could not be mistaken.   He has shared the Fate of honest Patriots in
all Times of Corruption in being persecuted.   But
I am satisfied the People in the Eastern States entertain an high opinion of his Integrity & Abilities.   I
hope he will meet with Justice in Congress.   I think
he merits Applause.

Please to pay my Respects to Mrs Lee—your
Brother Col° Frank & others to whom they are due.
I will write as often as I can.   Adieu & be assured
that I am affectionately
                    Your Friend

TO SAMUEL COOPER.

[MS., Samuel Adams Papers, Lenox Library.]

PHILAD^A Novr 7 1780

My dear Sir
    Your favor of the 21st of Septr was deliverd to me by

my very worthy Friend Mr Arthur Lee who came to this City about a Fortnight ago. The Respect which you say was paid to him by the principal Gentlemen in Boston is exceedingly pleasing to me, because, from an intimate & confidential Correspondence with him for ten years, I am convincd that he was among the most early and consistent American Patriots. His inflexible Virtue in the first Stages of our Contest renderd him obnoxious to the great & powerful in England, and equally of late to interrested Persons in France & their Connexions in America. My Friendship for him is not private; it is grounded altogether on publick Principles. You tell me, his short Residence in the State of Massachusetts, has been very far from diminishing that Estimation in which the People held him there. I should have been indeed sorry if it had been otherwise; for his great Services to *them* in particular, had justly merited their Esteem. I rejoyce that *my own* Countrymen are not ungrateful. I hope they will always be too knowing and too just, either to pay servile Hommage to the weak and wicked, or to withhold the Marks of their Approbation due to the wise and good.

You have doubtless before this time been informd that Congress have called on the States to take immediate and effectual Measures to fill up the Army with their respective Quotas during the War. They have since orderd a Tax to the Value of Six Millions of Dollars in Specie; to be paid partly in specifick Articles for the Supply of the Army, and the Remainder in Gold & Silver or Bills of the new Emission. Their Design is to have a permanent Army, and to provide adequate Magazines for its subsistence without Delay. We have often a Choice of Difficulties presented to us. I think, upon the whole, we have in this Instance fixed upon the best Method. At least it appears to me to be the surest, considering all our Circumstances. And I am the more satisfied, because I understand that our Legislature have anticipated the Measure and already begun to assess the Towns for their respective Proportions of the specifick Articles. Had our Money been stable we might have contracted for the Supply of our Army; but the Paper, as all the World knows, is depreciated, for which we are in part obligd to our Enemies, who are dexterous in counterfeiting.

Our Affairs in N Carolina wear a more agreable Aspect than they did a few Weeks ago. The Enemy, you have heard, are got into Chessapeak Bay. It is said they are landed at Portsmouth & Hampton & that they burn all before them. It is also said that the Militia turned out with great Spirit, but we have had no official Letters by the last post. Although we are pressd with Difficulties, we are in chearful Spirits and by the Blessing of Heaven Expect to overcome them. Adieu my dear Sir, and believe me to be affectionately,

Your Friend,

Be pleasd to acquaint M^{rs} A that
I am in good Health.

TO MRS. ADAMS.

[MS., Samuel Adams Papers, Lenox Library.]

PHILAD^E Nov_r 11th 1780

MY DEAR BETSY

I have receivd no Letter from you since the 9th of October. Some Accident prevented the Arrival of the Eastern Post last Monday and he is now not expected till the next. I hope I shall then receive a Line from you, to let me know at least that you are well. If you do not acknowledge the Receipt of my Letter of the 10th of October, I shall conclude that it fell into wrong hands: for the Post that took Charge of the Letters from hence of that Date, was robbd of his Mail in Connecticut and it was carried to New York. I am uncertain whether I sent that Letter to the Post Office, or deliverd it to Mr Torry who left this City about the same time. If the Enemy have filchd it, their publishing it would do no good to them nor Injury to me or any one else. Indeed it was an harmless thing, and worth no ones Notice but yours, and yours, only as it was intended to inform you that I was then, as I am at this Time, in good health. I flatter myself you are always gratified when I can give you this Intelligence.

Novr 13th

The Post is just arrivd & has not brought me a Letter from you—his latest Letters and Papers are dated the 26th of Octob^r. By the next we expect to receive Accounts of the Organization of our Government under the new Constitution, in all its Splendor— to see the Speech from the Chair—the Answers from

the several Branches of the Legislature—congratulatory Addresses &ᶜ, &ᶜ. I have been anxious, lest our
Countrymen should misjudge in the Choice of their
first Governor. They are grateful; and I was affraid
that from the Goodness of their Hearts they might
be inducd to give their Suffrages for a Man, who,
they might conceive had done them eminent Services
in other Stations, without a due Consideration whether
he possesses those excellent Qualities which should
characterize and dignify their chiefe Magistrate. Our
present Governors may probably stamp the moral as
well as political Character of the People. I shall most
heartily rejoyce, if the "*Abilities and disinterested
Zeal*" of the Gentleman called to fill the Chair prove
adequate to the strong Expectations of my fellow
Citizens in Boston, expressd in their late Vote of
Thanks. But why do I trouble you with a Subject of
this Nature? Let me ask you before I finish this
Letter—Are you in Health? Have you a Sufficiency
of Fire wood & other Necessaries for the approaching
cold Season? Are your Family Cares alleviated with
the Visits & chearful Conversation of your Friends
and mine? You must answer me these Questions, for
I am greatly interrested in them. My Love to my
Family and Friends. Adieu my Dear. Believe me
to be most sincerely and affectionately

Your,

TO JAMES WARREN.

[MS., Samuel Adams Papers, Lenox Library.]

PHILAD^E NOVR 20 1780

MY DEAR SIR

In your Letter of the 17th of Septr which is still before me, you say "the Tongue of Malice has always
been employd against me"; and in mentioning it you
discover the Feelings of a Friend. It may perhaps
in some Measure relieve those Feelings if I tell you,
that it serves to make me more watchful over my self,
lest by any Misconduct I might afford Occasion to
the malicious Man to say things of me which would
give me just Cause to be ashamd. It is said to be a
Misfortune to a Man, when all speak well of him. Is
it then an Advantage to a Man to have Enemies?
It may be so if he has wisdom to make a good Use
of them. We are apt to be partial in our own Judgment
of our selves. Our Friends are either blind to our
Faults or not faithful enough to tell us of them. The
Malicious Man will speak all Manner of Evil against
us, and contrive Means to send it Post haste to our
Ears; and if among much Slander they say some
Truths, what have we to do, but correct past Errors
& guard against future ones. The Report which you
mention as propagated of me is groundless. Would
any Man in his Senses who wishes the War may be
carried on with Vigor, prefer the temporary and expensive Drafts of Militia, to a permanent and well
appointed Army! But Envy has no other Business
than to calumniate.—

Mr Penny has deliverd me your favor of the 2^d Instant. He has also brought us a Paper which exhibits a Picture of the Times. You express too much Resentment at the Ingratitude which you imagine has been shown to your Friend—that his Name is not to be found in any of the Lists—and especially, that he could not be supported in Competition with Mr Avery—Your Friend has no Claims on his Country, nor does he set himself in Competition with M^r A, who in some Respects is thought to be a necessary Man. He is one, whom, I confess, I regard for his Honesty and easy good Humour. We have been entertaind with the Speeches both before and after the putting on the Regalia; and we expect to see congratulatory Addresses from various Orders civil & ecclesiastical. I should pity the Governor if I thought him apt to be discomposd with the high Complimentary Stile. It is usual in all Honey Moons. I could wish to see, if we must have abundant Addresses, the manly Simplicity of Barcklay the Quaker in his Dedication to Charles the 2^d of England. Excepting that Instance, I do not recollect to have seen an Address to a great Man, that was not more or less, & very often deeply, tincturd with Flattery.—If the Town Clerk of Ephesus has treated me "with very great Disrespect," I am sorry *for him*. It gives me no Uneasiness on my own Account. If he "treats every one in that way who will not worship the Great Image," he leaves me in the best of Company—Company, which he may at another Time, find it his own Interest, if that governs him, to court & respect. We are even reduced to the Hutchinsonian Times, if a

Citizen shall think himself constraind to malign his *old* Friend, merely because the Great Man has been prevaild upon to mark him as *his* Enemy.—But the History of all Ages & all Countrys shows, that there is no Absurdity into which Idolatry will not lead Men. Remember me to My Friend Mr Gerry, & let him know that I have not forgot his Letters, & that I will write to him soon. Adieu my dear Sir.

Your affectionate,

Will you call on M^{rs} A & let her know that I am well.

TO THOMAS WELLS.[1]

[MS., Samuel Adams Papers, Lenox Library.]

PHILADELPHIA Novr 22 1780

MY DEAR MR WELLS

Although I have not yet acknowledgd the obliging Letter you wrote to me some time ago, I would not have you entertain a Doubt of my sincere Respect and the Confidence I place in you. I think I gave you the strongest Proof of this when I was last in Boston. From that Moment I have considerd myself particularly interested in your Wellfare. It cannot indeed be otherwise, since I then consented that you should form the most intimate Connection with the dear Girl whom I pride myself in calling my Daughter. I did this with Caution and Deliberation ; and having done it, I am now led to contemplate the Relation in

---

[1] A younger brother of Elizabeth Wells; he married the daughter of Adams. *Cf.* Vol. iii., p. 214.

which I am myself to stand with you, and I can [hardly] forbear the same Stile in this Letter, which I should take the Liberty to use if I was writing to her. The Marriage State was designd to complete the Sum of human Happiness in this Life. It some times proves otherwise; but this is owing to the Parties themselves, who either rush into it without due Consideration, or fail in point of Discretion in their Conduct towards each other afterwards. It requires Judgment on both Sides, to conduct with exact Propriety; for though it is acknowledgd, that the Superiority is & ought to be in the Man, yet as the Mannagement of a Family in many Instances necessarily devolves on the Woman, it is difficult always to determine the Line between the Authority of the one & the Subordination of the other. Perhaps the Advice of the good Bishop of Sᵗ Asaph on another Occasion, might be adopted on this, and that is, not to govern too much. When the married Couple strictly observe the great Rules of Honor & Justice towards each other, Differences, if any happen, between them, must proceed from small & trifling Circumstances. Of what Consequence is it, whether a Turkey is brought on the Table boild or roasted? And yet, how often are the Passions sufferd to interfere in such mighty Disputes, till the Tempers of both become so sowerd, that they can scarcely look upon each other with any tolerable Degree of good Humor. I am not led to this particular Mode of treating the Subject from an Apprehension of more than common Danger, that such Kind of Fricas will frequently take Place in that Connection, upon which, much of my

future Comfort in Life will depend. I am too well
acquainted with the Liberality of your Way of thinking, to harbour such a Jealousy; and I think I can
trust to my Daughters Discretion if she will only
promise to exercise it. I feel myself at this Moment
so domestically disposd that I could say a thousand
things to you, if I had Leisure. I could dwell on the
Importance of Piety & Religion, of Industry & Frugality, of Prudence, Œconomy, Regularity & an even
Government, all which are essential to the Well
being of a Family. But I have not Time. I cannot however help repeating Piety, because I think
it indispensible. Religion in a Family is at once its
brightest Ornament & its best Security. The first
Point of Justice, says a Writer I have met with, consists in *Piety;* Nothing certainly being so great a
Debt upon us, as to render to the Creator &
Preserver those Acknowledgments which are due
to Him for our Being, and the hourly Protection
he affords us.

Remember me to all Friends, and be assured that
I am

Yours

TO MRS. ADAMS.

[MS., Samuel Adams Papers, Lenox Library.]

PHILAD^A Novr 24 1780

MY DEAR BETSY

Yesterday I wrote to Mr Wells, and in haste because I was informd that Dr Craigie was then instantly setting off for Boston. As he has waited

another Day, I have the Opportunity of acknowledging
the Receipt of your Letters of the 25th of October &
the 8th of Novr which were brought to me by the Post.
You seem, my Dear, to express more Concern than I
think you ought, at certain Events that have of late
taken Place in the Common Wealth of Massachusetts.
Do you not consider that in a free Republick, the
People have an uncontroulable right of chusing whom
they please, to take their Parts in the Administration
of publick Affairs? No Man has a Claim on his
Country, upon the Score of his having renderd publick Service. It is the Duty of every one to use his
utmost Exertions in promoting the Cause of Liberty
& Virtue; and having so done, if his Country thinks
proper to call others to the arduous Task, he ought
chearfully to acquiesce, and to console himself with
the Contemplations of an honest Man in private Life.
You know, how ardently I have wishd for the Sweets
of Retirement. I am like to have my Wish.—You
are Witness that I have not raisd a Fortune in
the Service of my Country. I glory in being what
the World calls, a poor Man. If my Mind has ever
been tinctured with Envy, the Rich and the Great
have not been its objects. If I have been vain, Popularity, tho' I had as much of it as any Man ought
to have, is not the Phantome I have pursued. He
who gains the Approbation of the Virtuous Citizens.
I will own, may feel himself happy; but he is in
Reality much more so, *who knows he deserves it*,
Such a Man, if he cannot retreat with Splendor, he
may with dignity. I will trust in that all gracious
Being, who, in his own good Way, has provided us

with Food and Raiment; and having spent the greatest Part of my Life in Publick Cares, like the weary Traveller, fatigud with the Journey of the Day, I can rest with you in a Cottage. If I live till the Spring, I will take my final Leave of Congress and return to Boston. I have Reasons to be fixed in this Determination which I will then explain to you. I grow more domestick as I increase in years.

My worthy Friend Mr Arthur Lee, who just now favord me with a Visit, sends Respects to you and the Family.

I have forgot in my late Letters to tell you, that six Weeks ago, General Ward & my self changd our Lodgings, and are at the House of Mrs Miller. She is a well bred Woman, and my Situation is agreable. Col^o Palfrey who is with us is appointed Consul, and will soon go to France, when Mr Lovel will take the vacant Chamber. —— Adieu my dear.

Your affectionate,

TO ELBRIDGE GERRY.

[MS., Samuel Adams Papers, Lenox Library; the text, with variations, is in J. T. Austin, *Life of Elbridge Gerry*, vol. i., pp. 359–363.]

PHILAD^E Novr 27 1780

Let me intreat you, my dear Sir, not to think me unmindful of the several Favors I have receivd from you since I arrivd in this City. I hate Protestations among Friends, and the making Apologies is so formal a Business, that I know not in what Manner to begin it. Yet it seems necessary that I should say something in Excuse for my not having written to you. Shall I tell you of my trembling Hand, & how unfit an Instrument it is to guide a Pen? I do assure you that writing is on that Account become painful to me. I am perswaded you never doubted the Reality of my Friendship for you, and I solemnly affirm it has not abated a single Iota. Let this suffice on the Score of Apology, and permit me to hope that I shall receive your Letters frequently, while I remain here, which however will be only until next Spring. I shall then take my final Leave of Congress, & seek that Retirement from publick Cares, which my Country seems to point out for me, & to which my own Inclination leads me.

I perceive it has been in your Option to take a Seat in either House of the General Assembly, or return to Congress. I cannot say in which of these Departments you will have it in your Power to render the most substantial Service to the Publick. We feel the Want of you here; and yet I think you have wisely chosen a Seat for the present in the House of Representatives. Many Virtuous Men there may want that Information which you are able to give them. Possibly you may have much of the old Ground to go over again. More in my Opinion, is necessary to be done, than conquering our British Enemies in order to establish the Liberties of our Country on a solid Basis. Human Nature, I am affraid, is too much debas'd to relish those Republican Principles, in which the new Government of the Common Wealth of Massachusetts appears to be founded. And may it not be added, that the former Govern-

ment, I mean the last Charter, being calculated rather
to make *servile Men* than *free Citizens*, the Minds
of many of our Countrymen have been inurd to a
cringing Obsequiousness, too deeply wrought into
Habit to be easily eradicated? Mankind is prone
enough to political Idolatry. Such a temper is widely
different from that reverence which every virtuous
Citizen will show to the upright Magistrate. If my
Fears on this Head are ill grounded, I hope I shall
be excusd. They proceed from a cordial Affection
for that Country to the Service of which I have devoted the greatest Part of my Life—May Heaven
inspire the present Rulers with Wisdom & sound
Understanding. In all Probability they will stamp
the Character of the People. It is natural for sensible Observers to form an Estimate of the People
from the Opinion they have of those whom they set
up for their Legislators & Magistrates. And besides,
if we look into the History of Governors, we shall
find that their Principles & Manners have always had
a mighty Influence on the People. Should Levity &
Foppery ever be the ruling Taste of the Great, the
Body of the People would be in Danger of catching
the Distemper, and the ridiculous Maxims of the one
would become fashionable among the other. I pray
God we may never be addicted to Vanity & the Folly
of Parade! Pomp & Show serve very well to promote the Purposes of European & Asiatick grandeur,
in Countries where the Mystery of Iniquity is carried
to the highest Pitch, & Millions are tame enough to
believe that they are born for no other Purpose than
to be subservient to the capricious Will of a single

Great Man or a few! It requires Council & sound Judgment to render our Country secure in a flourishing Condition.—If Men of Wisdom & Knowledge, of Moderation & Temperance, of Patience Fortitude & Perseverance, of Sobriety & true Republican Simplicity of Manners, of Zeal for the Honor of the Supreme Being & the Welfare of the Common Wealth—If Men possessd of these & other excellent Qualities are chosen to fill the Seats of Government we may expect that our Affairs will rest on a solid & permanent Foundation.

I thank you my dear Sir, for mentioning my Family so affectionately in one of your Letters. Oblige them with your Visits as often as you can. Remember me to Col° Orne, who, I have Reason to think is among my Friends. Adieu and believe me to be most sincerely

Yours,

TO JOHN ADAMS.

[MS., Samuel Adams Papers, Lenox Library.]

PHILAD^A Decr 17. 1780

My dear Sir

I have written several Letters to you & M^r D [1] since the 28th of June when I last arrivd in this City. I think I committed one to the Care of our Friend Mr Laurens, who is unfortunately carried to England. Mr Palfrey, who is the Bearer of this, is appointed Consul in France; and besides his Consular Func-

---

[1] Francis Dana.

tions, he has it in charge to forward such Cloathing Arms &c as are or may be procured there for the Use of our Troops. Great Exertions have been made the year past, in which old Massachusetts has borne her full Share, to be in Readiness to cooperate with our Ally, in an Attempt to give our Invaders a decisive Blow. But the second Division of the french Squadron being blockd up in Brest, & a Reinforcement to the Enemy arriving from the West Indies, they have had the Superiority at Sea. This was not our only Misfortune; for had the whole naval Force arrivd which we expected, I am inclind to believe we should have faild for Want of a Sufficiency of Powder. By an unpardonable Neglect in somebody, that essential Article was not sent, as it ought to have been, in Season. I have called it an unpardonable Neglect. It appears so to me. My Judgment, however, may be too severe. I confess, I feel much chagrind, while I think that any thing has been omitted which might have been done, to have finishd the War with a glorious Campaign. But Disappointments, tho vexatious, ought not to disconcert us. They do not. No Difficulties should discourage us in the Support of a Cause, so righteous in the Sight of Heaven as I believe ours to be, and so interresting to Mankind. Our Creator has given us Understanding, Strength of Body and a Country full of Provisions. We must make a good Use of them, hoping that His blessing will crown our virtuous Struggle. He helps those who make proper Exertions to help themselves. Such Exertions are now making. The States are called upon for an Army of 35,000 Men ;

and from past Experience of the great Expence, as well as Inutility of temporary Drafts, they are resolvd to have a well appointed Army early in the Field & inlisted for the War. And effectual Measures are taken for the Purpose of providing Magazines in Season for its Subsistence. The People at large, as far as I can learn, are as determind as ever to support their Independence, & for that End to carry on the War with Vigor. If our Ally can furnish us with a decided naval Superiority, I think there will be the fairest Prospect of bringing this great Contest to a happy Conclusion the next year.—Altho' the Enemy have gaind the Possession of Charleston, they have not succeeded to their Wishes in that Quarter. They do not find the People so pliable as they flatterd themselves they should. Notwithstanding Cornwallis' boasting Letter to Lord George, of "a compleat Victory obtaind the 16ᵗʰ Instant by His Majesties Troops under my Command, over the rebel southern Army," that brave Army checkd the Progress of the Troops under his Command on the 16ᵗʰ of August; and the Militia have since, in several Instances, given him ample Proofs of a firm Attachment to the pub-lick Cause, as well as Bravery and Alertness which he did not expect, and which I believe have discon-certed their general Plan.—The Hands of those People, if not already, will very soon be taught to war & their Fingers to fight.

Arnolds Conspiracy was to have wrought Wonders, but gracious Heaven defeated it. We have so often seen in the Course of this Conflict, the remarkeable Interposition of divine Providence in our favor, as to convince me, that the Attempts of our Enemies to subdue us, will be but gnawing a File.

Your publick Letters have been well receivd. I have been favord with only two from you since you left Boston. One was deliverd to me by my worthy patriotick Friend Mr A Lee, & the other by the Count de Noailles, who lately spent a few Days in this City. He appears to be a most amiable young Nobleman, & I believe you have not said too much in the great Character you have given him. The very short time he stayed here & the Business I have been engagd in, prevented me the Honor, which I very much covetted, of conversing with him frequently.

Congress have appointed Colo John Laurens Envoy extraordinary at the Court of Versailes, & Mr Dana will be regularly informd that he is to go to Russia.

Before I conclude I must let you know, that the Ship which was set up in Massachusetts while you was there, and which, it was proposd, should be named, the *Oceana*,[1] has since been compleatly finishd and is now afloat. Her Materials are acknowledgd to be of the best kind, & well put together. It is said she will make a prime Sailer if not too taunt masted. Others say, that the Construction of her Hull is such as to require a lofty Sail. There are many Speculations about her. As I am not a Judge in the Matter, I am prudently silent & hear the Opinions of those who are Connoisseurs. All agree that her Owners have much at Stake, & that it will be a very great Oversight in them if they should ever risque her with unskilfull or unprincipled Officers or Pilots.

---

[1] The Massachusetts Constitution of 1780.

My due Regards to Mr Dana, & be assured that
I am very cordially his & your Friend.

TO JOHN ADAMS.

[MS., Samuel Adams Papers, Lenox Library.]

PHILADELPHIA Decr 20 1780

My dear Sir—

Mr Palfrey is just embarking, so I have only a few
Moments to inform you, that I have this Morning
been conversing with an old Man and an old Whig,
who has all his Days been an Inhabitant of South
Carolina & Georgia. He was taken Prisoner last
Summer & carried to New York, from whence he
lately came to this Place. And though his Fortune
would enable him to live here at Ease, he thinks he
can be useful to America by returning to that Part of
it, and at the Age of 73 has undertaken the long
Journey. He has always mixed with the People of
those States, & is well acquainted with their Temper
& Sentiments. He also has been much among the
Indians & is greatly beloved by them. This Account
I have had of him often from the Delegates of
Georgia & others whom I can confide in. The old
Gentleman tells me that the People of those States
are in general firmly attachd to the American Cause,
& most fervently deprecate their being finally seper-
ated from the United States. His Soul was refreshd
to hear me say that I did not apprehend any Danger
of it—that the Idea would, in my Opinion, be abom-
inated by the Eastern States, and, as far as I could
judge, by all the rest. He says, that the Creeks &

the Chictaws, which are the most numerous tribes of
Indians, consisting of at least 8 perhaps 10 thousand
Gun men, are our staunch Friends. The Heads of
them have lately spoken to him in this Language,
" We stand on the same Ground with you, we drink
the same Water, breathe the same Air . . you are the
Buds, & can there be Fruit if the Buds are nipped
off ? " These are forceable Words, which express
their own Sense of the *Necessity* of their Union with
us for their very Existence. They are a sagacious as
well as a powerfull People, & an Alliance & Friendship with them is of Importance to all the United
States. The People, of whatever Nation, who shall
possess Georgia & South Carolina, will be, *the Leaves
of their Trees.* It is my Opinion, that even a Thought
of leaving the Inhabitants of those States to be subject to any foreign Power, who so gallantly defended
themselves in the Beginning of this Contest, & have
lately sufferd so much for the Sake of *American*
Liberty, would not only be unjust to them, but in a
high Degree impolitick.

In every view we see the Necessity of a sufficient
Naval Force. A few Ships of War at the Bar of
Charlestown, & a Frigate or two in Stone River,
might at this time effect the Recovery of that City.
I need not inform *you*, what an Effect the Sight of a
Sixty Gun Ship would probably have at Penobscott.—
Do not our Enemies conceive the Idea of *Uti pos-
sidetis ?* And can there be Peace in America while
Britain holds a Foot of Ground in any Part of it ?

Adieu.

TO JOHN SCOLLAY.

[MS., Samuel Adams Papers, Lenox Library; a portion of the text, with modifications, is in W. V. Wells, *Life of Samuel Adams*, vol. iii., pp. 114, 115.]

PHILAD^E Decr 30 1780

My dear Sir

I receivd your favor of the 6th Instant, but not till the 25th. The Post has been very irregular of late, & our Letters grow old before we receive them. It is a Shame that the Mail has been catchd a second time in the same trap. I inclosd to you a Warrant on Mr Appleton for the Amount of your Demand for boarding the Orphans of our late Friend Genl Warren. I think I did not send the Letter by that Post. But being uncertain I informd you in a subsequent Letter of my having sent the Warrant, and desired you to inform me whether it had come safely to hand. I expect to hear from you in Answer to my last at least, & shall then conduct the Matter if necessary, as you have proposd.

Our Government, I perceive, is organizd on the Basis of the new Constitution. I am affraid there is more Pomp & Parade than is consistent with those sober Republican Principles, upon which the Framers of it thought they had founded it. Why should this new Œra be introducd with Entertainments expensive & tending to dissipate the Minds of the People? Does it become us to lead the People to such publick Diversions as promote Superfluity of Dress & Ornament, when it is as much as they can bear to support the Expense of cloathing a naked Army? Will Vanity & Levity ever be the Stability of Government, either in States, in Cities, or what, let me hint

to you is of the last Importance, in *Families ?* Of
what Kind are those Manners, by which, as we are
truly informd in a late Speech, " not only the freedom
but the very Existence of Republicks is greatly
affected ?" How fruitless is it, to recommend " the
adapting the Laws in the most perfect Manner possible, to the Suppression of Idleness Dissipation &
Extravagancy," if such Recommendations are coun
teracted by the Example of Men of Religion, Influence & publick Station ? I meant to consider this
Subject in the View of the mere Citizen. But I have
mentiond the sacred Word *Religion.* I confess, I am
surprizd to hear, that some particular Persons have
been so unguarded as to give their Countenance to
such kind of Amusements. I wish M^r —— would
recollect his former Ideas when his Friend Whitfield
thunderd in the Pulpit against Assemblies & Balls.
I think he has disclaimd Diversions, in some Instances, which to me have always appeard innocent.
Has he changd his Opinions, or has the Tendency of
things alterd ? Do certain Manners tend to quench
the Spirit of Religion at one time & are they harmless at another? Are Morals so vague as to be
sanctified or dispens'd with by the Authority of different Men ? He does not believe this. But I will
not be severe, for I love my Friend. Religion out of
the Question for the present. It was asked in the
Reign of Charles the 2^d of England, How shall we
turn the Minds of the People from an Attention to
their Liberties ? The Answer was, by making them
extravagant, luxurious, effeminate. Hutchinson advisd the Abridgment of what our People called Eng-

lish Liberties, by the same Means. We shall never
subdue them, said Bernard, but by eradicating their
Manners & the Principles of their Education. Will
the judicious Citizens of Boston be now caught in
the Snare, which their artful, insidious Enemies, a
few years ago laid for them in vain? Shall we ruin
ourselves by the very means, which they pointed out
in their Confidential Letters, tho even they did not
dare openly to avow them? Pownal, who was indeed
a mere Fribble, venturd to have his Riots & Routs at
his own house, to please a few Boys & Girls. Sober
People were disgusted at it, & his privy Councellors
never thought it prudent to venture so far as expensive Balls. Our Bradfords, Winslows & Win-
throps would have revolted at the Idea of opening
Scenes of Dissipation & Folly ; knowing them to be
inconsistent with their great Design, in transplanting
themselves into what they called this " Outside of the
World." But I fear I shall say too much. I love the
People of Boston. I once thought, that City would
be the *Christian* Sparta. But Alas! Will men never
be free ! They will be free no longer than while they
remain virtuous. Sidney tells us, there are times
when People are not worth saving. Meaning, when
they have lost their Virtue. I pray God, this may
never be truly said of my beloved Town. Adieu.
My Respects to M[rs] Scollay & Family & believe me
to be sincerely

Your Friend

If M[r] B A [1] thinks a Question from me worth his

---

[1] Benjamin Austin.

answering, ask him whether he has lost some valueable Books which I have seen in his Library, *the
Works of our illustrious Forefathers.*

TO RICHARD HENRY LEE.

[MS., Lee Papers, American Philosophical Society.]

PHILAD^E Jany 15th 1781

MY DEAR SIR

Your second Letter came to hand in due Season.
My much Esteemed Friend Mr Arthur Lee will take
the Charge of this.   I will say to you as I have said
to my Boston Friends, who are sollicitous to know
what Treatment he meets with here.   The more I
have conversd with him, the more I have been confirmd in a good opinion of him, and lamented the
Mistakes and Prejudices of some Men & the Wickedness of others. His Enemies, I think, dare not openly
attack his Reputation or Conduct. But the Whispers
of Envy & Malice, have sometimes Influence enough
to prevent the Justice due to the virtuous Citizen.
When this is the Case, it affords a Symptom of the
Decay of publick Spirit, more threatning to the
Liberties of a Common Wealth than Hosts of foreign
Enemies.   Monarchs have their Favorites who serve
as Pimps on their honest Subjects.   But Republicks
should examine the Conduct of their Servants with
an impartial Eye; and it discovers the Want of publick Virtue, as much, to withhold their Smiles from
the wise and good as to bestow them on the wicked
& unfaithful.   Mr Lee has as yet had neither Smiles

nor Frowns. I am still in hopes, he will meet with the Rewards which I am sure he would have receivd if he had returnd a few years ago. He will have them, when the Trustees of the Publick shall have Fortitude enough, to be uninfluencd by great Names & Characters given to Men of base & depraved Minds. You will ask, when that will be. Perhaps not in this Age. But the Historian will in some future time draw forth the Proofs of his Patriotism, & unprejudicd Posterity will acknowledge that Arthur Lee has borne a great Share in defending & establishing the Liberties of America. I say Posterity ; for I believe that a wiser Generation will enjoy the Fruits of the Toil of Patriots & Heroes in the present Day.

My Friend, we must not suffer any thing to discourage us in this great Conflict. Let us recur to first Principles without Delay. It is our Duty, to make every proper Exertion in our respective States to revive the old patriotick Feelings among the People at large, and to get the publick Departments, especially the most important of them, filled with Men of Understanding & inflexible Virtue. It would be indeed alarming, if the United States should ever entrust the Ship in which our all is at Stake, with inexperiencd or unprincipled Pilots. Our Cause is surely too interesting to Mankind, to be put under the Direction of Men, vain, avaricious or conceald under the Hypocritical Guise of Patriotism, without a Spark of publick or private Virtue. We may possibly be more in Danger of this, than many of our honest Citizens may imagine. Is there not Reason to appre-

hend, that even those who are inimical to our Cause
may steal into Places of the highest Trust ?   I need
not remind *you* that Men of this Character have had
Seats in Congress from the begining.   Where is Galloway, Low, Allen & Alexander ?—If it was so in
those Times of Vigilance & Zeal, how much more
is it to be expected, when the Love of many is waxen
cold, & their Minds are distracted with the Pursuit of Pleasure & exorbitant Riches.   We cannot be
perswaded to believe that bad Men have been sent by
their States with a View of giving a fatal Stab to our
Cause in its Infancy ; but is it unreasonable to suppose that their Elections were secretly influencd by
artful Men, with that Design.   Our most dangerous
Enemies may be in our Bosoms.

Mr Lee will inform you how Matters go on here.

I must let you know that when your Kinsman M^r
William Lee was in Boston in Sept 1779 he borrowed
five hundred Dollars of Moses Gill Esqr, and drew
his Bill on his Brother Mr George Lee of Westmoreland County.   I wish it may be paid on Sight, for it
was advancd on my Application.

My Regards to Mrs Lee &^c.   Adieu & believe me
to be

Your Friend

TO JOHN PITTS.

[MS., Samuel Adams Papers, Lenox Library.]

PHILAD. Jany 17 1781

MY DEAR SIR

Your favor of the 17th of Novr was duly receivd.

It bodes very ill to Government when Men are exalted to places of high trust through their own Sollicitations.   He only fills a place with Dignity, who is
invited to it by his Fellow Citizens, from the Experience they have had of his adequate Abilities, & who
does the Duties of it with Zeal & Fidelity.   Such a
Man, being conscious that neither Smiles, Intreaties,
Gifts, Intrigue nor any dishonorable Practices have
procured him his high Station, may rely on the People
who gave him their free Suffrages, to approve of his
honest Endeavors to serve them.   And having Nothing in View but that the Publick may be best servd,
he will chearfully resign his Place whenever the People shall make Choice of another whom they judge
more capable than he.   The People are certainly the
best Judges, who are most likely to render them
substantial Service ; & whoever interposes in their
Elections, with his own Sollicitations for himself, it is
to be feard, if he is of any Consequence, will in time
become a dangerous Party Man.   He ought therefore
to be despisd as an obtruder.   I hope there are not
many such Men in our Government.   I am sorry to
be informd that there are any.   They should be
watchd ; for if they have no evil Designs, their Vanity
may prompt them to do Mischief.   The Express
waits.   Adieu.

TO JAMES WARREN.

[MS., Samuel Adams Papers, Lenox Library.]

PHILAD^E Feb 1st 1781—

MY DEAR SIR

I have not had Leisure to write to you since the

20th of Novr. Indeed I am not willing to trust a
Confidential Letter to the Post, which has shame-
fully been catchd in the same Trap more than once.
I gladly embrace the opportunity by Mr Otis, with
whom I have had frequent & candid Conversations
concerning Men & Things. He will be able to tell
you some Truths which I do not think it prudent
to commit to Paper. You & I have been long
struggling for the Liberty of our Country. I believe its Independence will be finally acknowledgd
by the World. But are not many Nations England in particular called Independent? And do you
think the People of England are free. No People, in
my opinion can be long free who are not virtuous; and
it is no Sign of Virtue, when the Councils of an enlightned Country are directed by a foreign Influence.
If I were a Minister at a foreign Court, my Vanity
might be flatterd, in imagining that by having
Address enough to rule its Measures, I might fix myself in the Esteem and Confidence of my Country, but I
should entertain a contemptible Opinion of the Wisdom & Virtue of that Court if it would suffer me to
do it. The Councils of a Nation must be weak in
the extreme, or it must be reducd to the greatest
Degree of Dependence to submit to so servile a Condition. You will not think I have the remotest
Reference in what I now say, jealous as I allow my
self to be, to the Amphictyon of the United States of
America. It is presumd they will always have too
high a Sense of their Dignity to suffer themselves &
their Nation to be degraded. But when Peace is
happily settled & a Number of foreign Ministers are

about our Court, it will require Men of great Knowledge of the World & Experience in Affairs to penetrate their various Intrigues. I have been assured that the Court of France would be highly disgusted with any of its Ministers if they should improperly interfere in our Councils ; and indeed when I consider the Jealousy of a rising Republick, I think nothing would equal the Impolicy of their attempting it, but the Imprudence of Congress in submitting to it. —— But I am unexpectedly called off and Mr Otis is just going. I intended to have written to you largely but must omit it till the next opportunity. Pray inform my worthy Friend Capt Bradford that I must also omit writing to him, as I intended, for the same Reason.

your affectionate,

TO MRS. ADAMS.

[MS., Samuel Adams Papers, Lenox Library.]

PHILAD^E Feb. 1st 1781

MY DEAR BETSY

My last was by Major Clarkson. He is a young officer of military Merit. I wish you would entertain him with a Dish of Tea.

Our new Œra of Government, I fancy, has occasiond a Revolution in political Circles & a Change of Connections. I cannot otherwise account for the long Silence of my Friend Doctor Cooper. I used to correspond with him very confidentially. We indeed thought aloud together. But I have receivd only one Letter from him since I left Boston, which was deliverd to me by M^r A Lee. I considerd it as a Compliment to that most deserving Patriot, rather than a Letter of Friendship to me. I have written several Times to him, & once desired particular Information, which he might have given me without offending any Man, but he has not done it. I hope the Doctor does not think his Letters troublesome to me. He has no Reason to think so. But, he chuses to close the Correspondence, & you know, that I am disposd on such Occasions, to retaliate. It sometimes affects my Feelings, but I shall never be in Debt on that Score. You may let the D^r read this Letter if he pleases, but no other Person ; for when I think amiss of the private Conduct of a Friend, I let none know it, but him & you. Indeed I shall say nothing to you at present that I would not wish him to know. I employ no Pimps or Spies on my Fellow Citizens, & yet I hear of many things that are said & done in Boston. I may sometimes be misinformd, & I am always inclind to think I am, when I cannot reconcile what is said with the Honor & Integrity of Friendship. If M^r W C[1] has "spoken very disrespectfully" of me, I am sorry for *him.* It gives me no Pain on my Account because I deserve not his reproach. I know he is apt to be sanguine in his Opinions of Men, & his Zeal in Elections has been commendable. But as I did not interest myself at all in the late Elections he might have spared me. I have candidly declared, when I was asked in Boston, who I thought to be most endowd with those great

---

[1] William Cooper.

Qualities, which should characterize the first Magistrate of so respectable a Commonwealth. This is the Right, it is the Duty of every Citizen. And had I been present, I should most certainly have voted for that Candidate. I may have been mistaken in my Judgment; and, as it becomes a Citizen, I will, acquiesce in the Choice of a Majority of the People, who ought to know & prefer the fittest Person. If they do not, they are hardly worthy to be servd by any Man. I hope we shall never fall into those Dregs of Time, when it shall be the Custom for one Citizen to treat another ill, merely because a popular Man has markd him as *his* Enemy, or because others, for servile Purposes, have reported him as such. This may afford Sport for the Enemies of our Cause, who are laying the Snare with great Art & Industry. James Rivington has publishd in his Royal Gazette, that the Acrimony between Mr Hancock & me, was owing to his Attachment to General Washington, & my being on the Contrary, desirous of his Removal. This is an old Story which Men have believd and disbelievd as they pleasd, without much Concern of mine. It was a pityful Contrivance to render me obnoxious to the General & our common Friends. If there has been any Difference between M^r H and me, Rivington knows not the Origin of it. Mr Hancock never thought me an Enemy to Genl Washington. He never thought that I was desirous of his being removd, & therefore could never treat me with Acrimony on that Account. I never wishd for the Removal of General Washington, but if I had even attempted to effect it, it might have been an

Evidence of my Deficiency in Judgment, or Rash-
ness, but it could be no Evidence that I was his
Enemy. M^r W C may think that I am an Enemy to
Mr Hancock, because he may have heard that I pre-
ferd another as a Governor before him. At this
Rate, I must be thought an Enemy to every Man to
whom I cannot give the Preference for an exalted
Station for which few of the Many can be supposd to
be qualified. Ridiculous [&] mischievous as this is,
I am told that some carry their opinions further and
that it is not enough, that a Man who cannot consistently vote for a Governor is to be reckon'd his
Enemy, but he is for this Reason to be excluded from
every Department. Who could wish to hold a Seat
in Government on so slavish a Tenure? The People
of Massachusetts under the old Government have
seen enough of the mischievous Effects of the Governors having a Power to negative Elections & I
cannot see the Difference between this & his being
able to influence or prevent an Election by causing
it to be believd that a Candidate is *his* Enemy. He
who gives his Suffrage according to the Dictates of a
well informd Judgment, is certainly a virtuous Citizen.
And is it to be supposd that such a Man would withhold his Influence in favor of a wise Measure, because
a Gentleman is placed in the Chair by his Fellow
Citizens, whom he did not vote for? Such a Supposition savours so much of a Narrow, illiberal party
Spirit, that I should think no intelligent Man would
countenance it. If it should prevail, it would produce evil Consequences ; for some Men, if they are
made to believe their political Existence depends on

their being thought the Governors Friends, will not
easily prevail on themselves to risque that Existence
by giving him Advice, however salutary it might be,
& necessary for the Honor & Safety of the Commonwealth, if they think it will disgust *him*.

You may wonder, my Dear, that I send this Budget
of Politicks to you. I see no Reason why a Man
may not communicate his political opinions to his
Wife, if he pleases. But to tell you the truth I consider this Epistle, after the License I have already
given you, as indirectly addressd to the Friend I
have mentiond. I would gladly know his opinion,
Whether there is not more Parade among our Gentry
than is consistent with sober republican Principles.
Is it to imitate the Vanity of former times that every
order of Men have been so fond of addressing the
Governor? Are we to pay the same Ceremonies to
the next & the next? Will not such high Strains of
Panegyrick injure the Feelings of modest Men?
And if there should happen to be a weak Man, will
they not make him intollerably vain? Republicks
should adopt the Rule of another Society. The Yea
should be Yea, and the Nay, Nay, for whatsoever is
more than these cometh of Evil. Adieu.

TO MRS. ADAMS.

[MS., Samuel Adams Papers, Lenox Library.]

PHILADELPHIA Mar. 15 1781

My dear Betsy

Mr Bagnal, the Bearer of this Letter, this Moment

informs me, that he sets off in half an hour for Boston I am sorry he did not give me more timely Notice, because I chuse to write to my Confidential Friends by private Hands rather than the Post. I have in a Letter forwarded yesterday, given Notice to the General Assembly, of my Wish to return home as early as may be and requested to be relievd by one of my Colleagues or otherwise as may be thought proper. I expect to have General Wards Servant to attend me on my Journey. He is afterwards to return here. I am much concernd at the Dissentions in the New South Society, who have generally been remarkeable for Peace & Harmony. They should strive for a conciliatory Spirit as far as is consistent with good Conscience, condescend to each other in smaller Matters, and bear with each others Tempers.

I have not been unmindful of my Sons Situation, as mentiond in his Letter to me some time ago. He will see by the Journals of Congress (Sept. 30, 1780) that the officers in the Medical Department, are intitled annually to draw Cloathing from the Stores of the Cloathier General in the same Manner & under the same Regulations as are establishd for officers of the Line by a Resolution Novr 25, 1779—such Cloathing to be deliverd by the Cloathier General or any sub Cloathier in the State in which the officer to receive the Cloathing shall reside. I have sent the Journals of the Dates above mentiond, and wish Mr Davis or some other of my Friends would speak to Mr Ruggles, who I think is the Sub Cloathier in the State, in Behalf of my Son. I hope however that the Matter is already settled, & he gone to Newport. I am uneasy at his being absent from his Station any length of Time; for however necessary it may be, it may be turnd to the Disadvantage of his Character, which if I am not *flatterd*, he has hitherto kept unsullied. In this virtuous & important Struggle, he will remember that all of us must ruff it as well as we can.——The medical Committee inform me that it is the Duty of the State Cloathier to furnish him without the intervention of the Commander in Chiefe or Board of War.

Pray let Mrs Fogs know that Mr Lovel & I have done all we could for the Release of her Son who was made a Sea Prisoner & carried to New York. Our officers have some of them been sent to England, but not any of the Seamen, so that it is hoped he is still there. Many of them have died. They have lately been better treated than they were some time ago. The British Sea Officers are retaind in close Confinement here till we hear what is become of ours. We are in hopes there will soon be an Exchange of the whole.

Remember me to Friends——Adieu.

ARTICLE, UNSIGNED.

[*Boston Gazette*, April 2, 1781 ; a draft is in the Samuel Adams Papers, Lenox Library.[1]]

Extract of a Letter from the Southward.

"As we have a Constitution which is admired for its genuine Principles, I have been sollicitous to know,

---

[1] Endorsed by Adams : " The foregoing was sent to Mr Edes by the Post March 13, 1781."

whether our Countrymen at large partook of the
Spirit of those who formed it.   I have conceived
strong Hopes, that in organizing their Government
and electing Persons to fill the important Places of
Trust, no Consideration would avail, to govern their
Suffrages in Favour of any Candidate, unless he was
possessed of those Qualities which are necessary, to
enable him to perform the Duties of the Office to be
filled, to the Advantage of the Publick.   I have
flattered my self, that both the Governors and the
Governed would have lain aside the gawdy Trappings
of Monarchy, and put on that Simplicity which is the
Ornament and Strength of a free Republick.   How
far it has been done, I am not able to judge at this
Distance.   It is a great Satisfaction to me to be
informed, that some of the best Men in the Commonwealth have been elected into the Principal Departments of Government.   Men, who will dignify the
Character of our Country—who will revive and disseminate those Principles, moral and political, to
propagate which, our Ancestors transplanted themselves into this new World—Men who by the Wisdom
of their Councils and their exemplary Manners, will
establish the public Liberty on the Foundation of a
Rock.—These Men will secure to themselves more of
the Esteem of their virtuous, and even of their vicious
Fellow-Citizens, than they could by a thousand courtly
Addresses which are commonly the Breath of Vanity
and Adulation.—There is a charm in Virtue to force
Esteem.—If Men of a different Character have by
any Means been advanced to those hallow'd Seats,
who have even *sollicited* public Employments to give

a Scope to Views of Ambition and Avarice, Passions which have in all Ages been the Bane of human Society ; or, to gratify the raging Thirst for popular Applause, a Disease with which little minds are usually tormented, it is our Happiness that the Constitution requires *annual* Elections, and such Mistakes may be corrected at the next.

" I was sorry to hear, that the Number of Votes returned, the last Time, did not amount to a Quarter of the Number of qualified Electors in the Commonwealth.   The Choice of Legislators, Magistrates and Governors, is surely a Business of the greatest Moment, and claims the Attention of every Citizen. The Framers of our Constitution, while they gave due Attention to *Political* were not forgetful of *Civil* Liberty—that personal Freedom and those Rights of Property, which the meanest Citizen is intitled to, and the Security of which is the great End of political Society.   It was not indeed their Province to make particular Laws for these Purposes.   To do this, and to provide for the equal and impartial Execution of such Laws, agreeable to the Constitution, is the Duty of the Legislature.   Hence every Citizen will see, and I hope will be deeply impressed with a Sense of it, how exceedingly important it is to *himself*, and how intimately the welfare of *his Children* is connected with it, that those who are to have a Share in making as well as in judging and executing the Laws should be Men of singular Wisdom and Integrity. Such as are conscious that they are deficient in either of these Qualities, should even TREMBLE at being named as Candidates !   I hope the great Business of

Elections will never be left by the Many, to be done by the Few ; for before we are aware of it, that few may become the Engine of Corruption—the Tool of a Junto.—Heaven forbid ! that our Countrymen should ever be byass'd in their Choice, by unreasonable Predilections for any man, or that an Attachment to the Constitution, as has been the Case in other Countries, should be lost in *Devotion to Persons.* The Effect of this would soon be, to change the Love of Liberty into the Spirit of Faction. Let each Citizen remember, at the Moment he is offering his Vote, that he is not making a Present or a Compliment to please an Individual, or at least that he ought not so to do ; but that he is executing one of the most solemn Trusts in human Society, for which he is accountable to GOD and his Country.

"When the great Body of the People are determined not to be imposed upon by a false Glare of Virtues held before their Eyes, but, making up their own Minds, shall impartially give in their Suffrages, after their best Enquiries into the Characters of Candidates, for those whom they judge to be the fittest Persons, there will be no Danger that the generous Enthusiasm of Freedom, so characteristic of the People of Massachusetts, will ever sink into the Violence and Rage of Party, which has often proved fatal to free Republicks.'

TO CALEB DAVIS.[1]

[MS., Samuel Adams Papers, Lenox Library.]

PHILAD^E April 3 1781

DEAR SIR /

I have just receivd your favor of the 17th Ult° by

---

[1] Speaker of the House of Representatives of Massachusetts.

Mr Dugan. The Request he proposes to make to Congress for Liberty to bring his Effects from Ireland, cannot be complied with consistently with the inclosd ordinance, which strictly forbids all Intercourse between the Citizens of the United States & the Subjects of Great Britain. There have been so many undue Advantages taken from Indulgences of this Kind, as to render the Continuance of them unsafe to us and disgustful to our Ally. I shall always pay a due Regard to your Recommendations, and should have been particularly desirous of rendering Service to your Friend Mr Dugan whom I personally know & of whose Integrity I have no Reason to doubt.

Your Letter of the 23^d of Feby never came to hand; and I regret it the more, because you tell me, you then wrote fully of the State of Affairs in Boston which I should have been glad to have receivd. Let me observe to you as a private Friend, the Delegates of Massachusetts are by no means duly informd of what is done in their own State; & when they receive any kind of Information, it is not in a Manner adapted to give them Weight. I do not mention this on my own Account; for I intend very soon to take Leave of Congress & get myself excusd from any future Attendance. I will then explain the Hint I have now given you, more fully than I chuse to do in a Letter by *the Post*. You mention a certain Juncture when you wish me to return. I think I can discover your Motive and your old Partiality for me. I do assure you, I am not at all sollicitous about any thing of the Kind which your Letter seems to intimate. I have always endeavord to confine my Desires

in this Life within moderate Bounds, and it is time
for me to reduce them to a narrower Compass. You
speak of "Neglect," "Ingratitude" &ᶜ. But let us
entertain just Sentiments. A Citizen owes everything
to the Commonwealth. And after he has made his
utmost Exertions for its Prosperity, has he done more
than his Duty? When Time enfeebles his Powers &
renders him unfit for further Service, his Country, to
preserve its own Vigour will wisely call upon others;
and if he decently retreats to make Room for them
he will show that he has not yet totally lost his Understanding. Besides, there is a Period in Life when a
Man should covet the exalted Pleasure of Reflection
in Retirement.

I thank you, my dear Sir, for the information you
gave Mʳˢ A of Mʳ Dugans coming. Pray let her
know that I receivd her Letter & am well. My
Compᵗˢ to the Circle about you.

Your affectionate,

ARTICLE, UNSIGNED.

[*Boston Gazette*, April 16, 1781; a draft is in the Samuel Adams Papers,
Lenox Library.[1]]

Extract of a Letter from the Southward.

"BEFORE this will reach you, your Countrymen
will have finished the important business of electing
their Legislators, Magistrates and Governors for the
ensuing year. I hope they have made a wise choice.
At least, from the opinion I entertain of their virtue, I

---

[1] Endorsed by Adams: "The foregoing was sent to Mʳ Edes by the Post
Mar 27, 81."

am persuaded they have acted with all that deliberation and caution which the solemnity of the transaction required. They may then reflect, each one on his own integrity, and appeal to the Monitor within his breast, that he has not trifled with the sacred trust reposed in him by GOD and his country—that he has not prostituted his honor and conscience to please a friend or a patron —that he has not been influenced with the view of private emolument to himself and his family, but has faithfully given his vote for the candidate whom he thought most worthy the choice of free and virtuous citizens—I congratulate that Legislator, Magistrate & Governor, who *knows* that neither smiles, entreaties, gifts, dissimulation, intrigue, nor any base and dishonorable practices have procured him this exalted station. His fellow citizens, *unsollicited* by him, have called him into their service, from the opinion they have formed of his integrity and adequate abilities.—He feels himself happy in their opinion of him—happy is he indeed, if he *is conscious he deserves it.*

But our countrymen will not imagine, that having filled the several departments of government, they have no further concern about it. It is, I humbly conceive, their duty and interest to attend to the manner in which it is administered by those whom they have entrusted. How often has the finishing stroke been given to public virtue, by those who possessed, or seemed to possess many amiable virtues? GUS-TAVUS VASA was viewed by the Swedes as the deliverer of their country from the Danish yoke. The most implicit obedience, says the historian, was considered by them as a debt of gratitude, and a virtue.

He had many excellent qualities. His manners were conciliating — His courage and abilities great—But the people by an entire confidence in him suffered him to lay a foundation for absolute monarchy. They were charmed with his moderation and wisdom, qualities which he *really* possessed ; but they did not consider his ambition, nor had they a thought of his views. They found peace restored, order established, justice administered, commerce protected, and the arts and sciences encouraged, and they looked no further. They did not imagine, that he who had been the instrument of recovering the independence of their country, could be the very man who was to effect the ruin of their liberties. By the Constitution of Sweden their kings were elective, and the powers of the crown were exceedingly limited. The unsuspecting people even voluntarily gave up their right of election, and suffered *Gustavus* to enlarge the powers of the crown, and entail it in his own family ! This is the account which the history of Sweden has given us ; and it affords an instance among a thousand others, of the folly and danger of trusting even *good men* with power, without regarding the use they make of it. Power is in its nature incroaching ; and such is the human make, that men who are vested with a share of it, are generally inclined to take more than it was intended they should have. The love of power, like the love of money, increases with the possession of it ; and we know, in what ruin these baneful passions have involved human societies in all ages, when they have been let loose and suffered to rage uncontrouled— *There is no restraint like the pervading eye of the virtuous citizens.*—I hope therefore our countrymen will constantly exercise that right which the meanest of them is intitled to, and which is particularly secured to them by our happy constitution, of inquiring freely, but decently, into the conduct of the public servants. The very being of the Commonwealth may depend upon it. I will venture to appeal to the experience of ancient Republicks, to evince the necessity of it; and it is never more necessary than in the infancy of a Commonwealth, and when the people have chosen honest men to conduct their affairs. For, whatever is done at a time nearly contemporary with the constitution, will be construed as the best exposition of it; and a mistaken principle of a virtuous ruler, whose public conduct is generally good, and always supposed to be honestly intended, carries with it an authority scarcely to be resisted, and precedents are thus formed which may prove dangerous—perhaps *fatal.*"—

TO SAMUEL COOPER.

[MS., Samuel Adams Papers, Lenox Library.]

PHILAD^E Apr 23 1781

My dear Sir

I did not receive your favor of the 3^d Inst^t till yesterday ; a week later than Letters of the same Date from some others of my Boston friends were brought to me by the Post. As the Subject is delicate, I do not chuse to continue it in this Letter, which is to go thro a Channel provd from repeated Experience to be uncertain & unsafe. It was for this Reason that

I committed to the Care of a private friend, my
Letter to M^{rs} A of the 1st of Feby which she communicated to you.   I am glad she did it in a Manner
so acceptable.   Indeed I never found Reason to doubt
her Discretion.   What you have written is very
obliging & satisfactory to me.   I hope to have the
Pleasure of seeing you next Month.   We will then,
after our usual Manner, disclose each others Hearts.

Your Letter of the 31st Decr was not long ago deliverd to me by the Count Chartres.   He appears to
me to be an amiable & fine-spirited young Nobleman.
After a short stay here, he proceded with the Marq^{s}
de la Fayette to the Southward.

You will recollect a Design which I mentiond to
you respecting our Friend M^{r} L   , & the Omission
which, we were informd the Evening before I left
Boston, had happend thro Mistake.   I early wrote to
you & requested your Influence to have it rectified.
I have heard Nothing of it since.   In my Opinion the
most essential Interest of the Town of Boston will be
servd by it, & therefore I cannot look upon it as a
Matter of Indifference.   Not being acquainted with
that Gentleman in the early Times of our Contest, I
had by some means conceivd an Opinion of him not
so favorable ; but having had an Opportunity of critically observing him in the late Convention at Cambridge, I am satisfied he is a Virtuous Citizen, and
possessd of the genuine Principles of New England.
That Mr Rivington, if this Letter should fall into
his Hands, may not pretend to be at a Loss to know
what is here meant, I will inform him that the genuine
Principles of New England are Republican Prin-

ciples which have been admired by some of the greatest Characters, whom (if he is an Englishman) his Country can boast of. You & I, among others, have had the Honor of being abusd by Rivingtons Press. A labord Performance has lately crept out, called *the Times.* I have had a cursory reading of it. It appears to me so much like the Productions of certain Geniuses who figurd in Mr Popes Time, that had the Author been cotemporary with them, a Page might have been added to the Dunciad, to immortalize his Works. I will endeavor to get some Parts of it transcribd & carry them to Boston. I am sure the reading it would serve to divert rather than to give you the least Pain. My due Regards to Friends.

Your affectionate

TO THOMAS McKEAN.[1]

[MS., Historical Society of Pennsylvania.]

BOSTON Augt 29th 1781

MY HONORD FRIEND

I have not yet acknowledgd your obliging Letter of the 8th of July, deliverd to me by Mr Davidson. Bodily Indisposition prevented my writing, when he returnd. I fancy he settled his Affairs here to his own Satisfaction. He is much esteemd by those who were favord with his Company, & I hope he met with Nothing disagreable to him during his short Stay among us.

Col^o John Laurens with our Friend Mr Pain arrivd here a few Days ago from France. He left the Town

---

[1] President of Congress.

the Day after his Arrival. His Visit to me was so short that I could not converse with him so fully as I wishd. I hope he will be able to inform you of his complete Success in his Negociation. Will you be so kind as to give me such Intelligence as you may receive from him or any other Person from Europe. I wish to know the true State of our Affairs. Are we soon to have Peace? However desireable this may be, we must not wish for it on any Terms but such as shall he honorable & safe to our Country. Let us not disgrace our selves by giving just Occasion for it to be said hereafter, that we finishd this great Contest with an inglorious Accommodation. Things are whisperd here which, if true, will cause much Discontent. The Citizens of this Part of America will say, and judge, my dear Sir, whether it would not be just, that the fishing Banks are at least as important as Tobacco yards, or Rice Swamps, or the flourishing Wheat Fields of Pennsylvania. The Name only of Independence is not worth the Blood of a single Citizen. We have not been so long contending for Trifles. A *Navy* must support our Independence; and Britain will tell you, that *the Fishery* is a grand Nursery of Seamen. —I understand that G M,[1] is appointed Deputy Financier, R R L,[2] Secretary of foreign Affairs, and if G[1] S[3] is appointed to the War Department and G[1] M[4] to the Marine, there will be a compleat N Y Administration. It may be well to enquire, *what Influence* has brought this about, & whether so much Power

[1] Gouverneur Morris.   [2] Robert R. Livingston.
[3] Philip Schuyler.   [4] Alexander McDougall.

vested in the Citizens of any one State will excite the reasonable Jealousy of the rest. Adieu my Friend. Find a Moments Leisure to write to me.

TO THOMAS McKEAN.

[MS., Historical Society of Pennsylvania; a draft is in the Samuel Adams Papers, Lenox Library.]

BOSTON Sept 19 1781

MY HONORD FRIEND

The Bearer, Major Brown, is a Person who has deservd well of the United States, and has for that Reason the Esteem of Men of Distinction in this Commonwealth. He was formerly a Soldier in the British Service, and before the Commencement of Hostilities, he left that Service—Immediately after the Battle of Lexington he joynd the American Army in which his Zeal & Activity was signalizd—In July 1776 he servd as Major in the Militia of this State at Ticonderoga under Genl Gates—In 1777 he was appointed Depy Muster Master by Col Ward, and when the Convention Troops arrivd at Cambridge he was employd by Genl Heath as Town Major— He has Certificates of his Fidelity from that General as well as the Commissary of Musters Coll Ward— Your Attention to a Request he will make to Congress for Allowance for Depreciation (if you can find Leisure) will much oblige me.

Will you suffer me Sir, in great Haste, to offer a few indigested Hints for your Consideration. I take it for granted that a very great Majority of the People in Each of the United States are determind to support this righteous & necessary War, till they shall obtain their grand Object, an *undisputed* Sovereignty. This must hereafter be maintaind, under God, by the Wisdom and Vigour of *their own* Councils & *their own* Strength— Their Policy will lead them, if they mean to form any Connections with Europe, to make themselves respectable in the Eyes of the Nations by holding up to them the Benefits of their Trade— Trade must be so free to *all* as to make it the Interest of *Each* to protect it till they are able to protect it themselves—This, the United States must do by a Navy. Till they shall have erected a powerful Navy, they will be lyable to Insults wch may injure & depreciate their Character as a Sovereign & independent State ; & while they may be incapable of resenting it themselves, no friendly power may venture or care to resent it on their Behalf. The U. S. must then build a Navy. They have or may have all the Materials in Plenty—But what will Ships of War avail them without Seamen ? And Where will they find a Nursery for Seamen but in THE FISHERY ? Adieu my dear Sir. Your affectionate

TO HORATIO GATES.

[MS., Historical Society of Pennsylvania.]

BOSTON Oct 11th 1781

MY DEAR SIR

Altho' I am at this Juncture much pressd with publick Business, I will not omit writing a few Lines, to testify my sincere Regards for you—When I left you in Philadelphia last June, I regretted the disagreable

Situation you was then in—deprivd of the Prospect
of reaping fresh Laurels, when an active Campaign
was expected.   Whether a Court of Enquiry has yet
been called, agreable to your Wishes, I know not.
Till that is done, I say it without Flattery, our
Country will lose the Assistance of one of its most
able & faithful Servants.—We are at this Distance in
great Uncertainty of every thing that happens Southward of New York.   We hear of military Movements
& naval Engagements, but not of their Events—Pray
inform me of the Situation of publick Affairs, and of
your own as far as you shall think proper.   We hope,
& are even sanguine in our Expectations of great &
decisive Events in our favor—God grant we may not
be disappointed!   Doctor Gordon who kindly takes
the Care of this Letter, is well acquainted with the
Internal State of this Common Wealth—He knows
my Mind, & will communicate to you, more than I
can now do for Want of Leisure.   Adieu, & believe
me to be with the warmest Attachment——Your
unalterd Friend

TO WILLIAM HEATH.

[MS., Samuel Adams Papers, Lenox Library.]

BOSTON Nov^r [21] 1781

SIR

The Bearer of this Letter Mr Edgar called on me
the other Day with General Baylie of Vermont a Gentleman of undoubted Integrity & Attachment to the
Cause of our Country &[who]has renderd himself very
useful by the Intelligence he has obtaind from Canada since the Beginning of this War, & is well known

to the Commander in Chief of our Armies. Gen¹ Baylie earnestly wishes that Mᵣ Edgar may be introducd to Head Quarters because he thinks from what he has to say it will appear that if two Gentlemen who are now Prisoners in Canada whose Names he will mention to you may be exchangd they will be able to make a full Discovery to you, of the Plan of union which he says is actually compleated between the Govᵣ of Canada & the principal Leaders in Vermont. One of these Gentlemen General Baylie tells me he has long been acquainted with & confides in. It is possible you may be already sufficiently acquainted with this Matter; & there may be a Scheme of Policy on our Side which has not come to my Knowledge. In this Uncertainty I hope I shall be excusd troubling you with this Letter.

Mᵣ Edgar, according to his own Account was in the British Service on the Lakes in 1774, afterwards was at Detroit as a private Trader, when he renderd Services to Colᵒ Clark as an Intelligencer, became suspected he was sent a Prisoner to Montreal where he lay in Irons nine Months, & after two years Imprisonment, he made an Escape.

After congratulating you on the Divine Blessing afforded to the Allied forces under the Direction of his Excy Gen¹ Washington, I am &ᶜ

THE TOWN OF BOSTON TO THE SELECTMEN OF OTHER TOWNS.

[MS., Chamberlain Collection, Boston Public Library.]

GENTLEMEN

The Inhabitants of the Town of Boston legally

assembled, have taken into Consideration a Matter which they conceive all the other Maritime Towns in this & the Neighboring States are equally, and some of them more nearly interested than they. It is the Subject of the Fishery, and the great Importance of a Common Right therein being secured to the United States, whenever a Treaty of Peace shall be concluded. To flatter our selves with so happy a Prospect, so far as to neglect the necessary Preparations for another vigorous Campaign, would indeed be unbecoming the Wisdom of Americans; and yet, so important has been the Success of the allied Arms, the last year, that it would seem to be Madness in the Extreme for Britain any longer to persist in her unrighteous Claims. But Wisdom has forsaken her Councils.

We ought to presume, that the supreme Representative of these States will have an equal Regard in so momentuous a Crisis to the Rights of each Individual. We would not suggest the Contrary. But, may it not be supposd, that Persons whose Situation is remote from the Fishery, and who derive Advantages from it in its more distant Effects & not directly perceivable, are probably not so attentive to its unspeakeable Importance, as others who are immediately concernd, & depend upon it as the only Source of their Commerce & even their Subsistence? If this should be the Fact, Would not States so immediately interested in the Fishery as ours, be justly criminated by the others, if we should neglect seasonably to lay before them our own Sense of the Necessity of an express Article in a Treaty of Peace for its Security? Should we not be wanting to our selves in a most essential Point, & be chargeable by all Posterity, with sacrificing our and their invalueable Rights by unpardonable Carelessness ?   Such is the Sentiment of this Town. And though we would be far from obtruding this or any Sentiment of ours upon others, we cannot but think our selves justifyable in candidly recommending it to their serious Deliberation.

This Town have judgd it necessary to instruct their Representatives in the General Court on the Subject. The instructions are inclosd. Many other and cogent Reasons might have been urgd, & will undoubtedly be made Use of by you, if you shall think it proper to take the Matter into your Consideration.   Should we be so fortunate as to have your full Concurrence in Opinion with us, we assure our selves that we shall be equally fortunate in the Aid we shall receive from your Concurrent Exertions.

In the Name & by Order of the Town of Boston[1] in Meeting legally assembled December 14 1781.

TO JOHN ADAMS.[2]

[MS., Adams Papers, Quincy; a draft is in the Samuel Adams Papers, Lenox Library.]

BOSTON 18 Decʳ 1781

MY DEAR SIR

I have already written to you this Day by the Marquis de Lafayette. This passes thro the Hands of

---

[1] Signed, in the original as published, by William Cooper, Town Clerk. This letter and the instructions of the town of December 11, 1781, were printed in a pamphlet of three pages.   A copy is in the Boston Public Library.

[2] Addressed to Adams at Amsterdam.

Count de Noailles, whom you did me the Honor to introduce to me. I duly acknowledgd the Receipt of your Favor which he brought me ; but the Loss of my Letter was attended with an infinitely greater, that of Coll° Palfrey. I wrote to you largely by him.

The Son in Law of one of our good Friends has lately arrivd here from England, which gives great Disgust to more Persons than his near Relations conceive of. On his Arrival, the Governor & Council directed him to state his Reasons for going to England and returning hither without the Leave of Government. He stated his Reasons ; which in general were to render Service to the United States, particularly by removing the Ideas which the British Minister had conceivd of the Attachment of nine tenths of the Americans to that Government, and their Wishes to return to it. However frivolous this may appear to others, his nearest Friends speak of it, can you believe me, in a high Tone, and M^r —— told me that M^r —— was happy in being conscious not only of Innocence, but of great Merit.[1]—Those who hope for a Change of Person in our first Magistrate next Spring will be much embarrassd by this Circumstance. Adieu my Friend.

TO JOHN ADAMS.

[MS., Samuel Adams Papers, Lenox Library.]

BOSTON Decr 19 1781

MY DEAR SIR
    The Marquis La Fayette is so obliging as to take

---

[1] The draft at this point has the words: "the Affair is in the Hands of the Attourney General by the Direction of the Govr & Council."

the Care of this Letter, which, for the sake of him, the Count de Noailles and others our french Friends who take Passage with him in the Alliance, I hope will arrive safely. In the same Conveyance is a Packett intended for you from Congress, by which you will doubtless be informd of what has been doing there. It is six Months since I left Philadelphia; you cannot therefore expect I should give you any of the Intelligence of that City. I presume M^r L^1 makes known to you every thing interesting. I wrote to you frequently while I was there, but suppose all my Letters miscarried, as well as yours if you have written to me; for I have not receivd one for many Months. I except your favor by the Sieur de la Etombe, to whom I pay great Attention, both on Account of your Recommendation & his Merit. I give you Credit for a Packett of Gazzettes lately receivd, because I knew the Direction on the Cover to be your hand writing.

Matters go on here just as you would expect from your knowledge of the People. Zealous in the great Cause, they hesitate at no Labor or Expence for its Support. Anxious to have a Code of Laws for the internal Government, adapted to the Spirit of their new Constitution with which they continue to be highly pleasd, the General Court have appointed the supreme Judges with Mr Bowdoin who is *at present* at perfect Leisure, to revise the Laws and report necessary or proper Amendments. The two great Vacancies in the offices of President & Professor of Mathematicks &^c in our University are filled with

---

[1] Laurens.

Gentlemen of Learning & excellent Characters, the Revd Mr Willard of Beverly & the Revd Mr Williams. The Academy of Arts & Sciences is in a flourishing Way. A new Society is incorporated by the Name of the Medical Society. And this Metropolis has lately appointed a Committee, to consider the present Arrangement of the Schools & what further Improvements may be made, in which the better Education of female Children is designd to be comprehended. All these things I know are pleasing *to you*. Our People treat Foreigners of Merit who come among them, with good Humour & Civility, being desirous of adopting the virtuous Manners of others, and ingrafting them into our Stock. Laudable Examples on their side & ours will be productive of mutual Benefits. Indeed the Men of Influence must form the Manners of the People. They can operate more towards cultivating the Principles & fixing the Habits of Virtue than all the Force of Laws. This I think is verified in the Experience of the World; & should induce those People who exercise the Right of electing their own Rulers, to be circumspect in making their Choice. You are well enough acquainted with the Character of our first Magistrate to judge what Effects his Influence will have upon Manners.

Inclosd are some of the Proceedings of a late Town Meeting,[1] which I send to you as a private Citizen for your mere information. The Meeting was called in Consequence of a Letter receivd by our Selectmen from Marblehead, in which it was proposd that the Subject should be considerd in a Convention of the

---

[1] *Boston Record Commissioners' Report*, vol. xxvi., p. 214.

Maritime Towns. But this Town judgd it more proper to lay the Matter before the General Court, and have accordingly instructed their Representatives & recommended it to the others to take the same Method. They could not think it becoming in them to write to you (tho a fellow Citizen) on a Subject which concerns the American Republick. They have an entire Confidence in your Attachment to the Interest of the United States & of this which makes an essential Part of it.

The Count de Noailles tells me he has a Letter for you from your Family. Please to pay my due Regards to Mr Dana M^r Th——[1] &^c. I rejoyce to hear of the Welfare of one of your Sons, whom we had almost given up for lost. Mrs Adams sends Compliments Miss has changed her Name & left her Fathers House.

Your affectionate,

TO ALEXANDER McDOUGALL.

[MS., Samuel Adams Papers, Lenox Library.]

BOSTON May 13 1782.

My DEAR SIR

Your Favors of 10th Dec^r & 7th Feb last were severally deliverd to me by Major Gibbs & Dr Townsend. I am sometimes obligd to apologize for omitting to answer Letters in Season. You, I am perswaded, will be ready to believe that necessary Avocations have prevented my writing to you, for there can be no Doubt in your Mind, of the Sincerity of my Professions of Esteem & Friendship. The Present you sent

---

[1] John Thaxter, private secretary to John Adams.

me by Major Gibbs gratified me exceedingly. I intend to transmit it to my Posterity, as a Specimen of Spartan Frugality in an American General Officer. The Citizen & the Soldier are called to the Exercise of Self Denial and Patience, and to make the utmost Exertions in Support of the great Cause we are engagd in. Providence has highly honord our Patriots & Heroes in calling them into Existence at a Time when there is an Object worthy their Views. The Romans fought for Empire. The Pride of that haughty People was to domineer over the rest of Mankind. But this is not our Object. We contend for the Liberty of our Country and the Rights of human Nature. We hope to succeed in so righteous a Contest; and it is our Duty to acquire such Habits, and to cultivate in those who are to come after us such Principles and Manners as will perpetuate to our Country the Blessings which are purchasd with our Toils and Dangers.

I have been expecting your Confidential Letters under the Signature you proposd. Pray let me hear of the Event of the Court Martial, and as many particulars as are expedient—Compl^ts to your Lady.

Adieu.

TO JOHN LOWELL.

[*Historical Magazine*, 1st ser., vol. i., pp. 260, 261.]

BOSTON, May 15th 1782.

MY DEAR SIR,—

The General Court was prorogu'd Friday, the tenth instant, previous to which on the same day the Govr sent the Impost Bill to the house of Representatives with his objections and reasons against it stated in form. The house conceiving that the five days to which he was limited by the Constitution, had expired the preceding day, sent it back to him without reading the objections, as being in their opinion to all intent and purposes *a law.* It seems the bill had been sent to the Governor on Saturday. He excludes Sunday from the 5 days, in which the House differ in opinion. This matter of difference which arises from an incidental circumstance, would have been avoided if his Excellency had thought it convenient to have sent the bill to the House a day sooner. It is a subject of speculation among the political casuists. But how will it affect the great public for whose benefit it was intended? If the bill has become a law, how will it operate? What will be the opinion of Congress concerning it under its present circumstances? I wish to hear from you by return of this post.

Yesterday, this town made choice of the same gentlemen to represent them in the G. C. who had served them the last year, except that Mr. Lord[1] is chosen in the room of Mr. Davis.[2] No one doubts my personal regard for Mr. L., but I think it may be highly dangerous, and attended with very ill effects, to admit an undue influence of the Superintendent of Finance into the general assemblies of these states, and therefore could not help mentioning my objections, to such of the inhabitants as I had an oppor-

---

[1] The town records appear to indicate that John Rowe should have been named in this connection.

[2] Caleb Davis ; *cf.* page 253.

tunity of conversing with, against his agent's being chosen a member of ours. The post is just going. Your affectionate,

TO JOHN LOWELL.

[*Historical Magazine*, 1st ser., vol. i., p. 261.]

BOSTON, June 4ᵗʰ, 1782.

MY DEAR SIR,—

Last week the House of Representatives directed the attendance of the Secretary, and enquired of him whether he had forwarded the Impost Act to Congress. He answered he had not seen it since he left it on their table, in the last session. The House then sent a message to the Governor to the same purpose.

He returned a message acquainting them that he conceived the bill in the same light he had before, and could not send it to Congress as a law, or to that effect ; adding, that if the House would signify their desire of having it, the Secretary would be directed to lay it before them. The House stated the matter, and sent it to the Senate with the Governor's message and a vote to join a committee to consider them, and the Senate concurred ; the result of which is that the two houses have resolved, that the Governor did not return the bill to the late House of Representatives, where it had originated, within five days after it was presented to him by the late General Court, and therefore that it had passed all the forms prescribed by the Constitution to constitute it a law of the Commonwealth. What the next step will be, may, I think, be easily foreseen, that those who are against the law

upon principle, or those who would wish to gratify
the Govr, will move for a repeal of it, and have a new
bill brought in. But it is difficult for me to conceive
how a bill can be framed which will remove his
doubts, and answer the end of Congress.   You
remember that matter was once tried.   I must break
off abruptly.

Your affectionate,

TO ARTHUR LEE.

[R. H. Lee, *Life of Arthur Lee*, vol. ii., pp. 229, 230.[1]]

BOSTON, Nov. 21st, 1782.

MY DEAR SIR,—In the late session of our general
court, and in the hurry of important business, a petition was presented signed William Burgess, praying
to be naturalized. This gentleman very lately arrived from England, by way of Holland. The senate
declined sustaining his petition, and gave him leave
to withdraw it. A few days after, an authenticated
resolution of congress came to hand, recommending
it to the states not to admit any British subject *whatever*. Yet this man has had interest enough to prevail on the assembly to permit him to go to congress,
to have it decided there whether he comes within the
meaning of their resolution, because his arrival here
was prior to the reception of the resolution by this
government. If it should be thought there was in
this instance a want of attention, it must be imputed
to the circumstance I first mentioned. The general
court had before directed his departure from the
state ; requesting the governor however, to allow him

---

[1] A short note to Lee, also dated November 21, is in *Ibid.*, p. 231.

convenient time to prepare for his voyage, which appeared to me a sufficient indulgence. Some of our good citizens are disgusted at the favour shown to Mr. B. They say that being a partner with Messrs. Champion and Dickinson, the latter of whom is reported to have been always inimical to America by his residence here, he will probably be instrumental in the importation of as many English goods as he will be able to vend ; or in other words, that the new house in Boston will be nearly if not quite as convenient in the time of war, as the old house in London was in time of peace. Whether there will be any danger, congress will judge. Jealousy is a necessary political virtue, especially in times like these. Such a plan would gratify those among us who are still hankering after the onions of Egypt, and would sacrifice our great cause to the desire of gain. What need is there of our admitting (to use the language of congress) any British subject *whatever ?* Congress surely had some good reason when they so earnestly cautioned us against it. Our citizens are in more danger of being seduced by art, than subjugated by arms. I give you this notice that you may have an opportunity of conversing on the subject in your patriotic circles (if you think it worth while) in season. Mr. B. will set off next week in company with one of our new delegates, who I am satisfied will favour his cause. My friendly regards to Dr. Shippen, and my old friends in congress, if any such are there. Adieu.

Believe me to be very affectionately your friend,

TO ARTHUR LEE.

[R. H. Lee, *Life of Arthur Lee*, vol. ii., pp. 231, 232.]

BOSTON, Dec. 2d, 1782.

MY DEAR SIR,—A friend of mine to whom I give entire credit, who lived many years in Canada, and was well acquainted with the bearer of this letter, requests me to introduce him to you. After a long confinement in prison in Quebec, where he was used with great severity, he found means to make his escape, and came to this town. He is a Frenchman by birth, and was a very respectable merchant in Canada. When the attempt was made to gain that country in 1775, he privately aided our forces; the suspicion of which rendered him obnoxious to the British government, and was the real cause of his suffering. He will inform you of the state and circumstances of British affairs there, and will tell you it is an easy thing to unite that province with these states. Possibly he may be influenced in some degree by a just resentment of the ill-treatment he has received; but other intelligent persons acquainted with the people of Canada, have zealously affirmed the same to me. If it be so, it is hoped that a favourable opportunity to effect it will be embraced, if any such should offer. I need not hint to you the importance of that object. Adieu,

Your friend,

TO ARTHUR LEE.

[R. H. Lee, *Life of Arthur Lee*, vol. ii., pp. 232-234; a draft is in the Samuel Adams Papers, Lenox Library.]

BOSTON, Feb. 10th, 1783.

MY DEAR SIR,—It is a long time since I had the

pleasure of a letter from you. I hope you have not struck my name from the list of your correspondents. Mr. Stephen Higginson, who will deliver you this letter, is appointed a delegate of this state. He is a sensible and very worthy man, and I think entertains sentiments like yours. I am persuaded you will find him a valuable member, if his great modesty and diffidence of himself will allow him to step forward as far as his good understanding would lead him.

I feel myself constrained to mention to you the present situation of Capt. Landais, though not at his request, or the smallest intimation from him. He resides in this town, and sometimes calls to see me. As he appears to be an injured man, I wish that justice may be done to him; and I am the more solicitous about it, as I was, with your worthy brother Mr. R. H. instrumental in his first appointment in the American navy. Congress granted him 12,000 livres as a compensation for services he had performed, and ordered that he should be paid by Dr. F. in France; but for some reason which is or ought to be known, he has never received that sum. Much the greater part of his wages as commander of the Alliance remains unpaid. A large sum due to him for prize-money is stopped in the hands of some person or persons in France; which indeed is too common a complaint among those continental officers and seamen who have carried prizes into ports in Europe. He made a journey to Philadelphia to obtain a settlement of his accounts, and was offered by M^r. M.[1] three months' pay, and a certificate for the balance, which he

---

[1] Morris.

would not accept, because he really wanted the whole
of his wages to supply him with the necessaries of life.
I am sure that your own feelings of justice and humanity will plead an excuse for my troubling you with
this detail.   Perhaps his court-martial, by whose decree he was broken, were too severe.   If his conduct
in his last passage from France was blameable was
not his mind to the greatest degree irritated by the
treatment he met with there? and should not reasonable allowances have been made?   He thinks it was
an unrighteous decree.   He may judge partially ; I
know nothing of the matter.   If it was, is not the
wound given to his honour sufficiently severe?   But
even if it was just, should not a discarded officer be
immediately paid?   Should not congress demand the
reason why the prize-money has not been paid to
those to whom it has been long due?   Complaints of
this kind have to my knowledge spread from Philadelphia to Boston.   I am concerned for the honour of
congress.   These complaints may appear of little consequence; but I am afraid if they continue unattended
to, they will cast a dark shade over the public character.   The state of Landais' affairs will appear in his
own memorial to congress, which was rejected, and
perhaps may be on the files.   You will oblige me if
you will interest yourself (if leisure will admit
of it) as far as you may think just, in his favour.

I have been applied to by some of the inhabitants of
the island of Nantucket, and have promised them
to write to my friend respecting the whale fishery.
These people have been usually employed in that
branch of business chiefly.   They have greatly re-

duced the number of their vessels, since the commencement of the war, by which means they say they are
reduced to great distress and wish for some indulgence
from congress. Whether this can be consistently
granted, and in what manner, you will judge. The
delegates of this state, I believe, can inform you more
particularly of this matter. You are sensible of the
absolute dependence of this state upon the fishery for
its trade, and how great an advantage will accrue from
it to the United States, if they intend ever to have a
navy. I hope our peacemakers are instructed by all
means to secure a common right in it.

My respects to the Hon. Mr. Izard, if at Philadelphia, and other friends. Adieu, and believe me very
affectionately yours,

TO THE SELECTMEN OF BOSTON.

[MS., Chamberlain Collection, Boston Public Library.]

MARCH 10 1783

GENTLEMEN

Having been just now made acquainted by your
Messenger that the Freeholders and Inhabitants of
Boston assembled in Town Meeting,[1] have chosen me
their Moderator, I beg the Favor of you to inform
them, that I esteem my self greatly honourd by their
Choice ; but my Engagements in the Senate, which
it is not in my Power to dispense with, lay me under
a Necessity of praying that I may be excusd by the
Town.——

With the warmest Wishes for their Prosperity, I am
Gentlemen
Your obedient hbl Serv[t]

---

[1] *Boston Record Commissioners' Report*, vol. xxvi., p. 292.

TO ARTHUR LEE.

[MS., Samuel Adams Papers, Lenox Library.]

BOSTON Apr 21 1783

D^r S^r

I am indebted to you for several Letters which I have not acknowledged. The Anecdote you gave me in one of them relating to a Mr Mercer & Col^o Griffin in Virginia was very diverting to me. The People in this part of the Continent would never have fixed upon the Names of L^a L^e or A^1 to hold up to a publick Assembly as the Heads of a British Interest in America. It would not have been sooner believed here than another Story I have heard, that a certain french Politician of Consideration in America had expressd his high Displeasure with M^r S A for stiring up his Countrymen to attend to the Importance of our retaining a Common Right to the Newf^d L^d fishery. Many wonderful Tales are & will be told, some of which a Sight of the secret Journals of Congress would unravel. I think the sooner those Journals are pub-lishd the better. The People at large ought to know what that illustrious Body has been doing for them and the Part each Member has acted. We are now at Peace, God be thanked, with all the World—and I hope we shall never intermeddle with the Quarrels of other Nations. Let the U S continue in peace & Union, & in order to this Let them do Justice to each other. Let there be no longer secret Journals or secret Com^{tees}. Let the Debates in Congress be open and the whole of their transactions publishd weekly

---

[1] Laurens, Lee, Adams.

—this will tend to the speedy rectifying Mistakes &
preserving mutual Confidence between the People &
their Representatives.   And let Care be taken to prevent Factions in America, *foreign or domestick.*

Will you suffer me to recommend to you my good
friends & excellent fellow Citizens Mr Appleton
the Bearer of this Letter & his fellow Traveller M^r
Wendel.   My Regards.

Adieu.

TO BENJAMIN LINCOLN.

[MS., Samuel Adams Papers, Lenox Library.]

BOSTON May 1 1783

MY DEAR SIR

Coll° John Allan will deliver you this Letter.   This
Gentleman soon after the Commencement of the late
Hostilities, left his Connections in Nova Scotia which
were respectable there & took a decided part with us
against Great Britain.   In the Winter of 77 Congress
appointed him Superintendent or Agent for the
Indians in Nova Scotia & the Tribes to the Northward & Eastward thereof, with a Salary of 900 Dollars p Annum, & afterwards requested this State to
furnish him from time to time with needful Supplies.
The State raised an Artillery Company for the Defence of the Post of Machias & gave him the Command with a Col^s Commission.   Congress in Feb 81
if I mistake not, empowerd our supreme Executive to
enlarge that Comp^y to the Number of 65, officers included, & to officer the same with the express Nomi-

nation of Col° Allan to the Command. This Comp^y
was by the Resolve to be raisd cloathed subsisted &
paid as other officers & Soldiers of the U S. I believe Col° A has executed the trusts reposed in him
with Fidelity & to the Advantage of the Publick.
As this State has supplied him at the Expence of the
U S, I suppose that his Acco^ts which remain to be
settled, will as his former Acc^ts have been, be settled
in the first Instance by our Assembly when it meets.
He takes the Opp^ty in the Interval (the War being
finishd) to wait on Congress for their further Direction. Your Notice of him & Care that he may receive such Emoluments as he may be intitled to as an
officer will oblige me. I think he has too much Republican Pride to expect more than is reasonable
from *Congress*, & he is too much the Gentleman to
be troublesome to *you*. I write this without his
knowledge.

Another calls upon me. You will think me a Man
of Importance! But this is one of my Days of
Business. Is it not strange that an officer of the
American Army should apply to the Friendship of
one whom they have been led to look upon as their
Enemy? But—I am informd that Col° Badlam was
among the first who flew to Arms, that he has sus-
tained the Character of a meritorious officer. If he
has been unfortunate rather than faulty or if guilty of
a Fault it was attended with Circumstances very alle-
viating why should an officer of Merit at the very
close of the War be deprivd of the Benefits which
are allotted to others? I think I know your feelings
for that officer and perhaps your private Judgment of

his Case from your Letter to him which I have seen.
What Advantage can he expect from an Application
to this State? Would not a Recommendation to
Congress from Head Quarters in his favor answer
a much better Purpose? This is only a Hint to you.
Perhaps I am out of my Line. I will conclude this
Epistle with congratulating you most heartily on the
return of Peace with Liberty and Independence &
assuring you that I am affectionately

Yours

TO HORATIO GATES.

[MS., Emmet Collection, Lenox Library.]

Boston May 2 1783

My dear Sir

Our Friend Col° John Allan takes the Care of this
Letter and will deliver it to you. The War being
finishd, he is going to Philadelphia to receive such
Directions as Congress shall think proper to give to
him. You remember he was appointed in 77, Agent
of the St Johns & Nova Scotia Indians, and he has
since commanded an Artillery Company raised by this
State for the Defence of the Post at Machias, adopted
by Congress in Feb. 81 and cloathd subsisted & paid
as other Officers & Soldiers of the United States. He
has I doubt not, executed the Trusts reposed in him
with Fidelity, and I think is entitled to the Emoluments given to Officers of his Rank. I have
given him a Letter to the Secretary at War &^{c}.
Your Recommendation first gaind him the Confidence of Congress and your repeated Favor will still
be a substantial Advantage to him.

I most heartily congratulate you on the Return of Peace with Liberty & Independence.—Blessings for which Patriots have toiled & Heroes fought & bled. Our Country may now be happy if she is not wanting to her self. We have done our Duty. Future Generations can never curse the present for carelessly surrendering their Rights.

I beg you, my Friend, not to impute my long Silence to a faulty Cause. If you believe me to be a Man of Truth, be assured that I have constantly participated with you in good & ill Fortune. I shall ever rejoice that *you* was honord by Providence, in captivating Burgoyne & his whole Army—An Event which wrought the most happy Change in the Face of our Affairs in Europe, and which alone, in Spite of Envy, will give you a brilliant Page in History.

Mr Yancey is gone to South Carolina. I have written by him to my old Patriotick friend Gadsden and the stronger to enforce my Recommendation of Mr Yancey have mentiond him as one whom you regard.

Oblige me with your Letters for I am sincerely and affectionately

Your Friend
& very humble Servant,

TO ELBRIDGE GERRY.[1]

[J. T. Austin, *Life of Elbridge Gerry*, vol. i., pp. 408–410; a draft is in the Samuel Adams Papers, Lenox Library.]

BOSTON, Sept. 9, 1783.

MY DEAR SIR,

This is the first letter I have been able to write

[1] For a facsimile note by Adams to Gerry, dated September 11, 1783, see Brotherhead, *Signers of the Declaration of Independence* (1872), p. 172.

since I had the pleasure of seeing you, excepting a
short one to our delegates, informing them that the
general court had appointed a committee to correspond with them. Mr. Appleton and Mr. Rowe
are my colleagues in this business. The correspondence is to be very extensive. " Any other important
matter which relates to the being and welfare of the
United States ! " My bodily illness has prevented
my engaging in it. I wish the delegates would begin.
The welfare, and perhaps the being of the United
States, in my opinion, depends much upon congress
possessing the confidence of the people at large ; that
upon the administration of public affairs being mani-
festly grounded upon principles of equality and
justice, or upon the people being assured that congress merit their confidence. The war is now over,
and the people turn their eyes to the disposition of
their money, a subject, which I hope congress will
always have so clear a knowledge of, as to be able at
any time to satisfy the rational enquiries of the people.
To prevent groundless jealousies, it seems necessary
not only that the principal in that department should
himself be immaculate, but that care should be taken
that no persons be admitted to his confidence but
such as have the entire confidence of the people.
Should a suspicion prevail that our high treasurer
suffers men of bad principles or of no principles to be
about him and employed by him, the fidelity of congress itself would be suspected, and a total loss of
confidence would follow. I am much concerned for
the reputation of congress, and have laboured to support it because that body is and must be the cement

of the union of the states. I hope, therefore, they will always make it evident to reasonable men that their administration merits the public applause. Will they be able to do this, if they should cease to be very watchful over men whom they trust in great departments, especially those who have the disposition of the public moneys? Power will follow the pos- session of money, even when it is known that it is not the possessor's property. So fascinating are riches in the eyes of mankind! Were our financier, I was going to say, even an angel from heaven, I hope he will never have so much influence as to gain the ascendency over congress, which the first lord of the treasury has long had over the parliament of Britain; long enough to effect the ruin of that nation. These are the fears which I expressed in congress when the department was first instituted. I was told, that the breath of congress could annihilate the financier; but I replied, that the time might come, and if they were not careful it certainly would, when even congress would not dare to blow that breath. Whether these fears are the mere creatures of the imagination you will judge.

My regards to Dr. Holten and Mr. Higgenson, if he is still in Congress. Pray write to me often.

Adieu.

TO JOHN ADAMS.

[MS., Adams Papers, Quincy; the text is also in John Adams, *Works*, vol. ix., pp. 519–521.]

BOSTON Nov. 4 1783.

MY DEAR SIR

Col° John Trumbull, the Son of the worthy Gov-

ernor of Connecticutt is the Bearer of this Letter. I
give the Governor this Epithet, because I think his
faithful Services to our Country entitle him to it.
Yet even he has undergone the Suspicions of some,
unsupported by any solid Reasons that I have heard
of. We live in an Age of Jealousy, and it is well
enough. I was led to believe in early Life, that
Jealousy is a political Virtue. It has long been an
Aphorism with me, that it is one of the greatest Securities of publick Liberty. Let the People keep a
watchful Eye over the Conduct of their Rulers; for
we are told that Great Men are not at all times wise.
It would be indeed a Wonder if in any Age or Country they were always honest. There are however
some Men among us, who under the Guise of watchful Patriots, are finding Fault with every publick
Measure, with a Design to destroy that just Confidence in Government, which is necessary for the
Support of those Liberties which we have so dearly
purchas'd. Many of your Countrymen besides myself, feel very grateful to you and those of our Negociators who joyned you, in preventing the Tory
Refugees from being obtruded upon us. These
would certainly have increasd the Number of such
Kind of *Patriots* as I have mentiond, and besides,
their Return would have been attended with other
mischievous Effects. Mutual Hatred and Revenge
would have occasiond perpetual Quarrels between
them & the people & perhaps frequent Bloodshed.
Some of them, by Art and Address might gradually
recover a Character & in time an Influence, and so
become the fittest Instruments in forming Factions

either for one foreign Nation or another. We may be in Danger of such Factions, and should prudently expect them. One might venture to predict that they will sooner or later happen. We should therefore guard against the evil Effects of them. I deprecate the most favord Nation predominating in the Councils of America, for I do not believe there is a Nation on Earth that wishes we should be more free or more powerful than is consistent with their Ideas of their own Interest. Such a disinterested Spirit is not to be found in National Bodies; The World would be more happy if it prevaild more in individual Persons. I will say it for my Countrymen, they are, or seem to be, very grateful. All are ready freely to acknowledge our Obligations to France for the Part she took in our late Contest. There are a few who consider the Advantage derivd to her, by a total Seperation of Britain & the Colonies, which so sagacious a Court doubtless foresaw & probably never lost Sight of. This Advantage was so glaring in the first Stages of our Controversy, that those who then ran the Risque of exciting even an Appeal to Heaven rather than a Submission to British tyranny, were well perswaded that the Prospect of such a Seperation would induce France to interpose, and do more than she has done if necessary. America with the Assistance of her faithful Ally has secured and establishd her Liberty & Independence. God be praisd! And some would think it too bold to assert, that France has thereby saved the Being of her great Importance.—But if it be true why may we not assert it? A punctual Fulfillment of Engagements solemnly enterd into by

Treaty is the Justice, the Honor & Policy of Nations. If we, *who have contracted Debts*, were influenced only by Motives of sound Policy, we should pay them as soon as possible & provide sure & adequate Funds for the Payment of Interest in the mean time. When we have done this we shall have the Sense of Independence impressd on our Minds, no longer feeling that State of Inferiority which a wise King tells us the Borrower stands in to the Lender.

Your Negociation with Holland, as "my old Friend" observd, is all your own. The faithful Historian will do Justice to your Merits—Perhaps not till you are dead. I would have you reconcile yourself to this Thought. While you live you will probably be the Object of Envy. The leading Characters in this great Revolution will not be fairly marked in the present Age. It will be well if the leading Principles are rememberd long. You, I am sure, have not the Vanity, which Cicero betrayed, when he even urged his Friend Licinius to publish the History of the Detection of Cataline in his Life Time that he might enjoy it. I am far from thinking that Part of History redounds so much to the Honor of the Roman Consul, as the Treaty of Holland does to its American Negociator.

Decr 4th I intended to have committed the Care of the foregoing Letter to Mr Trumbull, but when he called on me I was confind to my Chamber by severe bodily Indisposition unable to attend even to the lightest Business. I am still kept at home, but hope soon to be abroad. Mr Jon^n Jackson will deliver this

to you if he meets you in London, otherwise he will
convey it by some safe hand. When I shall be certain of your being appointed for London, I will write
to you as often as I can. May Heaven bless you
My Friend as I am

affectionately yours

TO JOHN ADAMS.

[MS., Adams Papers, Quincy.]

Boston Feb 4 1784

My dear Sir/

I had laid up in my mind many things to say to
you, but an hours notice only of this opportunity and
the hurry of business in the General Court now sitting
prevents my communicating them to you at present.
The Son of Mr Nathl Appleton will deliver to you
this short epistle ; written for the sake of recommending him to your notice. He is a young gentleman
lately enterd into Business in the Commercial line.
My Affection for a young fellow Citizen, and Regard
for his Father an intimate friend & a Member of the
old committee of Correspondence of this town are
strong Inducements to me to take this method of
availing the Son of your Advice & Patronage. I
wrote to you the 4 Decr by Mr Jonathan Jackson &
will write again by the next opportunity. Your
Family was well a few Days ago. You will doubtless
have heard, before this will reach you, of the Death
of our good Friend Dr Cooper.

Adieu

TO ELBRIDGE GERRY.

[MS., Samuel Adams Papers, Lenox Library.]

BOSTON Feb 25 1784

MY DEAR SIR

When a Committee was appointed by the G C[1] to correspond with the Delegates in Congress for this C W[2] I proposd that the Correspondence sh[d] be carried on in a liberal Manner ; but it was apprehended that the Sentiments of the G C might be mistaken by the Com[e] & the Delegates thereby misled & so the Idea was drop'd & nothing material was left for the Court to do but to forward such Letters or papers as sh[d] be from time to time orderd by the Court. Had the Com[e] pursued the first proposal, I could have had no Share in the Correspondence having been exceedingly sick the greatest part of the Time from June to January. This I hope will apologize for my not having written to you & my other Friends in Congress ; which I mention because, not receiving your favors, I have been affraid you imputed my Omission to Neglect. In the September Session the Court thought fit to direct the Delegates officially to write to the Gov[r] once a fortnight which of Course dissolved the Corresponding Com[e], & since that time no Letters from the Delegates have been laid before the G C.

Your Letter of Sept 11 directed to the Com[e] was through mere forgetfulness omitted to be communicated in Season. This was attributed by some Persons of illiberal Minds & Party Spirit to an abominable Design to withhold from the Court the Sentiments of the Delegates respecting the Expediency of refus-

---

[1] General Court. [2] Commonwealth.

ing to yield Supplys to the Continental Treasury till Justice should be done us with Regard to the Old money now in our publick Treasury & private hands. I could not help diverting my self with the Ebullitions of apparent Zeal for the publick Good on this Occasion, and upon its being said by a Gent^n in Senate that it was the Subject of warm Conversation among the people without Doors I observed the Clamour w^d undoubtedly subside on *the Afternoon* of the *first Monday in April next.* Your Letter has since been very *prudently* published by an unknown Person in Edes' Paper.

Inclosd is a Letter to your Self from Col^o Scar Gridley. It seems he applied to this G C some time ago for Depretion of his pay while in the Service, upon which the Govr was requested to write to G W to make known to him the Rank held by Mr Gridley & . . . . but the Letter has never been written. I advisd him to write you on the Subject, & hope you will excuse my giving you the Trouble. As you are now near the Place of Residence of General Washington, perhaps it may not be inconvenient to you to write to him, in doing which you will gratify & oblige Mr Gridley.

I shall esteem a Letter from you one of the greatest favors being your very affectionate Friend,

TO JOHN ADAMS.

[MS., Adams Papers, Quincy ; a draft is in the Lenox Library.]

BOSTON April 16 1784

MY DEAR SIR

I have not receivd a Letter from you of a later

Date than the 10th of Septr last. Extracts of yours
to D G of the same Date have been handed about,
with a View, as I conceivd, of giving the Sanction of
your Opinion to that of others respecting the Tories.
It is often inconvenient, perhaps unsafe, to trust ones
Confidential Letters to indiscrete, however honest,
Friends. Detachd Parts of them being given out,
they may be made to bear a different Construction
from what was intended, and answer the Purpose of
interrested & designing Men. When the Recommendations of Congress in Pursuance of the 5th
Article of the Treaty were receivd here, they were
treated with great Decency & very seriously considerd. They were construed differently by Men of
Sense, who were above the Influence of old Prejudices
or of Party or Family Connections. This Difference,
I supposed, was owing to certain Ambiguities in the
Treaty, which I afterwards found had been acknowledgd in a joynt Letter to Congress of the 18th July,
in which it appeard that our Negociators had stu-
diously avoided any Expressions in the Articles of
the Treaty which sh^d amount to absolute Stipulations
in Favor of the Tories. From the first Sight I had
of the Articles, I have been of opinion that no such
Construction could fairly be put upon them, but that
it would finally lie with the several Legislatures of
the States, how far it would be proper to show
Lenity to them, and I was happy in being confirmd
in this Opinion by an Expression in your joynt Letter
to Congress Septr 10th—" it is much to be wishd that
the Legislators may not involve *all* the Tories in
Banishment and Ruin, but that such *Discrimination*

may be made as to intitle the Decisions to the Approbation of disinterested Men and dispassionate Posterity." In this View I early inculcated Moderation and Liberality towards them, as far as could be consistent with that leading Principle of Nature which ought to govern Nations as it does Individuals, Self Preservation. I cannot think that all can be admitted consistently with the Safety of the Commonwealth. I gave you my Reasons in my Letter of Nov. 4th. Nor can I believe you intended to be understood universally in your private Letter above referrd to. Some of them would be useful & good Citizens; others, I believe highly dangerous. Our Act passed in the late Session of the General Court declares them all Aliens, and excludes those of them who in a former Act were called Conspirators from residing among us. It restores the Estates of others which have not been confiscated and refers their coming to reside within the Commonwealth in the first Instance to the Governor with Advice of Council. The Licenses he may give are to be valid if approvd of by the General Court at the Session next after such License shall be given. It is thought that this will be a difficult Task for the Governor & Council, but a constant Attention to the publick Safety without Respect to Persons will prevent Difficulties. " Much, says your joynt Letter, will depend upon our Negociations with England." The sooner a Commercial Treaty is settled with that Nation the better, as it appears to me. Our General Court, in the late Session, thought of making Retaliation on England for her prohibiting Importations from

America into her West India Islands but in British Bottoms. They were sensible of the Difficulty in the Way of the United States coming into general Regulations of this Kind, & have written to their Delegates on the Subject. Should the States agree to give Congress a more extensive Power, it may yet be a great while before it is compleated; and Britain in the mean time seeing our Trade daily reverting to its old Channel, may think it needless and impolitick to enter into express Stipulations in favor of any Part of it while she promises her self the whole without them.

I am fully in the Sentiment expressd in your joynt Letter Sept 10th, that now we have regular & constitutional Governments, popular Committees and County Conventions are not only useless but dangerous. They served an excellent Purpose & were highly necessary when they were set up. I shall not repent the small Share I then took in them. But what think you of the District & State Conventions of the Cincinnati, & of the Cincinnati in Congress assembled? Do not these Assemblies convene expressly to deliberate & adopt Measures on great and National Concerns proper only for the Cognizance of the United States in Congress assembled, and the different Legislators & Officers of Government? And will they not, being an Order of *Military* Men, too soon proceed to *enforce* their Resolutions, not only to the lessening the Dignity of the States in the Eye of Europe, but the putting an End to their free Existence! The Order is very unpopular here. By the inclosd you will see the Sentiments of our Gen¹ Court. The Governor of S° Carolina in a

late Speech to his Assembly inveighs against them
with the Vehemence of Luther.

Adieu

TO JOHN ADAMS.

[MS., Adams Papers, Quincy ; a draft is in the Lenox Library.]

Boston April 17 1784

Dear sir

Several of my Fellow Citizens have desired me to
mention to you certain Difficulties they labour under &
to request that you would inform me whether it is
probable they can obtain Reliefe, among whom are D^r
Nathl Noyes & Capt Saml Dashwood.   Both of them
I believe you knew.   I inclose Mr Noyes^s Questions
as he has stated them himself.—Capt Dashwoods
Goods were taken from him by order of the Commanding officer of the British Troops when they left
this Town in 1776.   I need not trouble you to explain
as I doubt not you well remember the Circumstances
of these Matters.   It will be hard for such Persons to
pay the British Creditors for the same Goods which
the British Nation took from them for its own necessary Use & if I mistake not with a Promise to com-
pensate them, unless the Promise is complied with.

A few Lines on this Subject when you are at Leisure will very much oblige them as well as

Your Friend

TO ELBRIDGE GERRY.

[MS., Samuel Adams Papers, Lenox Library ; a text is in J. T. Austin, *Life of Elbridge Gerry*, vol. i., pp. 422–424.]

BOSTON April 19th 1784

MY DEAR SIR,

Mr Higginson was so obliging as to show me your Letter to him dated the 4th of March. I was happy in having adopted an opinion of the Cincinnati so similar to what I found yours to be. I think I am as sensible as any Man ought to be of the important Services of our late Army, and am very desirous that their full Share of Merit may be gratefully acknowledgd & rewarded by the Country. This would have been done, (for the Prejudice of the People against the Gratuity of five years pay began to subside) had they not adopted a Plan so disgustfull to the Common Feeling. It appears wonderful that they could imagine a People who had freely spent their Blood & Treasure in Support of their equal rights & Liberties, could so soon be reconciled to the odious hereditary Distinction of Families. This Country must be humiliated & debased to a great Degree, before they will patiently bear to see Individuals stalking with their assumed honorary Badges, & proudly boasting " These are the Distinctions of *our* Blood." I cannot think that many of our Officers entertained such an Idea of haughty Pre-eminence ; but the human Mind is so captivated with the Thought of being elevated above the ignoble Vulgar, that their Sons, if they should not themselves, when they perceive the Multitude grown giddy with gazing, may assume more than the mere Pageantry of Nobility. When Men begin to applaud themselves, they are not easily perswaded to believe they can take a greater Share of Honor than justly belongs to them. They will be pleasd with the Adulatory Addresses of other Men & flatter themselves that they are intitled to Power and Authority as well as the ostentatious Show of Superiority above their Equals. I confess I do not barely dislike the order. With you I think it dangerous & look upon it with the Eye of Jealousy. When the Pride of Family possesses the Minds of Men it is threatning to the Community in Proportion to the Good they have done. The unsuspecting People, when they are in a Mood to be grateful, will cry up the Virtues of their Benefactors & be ready to say, Surely those Men who have done such great things for us, will never think of setting up a Tyranny over us. Even Patriots & Heroes may become different Men when new & different Prospects shall have alterd their Feelings & Views ; and the undiscerning People may too late repent that they have sufferd them to exalt themselves & their Family upon the Ruins of the Common Liberty. The Cincinnati are very unpopular here ; you will wonder then that one of the Order has had a Majority of the Votes of this Town for a Senator for the County. I am affraid the Citizens are not so vigilant as they used and ought still to be. It was given out at the Moment of Election that he intended to withdraw himself from the Society. If he does, it may weaken their Influence—if not, he will probably destroy his own. You have doubtless seen the Sentiments of the General Court of the

Order.   The Reprobating Speech of the Governor of S° Carolina has been publishd in our papers.

I had the Pleasure of receiving by the same Post your several Letters of the 15th, 20th and 24th Ult°. If I have a Seat in the General Court the ensuing year, (which is uncertain) I shall (tho very reluctantly) communicate your Intention to leave Congress, unless you will gratify the earnest Wishes of your Friends by altering your Determination.   I assure you there is no Friend to our Country within my Circle who is not anxiously solicitous for your continuing there longer.   I was in hopes when you was prevailed upon again to take a Seat you would have held it at least two years.   Let me entreat you to release me from the obligation of complying with your Request.

I have written so much in Spite of my trembling hand, concerning the Cin[i], that I can at present only fulfill a Promise I gave our Navy officers, to inclose their Petition to Congress and to beg your Patronage of it.   They appear to me to be injurd or at least neglected Men.   It is certainly high time they should receive their Prize Money and Assurances of their Pay.   I will write you by M[r] Lowell (who sets off for Phil[a] in a few Days & intends making you a Visit) or by the Post speedily. M[rs] A desires her Compl[ts]

Adieu my Friend,

TO ELBRIDGE GERRY.

[MS., Samuel Adams Papers, Lenox Library ; a text with modifications is in J. T. Austin, *Life of Elbridge Gerry*, vol. i., pp. 424–427.]

BOSTON April 23 1784

MY DEAR SIR,

M[r] Lowel thinks he shall not be able to make you

a Visit at Annapolis as he intended, so I have not written by him. Is the Court of Appeals[1] of which he is a Member to continue now the War is over? I should think it a needless Expence. If ever there should be Occasion for it, a new Court might at any time be constituted. I observe by the inclosd, that the Cincinnati in Congress assembled are to meet at Philadelphia on the 5th of May & that General Washington is to preside. That Gentleman has an idea of the Nature & Tendency of the Order very different from mine, otherwise I am certain he would never have given it his Sanction. I look upon it to be as rapid a Stride towards an hereditary Military Nobility as was ever made in so short a Time. My Fears may be ill grounded, but if they are not, it is impossible for me not to think it a very great Misfortune to these States that he is a Member; for the Reputation he has justly acquired by his Conduct while Commander in Chiefe of our Armies, and the Gratitude & warm Affection which his Countrymen do & ought to feel towards him will give Weight to any thing he patronizes, & Lustre to all who may be connected with him. It is a Tribute due to the Man who has servd his Country well, to esteem him highly & confide in him. We ought not however to think any Man incapable of Error. But so it is with the Bulk of Mankind & even in a free Country. They will reprobate the Idea of implicit Faith; and at the same time, while the Impression of Gratitude is deep in their Minds, they will not admit of a Benefactor, which must be said of every Man, "*aliquando dormitat.*" I

---

[1] *Cf.* J. F. Jameson, *Essays in Constitutional History*, pp. 32 *et seq.*

would never inculcate a mean & envious Suspicion of
any Man especially of those who have renderd signal
Services to their Country. But there is a Degree of
Watchfulness over all Men possessd of Power or Influence upon which the Liberties of Mankind much
depend. It is necessary to guard against the Infirmities of the best as well as the Wickedness of the
worst of Men. Such is the Weakness of human Nature that Tyranny has oftener sprang from that than
any other Source. It is this that unravels the Mystery of Millions being enslavd by a few. What was
it that inducd the Cincinnati Gentlemen who have
undertaken to deliberate and act upon Matters which
may essentially concern "the Happinesss & future
Dignity of the American Empire," to admit foreign
Military Subjects into their Society? Was there not
Danger before that a foreign Influence might prevail
in America? Do not Foreigners wish to have Weight
in our Councils? Can such a Junction of Subjects
of different Nations (& those Nations widely different
in their principles of Government) to Deliberate upon
things which relate to the Union & national Honor,
the Happiness & future Dignity of *one* consist with
sound Policy? Are we sure that those foreign Nations will never have separate Views & very national
& interrested ones too, because they once united in
the same object & it was *accidentally* their mutual Interest to fight Side by Side? If the Cincinnati had
a Right to erect themselves into an order for the
national Purposes of their Institution, had they a
Right to call in foreign Aid for those Purposes? It
appears to me as impolitic, preposterous & dangerous

as it would be for the United States to invite &
admit a Delegation from that foreign Power into
their Congress.

I take Notice that the Committee of Congress
propose that the Gov^ts of the ten new States to be
formd shall be in *Republican* form & *shall admit no
Person to be a Citizen who holds any hereditary Title.*
I hope Congress will not fail to make this an indispensible Condition.

Your Letter of the 2^d relating to Col° Gridleys
Affair came to hand. I am obligd to you for the
Care you have taken.

Believe me to be y^r sincere & affectionate Friend,

TO NOAH WEBSTER.

[MS., Ford Collection, Lenox Library; a draft is in the Samuel Adams
Papers, Lenox Library.]

BOSTON April 30th 1784

SIR

I was favord with your Letter of 24th March, but
by a Multiplicity of Affairs, which, as it happened I
was at that Time engaged in, I was prevented returning an Answer so speedily as you desired. For this
Reason I afterwards thought an Answer would be of
no Importance. Decency alone should, however,
have induced me to have acknowledgd the Favor. I
hope you will excuse the Omission.

Some time in the Month of September last, a
Gentleman in Connecticutt requested me to give him
my Opinion of a Subject, perhaps too much altercated
in that State as well as this, The Commutation of

half Pay granted by Congress to the Officers of the
late Army for Life for full Pay during the Term of
five years.   I did not hesitate to say in Return, that
in my Opinion Congress was, in the Nature of their
Appointment, the sole Judge of the necessary Means
of supporting the late Army raised for the Defence of
our Common Rights against the Invasions of Great
Britain ; and if, upon their own deliberate Councils &
the repeated Representations of the Commander in
Chiefe of the Army, they judgd that the Grant of half
Pay for Life was a Measure absolutely necessary for
the Support of a disciplined Army for the Purpose
before mentiond, they had an undoubted Right to
make it ; and as it was made in behalf of the United
States by their Representative authorizd to do it,
each State was bound in Justice & Honor to comply
with it, even tho it should seem to any to have been
an ill judgd Measure ; because States & Individual
Persons are equally bound to fulfill their Obligations,
and it is given as Characteristick of an honest Man,
that " though he sweareth (or promiseth) to his own
hurt he changeth not."   I moreover acquainted him,
that although I was never pleasd with the Idea of
half Pay for Life, for Reasons which appeard satisfactory to myself, some of which I freely explaind to
him, yet I had always thought, that as the Opportuni-
ties of the Officers of the Army of acquiring moderate
Fortunes or making such Provision for their Families
as Men generally wish to make, were not equal to
those of their Fellow Citizens at home, it would be
but just & reasonable, that an adequate Compensation
should be made to them at, or as soon as conveniently

might be after, the End of the War; and that he might therefore conclude, that the Commutation, if it be an adequate Compensation had fully coincided with my Ideas of Justice & Policy.

Nothing was mentiond in his Letter to me, of the Nature or the Proceedings of County Conventions, & therefore I made no Observation upon them. I hope it will not be in the Power of any designing Men, by imposing upon credulous tho' well meaning Persons long to keep this Country, who may be happy if they will, long in a State of Discord & Animosity. We may see, from the present State of Great Britain, how rapidly such a Spirit will drive a Nation to destruction. It is prudent for the People to keep a watchful Eye over the Conduct of all those who are entrusted with Publick Affairs. Such Attention is the Peoples great Security.[1] But there is Decency & Respect due to Constitutional Authority, and those Men, who under any Pretence or by any Means whatever, would lessen the Weight of Government lawfully exercised, must be Enemies to our happy Revolution & the Common Liberty. County Conventions & popular Committees servd an excellent Purpose when they were first in Practice. No one therefore needs to regret the Share he may then have had in them. But I candidly own it is my Opinion, with Deferrence to the Opinions of other Men, that as we now have constitutional & regular Governments and all our Men in Authority depend upon the annual & free Elections of the People, we are safe without them. To say the

---

[1] At this point the draft included the words : "for the wisest & best of Men are liable to Error & Misconduct."

least, they are become useless. Bodies of Men, under
any Denomination whatever, who convene themselves
for the Purpose of deliberating upon & adopting
Measures which are cognizable by Legislatures only
will, if continued, bring Legislatures to Contempt
& Dissolution.   If the publick Affairs are illy
conducted, if dishonest or incapable Men have crept
unawares into Government, it is happy for us, that
under our American Constitutions the Remedy is at
hand, & in the Power of the great Body of the People.
Due Circumspection & Wisdom at the next Elections
will set all right, without the Aid of any self Created
Conventions or Societies of Men whatever.[1]   While
we retain those simple Democracies in all our Towns
which are the Basis of our State Constitutions, and
make a good Use of them, it appears to me we cannot be enslaved or materially injured.   It must however be confessd, that Imperfection attends all human
affairs.
>   I am
>   Sir
>   your very humble Servant

TO JOHN ADAMS.

[MS., Adams Papers, Quincy.]

BOSTON June 20 1784

DEAR SIR

   The Hurry of the General Court which is now
sitting prevents my writing a Letter at this Time.
   Your amiable Lady who with her Daughter em-

---

[1] At this point the draft included the words: "The whole People will not
probably mistake their own true Interests, nor err in their Judgment of the
Men to whom they may safely commit the Care of them."

barks this day will, I hope, deliver you this Note, which is only to express a fervent Wish that they may be favord in their Passage & shortly have a joyful Meeting with you.

It is a long time since I receivd a Letter from you. Adieu—Believe me

Your affectionate friend

& humble serv^t

TO JOHN ADAMS.

[MS., Adams Papers,[1] Quincy.]

BOSTON 2^d Dee^r 1784.

MY DEAR SIR

I received several of your Letters with Pleasure, particularly that of May, which I will answer at a Time of more Leisure. Captⁿ Dashwood of this Town is going to London, to sollicit Payment of the British Crown, for Goods taken from him when the Troops left the Town, not as forfeited, but under the Apprehension that they would be of Use to our Army, & with an Express Promise that they should be paid for. It appears to me to be among the *bona Fide* Debts mention'd in the Treaty, and if there may be on the Part of the Crown itself a Failure of a Compliance with a positive stipulated Article, it will be difficult for the Governments in America to prevail with their Citizens to think it reasonable that they should pay the just Debts owing from them to British Subjects.

---

[1] Although the copy actually transmitted, no part of this letter is in the autograph of Adams except the subscription and signature.

Dashwood has my Promise to write to you again on
the Subject & I must fulfill it.   It is with reluctance
that I give you this repeated Trouble, especially as I
know you must be press'd with Affairs of greater
National Importance.   You are best able to say
whether you can afford him Aid or not.   I have ventured to assure him, that if it be in your Power
consistantly to interpose your Influence, you will undoubtedly be disposd to do it.   What aggravates the
Misfortune of this Citizen if he should not obtain
Justice in England is that his British Crediter now
demands the Payment of his Debt with Interest, &
tho' this Sum is very small in Comparison with the
Value of the Goods taken from him, the Payment, as
he says & I suppose truly, will compleatly ruin him.

your affectionate

TO RICHARD HENRY LEE.

[MS., Lee Papers, American Philosophical Society; a draft is in the Samuel
Adams Papers, Lenox Library; a text is in W. V. Wells, *Life of Samuel Adams*,
vol. iii., pp. 214–217.]

BOSTON Decr 23 1784

My dear Sir

I congratulate our Country on the Choice Congress
has lately made of a President.   He who fills that
Chair is the most respected Citizen, and while he
performs his Duty well, he adorns the most dignified
Station in our Confederated Republick.

You observe in your Letter to me, that "at this
Moment, Moderation, Wisdom, Firmness & Attention are the Principles proper for our Adoption."   I

agree with you, and devoutly wish that every Man who has a Share in the Administration of publick Affairs may possess a large Portion of those & other great Qualities. They are in a particular Manner necessary to him who presides in the important Councils of the American Amphyction.

Congress has need to watch, lest the Commonwealth suffer Harm. I doubt not they will be assiduous in their Labours for the publick Wellfare; and I pray God they may be *His* honord Instruments in exalting to the highest Pitch of human Happiness that People, who have testified to the oppressed World, that by Patience, Fortitude & Perseverance the iron Rod can be wrested from the Arm of a Tyrant, and that all Nations may be free, if they will magnanimously contend for their Liberty.

By Gods Blessing on the Councils & the Arms of our Country, we are now rank'd with Nations. May He keep us from exulting beyond Measure! Great Pains are yet to be taken & much Wisdom is requisite that we may stand as a Nation in a respectable Character. Better it would have been for us to have fallen in our highly famed Struggle for our Rights, or even to have remaind in our ignoble State of Bondage hoping for better Times, than now to become a contemptible Nation. The World have given us an exalted Character, & thus have laid on us a heavy Tax! They have raised Expectations from us! How shall we meet those Expectations? They have attributed to us Wisdom! How shall we confirm them in their Opinion of us? Inexperiencd as we are in the Refinements of Nations, Can we expect to shine in the World as able Politicians? Shall we then be hacknied in the Path of Deception because some others famed for their Dexterity in Politicks have long trod that Path & thought they have gaind Advantage by it? Or, because it is said All Nations are selfinterested & that *No Friendship in Treaties* and National Transactions is almost as proverbial as *No Friendship in Trade,* shall we depart from that excellent Rule of Equity, the Observance of which should be characteristick of all Nations especially Republicks, as it is of all good Men, to do to others as we would have them do to us? Could we be in-ducd thus to prostitute ourselves, How should we appear in the Eyes of the Virtuous & Wise? Should there be found a Citizen of the United States so un-principled as to ask, What will become of us if we do not follow the corrupt Maxims of the World? I should tell him, that the Strength of a Republick is consolidated by its Virtues, & that Righteousness will exalt a Nation.

Was it true as some affirm, that the old World is absorbd in all kinds of Vice, unhumanizd & enslavd, it would indeed be a melancholly Subject to con-template, and I should think that common Prudence would dictate to a Nation situated as we are, to have as little to do with them as possible. Such indiscriminate Censure, however, may spring from Ignorance of the World or unreasonable Prejudice. Nations as well as Individuals have different Charac-ters. We should not forget the Friendship & Kindness of *One* because we have experiencd the Injustice & Cruelty of *Another*. But the Inconstancy of Friendship & even Infidelity has been seen often enough among Individuals to lead wise men to suppose it may happen in any Case & to exercise a kind of Circumspection, different from base Suspicion, consistent with the generous Sentiments of Friendship and, considering the Weakness of the human Mind, a necessary Guard.

Does not the true Policy, the Honor & Safety of our Country greatly depend upon a National Character consisting, among other Particulars, in Simplicity & Candor in all her Publick Transactions; shewing herself in reality friendly to those to whom she professes to be a Friend—A constant Regard to mutual Benefit in Commercial Treaties; suspecting the Honesty of those who will not deal with her on equitable Principles, & guarding her Trade against their selfish Designs by wise Commercial Laws—An exact & punctilious Fullfillment of Obligations on her Part to be performd by Virtue of *all* Treaties—and, An unalterable Determination to discharge her National Debts with all possible Speed.—If, my honord Friend, the leading Men in the United States would by Precept & Example disseminate thro' the lower Classes of People the Principles of Piety to God, Love to our Country & universal Benevolence, should we not secure the Favor of Heaven & the Honor & Esteem of the wise and virtuous Part of the World.

Great Britain, tho' she has concluded a Treaty of Peace with us, appears to be not a cordial Friend. She cannot forget her unparralled Injustice towards us & naturally supposes there can be no Forgiveness

on our Part. She seems to have meant Nothing
more than a Truce. A sensible Gentleman very lately
from Canada informs me, that General Haldiman who
is going to England, has orderd those Posts to be rein-
forcd, which by Treaty were to be deliverd to us. En-
croachments are made, as I apprehend, on our Eastern
Territories. Our Fishery may, under some frivolous
Pretence be next interrupted. Should we not guard
ourselves against British Intrigues & Factions. Her
Emissaries, under the Guise of Merchants, Repenting
Refugees, Schoolmasters, and other Characters, unless
Care is taken, may effect another & fatal Revolution.
The Commonwealth of England lasted twelve years,
and then the exiled King was restored with all the
Rage & Madness of Royalty !—A Caution to the Citi-
zens of the United States zealously to counteract the
Hopes our Enemies entertain of " Discord, Disunion,
& Apathy on our Part," to watch over the publick
Liberty & Safety with a jealous Eye, and to practice
the moral and political Virtues upon which the very
Existence of a Commonwealth depends.

Mrs. Adams desires me to present her respectful
Compliments to you & your Connections. I am with
great Esteem   Your affectionate Friend

TO RICHARD HENRY LEE.

[MS., Lenox Library.]

BOSTON March 24 1785[1]

MY HONORD FRIEND

Could I be perswaded to believe that by your long

---

[1] A letter by Adams to Elbridge Gerry, dated February 24, 1785, is in *Magazine of American History*, vol. xii., pp. 177, 178.

Silence you would intimate to me a Desire on your Part to put an End to our Epistolary Correspondence, you should never again be troubled with my Letters. But as I am not disposd to entertain unfavorable Thoughts of one whom I have valued as an unchanging Friend, I will now sollicit you in Behalf of two Persons both of whom I believe you will recollect, and whose Services to the United States, in their different Way, have in my Opinion been meritorious.

Mr Kirkland has for many years been a Missionary to the Indians of the six Nations under the Society in Scotland for promoting Christian Knowledge. He was recognizd by Congress & in 1779 was appointed by that Body to be Chaplain at Fort Stanwix; for this Cause that *Charitable* Society forbore to continue his usual Stipend. He had Influence sufficient to keep the Indians steadily attachd to the United States during the War, and you will judge Sir, of the Policy of engaging so useful a Man in the same Mission under Congress, lest another should be employed by that Society under the Pretext of promoting Christian knowledge among the Indians, [who] may be secretly instructed to instill into their Minds Prejudices in favor of Great Britain and dangerous to our Interest. Mr Kirkland is or soon will be in New York to state his Case to Congress.

Col° John Allan left a valueable Estate and powerful family Connections in Hallifax in the Beginning of the late War & took a decided Part with the United States. He had the Happiness of your Friendship when Congress sat in Baltimore; and was there appointed Superintendant of the Indians in the Eastern Department. I do not fear I shall dishonor myself by assuring you, that in my Opinion he has been a faithful & successful Servant of the Publick. He is gone to Congress to settle his Affairs. If it shall appear to you that I have not mistaken his true Character, your Sense of Justice will prevent the Necessity of any Sollicitation in his Behalf from, My dear Sir,

your unfeigned
& affectionate friend,

TO RICHARD HENRY LEE.

[MS., Lenox Library.]

Boston April 14 1785

My dear Sir

Give me Leave to introduce to you Mr Graham[1] the Bearer of this Letter & his Lady, Mrs Macauley Graham, who have honord this Town & highly gratified the virtuous Citizens by a residence of some Months past. We sometimes meet with genuine republican Sentiments in Persons born under Monarchy. It is truly mortifying when one meets with the reverse Character. I firmly believe that the benevolent Creator designd the republican Form of Government for Man. Will you venture so far as to say that all other Institutions that we know of are unnatural & tend more or less to distress human Societies? Will the Lion ever associ-

---

[1] On the same date Adams wrote to Washington, introducing Graham ; a manuscript is in the Lenox Library and also in the Library of Congress.

ate with the Lamb or the Leopard with the Kid till our favorite principles shall be universally establishd? I am with Truth & sincerity,

your affection^t friend,

TO JOHN ADAMS.

[MS., Adams Papers, Quincy.]

BOSTON July 2 1785

DEAR SIR

I cannot omit the Opportunity of writing by Monsr de la Etombe who is going to France & will take the Care of this Letter. You must not expect it to be a long one. There are many Things which I wish to say to you, but the Tremor of my Hand is so increasd that I am put to Difficulty to guide my Pen.

Our Merchants are complaining bitterly that Great Britain is ruining their Trade, and there is great Reason to complain; but I think much greater, to complain of too many of the Citizens thro' the Common wealth who are imitating the Britons in every idle Amusement & expensive Foppery which it is in their Power to invent for the Destruction of a young Country. Can our People expect to indulge themselves in the unbounded Use of every unmeaning & fantastick Extravagance because they would follow the Lead of Europeans, & not spend all their Money? You would be surprizd to see the Equipage, the Furniture & expensive Living of too many, the Pride & Vanity of Dress which pervades thro every

Class, confounding every Distinction between the Poor & the Rich and evincing the Want both of Example & Œconomy.

Before this reaches you, you will have heard of the Change in our chiefe Magistrate. I confess it is what I have long wishd for. Our new Governor[1] has issued his Proclamation for the Encouragement of Piety Virtue Education & Manners and for the Suppressing of Vice. This with the good Example of a first Magistrate & others may *perhaps* restore our Virtue.

Monsieur le Etomb's true Decency of Manners has done honor to your Letter of Recommendation.

M^rs A joins in sincere Respects to your Lady & Family.

Adieu my dear sir

TO JOHN ADAMS.

[MS., Adams Papers, Quincy; a draft, dated 1784, is in the Samuel Adams Papers, Lenox Library.]

BOSTON 16th Augt 1785

MY DEAR SIR

The Governour of this Commonwealth will transmit to you Copies of Letters which lately passed between him and Capt Stanhope Commander of the British Ship of War Mercury. This is the same Person, as I am told, who, when a Prisoner here in the early time of the War, was not too delicate in Point of Honor to break his Parole. The Governor however

---

[1] James Bowdoin, who had succeeded John Hancock.

had treated him from the Time of his Arrival with
the Civilities and Respect due to a Foreigner in his
Station, without personal or national Distinction.
The occasion of this Epistolary Correspondence which
the Governor was necessarily carried into by the
Petulance of Stanhope, was a Fricas which happened
on the Evening of the 31ˢᵗ Ultᵒ, between the [latter]
and a young Sailor who alledges that he and a Number of American Prisoners on board the Mercury had
been flogged by Stanhopes order for refusing to do
the Duty of Seamen. The Altercation caused the
People near to collect, and the Captain, either really
or pretending to be, apprehensive of Danger, hast'ned
away, a Number following excited by common Curiosity, till his Fears were quieted in the House of one
of his Friends and the Scene ended. This gave rise
to Stanhopes Letter the following Day. Whatever
his Opinion might be of his own Importance, the
Governor considerd him entitled only to the Common Protection of the Law, nor could he see any
Obstacle in the Captains Way to obtain legal Satisfaction if he had receivd Injury, which required the
extraordinary Interposition of Government; for Stanhope was the same Day abroad in the Town without
the least Molestation or appearing to be apprehensive of any Affront. Perhaps this Gentleman's Ideas
of Propriety of Conduct in the Governor might have
led him to expect he would take the Part of a Grand
Juryman or a Justice of the Peace, to enquire into
Misdemeanours, or decide on little Controversies
which frequently happen among Persons who know
not how to keep upon Terms with each other.

I should not have troubled you with this Detail, had it not seemed to me somewhat necessary. You know it was formerly usual for such kind of Men as Stanhope appears to be, to fly to their Ships from pretended Danger, and by false representations impose on their too credulous Government. Adieu my friend, & believe me

Yours

TO RICHARD HENRY LEE.

[Historical Magazine, 2d ser., vol. i., pp. 167, 168.]

Boston Decr. 17. 1785.

My dear Sir.

It gave much Pleasure to find that your Countrymen had again honour'd you with their Confidence in Congress. My most earnest wish is, that the Seats in that Sacred Hall may ever be filled with Men of true Wisdom. This Wish, I know, cannot be gratified when the United States shall become debased in Principles and Manners. How much then depends upon the Exertions of the present members to perpetuate the Honour and Happiness of our Country by guarding its Virtue!

I beg leave once more to trespass upon your Time by calling your attention to my Friend Captⁿ Landais. You and I patronized him when he first came into this Country: and I have never for a Moment repented of the small share I had in his Promotion in the American Navy, although he has met with the Fate which some-

times has been the Lot of honest Men, through the
errors, to say the least, of Courts. He had long suffered as other virtuous Men had, by a Faction on the
other side of the Atlantick, which found means to
extend itself to this Country, and as you well remember, to the very Doors of Congress!—But enough of
this—Your kind Assistance was greatly beneficial to
him in his late Application to Congress, and he and I
gratefully acknowledged it. But he remains still em-
barrassed, and as I conceive, not without Reason—His
Pay as Commander of the *Alliance* is offered to him
in a Certificate. But what is such a Piece of Paper
worth. If it be said, all our brave Sea Officers & Men
are thus to be paid, should it not be remembered, that
those who continued in the service to the end of the
War are allowed a Gratuity. This Allowance was Established several years after he left the Service, and
cannot include him, nor does he desire it—But he was
broke by a Court Martial—True. And if a private
Gentleman discharges his domestick servant even for
a Fault, does he not in Justice pay him his due wages?
And are not States bound by the Rules of Justice?
Captain Landais has been obliged to pay an interest on money he has borrowed for his support
and other necessary expenses, more than the Value of
his Pay, and the want of his just Dues has kept him out
of Business—He also suffers by a short Allowance of
Interest on the Gratuity granted to him for an impor-
ant service. Congress ordered 12,000 Livres to be
paid him for that service, *in France*. The Payment
there would have been and it was intended to be an
advantage to him. It was paid to him in America, and

not till the last year—Should not the interest on that sum have commenced in 1777 when the service was performed instead of 79 as it is now settled? But his greatest Grievance, in which indeed he is a sufferer in common with others is the Detention of Prize Money —You recollect this mysterious Business and how often we were written to, and very pressingly by my worthy Friend your Brother. We have been lately told that Capt. Paul Jones has received a large sum on that account. This Jones Captn. Landais looks upon as his inveterate Enemy & he has not the least Confidence in him—If you think as I do that he has a Right to authentick copies of Letters written by Jones to Congress or any of the Boards on an affair so interesting to him, on his proper application, your Advice to him on this as well as his other concerns will add to the obligations I am already under to you.

Will you be so kind as to transmit me the names of the present Members of Congress and the States they severally represent,—

I am

Your affectionate Friend [1]

TO JOHN ADAMS.

[MS., Adams Papers, Quincy; a text is in John Adams, *Works*, vol. ix., p. 547.]

BOSTON April 13 1786

DEAR SIR

Doctor Gordon is to deliver you this Letter.   He

[1] A letter by Adams to Rufus King, dated January 30, 1786, is in *Life and Correspondence of Rufus King*, vol. i., pp. 153, 154.

is going to the Land of his Nativity, wishing for the best Happiness of his own Country & ours and hoping that mutual Affection will be at length restored, as the only Means of the prosperity of both. As he determines to spend the Remainder of his Days in the Country where he was born, what rational Man who considers the Ties of human Nature will wonder, if "*Esto perpetua*" is his most ardent Prayer *for her*! But the Attachments he has made here, his private Friendships and the Part he has taken in our publick Cause afford Reason to believe that his second Wish is for us. I am affraid however, that the Doctor builds too much upon the Hopes of the Return of mutual Affection; for Can this exist without Forgivness of Injury, and Can his Country ever cordially forgive ours whom she intended to injure so greatly? Her very Disappointment will perpetually irritate her own Feelings and in Spite of Reason or Religion prevent her conceiving a Sentiment of Friendship for us. And besides, she will never believe that there is a Possibility that *we* can forgive *her*. We must therefore be content, at least for a great While to come, to live with her as a prudent Man will with one who indeed has professd a Friendship for him, but whose Sincerity he has Reason vehemently to suspect; guarding against Injury from him by making it his Interest to do as little as possible. This is an arduous Task our Country has committed to you. Trade is a Matter I have had so little to do with, that it is not in my Power to aid you in this more than in any one thing else. May He who has endued you with a Strength of Understanding which your Country confides in afford you all that Light which is necessary for so great an Undertaking !

The *Child* whom I led by the Hand with a particular Design, I find is now become a promising youth. He brought me one of your Letters.—God bless the Lad ! If I was instrumental at that Time of enkindling the Sparks of Patriotism in his tender Heart, it will add to my Consolation in the latest Hour.— Adieu my Friend. Mrs Adams desires your Lady & Family may be assured of her cordial Esteem & Love.

> Believe that I am very affectionately
> > Your Friend
> > & humble Servant

TO JOHN ADAMS.

[MS., Adams Papers, Quincy ; a draft, dated July 20, is in the Samuel Adams Papers, Lenox Library.]

BOSTON July 21 1786

MY DEAR SIR

There are two great Objects which I think should engage the Attention of Patriots here, & which appear to me to involve every thing else—to preserve entire our political Liberties, & to support our National Faith. To effect either of these Capital Ends, we must counterwork the Designs of Great Britain, who to say the least does not appear to be our most cordial Friend, by her Emissaries amongst us, to ruin both. The internal Enemies of this Country ridiculed our early Ideas of Opposition, embarrassd our Measures through the whole Conflict and prolonged the War. They had nearly broke up our Army in 1782, and they are now practicing the same Arts, by influencing many weak Men to withhold the necessary Aid of Taxes, to destroy the publick Faith. I should therefore think it very impolitick to increase their Number by admitting the Tory Refugees without *Discrimination.* Jonathan Philanthrop whom *you* well knew, with many others took a very active Part, & they were very successful in promoting the Designs of the British Government before the War; There are some among them who would be the fittest Instruments to be employed by that Court in tearing up, or rather undermining the Foundations of our newly erected Fabrick.—If you ask, What has thrown me into this Fit of Zeal against the Refugees? I answer, they already have or soon will in my opinion form a dangerous Faction. But I will be more explicit in my next.

This Letter I commit to the care of Mr Benj Austin jun^r whose Father and Connexions you are not unacquainted with. Adieu & believe me

your affectionate Friend

TO RICHARD HENRY LEE.

[MS., Lee Papers, American Philosophical Society; a draft is in the Samuel Adams Papers, Lenox Library; a text is in W. V. Wells, *Life of Samuel Adams*, vol. iii., pp. 251–253.]

BOSTON Decr 3^d 1787

MY DEAR SIR

I am to acknowledge your several Favours of the 5th and 27 of October, the one by the Post and the

other by our worthy Friend Mr Gerry. The Session of our General Court which lasted six Weeks,
and my Station there requiring my punctual & constant Attendance, prevented my considering the *new*
Constitution as it is already called, so closely as was
necessary for me before I should venture an Opinion.

I confess, as I enter the Building I stumble at the
Threshold. I meet with a National Government,
instead of a Federal Union of Sovereign States. I
am not able to conceive why the Wisdom of the Convention led them to give the Preference to the former
before the latter. If the several States in the Union
are to become one entire Nation, under one Legislature, the Powers of which shall extend to every Subject of Legislation, and its Laws be supreme &
controul the whole, the Idea of Sovereignty in these
States must be lost. Indeed I think, upon such a
Supposition, those Sovereignties ought to be eradicated from the Mind ; for they would be Imperia in
Imperio justly deemd a Solecism in Politicks, &
they would be highly dangerous, and destructive of
the Peace Union and Safety of the Nation. And can
this National Legislature be competent to make Laws
for the *free* internal Government of one People,
living in Climates so remote and whose " Habits &
particular Interests" are and probably always will be
so different. Is it to be expected that General Laws
can be adapted to the Feelings of the more Eastern
and the more Southern Parts of so extensive a
Nation ? It appears to me difficult if practicable.
Hence then may we not look for Discontent, Mis-
trust, Disaffection to Government and frequent

Insurrections, which will require standing Armies to suppress them in one Place & another where they may happen to arise. Or if Laws could be made, adapted to the local Habits, Feelings, Views & Interests of those distant Parts, would they not cause Jealousies of Partiality in Government which would excite Envy and other malignant Passions productive of Wars and fighting. But should we continue distinct sovereign States, confederated for the Purposes of mutual Safety and Happiness, each contributing to the federal Head such a Part of its Sovereignty as would render the Government fully adequate to those Purposes and *no more*, the People would govern themselves more easily, the Laws of each State being well adapted to its own Genius & Circumstances, and the Liberties of the United States would be more secure than they can be, as I humbly conceive, under the proposed new Constitution. You are sensible, Sir, that the Seeds of Aristocracy began to spring even before the Conclusion of our Struggle for the natural Rights of Men, Seeds which like a Canker Worm lie at the Root of free Governments. So great is the Wickedness of some Men, & the stupid Servility of others, that one would be almost inclined to conclude that Communities cannot be free. The few haughty Families, think *They* must govern. The Body of the People tamely consent & submit to be their Slaves. This unravels the Mystery of Millions being enslaved by the few ! But I must desist—My weak hand prevents my proceeding further at present. I will send you my poor Opinion of the political Structure at another Time. In the Interim oblige me with your

Letters; & present mine and M^rs A's best Regards
to your Lady & Family, Col° Francis, Mr A. L. if
with you, & other Friends, & be assured that I am
                    very affectionately yours

As I thought it a Piece of Justice
I have venturd to say that I had often
heard from the best Patriots from Virginia
that M^r G Mason was an early active
& able Advocate for the Liberties of
America.

TO RICHARD HENRY LEE.

[MS., Lee Papers, American Philosophical Society; a draft is in the Samuel
Adams Papers, Lenox Library.]

BOSTON April 22^d, 1789.
MY DEAR FRIEND
    You must not expect lengthy Letters from me for a
Reason which I have heretofore given you. Possibly,
however, I may trouble you with more frequent Letters. I hope the federal Congress is vested with
Powers adequate to all the great purposes of the
federal Union; and if they have such adequate Powers,
no true and understanding Federalist would consent
that they should be trusted with more—for more would
discover the Folly of the People in their wanton Grant
of Power, because it might, and considering the Disposition of the human Mind, without Doubt would be
wantonly [exercised to] their Injury and Ruin. The
Powers vested in Government by the People, the only
just Source of such Powers, ought to be critically de-
fined and well understood; lest by a Misconstruction

of ambiguous Expressions, and by interested Judges too, more Power might be assumed by the Government than the People ever intended they should possess. Few men are contented with less Power than they have a Right to exercise, the Ambition of the human Heart grasps at more. This is evinced by the Experience of all Ages.

Will you give me Leave to mention to you the Name of Leonard Jarvis, Esqr; a Gentleman to whose agreable Acquaintance, tho he is a native of this Town, I introduced myself by the Request of our worthy Friend General Whipple now deceased. Mr. Jarvis is a very sensible Republican, and an honest Man. He holds the Place of Comptroller General in this Commonwealth. I believe Mr. Dalton can shew you a Specimen of his Industry and Accuracy in Business. It is not by his Solicitation, or even knowledge that I write this. I am induced to it, because I think that good Men living at a Distance from the Seat of the federal Government, and capable of serving the United States should be made known.

Adieu my dear Sir.

TO THE LEGISLATURE OF MASSACHUSETTS.

[W. V. Wells, *Life of Samuel Adams*, vol. iii., pp. 284, 285 ; the text is also in the pamphlet *Resolutions of the General Court* (Boston, 1789), p. 7.]

May 27, 1789.[1]

MR. PRESIDENT,—

I have been politely notified by a joint committee of the two branches of the General Court that, having examined the returns of the votes for a Lieutenant-

---

[1] Upon taking the oath as Lieutenant-Governor of Massachusetts.

Governor of the Commonwealth, it appears that a majority of the electors have seen fit to give me their suffrages.

I am impressed with a warm sense of the honor done me, and it is a pleasing reflection, in my own mind, that I have this testimonial of the confidence of my countrymen, without my solicitation or interference in any manner to obtain it.

I rejoice in the freedom of our elections; and it affords me particular satisfaction to be invited to take a share in government by citizens possessed of the most lively feelings of natural and civil liberty, and enlightened with the knowledge and true ends of civil government, who, in conjunction with their sister States, have gloriously contended for the rights of mankind, and given the world another lesson, drawn from experience, *that all countries may be free*, since it has pleased the righteous Governor of the universe to smile upon their virtuous exertions, and crown them with independence and liberty.

If it be not improper on this occasion, may I beg leave to express a devout and fervent wish that gracious Heaven may guide the public councils of the great confederated commonwealth, and the several free and independent republics which compose it, so that the people may be highly respected and prosperous in their affairs abroad, and enjoy at home that tranquillity which results from a well-grounded confidence that their personal and domestic rights are secure.

I feel, sir, a diffidence of my own abilities, and am anxious but in certain events they may be found in-

adequate to the importance of the duties I may be
called to perform ; but relying on the aid of Divine
grace, and hoping for the justice, candor, and liberal
sentiments of the General Court and of my fellow-
citizens at large, I venture to accept the trust, and
am now ready to be qualified in the mode prescribed
by the Constitution.

TO RICHARD HENRY LEE.

[MS., Lee Papers, American Philosophical Society.]

BOSTON July 14th, 1789.

DEAR SIR

I have not lately received a Line from you, and am
ready to impute it to the Multiplicity of Affairs in
which your Mind is employed.   You must not expect
that I shall be even with you upon the epistolary
Score, for the Reason which I have heretofore given
you.   I wish to know from *you* the State of federal
Affairs as often as your Leisure may admit.[1]   We or-
ganize our State Governments, and I heartily wish
that their Authority and Dignity may be preserved
within their several Jurisdictions, as far as may be
consistent with the Purposes for which the federal
Government is designed.   They are in my opinion
petit Politicians who would wish to lessen the due
Weight of the State Governments ; for I think the
federal must depend upon the Influence of these to
carry their Laws into Effect ; and while those Laws
have for their *sole* Object the promoting the purposes

---

[1] Lee was at this time in the United States Senate.

of the *federal* Union, there is Reason to expect they
will have the due Support of the State Authorities.
Places are now become the Object of Multitudes ; I
mentioned to you in a former Letter the name of
Leonard Jarvis, Esqr whom I hope you will not forget.
Israel Keith, Esqr wishes to have the Place of Mar-
shall within this District.   He is a Gentleman of the
Law, and was during the War Aid de Camp to Gen-
eral Heath, who I understand has recommended him
to the President.   You will gratify the wishes of M^r
Keith as far as shall consist with your own Ideas of
Propriety ; and be assured, that I am sincerely

Your Friend,

P. S.   I have been informed that Mr Edward
Church a Native of this Town, but now an Inhabitant
of Georgia is in the City of New York.   I take him to
have been a steady Friend to the Liberties of our
Country, and a man of Sense and Integrity.   If it will
not weary you with Applications I will beg your
Notice of him, and after your own Inquiries afford him
your Influence, if you shall think it proper, in promoting him to a suitable Employment under Congress
in the State of Georgia.   This I mention without his
Sollicitation, or even Knowledge.

TO ELBRIDGE GERRY.

[MS., Samuel Adams Papers, Lenox Library.]

Boston Augt 22 1789

My dear Sir

I wrote to you hastily two days ago, & as hastily
venturd an Opinion concerning the Right of Congress to controul a Light-house erected on Land be-

longing to this sovereign & independent State for its own Use & at its own Expence.   I say *sovereign &* *independent*, because I think the State retains all the Rights of Sovereignty which it has not expressly parted with to the Congress of the United States—a federal Power instituted *solely* for the Support of the federal Union.

The Sovereignty of the State extends over every part of its Territory.   The federal Constitution expresses the same Idea in Sec. 8, Art. 1.   A Power is therein given to Congress "to exercise like Authority," that is to exercise exclusive Legislation in all Cases whatsoever, "over all places purchased by *the Consent of the Legislature* in which the same shall be, for the Erection of Forts, Magazines, and other needful Buildings," among which Light-houses may be included.   Is it not the plain Conclusion from this Clause in the Compact, that Congress have not the Right to exercise exclusive Legislation in all Cases whatsoever, nor even to purchase or controul any part of the Territory within a State for the Erection of needful Buildings unless it has the Consent of its Legislature.   If there are any such Buildings already erected, which operate to the General Welfare of the U S, and Congress by Virtue of the Power vested in them have taken from a State for the general Use, the necessary Means of supporting such Buildings it appears to be reasonable & just that the U S should maintain them ; but I think that it follows not from hence, that Congress have a right to exercise any Authority over those buildings even to make Appointments of officers for the immediate Care of them or furnishing them with necessary Supplies. I wish to have your Opinion if you can find Leisure.

I hope Congress, before they adjourn, will take into very serious Consideration the necessary Amendments of the Constitution. Those whom I call the best—the most judicious & disinterested Federalists, who wish for the perpetual Union, Liberty & Happiness of the States & their respective Citizens, many of them if not all are anxiously expecting them. They wish to see a Line drawn as clearly as may be, between the federal Powers vested in Congress and the distinct Sovereignty of the several States upon which the private & personal Rights of the Citizens depend. Without such Distinction there will be Danger of the Constitution issuing imperceptibly and gradually into a consolidated Government over all the States ; which, altho it may be wished for by some was reprobated in the Idea by the highest Advocates for the Constitution as it stood without Amendm^{ts}. I am fully persuaded that the population of the U S liv^g in different Climates, of different Education and Manners, and possest of different Habits & feelings under one consolidated Governm^t can not long remain free, or indeed remain under any kind of Govern^t but despotism.

You will not forget our old Friend Devens, and if you please mention him to M^r R H Lee.

Adieu my dear Friend and believe me to be sincerely your,

P. S.   The joint regards of M^{rs} A & myself to Mrs Gerry.

TO RICHARD HENRY LEE.

[MS., Lee Papers, American Philosophical Society; a draft is in the Samuel Adams Papers, Lenox Library.]

BOSTON August 24ᵗʰ 1789.

MY DEAR SIR

Your very acceptable Letter of the 8ᵗʰ Current came to me by the Post. You flatter me very much when you tell me that any sentiment of mine can please you. I have always been apprehensive that through the weakness of the human Mind often discovered even in the wisest and best of Men, or the perverseness of the interested, and designing, in as well as out of Government; Misconstructions would be given to the federal constitution, which would disappoint the Views, and expectations of the honest among those who acceded to it, and hazard the Liberty, Independence and Happiness of the People. I was particularly affraid that unless great care should be taken to prevent it, the Constitution in the Administration of it would gradually, but swiftly and imperceptably run into a consolidated Government pervading and legislating through all the States, not for federal purposes *only* as it professes, but in all cases whatsoever: such a Government would soon totally annihilate the Sovereignty of the several States so necessary to the Support of the confederated Commonwealth, and sink both in despotism. I know these have been called vulgar opinions, and prejudices: be it so—I think it is Lord Shaftsbury who tells us, that it is folly to despise the opinions of the Vulgar; this Aphorism, if indeed it is his, I eagerly catched from a *Nobleman* many years ago, whose writings on some accounts, I never much admired. Should a strong *Federalist* as some call themselves see what has now dropt from my Pen, he would say that I am an Antifed, an *Amendment Monger* &c; those are truly vulgar terms, invented and used by some whose feelings would be sorely wounded to be ranked among such kind of Men, and invented and used for the mean purpose of deceiving, and entrapping others whom *they* call the Vulgar; but in this *"enlightned"* Age one should think there was no such *Vulgar* to be thus amused, and ensnared. I mean, my friend, to let you know how deeply, I am impressed with a sense of the Importance of Amendments; that the good People may clearly see the distinction, for there is a distinction, between the *federal* Powers vested in Congress, and the *sovereign* Authority belonging to the several States, which is the Palladium of the private, and personal rights of the Citizens. I freely protest to you that I earnestly wish some Amendments may be judiciously, and deliberately made without partial or local considerations—that there may be no uncomfortable Jarrings among the several Powers; that the whole People may in every State contemplate their own safety on solid grounds, and the Union of the States be perpetual. I hope that you have recovered your health, so valuable to our Country. Your Letter requires a further Consideration. I will at present only express my astonishment at the strange and absurd Opinion of our former *re-*

publican Connecticut friend. Tempora mutantur, et
hic mutatur in illis.

Your friend,

TO RICHARD HENRY LEE.

[MS., Lee Papers, American Philosophical Society ; a draft is in the Samuel
Adams Papers, Lenox Library.]

BOSTON Augt 29th. 1789.

MY DEAR SIR

The Power of removing federal Officers at the
Pleasure of the President is to be found the Constitution or it is not. If it is, What Need was there of
an Act or Decision of Congress to authorize it? But
if it is not, could Congress give so important a Power?
What have the United States been contending for?
Liberty. This is the great Object of their State
Governments, and has not the federal Constitution
the same Object in View? If therefore a Doubt
arises respecting the Exercise of any Power, no Construction, I conceive, should militate with the main
Design, or Object of the Charter. If there is a total
Silence in the Constitution, is it not natural to conclude that an Officer holding during Pleasure is
removable by the same Power which appointed him,
whether vested in a single Person, or a joint Number?
I am sensible, it is said, that a single Person, being
amenable for his Exercise of Power will use the utmost Circumspection. This may be true, but may
not this Idea be carried too far in Practice? May
not some Powers vested in a single Man give him

such Weight and Influence as to render any Restraint
from his feeling himself amenable of little, or no
Effect.   If this Power lodged in the Discretion of a
single Person will afford a greater Security against
Corruption because of his Amenability, why should
not the Power of appointing as well as removing Of-
ficers be given to him?   In the one Case the gracious
Hand may be held forth, in the other, the threatning
Rod ; and both may be used for improper Purposes.
In England, " the King can do no wrong " is a Maxim.
His Ministers are made accountable for him ; and
how often have corrupt Ministers and Councellors
been brought to the Block for Follies and Crimes
committed by their Royal Masters who can do no
Wrong?   And it may also be asked, how often such
Ministers and Councellors have found Means to get
themselves screened from Punishment through the
Influence of their Masters, by procuring Parliamen-
tary Sanctions to such Crimes and Follies?   But in
the Removal of Officers the President has not a Constitutional Council.   He must therefore be solely
accountable.   I need not tell *you* who have known so
thoroughly the Sentiments of my Heart, that I have always had a very high Esteem for the late Commander
in Chief of our Armies ; and I now most sincerely believe that while President Washington continues in
the Chair he will be able to give to all good Men a
satisfactory Reason for every Instance of his public
Conduct.   I feel myself constrained contrary to my
usual Manner to make *Professions* of Sincerity on this
Occasion because Dr Gordon in his History of the
Revolution, among many other Anecdotes innocent

and triffling enough, has gravely said, that I was concerned in an Attempt to remove General Washington
from Command; and mentions an anonymous Letter
written to your late Governor Henry which I affirm I
never saw nor heard of till I lately met with it in reading the History[1]—This is a Digression to which a Man
of my years is liable. Who will succeed the present
President for it is the Lot of Man to die? Perhaps
the next and the next may inherit his Virtues. But
my Friend, I fear the Time will come, when a Bribe
shall remove the most excellent Man from Office for
the Purpose of making Room for the worst. It will
be called an Error in Judgment. The Bribe will be
concealed. It may however be vehemently suspected
& who, in Times of great Degeneracy will venture to
search out and detect the corrupt Practices of great
Men? Unless a sufficient Check is provided and
clearly ascertained for every Power given, will not
the Constitution and the Liberties of the Citizens for
want of such Checksbe finally subverted.

A Gentleman of this Place who has suffered much
for his Attachment to our Cause I conceive has Documents in his Hands which would be of Importance
in the Settlement of the Eastern Boundary of the
United States which appears to have been encroached
upon by the British. I wrote so long ago as last
April to M[r] Dalton respecting this Gentleman; but
have never received an Answer. He I suppose is
able to give you an Account of M[r] Boyd the Name
of the Gentleman referred to. I wish you would

---

[1] William Gordon, *History of the American Revolution*, (3rd Amer. edit.) vol.
ii., p. 306.

converse with Mr Dalton upon the Subject. The
Vice President however is probably able, and un-
doubtedly disposed to give you the fullest Account.
I am sincerely yours

P. S. Pray write to me and let me know the State
of your Health, & pay my affectionate Regards to
your Brother the Doctor.

TO THE LEGISLATURE OF MASSACHUSETTS. MAY 28, 1790.[1]

[W. V. Wells, *Life of Samuel Adams*, vol. iii., pp. 288, 289; a text is in the
Massachusetts Archives.]

MR. PRESIDENT,—

Having been regularly informed that a majority of
the late electors in the several towns and districts
within this Commonwealth have honored me with
their suffrages for the office of Lieutenant-Governor,
I now present myself before the two branches of the
General Court to be qualified as the Constitution
directs. I do the more readily obey this *repeated* call,
because I cannot help flattering myself that it has
proceeded from a persuasion in the minds of my
fellow-citizens of the attachment of my heart to their
rights and liberties, and my earnest desires that they
may be perpetuated. My fellow-citizens may be
assured that I feel that attachment and the strength
of those• desires. The first of my wishes, as they
respect this life, is for our country; and the best of

---

[1] Upon taking office as Lieutenant-Governor, to which office he was also
elected in 1791 and 1792.

my feeble abilities shall be ever employed for her prosperity.

I shall presently be called upon by you, sir, as it is enjoined by the Constitution, to make a declaration upon oath (and shall do it with cheerfulness, because the injunction accords with my own judgment and conscience) that *the Commonwealth of Massachusetts is, and of right ought to be, a free, sovereign, and independent State.* I shall also be called upon to make another declaration, with the same solemnity, *to support the Constitution of the United States.* I see the consistency of this, for it cannot have been intended but that these Constitutions should mutually aid and support each other. It is my humble opinion that, while the Commonwealth of Massachusetts maintains her own just authority, weight, and dignity, she will be among the firmest pillars of the Federal Union.

May the administration of the Federal government, and those of the several States in the Union, be guided by the unerring finger of Heaven ! Each of them and all of them united will then, if the people are wise, be as prosperous as the wisdom of human institutions and the circumstances of human society will admit.

TO JOHN ADAMS.

[MS., Adams Papers, Quincy.[1]]

BOSTON Septem^r 2^d 1790

S^r

I have not written a single line to any friend in, or

---

[1] The body of this letter, like several in the later years, was not in the autograph of Adams.

out of Congress during the late session, having been prevented by my old nervous disorder, and am now dictating this to a confidential friend, whom you well know.

Cap^n Nathaniel Byfield Lyde who commanded the Ship in which your Lady sailed to England has informed me that a number of Vessells are to be built, and employed to guard the coast for a preventing of breaches of the act of trade ; and he requests me to ask the favour of you to mention his Name to the President of the United States for a command. I now gratify his request, which is my apology.

I hope you, and your connections are in good health, and spirits. Mrs Adams joins me in due Regards to yourself, and Lady.

I am, dear sir, with much Esteem, and respect,

Your affectionate friend,

TO JOHN ADAMS.

[MS., Adams Papers, Quincy; a draft is in the Samuel Adams Papers, Lenox Library ; the text is in John Adams, *Works*, vol. vi., pp. 412–414, W. V. Wells, *Life of Samuel Adams*, vol. iii., pp. 300–302 ; *cf.* Department of State, Bureau of Rolls and Library, *Bulletin* No. 8, p. 15.]

BOSTON Octr 4th 1790

DEAR SIR

With pleasure I received your Letter of Septr 12th ; and as our good friend, to whom I dictated our last is yet in Town, I have requested of him a second favour.

You ask what the World is about to become ? and, Is

the Millenium commencing? I have not studied the
Prophesies, and cannot even conjecture. The Golden
Age so finely pictured by Poets, I believe has never
yet existed; but in their own imaginations. In the
earliest periods, when for the honor of human nature,
one should have thought, that man had not learnt to
be cruel; what Scenes of horror have been exhibited
in families of some of the best instructors in Piety
and morals! Even the heart of our first father was
grievously wounded at the sight of the murder of
one of his Sons, perpetrated by the hand of the other.
Has Mankind since seen the happy Age? No, my
friend. The same Tragedys have been acted on
the Theatre of the World, the same Arts of torment-
ing have been studied, and practiced to this day;
and true religion, and reason united have never
succeeded to establish the permanent foundations
of political freedom, and happiness in the most
enlightened Countries on the Earth. After a
compliment to Boston Town meetings, and our
Harvard College as having "set the universe in
Motion"; you tell me Every Thing will be pulled
down; I think with you, "So much seems certain,"
but what say you, will be built up? Hay, wood and
stubble, may probably be the materials, till Men shall
be yet more enlightened, and more friendly to each
other. "Are there any Principles of Political Architecture?" Undoubtedly. "What are they?" Philosophers ancient, and modern, have laid down different
plans, and all have thought themselves, masters of the
true Principles. Their Disciples have followed them,
probably with a blind prejudice, which is always an

Enemy to truth, and have thereby added fresh fuel
to the fire of Contention, and increased the political
disorder.   Kings have been deposed by aspiring
Nobles, whose pride could not brook restraint.   These
have waged everlasting War, against the common
rights of Men.   The Love of Liberty is interwoven
in the soul of Man, and can never be totally extin-
guished ; and there are certain periods when human
patience can no longer endure indignity, and oppression.   The spark of liberty then kindles into a flame ;
when the injured people attentive to the feelings of
their just rights magnanimously contend for their compleat restoration.   But such contests have too often
ended in nothing more than " a change of Impostures,
and impositions " .   The Patriots of Rome put an End
to the Life of Cæsar ; and Rome submitted to a Race
of Tyrants in his stead.   Were the People of England free, after they had obliged King John to concede
to them their ancient rights, and Libertys, and promise to govern them according to the Old Law of the
Land ?   Were they free, after they had wantonly deposed their Henrys, Edwards, and Richards to gratify
family pride ?   Or, after they had brought their first
Charles to the block, and banished his family ?   They
were not.   The Nation was then governed by Kings,
Lords, and Commons, and its Libertys were lost by a
strife among three Powers, soberly intended to check
each other, and keep the scales even.   But while we
daily see the violence of the human passions controul-
ing the Laws of Reason and religion, and stifling the
very feelings of humanity ; can we wonder, that in such
tumults little or no regard is had to Political Checks

and Ballances? And such tumults have always happened within as well as without doors. The best
formed constitutions that have yet been contrived by
the wit of Man have, and will come to an End—because
" the Kingdoms of the Earth have not been governed
by Reason." The Pride of Kings, of Nobles, and
leaders of the People who have all governed in their
turns, have disadjusted the delicate frame, and thrown
all into confusion. What then is to be done ?—Let
Divines, and Philosophers, Statesmen and Patriots
unite their endeavours to renovate the Age, by im-
pressing the Minds of Men with the importance of ed-
ucating their *little boys*, and *girls*—of inculcating in the
Minds of youth the fear, and Love of the Deity, and
universal Phylanthropy ; and in subordination to these
great principles, the Love of their Country—of instructing them in the Art of *self* government, without
which they never can act a wise part in the Government of Societys great, or small—in short of leading
them in the Study, and Practice of the exalted Virtues
of the Christian system, which will happily tend to
subdue the turbulent passions of Men, and introduce
that Golden Age beautifully described in figurative
language ; when the Wolf shall dwell with the Lamb,
and the Leopard lie down with the Kid—the Cow,
and the bear shall feed ; their young ones shall lie
down together, and the Lyon shall eat straw like the
Ox—none shall then hurt, or destroy ; for the Earth
shall be full of the Knowledge of the Lord. When this
Millenium shall commence, if there shall be any need
of Civil Government, indulge me in the fancy that it
will be in the republican form, or something *better*.

I thank you for your Countenance to our friend Lyde. Mrs Adams tells me to remember her to yourself, Lady, and connections ; And be assured that I am sincerely

your friend,

TO JOHN ADAMS.

[MS., Adams Papers, Quincy ; a draft is in the Samuel Adams Papers, Lenox Library ; the text with variations is in John Adams, *Works*, vol. vi., pp. 420–426, W. V. Wells, *Life of Samuel Adams*, vol. iii., pp. 308–314 ; *cf.* Department of State, Bureau of Rolls and Library, *Bulletin* No. 8, p. 16. Certain texts give the date as November 20.]

BOSTON Novem^r 25th 1790

My dear Sir

I lately received your Letter of the 18th of October.—The Sentiment, and observations contained in it demand my attention.

A Republic, you tell me, is a Government in which "the People have an essential *share* in the sovereignty ;" Is not the *whole* sovereignty, my friend, essentially in the People? Is not Government designed for the Welfare and happiness of all the People? and is it not the uncontroulable essential right of the People to amend, and alter, or annul their Constitution, and frame a new one, whenever they shall think it will better promote their own welfare, and happiness to do it? That the Sovereignty resides in the People is a political doctrine which I have never heard an American Politician seriously deny. The Constitutions of the American States reserve to the People the exercise of the rights of Sovereignty ; by the annual, or biennial elections

of their Governours, Senators, & Representatives;
and by empowering their own Representatives to
impeach the greatest officers of the State, before the
Senators who are also chosen by themselves.

We the people is the stile of the federal Constitution. They adopted it; and conformably to it, they
delegate the exercise of the Powers of Government
to particular persons, who, after short intervals resign
their Powers to the People, and they will re-elect
them, or appoint others, as[1] they think fit.

The American Legislatures are nicely balanced:
They consist of two branches, each having a check
upon the determinations of the other: they sit in different chambers, and probably often reason differently
in their respective chambers, on the same question—
if they disagree in their decisions, by a conference
their reasons, and Arguments are mutually communicated to each other: Candid explanations tend to
bring them to agreement; and then according to the
Massachusetts constitution, the matter is laid before
the first Magistrate for his revision. He states objections, if he has any, with his Reasons, and returns
them to the Legislators, who by larger Majorities
ultimately decide. Here is a mixture of three Powers
founded in the Nature of Man; calculated to call
forth the rational Faculties in the great points of
Legislation, into exertion; to cultivate mutual Friendship, and good humour; and finally to enable them
to decide, not by the impulse of passion, or party
prejudice, but the calm Voice of Reason, which is the

---

[1] The draft at this point reads: " as in their own enlightened Judgments
shall best serve the great End of Government the good of the whole People."

Voice of God :—In this mixture you may see your
"natural, and actual Aristocracy among mankind,"
operating among the several Powers in Legislation,
and producing the most happy Effects. But the Son
of an excellent Man may never inherit the great
qualities of his father ; this is common observation,
and there are many instances of its truth : Should
we not therefore conclude that hereditary Nobility is
a solecism in Government ? Their Lordships Sons,
or Grandsons may be destitute of the faintest feelings
of honor, or honesty ; and yet retain an essential
share in the Government by right of inheritance from
Ancestors, who may have been the Minions of ministers—the favourites of Mistresses, or Men of real,
and distinguished Merit. The same may be said of
hereditary Kings ; Their Successors may also become
so degenerated, and corrupt, as to have neither inclination, nor capacity to know the extent, and Limits
of their own Powers, nor consequently those of others.
Such kind of Political Beings, Nobles, or Kings,
possessing hereditary right to essential shares in an
equipoized Government are very unfit persons to
hold the scales ; Having no just conception of the
Principles of the Government, nor of the part which
they, and their copartners bear in the administration ;
they run a wild career, destroy the checks, and ballances, by interfering in each others departments, till
the Nation is involved in confusion, and reduced to
the danger, at least, of Bloodshed to remove a Tyranny, which may ensue. Much safer is it, and much
more does it tend to promote the Welfare and happiness of Society to fill up the offices of Government

after the mode prescribed in the American Constitution, by frequent Elections of the People. They may indeed be deceived in their choice; they sometimes are; but the Evil is not incurable; the Remedy is always near; they will feel their mistakes, and correct them.

I am very willing to agree with you in thinking, that improvement in Knowledge, and Benevolence receive much assistance from the principles, and Systems of good Government: But is it not as true that without knowledge, and benevolence Men would neither have been capable or disposed to search for the principles, or form the System—Should we not, my friend, bear a gratefull remembrance of our pious and benevolent Ancestors, who early laid plans of Education; by which means Wisdom, Knowledge, and Virtue have been generally diffused among the body of the people, and they have been enabled to form and establish a civil constitution calculated for the preservation of their rights, and liberties. This Constitution was evidently founded in the expectation of the further progress, and "extraordinary degrees" of virtue. It injoyns the encouragement of all Seminaries of Literature, which are the nurseries of Virtue depending upon these for the support of Government, rather than Titles, Splendor, or Force. Mr Hume may call this a "Chimerical Project." I am far from thinking the People can be deceived by urging upon them a dependance on the more general prevalence of Knowledge, and Virtue: It is one of the most essential means of further, and still further improvements in Society, and of correcting, and amending

moral sentiments, and habits, and political institutions ; till "by human means" directed by divine influence, Men shall be prepared for that "happy, and
holy State" when the Messiah is to reign.

"It is a fixed Principle that all good Government
is, and must be Republican." You have my hearty
concurrence ; and I believe we are well enough acquainted with each others Ideas to understand what
we respectively mean when we "use the Word with
approbation." The Body of the People in this
Country are not so ignorant as those of England
were in the Time of the Interregnum Parliament.
They are better educated : they will not easily be
prevailed upon to believe that a Republican is "as
unamiable as a Witch, a Blasphemer, a Rebel, or a
Tyrant." They are charmed with their forms of
Government, in which is admitted a mixture of Powers
to check the human passions, and controul them from
rushing into exorbitances. So well assured are they,
that their liberties are best secured, by their own frequent, and free Election of fit persons to be the
essential sharers in the administration of their Government, and that this form of Government is
truly *Republic*, that the body of the People will not
be perswaded nor compelled to "renounce, detest,
and execrate the very Word Republican as the
English do." Their Education has "confirmed them
in the opinion of the necessity of preserving, and
strengthening the Dykes against the Ocean, its
Tydes, and Storms," and I think they have made
more safe, and more durable Dykes, than the English
have done.

We agree in the Utility of universal Education, but "will nations agree in it as fully, and extensively as we do"? Why should they not? It would not be fair to conclude, that because they have not yet been disposed to agree in it, they never will. It is allowed, that the present age is more enlightened than former ones. Freedom of enquiry is certainly more encouraged: The feelings of humanity have softned the heart: The true principles of civil, and religious Liberty are better understood: Tyranny in all its shapes, is more detested, and bigotry, if not still blind, must be mortified to see that she is despised. Such an age may afford at least a flattering Expectation that Nations, as well as individuals, will view the utility of universal Education in so strong a light as to induce sufficient national Patronage, and Support. Future Ages will probably be more enlightned than this.

The Love of Liberty is interwoven in the Soul of Man. "So it is in that of a Wolf;" However irrational, ungenerous, and unsocial the love of liberty may be in a rude Savage, he is capable of being enlightned by Experience, Reflection, Education, and civil, and Political Institutions. *But the* Nature of the Wolf is, and ever will be confined to running in the forest to satisfy his hunger, and his brutal appetites; the Dog is inclined in a more easy way to seek his living, and fattens his sides with what comes from his masters kitchen. The Comparison of La Fontaine is in my opinion ungenerous, unnatural, and unjust.

Among the Numbers of Men, my friend, are to be

found not only those who have "preferred ease,
slumber, and good chear to liberty"; but others, who
have eagerly sought after Thrones, and Sceptres,
hereditary shares in Sovereignty Riches, and Splendor, Titles, Stars, Garters, Crosses, Eagles, and many
other childish play things, at the expence of real Nobility, without one thought, or care for the liberty,
and happiness of the rest of Mankind. "The People,
who have no property feel the Power of governing
by a majority; and even attack those who have property." "The injured Men of Property recur to finess,
trick, and Stratagem," to outwit them: True; These
may proceed from a Lust of domination in *some* of
both parties. Be this as it may; It has been known,
that such deceitful tricks have been practiced by some
of the rich upon their unsuspecting fellow Citizens;
to turn the determination of Questions, so as to
answer their own selfish purposes. To plunder or
filch the rights of Men are crimes equally immoral,
and nefarious; though committed in a different manner: Neither of them is confined to the Rich, or the
Poor; they are too common among both. The
Lords as well as the commons of Great Brittain by
continued large majorities endeavoured by Finess,
Tricks, and Stratagems, as well as threats to prevail
on the American Colonies to surrender their Liberty
and Property to their disposal. These failing, they
attempted to *plunder* our rights by force of Arms.
We feared their Arts more than their Arms. Did
the Members of that hereditary House of Lords, who
constituted those repeated majorities, then possess
the spirit of Nobility? Not so, I think: That Spirit

resided in the *illustrious* Minorities in both Houses.
But "by Nobles" who have prevented "one hideous
Despotism as horrid as that of Turkey from falling
to the lot of every Nation of Europe"; you mean
not peculiarly an hereditary Nobility, or any particular Modification, but "the natural, and actual
Aristocracy among Mankind;" The existence of
which, I am not disposed to deny. Where is this
Aristocracy to be found? Among Men of all Ranks
and Conditions. The Cottager may beget a wise
Son; the Noble, a Fool: The one is capable of
great Improvement—the other not. Education is
within the Power of Men, and Societys of Men.
Wise, and judicious Modes of Education, patronized,
and supported by communities, will draw together
the Sons of the rich, and the poor, among whom it
makes no distinction; it will cultivate the natural
Genius, elevate the Soul, excite laudable Emulation
to excel in Knowledge, Piety, and Benevolence, and
finally it will reward its Patrons, and Benefactors by
sheding its benign Influence on the Public Mind.
Education inures Men to thinking and reflection, to
reasoning and demonstration. It discovers to them
the moral and religious duties they owe to God, their
Country and to all Mankind. Even Savages might,
by the means of Education, be instructed to frame
the best civil, and political Institutions with as much
skill and ingenuity, as they now shape their Arrows.
Education leads youth to "the Study of human nature, society, and universal History" from whence
they may "draw all the Principles" of Political Architecture, which ought to be regarded. All Men are

"interested in the truth." Education by showing
them "the End of all its consequences" would induce, at least, the greatest numbers to inlist on its
side. The Man of good understanding who has been
well educated, and improves these advantages as far
as his circumstances will allow, in promoting the happiness of Mankind, in my opinion, and I am inclined
to think in yours is indeed "well born." It may be
"puerile, and unworthy of Statesmen" to declame
against *Family Pride;* but there is and always has
been such a ridiculous kind of Vanity among Men.
"Statesmen know the evil, and danger is too serious
to be sported with." I am content they should be
put into one hole; as you propose, but I have some
fears that your Watchmen on each side will not well
agree. When a Man can recollect the *Virtues* of his
Ancestors; he certainly has abundantly more solid
satisfaction than another who boasts that he sprang
from those, who were *rich*, or *noble;* but never discovers the least degree of Virtue, or true worth of
any kind. "Family Popularity," if I mistake not,
has its source in family pride; It is by all means
sought after that hommage may be paid to the name
of the Title or Estate, to supply the want, in the
possessor, of any great, or good quality whatsoever.
There are *individuals* among Men, who study the art
of making themselves popular, for the purpose of
getting into Places of Honour, and Emoluments, and
by these means of gratifying hereafter the noble Passion—Family Pride. Others are so inchanted with
the Musick of the sound, that they conceive it to be
supreme felicity. This is indeed Vanity of Vanities,

and if such deluded Men ever come to their Senses, they will find it to be vexation of Spirit. When they reflect on their own folly, and injustice in having received the breath of Applause with avidity, and great delight, for Merrit which they are conscious they never had; and that many who have been the loudest in sounding their praises, had nothing in view, but their own private, and selfish interests, it will excite in them the feelings of shame, remorse, and self contempt.

The truly virtuous Man, and real Patriot, is satisfied with the approbation of the wise, and discerning; he rejoices in the contemplation of the Purity of his Intentions, and waits in humble hope for the Plaudit of his final Judge.

I shall hardly venture again to trespass on the Benevolence of our Confidential Friend—you will not be sorry; it will afford you Reliefe, for in common Civility you *must* be at the Trouble of reading ones Epistles. I hope there will be a Time when we shall have " sweet Communion " together. In the mean Time let me not lose the Benefit of your valueable Letters. Adieu. Believe me
Your sincere Friend

TO THE LEGISLATURE OF MASSACHUSETTS. JANUARY 17, 1794.

[*Independent Chronicle*, January 20, 1794; the text is in W. V. Wells, *Life of Samuel Adams*, vol. iii., pp. 324–328, and in the Massachusetts Archives.]

FELLOW-CITIZENS OF THE TWO
    BRANCHES OF THE LEGISLATURE,
    IT having pleased the Supreme Being, since your

last meeting, in His holy providence to remove from this transitory life, our late excellent Governour Hancock, the multitude of his surviving fellow-citizens, who have often given strong testimonials of their approbation of his important services, while they drop a tear, may certainly profit by the recollection of his virtuous and patriotic example.

You are sensible, that on this melancholly event, our Constitution directs that the Lieutenant Governour,[1] for the time being, shall perform all the duties which were incumbent on him, and exercise all the powers and authorities, during the vacancy of the chair, which by the Constitution, he was vested with when personally present. Diffident as I am of my abilities, I have yet felt myself constrained, to undertake the performance of those duties, and the exercise of those powers and authorities, in consequence of a sovereign act of God. To Him I look for that wisdom which is profitable to direct. The Constitution must be my rule, and the true interest of my Constituents, whose agent I am, my invariable object.

The people of this Commonwealth, have heretofore been possessed of the intire sovereignty within and over their own territories. They were "not controulable by any other laws than those to which their constituted representative body gave their consent." This, I presume, was the case in every other State of the Union.—But, after the memorable declaration of their Independence was by solemn treaty, agreed to and ratified by the British King, the only power that

---

[1] Hancock died October 8, 1793, and Adams became Governor; he was thereafter elected to that office in the years 1794, 1795, and 1796.

could have any pretence to dispute it, they considered
themselves decidedly free and independent of all other
people. Having taken rank among nations, it was
judged that their great affairs could not well be conducted under the direction of a number of distinct sovereignties. They therefore formed and adopted a
Federal Constitution ; by which certain powers of sovereignty are delegated and entrusted to such persons
as they shall judge proper from time to time to elect ;
to be exercised conformably to, and within the restric-
tions of the said Constitution, for the purposes of
strengthening and confirming the Union, and promoting the safety and happiness of the confederate
Commonwealth. All powers not vested in Congress,
remain in the separate States to be exercised according
to their respective Constitutions.—Should not unre-
mitting caution be used, least any degree of interference or infringement might take place, either on the
rights of the Federal Government on the one side, or
those of the several States on the other. Instances of
this kind may happen; for infallibility is not the lot of
any man or body of men, even the best of them on earth.
The human mind in its present state, being very im-
perfect, is liable to a multitude of errors. Prejudice,
that great source of error, often creeps in and takes
possession of the hearts of honest men, without even
their perceiving it themselves. Honest men will not
feel themselves disgusted, when mistakes are pointed
out to them with decency, candor and friendship, nor
will they, when convinced of truth, think their own
dignity degraded by correcting their own errors.

Among the objects of the Constitution of this

Commonwealth, Liberty and Equality stand in a con-
spicuous light. It is the first article in our Declaration of rights, " all men are born free and equal, and
have certain natural, essential and unalienable rights."
In the supposed state of nature, all men are equally
bound by the laws of nature, or to speak more properly, the laws of the Creator :—They are imprinted
by the finger of God on the heart of man. Thou
shall do no injury to thy neighbour, is the voice of
nature and reason, and it is confirmed by written revelation. In the state of nature, every man hath an
equal right by honest means to acquire property, and
to enjoy it ; in general, to pursue his own happiness,
and none can consistently controul or interrupt him
in the pursuit. But, so turbulent are the passions of
some, and so selfish the feelings of others, that in
such a state, there being no social compact, the weak
cannot always be protected from the violence of the
strong, nor the honest and unsuspecting from the arts
and intrigues of the selfish and cunning. Hence it is
easy to conceive, that men, naturally formed for society, were inclined to enter into mutual compact for
the better security of their natural rights. In this
state of society, the unalienable rights of nature are
held sacred :—And each member is intitled to an
equal share of all the social rights. No man can of
right become possessed of a greater share : If any
one usurps it, he so far becomes a tyrant ; and when
he can obtain sufficient strength, the people will feel
the rod of a tyrant. Or, if this exclusive privilege
can be supposed to be held in virtue of compact, it
argues a very capital defect ; and the people, when

more enlightened, will alter their compact, and extinguish the very idea.

These opinions, I conceive to be conformable to the sentiments held up in our State Constitution. It is therein declared, that Government is instituted for the common good ; not for the profit, honor or private interest of any one man, family, or class of men. And further, all the inhabitants of this Commonwealth, having such qualifications, as shall be established by their Constitution, have an equal right to elect or be elected for the public employments.

Before the formation of this Constitution, it had been affirmed as a self evident truth, in the declaration of Independence, very deliberately made by the Representatives of the United States of America in Congress assembled that, " all men are created equal, and are endowed by their Creator with certain unalienable rights." This declaration of Independence was received and ratified by all the States in the Union, and has never been disannulled. May we not from hence conclude, that the doctrine of Liberty and Equality is an article in the political creed of the United States.

Our Federal Constitution ordains that, no title of nobility shall be granted by the United States. The framers of that Constitution probably foresaw that such titles, vain and insignificant in themselves, might be in time, as they generally, and I believe always have been, the introductory to the absurd and unnatural claims of hereditary and exclusive privileges.

The Republic of France have also adopted the same principle, and laid it as the foundation of their

Constitution. That nation having for many ages groaned under the exercise of the pretended right claimed by their Kings and Nobles, until their very feelings as men were become torpid, at length suddenly awoke, from their long slumber, abolished the usurpation, and placed every man upon the footing of equal rights. "All men are born free and equal in rights," if I mistake not, is their language.

From the quotations I have made, I think it appears, that the Constitutions referred to, different as they may be in forms, agree altogether in the most essential principles upon which legitimate governments are founded. I have said essential principles, because I conceive that without Liberty and Equality, there cannot exist that tranquillity of mind, which results from the assurance of every citizen, that his own personal safety and rights are secure :—This, I think is a sentiment of the celebrated Montesquieu; and it is the end and design of all free and lawful Governments. Such assurance, impressed upon the heart of each, would lead to the peace, order and happiness of all. For I should think, no man, in the exercise of his reason would be inclined in any instance to trespass upon the equal rights of citizens, knowing that if he should do it, he would weaken and risque the security of his own. Even different nations, having grounded their respective Constitutions upon the afore-mentioned principles, will shortly feel the happy effects of mutual friendship, mutual confidence and united strength. Indeed I cannot but be of opinion, that when those principles shall be rightly understood and universally established, the whole family and brotherhood of man will then nearly approach to, if not fully enjoy that state of peace and prosperity, which ancient Prophets and Sages have foretold.

I fear I have dwelt too long upon this subject. Another presents itself to my mind, which I think is indeed great and important ; I mean the education of our children and youth. Perhaps the minds even of infants may receive impressions, good or bad, at an earlier period than many imagine. It has been observed, that "education has a greater influence on manners, than human laws can have." Human laws excite fears and apprehensions, least crimes committed may be detected and punished : But a virtuous education is calculated to reach and influence the heart, and to prevent crimes. A very judicious writer, has quoted Plato, who in shewing what care for the security of States ought to be taken of the education of youth, speaks of it as almost sufficient to supply the place both of Legislation and Administration. Such an education, which leads the youth beyond mere outside shew, will impress their minds with a profound reverence of the Deity, universal benevolence, and a warm attachment and affection towards their country. It will excite in them a just regard to Divine Revelation, which informs them of the original character and dignity of Man ; and it will inspire them with a sense of true honor, which consists in conforming as much as possible, their principles, habits, and manners to that original character. It will enlarge their powers of mind, and prompt them impartially to search for truth in the consideration of every subject that may employ their thoughts ; and among other branches of knowledge, it will instruct them in the skill of political architecture and jurisprudence ; and qualify them to discover any error, if there should be such, in the forms and administration of Governments, and point out the method of correcting them. But I need not press this subject, being persuaded, that this Legislature from the inclination of their minds, as well as in regard to the duty enjoined by the Constitution, will cherish " the interest of Literature, the Sciences and all their Seminaries."

Fellow-Citizens,

Legislation is within your department; yet the Constitution assigns a part to be taken by the Governor when Bills, and Resolves intended to operate as Laws, shall be presented to him, which is, merely to state objections if he has any, of which the Legislature will judge and finally determine. Let me in treat you to dispatch the weightier business, so early in the session, as to afford me opportunity to perform my duty, with due consideration and care.

I have communications to make, such as the state of the Treasury—of the military stores belonging to the Commonwealth, and others, which I will transmit to you by the Secretary.

SAMUEL ADAMS.

PROCLAMATION. FEBRUARY 19, 1794.

[*Independent Chronicle*, March 6, 1794 ; No. 3764 of the Leffingwell sale appears to have been a manuscript of this text.]

Commonwealth of Massachusetts [Seal]

BY HIS HONOR SAMUEL ADAMS, ESQ., LIEUTENANT-GOVERNOR AND COMMANDER IN CHIEF OF THE COMMONWEALTH OF MASSACHUSETTS

A PROCLAMATION FOR A DAY OF PUBLIC FASTING, HUMILIATION, AND PRAYER.

IT having been the invariable practice from time to time when our pious and renowned ancestors took possession of this land, at the approaching season of the year, to set apart a day publickly to acknowledge an entire dependence on the Father of all Mercies for every needful blessing, and to express sorrow and re-penntace for the manifold transgressions of His Holy Laws : And the Practice being highly becoming all people, especially those who profess the Christian Religion :

I HAVE thought fit, by, and with the advice of the Council to appoint THURSDAY, the *Seventeenth* day of *APRIL* next, to be observed throughout this Common-wealth, as a day of PUBLIC FASTING, HUMILIATION and PRAYER ; earnestly exhorting the Ministers of Religion to assemble with their respective Congregations on the same day—that deeply lamenting our ingratitude to our Heavenly Father, to whom we are under all possible obligations, and our many deviations from those right and safe Paths, into which, as our Supreme Governor, HE hath plainly directed us, we may with one heart and voice humbly implore His gracious and free pardon, thro' JESUS CHRIST, supplicating His Divine aid that we may become a reformed and happy people.   At the same time humbly beseeching HIM, mercifully to regard our lives and health, so that no infectious and mortal distemper may prevail amongst us : To favour our land with the alternate benefits of rain and warmth of the Sun ; and that our hopes of a plentiful harvest may not be disappointed by devouring insects, or any other calamity :—To prosper our trade and fishery, and the labor of our hands :—To protect our navigation from the rapacious hands of invaders and robbers on the seas, and graciously to open a door of deliverance to our fellow-citizens in cruel captivity in a land of Barbarians :—To continue and confirm our civil and religious liberties ; and for that great purpose to bless and direct our great University, and all Seminaries and Schools of education:— To guide and succeed the Councils of our Federal Government, as well as those of the several States in the Union, that under their respective Constitutions they may be led to such decisions as will establish the liberty, peace, safety, and honor of our country :— To inspire our friends and allies, the Republic of France, with a spirit of wisdom and true religion, that relying on the strength of His Almighty Arm, they may still go on prosperously till their arduous conflict for a government of their own, founded on the just and equal rights of men, shall be finally crowned with success :—And above all, to cause the Religion of JESUS CHRIST, in its true spirit, to spread far and wide, till the whole earth shall be filled with His glory.

And I do earnestly commend that all unnecessary labor and recreation be suspended on said day.

GIVEN *at the* Council-Chamber, *in* Boston, *the*

Nineteenth day of February *in the year of our* LORD, *One Thousand Seven Hundred and Ninety-Four, and in the* Eighteenth *Year of the* Independence *of the* United States *of* America.

SAMUEL ADAMS.

By His Honor's command, with the advice and consent of the Council, JOHN AVERY, jun. *Secr'y.*

GOD *save the Commonwealth of* Massachusetts.

TO THE LEGISLATURE OF MASSACHUSETTS. MAY 31, 1794.

[*Independent Chronicle*, June 2, 1794 ; a draft is in the Samuel Adams Papers, Lenox Library, and two manuscript texts (those sent to the Senate and House respectively) are in the Massachusetts Archives.]

FELLOW-CITIZENS !

While I attempt a short, but very respectful address to the two Branches of this new General Court, I cannot help expressing a great satisfaction in the continuance of the right which the citizens of the Commonwealth at large enjoy, of exercising their own sovereignty. In pursuance of the direction of our Constitution, which is expressive of their will, they have again in their anniversary meetings, made their free elections of such persons as they have judged meet to administer their public affairs. In this great transaction, they must surely have felt their own dignity ; and however different their sentiments may have been with regard to the men of their choice, each elector having given his suffrage according to the dictates of his own conscience, must enjoy the consoling reflection of having honestly done his duty.

Those in whom the people have placed their confidence, it is presumed will faithfully watch over, and guard their general interests, and take care that the liberties and the sovereignty of right belonging to this Commonwealth, shall suffer no diminution.

Fellow-Citizens !

We are met at a very critical period—The baneful influence of war in Europe, has already too far extended itself into this remote region. A war of Kings and Nobles against the equal Rights of Men. Their first object was to controul the common right of all civil societies, by frustrating the attempt of a magnanimous nation, to establish a Constitution of government for themselves, according to their own mind : More lately the nefarious design has been to crush the new formed Republic in its infancy :—But the GOD of Armies, who favors the brave in a righteous cause, has hitherto appeared for its protection, and crowned the astonishing efforts of its defenders with astonishing victories.

Great Britain takes an active part with the mighty combination of Kings. Indeed it does not appear that she has yet made a demand on our confederate Republic to join the league. A demand which we are well informed she has made upon some of the neutral Republics of Europe. But, whilst we have preserved the most strict neutrality towards the belligerent powers of Europe, in observance of treaties made under the authority of the United States, which are the supreme law of the land, she, for the sake of aiding the cause in which she is so deeply engaged, has employed her naval force in committing depredations on our lawful and unprotected commerce. Thus in fact, she has commenced hostilities. The Federal Government, although very solicitous if possible, to prevent the calamities of war, have meditated measures preparatory for the event. The papers and communications which I have received on this subject, shall be laid before you.

It was a declared intention of the people of the United States, when they adopted our present constitution, "to form a more perfect union"—an important object indeed. The deliberate voice of the people is commonly the voice of reason—the voice of the people ought therefore to be attended to. Union, formed upon the genuine republican principles and views of our political institutions, by combining our strength, will have a powerful tendency in a time of war to reduce an unreasonable enemy to terms of Justice, and the re-establishment of tranquility ; and in peace to secure the blessings of equal liberty to the present and future generations.

Fellow-Citizens !

It is my sincere and ardent wish, and I have a strong persuasion in my own mind, that wisdom and public spirit will guide you in all your deliberations and decisions. I will endeavor seasonably to dispatch such business as you shall lay before me during this session, and at all times, to support the true dignity of this Commonwealth in the station in which I have the honor of being placed, by a vigilant attention to its essential duties.

SAMUEL ADAMS.

TO THE LEGISLATURE OF MASSACHUSETTS. JUNE 4, 1794.

[*Independent Chronicle*, June 5, 1794; a text is in the Massachusetts Archives.]

GENTLEMEN OF THE SENATE AND
HOUSE OF REPRESENTATIVES,

By an Act of the Legislature passed on the fourteenth of March, 1785, intitled "An Act[1] providing a place of confinement for thieves, and other convicts to hard labor;" it is provided "that the Island within the harbor of Boston, commonly called Castle-Island, shall be a place for the reception, and secure confinement of all such persons as shall be sentenced for confinement and hard labor, for the term of their natural lives, or for any shorter space pursuant to the laws of the Commonwealth."

According to this, and subsequent laws, a great number of persons have been sentenced to confinement and hard labor; there are a number of them at this time under sentences, some for the term of their lives, and others for a shorter space of time.—There are particular regulations provided by the Legislature of the Commonwealth, and particular modes of discipline instituted for the government of such convicts.

This mode of punishment has been found by experience to be of great utility in the preservation of good order, and the producing of safety in the Commonwealth, and has a manifest tendency to render unnecessary those sanguinary punishments which are too frequently inflicted in other Governments.

The situation of our country now calls for fortifica-

[1] Chapter 32.

tions on our seacoasts ; and the President of the
United States has communicated the Act of Congress
for erecting forts in the harbor of Boston, which now
lies before you.   The fortification on Castle Island is
very ancient, and has always been supported by this
Government.   It is a prison for certain purposes, by
an act of the legislature of the Commonwealth, which
puts it out of my power, if I was disposed to do it, to
deliver the controul over to any other hands.   Should
that place, by act of the General Court, be given over
to the controul of the military department of the general Government, the convicts under sentence, must be
discharged, or another place of confinement be provided for them.   No government can assign the
execution of sentences passed by it to the officers of
another government, because such officers would be
under no obligation to execute the laws of a government of which they are totally independent, nor can
they be held amenable to it for any excesses, or op-
pressions in their conduct.   That fortification being
thus appropriated by the Legislature, and yet being
convenient as a place of defence, I submit it to you,
gentlemen, to determine, whether it will not be for the
interest of the Commonwealth in particular, and the
United States in general, to have it repaired at the expence of this government.   The expence will not be
great, and the utility, if not the indispensible necessity
of holding it under the controul of this state, in the
same manner, and for the same purposes for which
it has been held for several years last past, is very
obvious.

Samuel Adams.

PROCLAMATION.   NOVEMBER 3, 1794.

[*Independent Chronicle*,   November 6, 1794.]

By Authority [Seal] *Commonwealth of Massachusetts.*

BY THE GOVERNOR.

A PROCLAMATION.

IT being provided by the Seventeenth Article of the Treaty of Amity and Commerce, now subsisting between the United States of America and the French Republic, " That no shelter or refuge shall be given in the ports of either of said nations to such as shall have made prize of the subjects, people or property of either of the parties ; but if such shall come in, being forced by stress of weather, or the dangers of the sea, all proper measures shall be vigorously used, that they go out and retire from thence as soon as possible." [1]   And the Secretary of State for the Government of the said United States, having by his letter of the 10th of October last, informed me that " M. Fauchet, the Minister of the French Republic, near the United States, apprehends from circumstances which have been experienced that unless prompt and decisive measures are adopted in the several ports in regard to vessels hostile to the French Nation, and bringing in French prizes, the branch before recited, of the Treaty, will become null :" And the said Secretary having requested that measures may be taken to preserve that branch of the Treaty inviolate, by Vessels hostile to the French Nation receiving comfort in the out-ports of the Commonwealth :

---

[1] The quotation is not exact, although substantially correct.

I HAVE THEREFORE, in compliance, with the
request of the Government of the United States,
thought fit to issue this Proclamation, requiring all
Officers, Civil and Military, within this Commonwealth, to take all legal and proper measures, and
to use and practice all diligence, for the effectual
support of the above recited Article in the said Treaty.

AND I do hereby enjoin it upon them to prevent
any breach thereof, if such should be attempted in any,
and especially those ports distant from the Capital,
and immediately to give information of the same, with
their proceedings thereon, to the Governor and Commander in Chief of the Commonwealth, that such
further measures may be taken, if any shall be necessary, as may be suited to the faith of Nations, and
the solemnity of National Treaties—And I have reason to expect that the good people of the Commonwealth will cheerfully afford their aid in support of the
Laws of the land.

*Given at Boston, in the said Commonwealth, the
third day of November, in the Year of our Lord, One
Thousand Seven Hundred and Ninety-four, and in
the Nineteenth Year of the Independence of the United
States of America.*

SAMUEL ADAMS.

Attest,

JOHN AVERY, jun. Sec'y.

TO THE LEGISLATURE OF MASSACHUSETTS. JANUARY 16, 1795.

[*Independent Chronicle*, January 19, 1795 ; the copies sent to the two houses
are in the Massachusetts Archives.]

I am happy, fellow citizens, to meet you in General

Court assembled, on the day to which, according to your request, you have stood adjourned. By the Constitution, the Governor, with the advice of Council, during the session of the General Court, hath full authority to adjourn them to such times as the two branches may judge most convenient.

The people of this Commonwealth, in their declaration of rights, have recorded their own opinion, that the Legislature ought frequently to assemble for the redress of grievances, correcting, strengthening and confirming the Laws, and making new Laws, as the common good may require.—The Laws of the Commonwealth are intended to secure to each and all the Citizens, their own rights and liberties, and the property which they honestly possess. If there are any instances wherein the Laws in being, are inadequate to these great and capital ends, your eye will discern the evil, and your wisdom will provide a suitable remedy. It shall be my endeavour, as indeed it is my duty, carefully to revise and readily approve your Bills and Resolves, which may be calculated for the public good.

By the late returns of the votes for Representatives to serve the Commonwealth in Congress, there were several districts in which no choice had been effected. I immediately issued precepts according to law, requiring the several towns within those Districts to meet on a day now past, in order to complete their elections. I cannot but recommend to your consideration, whether it may not be necessary more effectually to guard the elections of public agents and officers against illegal practices. All elections ought

to be free, and every qualified elector who feels his
own independence as he ought, will act his part according to his best, and most enlightened judgment.
Elections are the immediate acts of the people's sovereignty, in which no foreigners should be allowed to
intermeddle. Upon free and unbiassed elections, the
purity of the government, and consequently the safety
and welfare of the citizens, may I not say altogether
depend.

If we continue to be a happy people, that happiness must be assured by the enacting and executing
of reasonable and wise laws, expressed in the plainest
language, and by establishing such modes of education as tend to inculcate in the minds of youth, the
feelings and habits of "piety, religion and morality,"
and to lead them to the knowledge and love of those
truly Republican principles upon which our civil institutions are founded. We have solemnly engaged
ourselves, fellow citizens, to support the Constitution of
the United States, and the Constitution of this Commonwealth. This must be reconcileable in the mind
of any man, who judiciously considers the sovereign
rights of the one as limited to federal purposes, and
the sovereign rights of the other, as acting upon and
directing the internal concerns of our own Republic.

We have been under apprehensions of being made
a party in the dissolating contest in Europe. Permit
me just to observe, that the first and main principle
which urged the Combined Powers to enter into the
contest, is in my own opinion unsupportable by reason
and nature, and in violation of the most essential
right of nations and of men. The repeated acts of

violence which have been committed on the property
of American citizens, might in the opinion of some,
have justified reprisals ; but the policy of the Federal
Government has directed to other measures.   The
wisdom of our own Councils, with the unexampled
successes of our magnanimous Ally, the Republic of
France, afford the strongest ground of hope, that
under the continued smiles of Divine Providence,
peace and tranquility, so interesting to a rising
Republic, will in the end be firmly established.

The business of fortifying certain harbors within
this Commonwealth, according to an act of Congress,
was left unfinished in your last session.   It is indeed
probable, that the danger which produced that measure, has nearly subsided ; but the law still exists, and
in my opinion it cannot be carried into constitutional
effect in this Commonwealth, without the aid of the
Legislature of the same.   I am led to this opinion
by contemplating the first article of the Constitution
of the United States, which establishes the powers of
Congress and which particularly authorises them to
exercise exclusive legislation in all cases whatever,
over all places purchased by the consent of the Legislature of the States, in which the same shall be for
the erection of Forts Magazines, and other public
buildings.

Those who wish to persuade the world to believe,
that a free representative Republic cannot be supported, will no doubt make use of every art to injure,
and by degrees to alter, and finally to eradicate the
principles of our free Constitutions : But the virtuous
and enlightened citizens of this Commonwealth, and

of all united America, have understanding and firmness, sufficient to support those Constitutions of Civil
Government which they have themselves formed,
and which have done them so much honor in the
estimation of the world.

It is with pain that I mention the insurrection
which has lately taken place in a sister state.[1] It was
pointed more immediately at an act of the Federal
Government. An act of that government, as well as
of the governments in the Union, is constitutionally
an act of the people, and our Constitutions provide a
safe and easy method to redress any real grievances.
No people can be more free under a Constitution
established by their own voluntary compact, and
exercised by men appointed by their own frequent
suffrages. What excuse then can there be for for-
cible opposition to the laws? If any law shall prove
oppressive in its operation, the future deliberations
of a freely elective Representative, will afford a constitutional remedy. But the measures adopted by
The President of the United States, supported by
the virtue of citizens of every description, in that,
and the adjacent states, have prevailed, and there is
an end of the insurrection. Let the glory be given
to Him, who alone governs all events, while we express the just feelings of respect and gratitude due to
all those, whom He honours as instruments to carry
into effect his gracious designs.

I congratulate you on the success which the forces
of the United States, have lately had against the

---

[1] The " whisky insurrection," in Pennsylvania.

hostile Indians. It is my hearty wish that by the blessing of Heaven, an end may be put to this expensive war, by an agreement between the parties, upon the permanent principles of justice, honor, good neighborhood, & true friendship.

The Constitution of this Commonwealth, having provided that the General Court which shall be in the year of our Lord, one thousand seven hundred and ninety five, shall issue precepts for collecting the sentiments of the people in regard to its revision.— And as this Court is within the year mentioned, you will be pleased to decide, whether it was intended by the people that this business should be done by the General Court which shall be elected within that year, or whether it is your duty to attend to it.

I will lay before you several papers transmitted to me by the Treasurer and other matters which may occur during the Session by subsequent messages.

Samuel Adams.

TO JEREMY BELKNAP.

[*Collections* of Massachusetts Historical Society, 1st ser., vol. iv., p. 83; a draft is in the Samuel Adams Papers, Lenox Library.]

Boston, March 30, 1795.

Sir,

I received your note, stating what Dr. Kippis had asserted, respecting a recommendation of Dr. Franklin, minister from America in France, in the year 1779, to the American cruisers, to treat Capt. Cook, on his expected return from a voyage of discoveries, as a friend, and not an enemy; assuring them, that in so doing, they would obtain the approbation of Congress. But that the Doctor was mistaken, for that assembly, at least the greater part of them, instantly reversed the order of Dr. Franklin, and directed, that a special order should be taken, to seize Capt. Cook, if an opportunity for doing it occurred.

You request me to give you a certificate respecting the matter, and to express the years when I was in Congress.—I was a member from the first sitting of Congress, in the year 1774, until the Spring of the year 1781. It was my constant practice, once in twelve or fifteen months, to make a short visit to my constituents. In the year 1779, I was detained in Boston a much longer time than usual, by a fit of sickness; in which time, I constantly received from Mr. Lowell, and my other colleagues, information of the most material transactions of Congress. I do now declare to you, that I do not recollect, either while I was present in Congress, or from any of my colleagues, while I was absent, that the orders he (Dr. Franklin) had given to the American cruisers were instantly or ever reversed, or that it was directed by Congress, that a special order should be taken to seize Capt. Cook, if an opportunity for so doing it occurred.

It appears to me that Dr. Kippis must have been misinformed. I am, with respect, your friend and humble servant,

---

TO THE LEGISLATURE OF MASSACHUSETTS.   JUNE 3, 1795.

[*Independent Chronicle*, June 4, 1795; a text is in the Massachusetts Archives.]

FELLOW CITIZENS,

The honor which the people have again conferred

on me, by a majority of their votes for a Governor of
this respectable Commonwealth, while it excites the
warm feelings of gratitude in my heart, it reminds me
of the arduous task I am called to undertake, and the
many attentions which are requisite for a performance
of the great duties of the station. Having already
been qualified agreeable to the Constitution and
Laws, next to a dependence upon Him who is the
Fountain of all Wisdom, I must rely upon your
candor, and that of my Fellow Citizens at large.

The sovereignty of a nation, always of right, resides
in the body of the People ; and while they have delegated to their freely elected Legislative, the power of
exercising that sovereignty in their behalf, the Executive department, as well as the Magistrates who are
appointed to render the Constitution efficient by
carrying the laws into effect, are no less important to
the people. For what avails the making of good
and wholesome laws, unless they are duly executed.
As the happiness of civil society may in a great
measure depend upon a wise and a consistent harmony between the various branches of the Government ; a free communication may have a tendency to
cultivate and extend the blessings of friendship and
good humor. Indeed our constituents, under whose
authority and for whose benefit we are to exercise
the functions of our different departments, have a
right to expect from us, as their public agents, to
avow our principles and intentions, and make them
acquainted with the true situation of their public
affairs.

In the addresses from the Chair, while it was filled

by Royal appointment, uniform attempts were made
to strengthen the prerogatives of the Crown, and to
bring the people obsequiously at the foot of the
Throne, for privileges holden by sufferance : Surely
it becomes us, in our happy state of Independence, to
turn our attentive minds to the great objects of securing the equal rights of the citizens, and rendering
those constitutions which they have voluntarily established, respectable and efficacious.

Our ancestors, when under the greatest hardships
and perils, they opened to us the wilderness, they took
possession of, and left for us an inheritance, one of
the best countries under the sun.   Amidst their toil,
and fatigue they extended their views, and early laid
the foundation of Civil Liberty.   Although they had
in prospect, the instruction of future youth in all liter-
ary science, they considered morality and real goodness of heart, as the great basis upon which the best
interests of a nation could be safely laid.   Under this
idea, they also provided for the institutions of Public
Worship, and the support of teachers in Piety, Religion and Morality.   The great increase of our numbers
& happiness, is a standing witness to the world, of the
wisdom of their measures.   Oppressed as they were by
the supercilious haughtiness of royal prerogative, and
considered as a contemptible people at a distance from
the favors of the Crown, and the flattering smiles of
courtiers, their perseverance has in effect raised us, by
the blessing of Providence, to an exalted degree of
prosperity and glory.

Fellow Citizens, we have a regular exercise of our
Federal and State Governments ; and we owe our un-

ceasing gratitude to the Supreme Ruler of the Universe, who safely carried us through our arduous struggle for freedom, for which other nations are now contending, at the expence of their blood and treasure. We cannot but rejoice that the principles for which we contended, and which are constitutionally established in United America, are irresistibly spreading themselves through two mighty nations in Europe. We are now able to embrace those powerful sister Republics ; and what adds much to our joy on this occasion is, that those nations became allied to us in an hour, when we were engaged in our hard conflict with an oppressive tyranny.

We ardently wish that the nations of the earth may sheath the sword of war, and we as ardently pray, that the equal rights of men may go hand in hand with peace. If our Federal Government shall with magnanimity and firmness, support the principles of a free elective Representative Government, and our honour and faith with our allies, and yet maintain peace with all nations upon the principles of sound policy, and terms honourable and safe to our country, it will be an acknowledged approximation to that perfection in practical politics, which all people should most earnestly covet.

It is with satisfaction that I have observed the patriotic exertions of worthy citizens, to establish Academies in various parts of this Commonwealth. It discovers a zeal highly to be commended. But while it is acknowledged, that great advantages have been derived from these institutions, perhaps it may be justly apprehended, that multiplying them, may have a tendency to injure the ancient and beneficial mode of Education in Town Grammar Schools. The peculiar advantage of such schools is, that the poor and the rich may derive equal benefit from them ; but none excepting the more wealthy, generally speaking, can avail themselves of the benefits of the Academies. Should these institutions detach the attention and influence of the wealthy, from the generous support of town Schools, is it not to be feared that useful learning, instruction and social feelings in the early parts of life, may cease to be so equally and universally disseminated, as it has heretofore been. I have thrown out these hints with a degree of diffidence in my own mind. You will take them into your candid consideration, if you shall think them worthy of it. In support of the public Schools, from whence have flowed so many great benefits, our University has from its infancy furnished them with well educated and fit persons to fill the places of Instructors ; and they, in return, have yearly brought forward fit pupils for the further instruction of the University.—The University therefore claims a place among the first attentions of the public.

The citizens of the Commonwealth have lately had before them a question of the expediency of revising, at this period, the form of our present Constitution. The conduct of the citizens on this occasion, has given full proof, that an enlightened, free and virtuous people, can as a body, be the keepers of their own Liberties, and the guardians of their own rights. On which side soever the question may have been decided, I have the pleasure of being informed that it has been discussed with propriety, calmness and deliberation. If the event should be in favour of a Convention, a future revision may be made at such period as may be most fit and convenient, and there may be opportunity, in the mean time, for the citizens at their leisure, to make their own remarks upon the Constitution, in its operation, and thus prepare themselves for cool deliberation, at another revision. Should the determination be otherwise, I think it will clearly follow, that the citizens are happy under the present Constitution, and that they feel themselves well assured, that if there should be a future necessity for it, they can, in a peaceable and orderly manner, revise, alter and amend it at their pleasure.

A compleat, perfect and permanent system of jurisprudence, is one of the greatest blessings which our country can possess. To have justice administered promptly and without delay, is to gather the best fruits of a free and regular Government. Uncorrupted Juries are an effectual guard against the violations of our rights and property. Having an Executive annually elected, and the Legislative elected as often, the one branch of which is the grand inquest of the Commonwealth, and the other branch to be constituted a Court, as there may be occasion, to try and determine upon impeachments, we may be secured against impartiality in the fountain, and corruption in the streams of justice. The Legislative will examine all the machinery by which the Government acts : Too frequent speculative experiments may tend to render the motions unsteady, and to annex insecurity to property. Where there are no radical defects, a long exercise of Judicial Authority, in any particular mode, brings the feelings of the people in unison with it, and fixes habits to which they have been accustomed.

While we expect from our Judges and Magistrates and other civil officers that justice be administered with alacrity and impartiality, should we not be careful that ample justice be done to them. The administration of justice should indeed be without oppressive or unnecessary expences on the people ; but the Ministers of justice should have an equitable reward for their services. If therefore from accident or peculiar or temporary circumstances, the established rewards are inadequate, I doubt not but you will determine, that what is fit and proper, will be done. The Executive should be enabled to find men of superior knowledge and integrity, who may be inclined to fill the important places in the Civil Departments, as they shall become vacant. On such appointments, the dignity and just authority of the Government very materially depends.

The Legislative will no doubt continue to guard the public credit, by adequate provisions for discharging the interest and finally sinking the principal of our public debt. The sale of our vacant Lands, and the debts due to the Treasury, will contribute to ease the people from too great a burthen of direct taxes. The Treasurer's statements will ascertain the demands necessary for the ensuing year.

I must intreat you to give me opportunity to revise such Bills and Resolves as you may think proper to lay before me, to which I shall cheerfully attend, and do all within my power to dispatch the public business, and render the session agreeable to you, and beneficial to the Commonwealth.

Let us, Fellow Citizens, cultivate a due observance of the Laws which are constitutionally made by the authority of this Government, as well as those of the Federal Government, agreeable to the Constitution of the United States. Let us transmit our Liberties, our Equal Rights, our Laws and our free Republican Constitutions, with their various concomitant blessings, to those who are coming upon the stage of action, and hope in God, that they will be handed down, in purity and energy, to the latest posterity.

SAMUEL ADAMS.

ADDRESS JULY 4, 1795.

[*Independent Chronicle*, July 6, 1795.]

FELLOW CITIZENS,

The Representatives of the people in the General Court assembled did solemnly Resolve, that an Edifice be erected upon this spot of ground for the purpose of holding the Public Council of the Commonwealth of *Massachusetts*. By the request of their Agents and Commissioners, I do now lay the Corner Stone.

May the Superstructure be raised even to the top Stone without any untoward accident, and remain permanent as the everlasting mountains.—May the principles of our excellent Constitution, founded in nature and in the Rights of Man be ably defended here : And may the same principles be deeply engraven on the hearts of all citizens, and thereby fixed unimpaired and in full vigor till time shall be no more.

PROCLAMATION.   OCTOBER 14, 1795.

[*Independent Chronicle*, October 19, 1795.]

Published by Authority [Seal] *Commonwealth of Massachusetts.*

BY THE GOVERNOR.

A PROCLAMATION FOR A DAY OF PUBLIC THANKSGIVING AND PRAISE.

FORASMUCH as the occasional meeting of a People for the exercise of Piety and Devotion towards God, more especially of those who enjoy the Light of Divine Revelation, has a strong tendency to impress their minds with a sense of Dependence upon HIM and their Obligations to HIM.

I have thought fit, according to the ancient and laudable Practice of our renowned ancestors, to appoint a day of Public Thanksgiving to God, for the great benefits which HE has been pleased to bestow upon us, in the Year past.   And I do by advice and consent of the Council, appoint THURSDAY the *Nineteenth* day of November next, to be observed as a DAY of PUBLIC THANKSGIVING and PRAISE throughout this Commonwealth : Calling upon the Ministers of the Gospel of all Denominations, with their respective Congregations to assemble on that Day to offer to God, their unfained Gratitude, for his great

Goodness to the People of the United States in general, and of this Commonwealth in particular.

More especially in that he hath in his Good Providence united the several States under a National Compact formed by themselves, whereby they may defend themselves against external Enemies, and maintain Peace and Harmony with each other.

That internal tranquillity has been continued within this Commonwealth ; and that the voice of Health is so generally heard in the habitations of the People.

That the Earth has yielded her increase, so that the labours of our industrious Husbandmen have been abundantly crowned with Plenty.

That our Fisheries have been so far prospered.— Our Trade notwithstanding obstructions it has met with, has yet been profitable to us, and the works of our Hands have been established.

That while other nations have been involved in War, attended with an uncommon profusion of Human Blood, we in the course of Divine Providence, have been preserved from so grievous a Calamity, and have enjoyed so great a measure of the Blessing of Peace.

And I do recommend that together with our Thanksgiving, humble Prayer may be offered to God, that we may be enabled, by the subsequent obedience of our Hearts and Manners, to testify the sincerity of our professions of Gratitude, in the sight of God and Man ; and thus be prepared for the Reception of future Divine Blessings.

That God would be pleased to Guide and Direct the Administration of the Federal Government, and those of the several States, in Union, so that the whole People may continue to be safe and happy in the Constitutional enjoyment of their Rights, Liberties and Privileges, and our Governments be greatly respected at Home and Abroad.

And while we rejoice in the Blessing of Health bestowed upon us, we would sympathize with those of our Sister States, who are visited with a Contagious and Mortal Disease ; and fervently supplicate the FATHER of Mercies that they may speedily be restored to a state of Health and Prosperity.

That HE would in HIS abundant Mercy regard our fellow Citizens and others, who are groaning under abject Slavery, in Algiers, and direct the most effectual measures for their speedy Relief.

That HE would graciously be pleased to put an end to all Tyranny and Usurpation, that the People who are under the Yoke of Oppression, may be made free ; and that the Nations who are contending for freedom may still be secured by HIS Almighty Aid, and enabled under HIS influence to complete wise systems of Civil Government, founded in the equal Rights of Men and calculated to establish their permanent Security and Welfare.

And Finally, that the Peaceful and Glorious Reign of our Divine Redeemer may be known and enjoyed throughout the whole Family of Mankind.

And I do recommend to the People of this Commonwealth, to abstain from all such Labour and Recreation, as may not be consistent with the Solemnity of the said Day.

Given at the Council-Chamber, in *Boston*, the

fourteenth Day of *October* in the Year of our LORD, One Thousand seven Hundred and Ninety-five, and in the Twentieth Year of the Independence of the United States of *America*.

SAMUEL ADAMS.

True Copy—*Attest*,
JOHN AVERY, jun. *Sec'ry*.
God save the Commonwealth of Massachusetts!

TO THE LEGISLATURE OF MASSACHUSETTS. JANUARY 19, 1796.

[*Independent Chronicle*, January 21, 1796; two texts are in the Massachusetts Archives.]

FELLOW CITIZENS,

I CANNOT but congratulate you upon the many blessings which the bountiful hand of Providence has bestowed upon us since your adjournment.

We with our Fellow Citizens at large have observed a day solemnly to recognize these blessings; and if sincere obedience to our gracious Benefactor, shall accompany the gratitude which we then professed, we may humbly rely upon him that he will continue his divine favors to the citizens at large, and direct the public councils of our Nation and Commonwealth to such measures as shall be productive of the safety and welfare of all.

In my former address to this General Court I mentioned the duty required by the Constitution, frequently to revise the laws, and amend such of them as may still be necessary to secure the lives, liberty

and property of the citizens—The importance of civil
commutative justice and the good policy of making
adequate compensations to those who administer well
—and the great advantages of cherishing the interests
of literature and the sciences, and all seminaries of
them among the body of the people.   Upon these I
shall not now enlarge.

Agriculture and Commerce mutually depend upon
each other.   As foreign markets are supplied from
our fields, it is an object of importance, that the
transportation of heavy articles, and means of communication from one part of the State to another,
may be rendered as easy and cheap as the nature of
the country will admit.   By the spirit of enterprize,
which so remarkably animates the citizens, countenanced by the Legislature, much has been done and
is still doing in various parts of the Commonwealth.

The improvement of Arts and Manufactures is of
interesting moment.   The encouragement of such
manufactures *in particular*, as will diminish the consumption of Foreign Articles and exhibit a real balance in our favor, is the common concern of the whole
Union—Such encouragement as will spread the spirit
of Industry individually through the body of the people, will tend to increase their happy feelings of Independence, and give them an exalted idea of the *truly
noble* character of Free Citizens.   Industry naturally
leads to sobriety of sentiment, rectitude of manners,
a due observance of wise and constitutional laws, and
of course to public and private virtue.

Fellow Citizens,

It is wisdom often to recur to first principles.

The people of this Commonwealth, as well as those
of the United States, have voluntarily formed such
constitutions of government, as they have judged well
adapted to secure their own political safety.—These
Constitutions are founded upon the same principles;
and they avow the great and fundamental political
truth that all power is derived from the people. As
these and all new forms of Government which recognize principles, never reduced to practice until the
period of our illustrious Revolution must be in their
nature *experiments*, the provision of a peaceable and
constitutional remedy for such defects as experience
may point out, is with great propriety established in
our State and National Governments.—The citizens
of this Commonweath, have lately discovered their
acquiescence under their Constitution as it now
stands.   But it still remains recorded in our declaration of rights, that the people *alone* have an incon-
testible, unalienable and indefeasible right to institute
government; & to reform, alter, or totally change the
same when their protection, safety, prosperity and
happiness require it.   And the Federal Constitution,
according to the mode prescribed therein has already
undergone such amendments in several parts of it, as
from *experience* has been judged necessary.

The Government of the United States is entrusted
solely with such powers as regard our safety as a nation; and all powers not given to Congress by the
Constitution remain in the individual States and the
people.   In all good Governments the Legislative,
Executive and Judiciary powers are confined within
the limits of their respective Departments.   If there-

fore it should be found that the Constitutional rights of
our federal and local Governments should on either
side be infringed, or that either of the Departments
aforesaid should interfere with another, it will, if continued, essentially alter the Constitution, and may in
time, I hope far distant, be productive of such con-
vulsions as may shake the political ground upon
which we now happily stand.

Under these impressions, I cannot forbear to mention to you a subject which has lately arrested the
public attention and employed the pens of ingenious
men of different sentiments concerning it. In dis-
cussing a subject so exceedingly momentous as a
national Treaty, no personal attachment or prejudice,
no private or selfish feelings, no arts of deception
should be suffered to intermingle : Truth should be
the object, and reason the guide.

By the Constitution of the United States, it is provided, that all Legislative powers therein granted,
shall be vested in a Congress, to consist of a Senate
and a House of Representatives. These several
branches have, and exercise a positive negative upon
each other : No Legislative act, therefore, can pass
without their joint concurrence. But in another part
of the Constitution, under the head of Executive, *the
President* has the power with the advice and consent
of the Senate, provided two thirds of the Senate
present, concur, to make Treaties ; and all Treaties
which are made or shall be made under the authority
of the United States, shall be among the Supreme
Laws of the Land : The Senate therefore partakes
with the Executive, so far as to advise and consent ;

but the most popular branch of Congress has no concern therein. I do earnestly recommend to you to turn your attention to those parts of the Constitution, at least, which relate to the Legislative and Executive powers, and judge for yourself, whether they may not be construed to militate with each other and lead to an absurd conclusion—that there actually exists in the Government of the United States, two distinct and decisive Legislatives.

I am far from being desirous that unnecessary alterations of our Constitution, should be proposed : but it is of great consequence to the liberties of a nation, to review its civil Constitution and compare the practice of its administrators with the essential principles upon which it is founded. We, fellow-citizens, are under the strongest obligations, from the solemnity of our mutual compacts, and even our sacred oaths, with a watchful eye at every point to defend and support our Constitutions ; and to strengthen the essential principles upon which they are founded, when it shall be needful, falls in my opinion within those solemn obligations.

I hope, fellow-citizens, that what I am now about to say will not be deemed improper.

I have been accustomed to speak my mind upon matters of great moment to our common country with freedom ; and every citizen of the United States has the same right that I have. I may never hereafter have an opportunity of publicly expressing my opinion on the Treaty made with the Court of London : I am therefore constrained with all due respect to our Constituted Authority to declare, that the Treaty appears to me to be pregnant with evil. It controuls some of the powers specially vested in Congress for the security of the people; and I fear that it may restore to Great Britain such an influence over the Government and people of this country as may not be consistent with the general welfare. This subject however it is expected will come before the Congress whose immediate province it is to discuss it, and to determine, so far as it may be in their power, as they shall think, for the safety and welfare of the *people*.

I shall use my best endeavor to dispatch the business which you shall lay before me. And it is my cordial wish that all your decisions may tend to the prosperity of the Commonwealth, and afford to you the most agreeable reflections.

SAMUEL ADAMS.

TO THE LEGISLATURE OF MASSACHUSETTS. MAY 31, 1796.

[*Independent Chronicle*, June 2, 1796; two texts are in the Massachusetts Archives.]

FELLOW CITIZENS,

It is not my intention to interrupt your business by a lengthy Address. I have requested a meeting with you at this time, principally with a view of familiarizing the several branches of government with each other, of cultivating harmony in sentiment upon constitutional principles, and cherishing that mutual friendship which always invites a free discussion in matters of important concern.

The Union of the States is not less important than that of the several departments of each of them. We have all of us recently laid ourselves under a sacred obligation to defend and support our Federal and State Constitutions : A principal object in the establishment of the former, as it is expressed in the preamble, was " to form a more perfect Union : " To preserve this Union entire, and transmit it unbroken to posterity, is the duty of the People of United America, and it is for their lasting interest, their public safety and welfare. Let us then be watchful for the preservation of the Union, attentive to the fundamental principles of our free Constitutions, and careful in the application of those principles in the formation of our laws, lest that great object which the people had in view in establishing the independence of our country, may be imperceptibly lost.

The Members of the General Court, coming from all parts of the Commonwealth, must be well acquainted with the local circumstances and wants of the citizens; to alleviate and provide for which, it is presumed you will diligently enquire into the state of the Commonwealth, and render such Legislative aid as may be found necessary, for the promoting of useful improvements, and the advancement of those kinds of industry among the people, which contribute to their individual happiness, as well as that of the public.—Honest industry, tends to the increase of sobriety, temperance and all the moral and political virtues—I trust also that you will attend to the general police of the Commonwealth, by revising and making such laws and ordinances, conformably to our Constitution, as in your wisdom you may think further necessary to secure as far as possible, the safety and prosperity of the people at large.

It is yours, Fellow Citizens, to legislate, and mine only to revise your bills, under limited and qualified powers; and I rejoice, that they are thus limited :— These are features which belong to a free government alone.

I do not, I ought not to forget that there are other important duties constitutionally attached to the Supreme Executive—I hope I shall be enabled within my department, with the continued advice of a wise and faithful Council, so to act my part, as that a future retrospect of my conduct may afford me consoling reflections; and that my administration may be satisfactory to reasonable and candid men, and finally meet with the approbation of God, the Judge of all.—May his wisdom preside in all our Councils and deliberations, and lead to such decisions as may be happily adapted to confirm and perpetuate the public liberty, and secure the private and personal rights of the citizens from suffering any injury.

I shall further communicate to you by subsequent message as occasion may offer.

SAMUEL ADAMS.

PROCLAMATION.   OCTOBER 6, 1796.

[*Independent Chronicle*, October 17, 1796.]

Published by Authority [Seal] *Commonwealth of Massachusetts.*

BY THE GOVERNOR.

A PROCLAMATION FOR A DAY OF PUBLIC THANKSGIVING.

WHEREAS it has pleased God, the Father of all

Mercies, to bestow upon us innumerable unmerited favours in the course of the year past; it highly becomes us duly to recollect his goodness, and in a public and solemn manner to express the greatful feelings of our hearts:

I have therefore thought fit, with the advice and consent of the Council, to appoint THURSDAY the 15th day of *December* next, to be observed as a Day of PUBLIC THANKSGIVING and PRAISE to our Divine BENEFACTOR throughout this Commonwealth—Calling upon the Ministers of the Gospel, with their respective Congregations, and the whole body of the People, religiously to observe the said Day by celebrating the Praises of that all-gracious Being, of whose Bounty we have experienced so large a share.

He hath prevented Epidemical Diseases from spreading, and afforded us a general state of Health. *He* hath regarded our Pastures and Fields with an Eye of the most indulgent Parent, and rewarded the Industry of our Husbandmen with a plentiful Harvest.

Notwithstanding the unreasonable obstructions to our trade on the seas, it has generally been prosperous and our fisheries successful.

Our civil Constitutions of Government, formed by ourselves, and administered by Men of our own *free Election*, are by His Grace continued to us. And we still enjoy the inestimable Blessings of the Gospel and right of worshipping God according to *His* own Institutions and the honest dictates of our Consciences.

And, together with our thanksgiving, earnest Supplication to God is hereby recommended for the forgiveness of our Sins which have rendered us unworthy of the least of his Mercies ; and that by the sanctifying influence of his Spirit, our hearts and manners may be corrected, and we become a reformed and happy People—That he would direct and prosper the Administration of the Government of the United States, and of this and the other States in the Union. That he would still afford his Blessings on our Trade, Agriculture, Fisheries and all the labours of our hands. That he would smile upon our University, and all Seminaries of Learning—That Tyranny and Usurpation may everywhere come to an end—That the Nations who are contending for true liberty may still be succeeded by his Almighty aid—That every Nation and Society of Men may be inspired with the knowledge and feeling of their natural and just rights, and enabled to form such systems of Civil Government as shall be fully adopted to promote and establish their Social Security and Happiness—And, finally, that in the course of God's Holy Providence, the great Family of Mankind may bow to the sceptre of the Prince of Peace so that mutual Friendship and Harmony may universally prevail.

And I do recommend to the People of this Commonwealth to abstain from all such Labours and Recreations as may not be consistent with the Solemnity of the said Day.

Given at the Council Chamber in Boston, this sixth day of October, in the year of our Lord, one Thousand seven Hundred and Ninety-six, and in the twenty-first

Year of the Independence of the United States of America.

SAMUEL ADAMS.

Attest

JOHN AVERY, *Sec'ry*

GOD save the Commonwealth of Massachusetts !

TO THE LEGISLATURE OF MASSACHUSETTS. NOVEMBER 17, 1796.

[*Independent Chronicle*, November 21, 1796 ; two texts are in the Massachusetts Archives.]

You are sensible, Fellow Citizens, that the principal motive which induced your adjournment to the 16th current, was to transact the business prescribed by law, respecting the Electors of a President and Vice-President of the United States of America.

Not being able to determine in my own mind, whether you would probably be inclined to begin the business of a winter session at this season, or not, I did, by the advice of the Council, appoint a later day for a Public Thanksgiving, than has been usual ; intending thereby, to afford you an opportunity to finish the business above mentioned, and, if you should then think it proper, keep the festival in your respective families. This matter, however, it becomes me to leave to your own discretion. Which ever, you may determine upon, while you continue this session, I will endeavour to finish the business which you may lay before me, with all convenient dispatch, always considering, that harmony and union among the several branches and governmental powers, consistent with their respective Constitutional rights and duties, to be essential to the security and welfare of our constituents at large.

SAMUEL ADAMS.

TO THE SENATE OF MASSACHUSETTS.   NOVEMBER 23, 1796.

[*Independent Chronicle*, November 28, 1796.]

GENTLEMEN OF THE SENATE,

HAVING had before me a Resolve of the 22d inst. providing for filling up any vacancies in the Electors of President and Vice President of the United States, which may be occasioned by death or resignation before the time of their meeting for the purpose of giving their suffrages, have permaturely approved the same; since which, having more fully considered the subject, I find a strong objection operating upon my mind, and I have erased my name: That the Electors chosen by the People and their Representatives for the great and important purpose of electing a President and Vice-President of the United States, should have the power of filling up vacancies in their own body, under any circumstances whatever, appears to be dangerous to the Liberties of the People, and ought not to form a precedent in a free government. If upon further deliberation you should be of my opinion, I shall be happy to concur with you, in a mode more consonant to the spirit of our government.

SAMUEL ADAMS.

TO THE LEGISLATURE OF MASSACHUSETTS. NOVEMBER 24, 1796.

[*Independent Chronicle*, November 28, 1796 ; a text is in the Massachusetts Archives, and a draft is in the Samuel Adams Papers, Lenox Library.]

Gentlemen of the Senate,
*   and Gentlemen of the House of Representatives.*

BY a Message, which I yesterday laid before the Senate, I gave a full, free and candid account of my proceedings respecting a Resolve of the two Houses, for filling up vacancies which may possibly happen in the Electors of President and Vice-President of the United States.

My mode of conduct on this occasion, I know is, and I flatter myself, will be considered, to be as well the result of an ardent wish to preserve free, important and secure the Elections of those very important Officers, as a desire to dispatch the business at this juncture before the Legislature.—I wish to promote the true interest of my country—I have no other object in view; and therefore, it can be of no consequence to me, in what mode this question is discussed nor in what form your opinions shall be expressed. I am not, at present, for supporting the idea that after the Resolve had been signed by me, and delivered to the Secretary, that it was not a formal act of government. Be that as it may—the question is now properly before the General Court, and if the Resolve, to which I have made an objection, was, under all considerations an Act of the Government upon my signing the same, the only question now is whether it ought to be repealed, and another provision made for the same object ?

My objection to the Resolve, or my reason why it should be repealed, (if it is one) is, that a delegation by the Legislature to the Electors appointed by the Citizens in their individual capacity for the Election of President and Vice President, to fill up vacancies in their own number, by death or resignation, is a dangerous power, and tends to the establishing a dangerous Precedent; but should my fellow citizens of the Senate and House, think differently from me, while I shall feel quite contented with your decision, I shall be happy, that I have candidly acknowledged an error in signing that Resolve, and yet done, with firmness, what has appeared to me as the true interest of the State of which I am a Member, and of a Nation of which I am a Citizen.

SAMUEL ADAMS.

TO THE LEGISLATURE OF MASSACHUSETTS. JANUARY 27, 1797.

[*Independent Chronicle*, January 30, 1797; a text is in the Massachusetts Archives].

FRIENDS AND FELLOW-CITIZENS,

SINCE your last adjournment, the President of the United States has officially announced to the Legislature of the Union his determination to retire from the cares of public life.—When a citizen so distinguished by his country withdraws himself from the Councils of the Nation, and retires to peaceful repose, it must afford very pleasurable feelings in his own mind, to be conscious of the good will of the people towards him—how much more consoling must his feelings be, in reflecting that he has served them many years with purity of intention and disinterested zeal. We sincerely wish him tranquility in his retirement and strong consolation in the latter stage of life.

In pursuance of the provision in the Constitution, the people have recently exercised their own sovereign power in the election of another President. Elections to offices, even in the smallest Corporations, are and ought to be deemed highly important; of how much more importance is it, that elections to the highest offices in our extensive Republic, should be conducted in a manner and with a spirit becoming a free, virtuous and enlightened people, who justly estimate the value of their sacred rights. In the late elections, the people have turned their attention to several citizens, who have rendered eminent services to our federal Commonwealth in exalted stations. Upon which ever of the Candidates the lot may have fallen, the people have reason to expect, that his administration will be strictly conformable to the letter and true intent of the Constitution, that it may long continue to be the guarantee of our freely elective Republican Government.—On fair and uncontrouled elections, depend, under God, the whole superstructure of our government—should corruption ever insert itself in our elections, there would be great danger of corruption in our governments.—Although it is not long since the subject of elections was under the consideration of the Legislature, and a law passed for the purpose of further security to the people in the free exercise of this invaluable right; yet give me leave to suggest for your consideration, whether still further securities may not be provided, so that the rightful electors may not be frustrated in their honest intentions. That elections may not be contaminated by strangers, or unqualified persons, may it not be necessary that every man may be known, as far as possible, when he presents himself to give his vote; this may be more especially important in our seaports and other populous towns, in which many foreigners of all sorts frequently reside. I would be far from dictating to you, but I would submit to your judgment whether, considering the liberality of this country to foreigners, and the frequency of their naturalizations, it may not be eligible that such foreigners should be required when they offer their votes to the Selectmen of the towns, to produce authentic certificates from the Courts, by which they were endowed with so high a privilege, as a test of their citizenship.

As Piety, Religion and Morality have a happy influence on the minds of men, in their public as well as private transactions, you will not think it unseasonable, although I have frequently done it, to bring to your remembrance the great importance of encouraging our University, town schools, and other seminaries of education, that our children and youth while they are engaged in the pursuit of useful science, may have their minds impressed with a strong sense of the duties they owe to their God, their instructors, and each other, so that when they arrive to a state of manhood, and take a part in any public transactions, their hearts having been deeply impressed in the course of their education with the moral feelings—

such feelings may continue and have their due weight through the whole of their future lives.

Permit me to call your attention to the subject of the Militia of the Commonwealth.—A well regulated militia " held in an exact subordination to the civil authority and governed by it," is the most safe de fence of a Republic.—In our Declaration of Rights, which expresses the sentiments of the people, the people have a right to keep and bear arms for the common defence. The more generally therefore they are called out to be disciplined, the stronger is our security. No man I should think, who possesses a true republican spirit, would decline to rank with his fellow-citizens, on the fancied idea of a superiority in circumstances : This might tend to introduce fatal distinctions in our country. We can all remember the time when our militia, far from being disciplined, as they are at present, kept a well appointed hostile army for a considerable time confined to the capital ; and when they ventured out, indeed they took possession of the ground they aimed at, yet they ventured to their cost, and never forgot the battle of Bunker Hill. The same undisciplined militia under the command and good conduct of General Washington, continued that army confined in or near the capital, until they thought proper to change their position and retreated with haste to Halifax.—If the Militia of the Commonwealth can be made still more effective, I am confident that you will not delay a measure of so great magnitude. I beg leave to refer you to the seventeenth article in our Declaration of Rights, which respects the danger of standing armies

in time of peace. I hope we shall ever have virtue
enough to guard against their introduction.—But may
we not hazard the safety of our Republic should we
ever constitute, under the name of a select militia, a
small body to be disciplined in a camp with all the
pomp & splendor of a regular army? Would such
an institution be likely to be much less dangerous to
our free government and to the morals of our youth,
than if they were actually enlisted for permanent service? And would they not as usual in standing
armies feel a distinct interest from that of our fellow-
citizens at large? The great principles of our present
militia system are undoubtedly good, constituting one
simple body, and embracing so great a proportion of
the citizens as will prevent a separate interest among
them, inconsistent with the welfare of the whole.—
Those principles, however, I conceive should equally
apply to all the active citizens, within the age prescribed by law.—All are deeply interested in the
general security; and where there are no invidious
exemptions, partial distinctions or privileged bands,
every Man, it is presumed, would pride himself in
the right of bearing arms, and affording his personal
appearance in common with his fellow-citizens. If
upon examination you shall find, that the duties in-
cident to our present system bear harder on one class
of citizens, than on another, you will undoubtedly endeavour, as far as possible, to equalize its burthens.

FRIENDS AND FELLOW-CITIZENS,

I THINK it a duty incumbent upon me to acquaint
you, and our fellow-citizens at large, that having

arrived to a stage of life, marked in holy writ, and verified by constant experience, as a time of labour and sorrow; it is highly proper both upon my own account, as well as that of the public, to decline the future suffrages of my fellow-citizens for the office I have now the honor to sustain.[1]   I have had this in contemplation near a twelve month past.   The infirmities of age render me an unfit person in my own opinion, and very probably in the opinion of others, to continue in this station; and I mention it now, that those of the electors who may probably be too warmly attached to me, may not nullify their own votes by giving them for me.   I have always been convinced that many others might have been found to fill my place with greater advantage to the Commonwealth than is now or ever has been in my power.—In the Civil Department during the times of War and of Peace, I have served her in various stations to the best of my ability, and I hope with general approbation; and I can say with truth, that I have not enriched myself in her service.—My warmest thanks are justly due to my constituents for the confidence they have repeatedly placed in me.—When I shall be released from the burthens of my public station, I shall not forget my country.— Her welfare and happiness, her peace and prosperity, her liberty and independence will always have a great share in the best wishes of my heart.

I will endeavour to consider the business you may lay before me with fidelity and dispatch.

SAMUEL ADAMS.[2]

[1] In May, 1797, Adams was succeeded as governor by Increase Sumner.
[2] There are in the Massachusetts Archives additional papers by Adams which

PROCLAMATION. MARCH 20, 1797.

[*Independent Chronicle*, March 30, 1797 ; the text is in W. V. Wells, *Life of Samuel Adams*, vol. iii., pp. 365, 366.]

By Authority.   Commonwealth of Massachusetts.

BY THE GOVERNOR,

A PROCLAMATION FOR A DAY OF SOLEMN FASTING AND PRAYER.

IT having been the invariable practice derived from the days of our renowned ancestors, at this season of the year to set apart a Day of Public Fasting and Prayer : And the practice appearing to be in

---

have here been omitted, but certain of which may well be noted, as follows: 1782, October 15, statement as to funds for South Carolina and Georgia ; 1790, May 28, letter accepting office of Lieutenant Governor ; 1794, February 3, veto message ; 1795, February 18, veto message ; 1795, June 12, message on the resignation of Major General Lithgow ; 1795, June 17, message upon the election of an additional major general ; 1795, June 22, message as to suspicious vessel in Boston Harbor ; 1796, February 2, message on petition of Willard Griffith ; 1796, February 24, message as to suit on bond of S. Ely ; 1796, February 27, message as to vacancies in excise offices ; 1796, June 1, message as to the Massachusetts-Connecticut boundary ; 1796, June 1, message as to troubles in Hancock County ; 1796, November 22, message as to vacancies in Council ; 1797, February 1, message on the militia system ; 1797, February 13, message on the Nantucket Bank.

The *Independent Chronicle* contains the following papers which have not been used: 1794, June 27, proclamation upon rioting in Boston ; 1795, June 21, proclamation as to the burning of the " Betsey" ; 1795, June 26, proclamation offering a reward in connection with the " Betsey."

The *Life of Samuel Adams*, by W. V. Wells, vol. iii., pp. 379–381, contains the will of Samuel Adams, dated December 29, 1790, and also a number of letters printed only in part, which have not been used.

There have also been omitted a number of relatively unimportant papers, such as a brief committee report of November 30, 1785 (Manuscript Documents, 1785, Boston City Clerk's office) ; a brief letter to Elbridge Gerry, recommending Thomas Melville, February 20, 1789 (Emmet Papers, Lenox Library) ; a note of introduction to John Adams, June 18, 1782 (Washburn Papers, Massachusetts Historical Society) ; two letters to Thomas McKean, November 7, 1781, and June 7, 1782, and one to Woodbury Langdon,

itself productive, if well improved, of happy effects on the public mind—

I have therefore thought fit, by & with the advice and consent of the Council, to appoint *Thursday, the FOURTH day of May next ensuing, to be observed and improved throughout this Commonwealth for the purpose of* PUBLIC FASTING AND PRAYER: Earnestly recommending to the Ministers of the Gospel with their respective Congregations *then* to assemble together and seriously to consider, and with one united voice confess our past sins and transgressions, with holy resolutions, by the Grace of God, to turn our feet into the path of His Law— Humbly beseeching him to endue us with all the Christian Spirit of Piety, Benevolence and the Love of our Country; and that in all our public deliberations we may be possessed of a sacred regard to the fundamental principles of our free elective civil Constitutions—That we may be preserved from consuming Fires and all other desolating Judgments.

And as at this season the general business of the year commences, it seems highly proper humbly to implore the divine blessing on our Husbandry, Trade, and Fishery, and all the labour of our hands—On our University and Schools of Education—On the

September 1, 1784 (Library of the Historical Society of Pennsylvania); a note of introduction to Richard Henry Lee, December 9, 1784 (Lee Papers, American Philosophical Society); and a brief note to Rochambeau, May, 17, 1794 (Library of Congress). A few original manuscripts, such as a letter of November 8, 1784, to John Avery and a letter of January 22, 1794, to George Clinton, have passed into private hands at auction sales. Certain manuscripts have been withheld by their owners; but in most instances the entire text of the same has been available, so that it is believed that all the important existing materials of Adams have been comprised in these volumes.

Administration of the Government of the United States and of this and the other States of the Union —On the foreign relations of the United States ; and in a particular manner that all misunderstanding between them and a Sister Republic may be happily, so adjusted as to prevent an open Rupture, and establish Peace.

And as it is our duty to extend our wishes to the happiness of the great Family of Man, I concede we cannot better express ourselves than by humbly supplicating the Supreme Ruler of the World—That the rod of tyrants may be broken into pieces, and the oppressed made Free—That wars may cease in all the Earth, and that the confusions that are and have been among the Nations may be overruled for the promoting and speedily bringing on that holy and happy period, when the Kingdom of our Lord and Saviour Jesus Christ may be everywhere established, and all the people willingly bow to the Sceptre of Him who is the Prince of Peace.

And I do hereby recommend that all unnecessary labour and recreation may be suspended on the said day.

Given at the Council Chamber in Boston, this 20th day of March, in the Year of our Lord one thousand seven hundred and Ninety seven, and in the twenty first Year of the Independence of the United States of America.

SAMUEL ADAMS.

Attest, JOHN AVERY, *Secretary.*

GOD SAVE THE COMMONWEALTH OF MASSACHUSETTS !

TO JOHN ADAMS.

[MS., Adams Papers, Quincy.]

BOSTON April 17th 1797

SIR

I am loth to trespass one moment upon your time, which at present must be very precious. But I am induced even to offer Mr Wyllys this recommendatory Letter to you. He is a native of our Commonwealth, and lately a traveller in Europe. Tho his travels have been merely on Mercantile Business, he appears to be very intelligent, observing, and impartial. He has seen Italy; and conversed among others with Genl Buonoparte and the Pope. He has visited a number of the Italian States, also Algiers and France.—I flatter myself you will be pleased with his conversation and hope you will find it usefull to you. This is the only motive for my addressing a Letter to you at this Time. I congratulate you as the first Citizen of the United States—I may add of the World. I am my dear Sir, notwithstanding I have been otherwise represented in party papers.

Your Old and unvaried Friend,

TO THOMAS JEFFERSON.

[MS., Library of Congress ; a draft is in the Samuel Adams Papers, Lenox Library.]

BOSTON, April 24th, 1801

MY VERY DEAR FRIEND

Your Letter of the 29th of March came duly to my hand. I sincerely congratulate our Country on the arrival of the day of Glory which has called *you* to the first office in the administration of our federal Government. Your warm feeling of friendship must certainly have carried you to a higher tone of expression than my utmost merits will bear. If I have at any time been avoided or frowned upon, your kind ejaculation in the language of the most perfect friend of Man, surpasses every injury. The Storm is now over, and we are in port, and I dare say, the ship will be rigged for her proper service; she must also be well man'd and very carefully officered. No man can be fit to sustain an office who cannot consent to the principles by which he must be governed. With you, I hope, we shall once more see harmony restored; but after so severe and long a storm, it will take a proportionate time to still the raging of the waves. The World has been governed by prejudice and passion, which never can be friendly to truth; and while you nobly resolve to retain the principles of candour and of justice, resulting from a free elective Representative Government, such as they have been taught to hate and despise; you must depend upon being hated yourself, because they hate your principles, not a man of them dare openly to despise you; your inaugural speech, to say nothing of your eminent services to the acceptance of our Country, will secure you from contempt. It may require some time before the great body of our fellow citizens will settle in harmony good humour and peace. When deep prejudices shall be removed in some, the self interestedness of others shall cease and many honest Men, whose minds' for want of better information have been clouded, shall return to the use of their own understanding,

the happy and wished for time will come. The Eyes
of the people have too generally been fast closed from
the view of their own happiness, such alass has been
always the lot of Man! but Providence, who rules
the World, seems now to be rapidly changing the
sentiments of Mankind in Europe and America.
May Heaven grant that the principles of Liberty
and virtue, truth and justice may pervade the whole
Earth. I have a small circle of intimate friends,
among whom Doct^r Charles Jarvis is one; he is a
man of much information and great integrity. I
heartily wish there may be an epistolary correspondence between him and you. I should have written
this Letter before, had not my faithfull friend and
amanuensis John Avery, who is your friend as well
as mine, been occupied in the business of his office of
Secretary of this Commonwealth, which he attends
with great punctuality and integrity. It is not in my
power my dear friend, to give you council; an Old
Man is apt to flatter himself, that he stands upon an
equal footing with younger Men; he indeed cannot
help feeling that the powers of his Mind, as well as
his body are weakened; but he relies upon his memory, and fondly wishes his young friends to think that
he can instruct them by his Experience, when in all
probability he has forgot every trace of it, that was
worth his memory. Be assured, that my esteem for
you is as cordial, if possible, as yours is to me.
Though an Old Man cannot advise you, he can give
you his Blessing. You have devoutly my Blessing
and my Prayers.

My dear Mrs. Adams will not suffer me to close

this Letter, till I let you know, that she recollects the pleasure and entertainment you afforded us, when you was about to embark for France, and hopes that your administration may be happy to yourself and prosperous to our Country.

TO THOMAS JEFFERSON.

[MS., Library of Congress; a draft is in the Samuel Adams Papers, Lenox Library.]

BOSTON Novem^r 18th 1801

MY DEAR FRIEND

Doct^r Eustis will be so kind as to deliver you this Letter.—I am persuaded you will find him a man of a candid and fair Mind and liberal sentiments.

I congratulate you on the return of Peace. The War both in America and Europe was designed by Tyrant Kings to exterminate those rights and liberties which the Gracious Creator has granted to Man, and to sink the happiness resulting therefrom in ruin and oblivion.—Is there not, my friend, reason to believe, that the principles of Democratic Republicanism are already better understood than they were before; and that by the continued efforts of Men of Science and Virtue, they will extend more and more till the turbulent and destructive Spirit of War shall cease?—The proud oppressors over the Earth shall be totally broken down and those classes of Men who have hitherto been the victims of their rage and cruelty shall perpetually enjoy perfect Peace and Safety till time shall be no more.

I am

Your cordial friend

TO THOMAS PAINE.

[W. V. Wells, *Life of Samuel Adams*, vol. iii., pp. 372, 373.]

BOSTON, November 30, 1802.

SIR,—

I have frequently with pleasure reflected on your services to *my* native and *your* adopted country. Your Common Sense, and your Crisis, unquestionably awakened the public mind, and led the people loudly to call for a declaration of our national independence. I therefore esteemed you as a warm friend to the liberty and lasting welfare of the human race. But when I heard you had turned your mind to a defence of infidelity, I felt myself much astonished and more grieved, that you had attempted a measure so injurious to the feelings and so repugnant to the true interest of so great a part of the citizens of the United States. The people of New England, if you will allow me to use a Scripture phrase, are fast returning to their first love. Will you excite among them the spirit of angry controversy at a time when they are hastening to amity and peace? I am told that some of our newspapers have announced your intention to publish an additional pamphlet upon the principles of your Age of Reason. Do you think that your pen, or the pen of any other man, can unchristianize the mass of our citizens, or have you hopes of converting a few of them to assist you in so bad a cause? We ought to think ourselves happy in the enjoyment of opinion, without the danger of persecution by civil or ecclesiastical law. Our friend, the President of the United States, has been calumniated for his liberal sentiments by men who have attributed that liberality to a latent design to promote the cause of infidelity. This, and all other slanders, have been made without the least shadow of proof. Neither religion nor liberty can long subsist in the tumult of altercation, and amidst the noise and violence of faction. *Felix qui cautus.* Adieu.

INDEX

[Entries in heavy-faced type indicate pages at which are printed letters to the person named, or articles over the pseudonym indexed.]

A

Adams, Amos, III., 222
Adams, Elizabeth, III., **214**, **215**, **217**, **220**, **221**, **227**, **239**, **266**, **270**, 293, **318**, **320**, **325**, **327**, **333**, 348, **362**, **367**, **372**, 376, 381, **399**, **403**, **408**, **411**; IV., 14, **21**, **24**, **41**, **50**, **58**, **65**, 66, **77**, 87, **95**, **128**, **137**, 143, 206, 209, 211, 218, **219**, 223, **225**, **244**, **248**, 255, 259, 271, 300, 312, 316, 322, 326, 332, 340, 344
Adams, Hannah, III., **214**, 216, 220; IV., **56**, **200**, 271
Adams, John, I., 13, 397; II., 65, 430; III., 25, 175, 176, 178, 226, 253, **258**, 267, 268, 299, 306, **309**, **310**, **311**, 321, **342**, 352, 356, 393, **416**; IV., **39**, 79, 89, 119, 120, **131**, **176**, **182**, **187**, **199**, **230**, **234**, **267**, **268**, 271, .287, 291, 293, 297, 306, 307, **315**, **316**, **320**, 322, **339**, **340**, **344**, 405, **408**
Adams, Samuel, Jr., III., 214, 220, 239; IV., 24
Adventure, The, IV., 155
Alamance, II., 197
Albany, N. Y., III., 332, 345, 383
Aldrich, III., 391
"Alfred," I., **386**
Algiers, IV., 385
Allan, John, IV., 282–284, 313
Allen, Ethan, IV., 9, 17, 184
Allen, Joseph, II., **268**
Alliance, The, IV., 144, 145
Allston, John, III., 209
Amboy, N. J., III., 375, 377, 378
Amelia county, Va., III., 178
Amherst county, Va., III., 224

Amory, John, IV., 18
Anderson, Jemmy, IV., 75
Andros, Edmund, I., 72, 138, 339; II., 248
Annapolis, Md., IV., 301
Annapolis, N. S., I., 32, 42, 143, 181
Anne, Queen, I., 33
Anstruther, Lt. Col., IV., 17
"Appeal to the World, An," I., 396; II., 238
Appleton, Nathaniel, III., 347; IV., 19, 291
Aquitaine, II., 440
Archer, Edward, III., **174**
Arnold, Benedict, III., **228**, 331; IV., 170, 210
Attucks, Crispus, II., 77, 109, 110
Augusta county, Va., III., 225
Austin, Benjamin, IV., **132**, 238
Austin, Benjamin, Jr., IV., 323
Austin, John L., IV., 176, 188
Austin, II., 146, 147
Avery, John, IV., 180, 222, 363, 369, 386, 396, 406, 407, 410

B

Bacon, II., 13
Bacon, Edward, III., 1, 2
Bailey, James, II., 131, 147
Baillie, Colonel, III., 290
Baltimore, Lord, II., 407
Baltimore, Md., III., 202, 204, 253, 270, 271, 326; IV., 13, 19, 313
Bannister, Jonathan, III., **178**
Barnard, John, I., 304
Barnstable, Mass., III., 1, 2
Barre, Isaac, I., 12, **332**, 396
Barrell, William, III., 221, 223
Barret, John, II., 7
Barrett, John, III., 148, 153

Bass, Jedediah, II., 159
Bass, Major, III., 401
Beaumarchais, IV., 118, 119, 134
Beaver, The, II., 241
Belcher, Jonathan I., 126, 127
Belknap, Jeremy, II., 95, 97;
   III., 306; IV., **374**
Bell, General, III., 316
"Benevolus," II., 172–175
Berkenhaupt, *see* Berkenhout
Berkenhout, IV., 55, 72, 97,
   101, 109
Berkshire county, Mass., IV., 152,
   153, 192, 194, 195
Berlin, IV., 3
Bernard, Francis, I., 98, 101, 152,
   166, 229, 248, 304, 305, 334,
   335, 337–339, 349, 353, 354,
   357, 367, 368, 370, 371, 377,
   378, 380, 385, 393, 396, 398,
   401–403, 405–407, 410, 411,
   417, 418, 420, 421, 423, 425,
   426–428, 431, 434, 436, 439,
   440–445; II., 3, 37, 47,
   48, 58, 72, 88, 165, 175,
   185, 192, 196, 197, 203, 209,
   211, 213, 214, 223, 233, 238–
   241, 243, 244, 247, 281, 282,
   285, ⸮312, 340, 364; III., 19,
   172, 184; IV., 55, 238
Bethune. Nathaniel, I., 1
Betsey, The, III., 194; IV., 405
Beverly, Mass., IV., 270
Beverly, Robert, III., 200
Biddeford, Me., III., 257
Bilboa, IV., 165
Billerica, Mass., III., 207
Birmingham, Eng., I., 66
Black, William, III., **191**
Blackstone, William, I., 317; II.,
   235, 355, 356, 434
Board of War, IV., **125**
Bollan, William, I., 131, 396,
   397; IV., 184
Bolling, Robert, III., **178**
Boston, Mass, I., 1, 7, 8, 12, 13,
   21, 26, 34, 39, 56, 59, 60, 61,
   71, 89, 97, 108, 111, 130, 132,
   152, 153, 199, 201, 213, 241,
   242, 245, 248, 260–263, 301–
   304, 319, 329, 332, 336, 338,
   340, 346, 347, 349, 351, 352,
   355, 360, 362–364, 368, 372, 377–
   379, 392, 393, 396–398, 406–
   408, 412, 413, 416, 422–424,
   427, 435, 436, 438, 442, 444–
   446; II., 7–11, 19–21, 24, 25,
   27, 31, 32, 35, 48–50, 56, 60,
   64–66, 69, 89, 92, 100, 111,
   134, 163, 164, 169, 173, 189,
   192, 230, 238–241, 243, 245,
   264, 274, 282, 304–306, 310,
   311, 327, 328, 330, 337, 339,
   340, 342, 346–348, 369–371,
   374, 379, 380, 387, 389, 392,
   394, 395, 426, 431; III., 1–3,
   12–14, 16–20, 25, 28, 32–37,
   39–42, 44, 48, 50, 52, 58, 62,
   67, 69–74, 78–80, 82, 85, 92,
   94, 97, 99, 103, 104, 106–117,
   119, 120, 122, 125, 127–130,
   132–136, 139–143, 145–154,
   156, 158, 160–167, 169, 172,
   174, 175, 177, 178, 181–183,
   187–190, 193, 194, 198, 200–
   205, 210, 215–218, 220, 222,
   223, 225, 233, 239, 248, 249,
   255, 274, 275, 277–279, 284–
   292, 306, 311–314, 319, 320,
   322, 324, 332, 333, 338, 339,
   345, 348, 350, 355, 356, 359,
   361, 364, 365, 367, 368, 372,
   373, 376, 394, 395, 398, 408,
   410, 416; IV., 10, 15, 39–41,
   50, 52, 54, 59, 61–64, 66, 67,
   75, 77, 102, 108, 110, 129, 137,
   150, 152, 154, 157, 159, 166,
   172, 182, 187, 199, 202, 206,
   209, 217, 220, 225, 227, 233,
   238, 239, 241, 245, 249, 254,
   258–260, 265, 267, 279, 280,
   341, 366, 367, 375, 385, 405
"Bostonian, A," I., **336**
Bowdoin, James, II., 10, 102,
   110, 163; III., **240**; IV., **54**,
   99, 183, **191**, **201**, 210, 269, 316
Bowers, Jerathmeel, I., 106, 114,
   153, 184, 355; II., 171
Bowler, Metcalfe, I., 188
Bowman, Archibald, II., 122
Boylston, Thomas, I., 99, 100;
   III., 252
Bradford, John, IV., **57**
Braintree, Mass., III., 260, 271;
   IV., 8, 40
Brewer, James, II., 131, 147
Brickett, James, III., 341
Bridgham, Ebenezer, II., 147, 157,
   161
Bristol, Eng. I., 304; III., **48**

Bromfield, III., 244
Bromfield, Henry, III., **410**
Brookfield, Mass., III., 152; IV., 24
Brookline, Mass., III., 74, 109
Broome, Samuel, III., 72
Brown, Gowen, III., 239
Brown, John, III., **182**
Brown, Major, III., 233, 240
Brown, Moses, II., 389
Brown, Woodbridge, II., 168
Bruce, James, III., 72
Bruce, III., 398, 399
Brunswick, N. J., III., 323, 371, 372, 375–378, 383
Bucks County, Pa., III., 225
Buenos Ayres, II., 168
Bulkley, John, II., 130
Bunker Hill, III., 227, 324, 384, 411; IV., 171
Burch, William, I., 401, 405
Burgess, William, IV., 275, 276
Burgoyne, John, III., 372, 382, 383, 385, 401, 403, 405, 410, 413; IV., **12, 13,** 17, 20, 21. 38, 48, 285
Burke, Edmund, I., 300
Burnet, William, I., 127; II., 23, 24
Burrill, Ebenezer, II., 426
Bush, IV., 44

C

Cadiz, IV., 89, 165
Caldwell, James, II., 77, 108, 118
Calef, Captain, III., 39
Caligula, I., 96
Callander, Eliezer, III., 225
Calvin's Case, II., 439
Cambridge, Mass., I., 346, 360; II., 9, 20, 25–28, 34, 50, 63, 64, 69, 173, 174, 188, 311, 349, **392,** 393; III., 74, 109, 183, 215, 217, 227, 230; IV., 262
Camden, Earl of, I., 152, **173,** 282; II., 301; III., 119
Campbell, Archibald, III., 342, 343, 362; IV., **9,** 17, 216
Canada, I., 11, 32, 33, 145, 158, 283; III., 186, 187, 197, 212, 213, 274, 275, 294–297, 304, 318; IV., 10, 90, 128, 149, 264, 265, 277, 312
"Candidus," I., **254, 259, 268, 278, 291, 309;** II., 172, 176,
186, 193, 198, 204, 212, 222, 237, 246, 250, 268, 281, 287, 293, 295, **297, 298, 313, 322, 382;** III., 28, **130,** 134, **261**
Cape Ann, III., 409
Cape Breton, I., 50
Cariel's Ferry, N. J., III., 372, 377
Carleton, Guy, III., 275, 278, 330, 335, 345
Carlisle, Earl of, IV., **25**
Carmichael, William, IV., 40
Carr, Patrick, II., 77, 110, 119. 144
Carroll, John, II., 147
Carthage, IV., 2
Cary, Archibald, III., **176**
Cary, Richard, II., 57, 66
Cecil county, Md., III., 203, 204 224
Charles I., I., 27, 163, 204, 257, 317; II., 235, 292, 293, 408, 410, 435, 449
Charles II., I., 158, 204, 317; II., 288, 408, 416, 417; IV., 237
Charles VII., II., 333
Charleston, S. C., II., 64; III., 143, 410; IV., 232, 235
Charlestown, Mass., I., 204, 205, 207; II., 57; III., 74, 109, 129, 220
Chartres, IV., 259
Chase, Colonel, IV., 8
Chatham, Earl of, I., 152, **180**
"Chatterer, A," II., **35, 39, 43, 70**
Chauncy, Charles, I., 323, 324, 326; III., **155,** 196, 303, 317; IV., **108**
Checkley, Elizabeth, III., 214
Checkley, Richard, III., 223; IV., 122
Checkley, William, II., **380;** III., **127, 215**
Chelsea, Mass., III., 261; IV., 169
Chesapeake Bay, III., 406; IV., 120, 218
Chesterfield county, Va., III., 176, 177
Chittenden, Thomas, IV., 203
"Chronus," II., 281, 282, 284–286, 288, 291, 293–295, 297, 298, 300, 302, 304, 305, 313–316, 318–326; III., 29
Church, Benjamin, II., 342, 370, 374; III., 13 215, 220

Church, Edward, I., 212, 213; IV., 330
Clarke, Richard, III., 71
Clarkson, Levinus, III., 143
Clinton, George, IV., 15, 125, 126, 406
Clinton, Henry, III., 330, 331, 345; IV., 25, 28, 75, 105, 195
Clymer, George, III., 72
Coffin, Hezekiah, III., 72
Coke, I., 157, 271; II., 325, 326, 355, 437, 439
Cole, John, II., 389
Collins, Stephen, III., 172
Collson, III., 48, 270
Colrain, ·Mass., III., 145
Colt, Peter, III., 417
Commissioners of the Customs, I., 216, 396
Commissioners of the Treasury, I., 152, 193
"Common Sense," III., 261; IV., 412
Confederation, Articles of, IV., 4, 6, 11, 18
Confederacy, The, IV., 120, 151
Connecticut, I., 188; II., 64, 111; III., 115, 336, 337, 358; IV., 153, 154, 192, 219, 303, 335, 405
Connecticut Committee of Correspondence, III., 63, 107–109, 114
Connecticut River, III., 290
Conway, Henry S., I., 12, 81, 88, 98, 101, 152, 189
Cooper, Samuel, III., 267, 273, 281, 301, 353, 388; IV., 104, 111, 115, 118, 123, 126, 148, 206, 216, 244, 258
Cooper, William, I., 7, 397; II., 351, 394; III., 12, 133; IV., 66, 126, 245, 247, 267
Cornwall, Daniel, II., 131
Cornwallis, John, IV., 232
Coryell's Ferry, *see* Cariel's Ferry
Cotton, John, I., 369; II., 266, 296
"Cotton Mather," II., 276
Coudray, III., 378, 379; IV., 14, 70
Cox, John, II., 105, 114
Crafts, Colonel, III., 393, 412
Craigie, IV., 225
Cromwell, Oliver, I., 317
Cross Creek, IV.. 207

Crouch, Henry, III., 410
Crown Point, III., 310, 318
Culpeper, Lord, II., 408
Cumberland county, Mass., I., 239; IV., 163
Cumberland county, Pa., III., 225
Cumberland county, Va., III., 177
Cunningham, IV., 144
Curtenius, Peter T., III., 165
Cushing, Thomas, I., 1, 7, 33, 34, 71, 153, 184, 241, 247, 346, 354, 397; II., 11, 18, 19, 65, 370; III., 24, 37, 63, 67, 100, 103, 107, 156, 173, 175, 176, 191, 203, 210, 268, 269, 374; IV., 6, 148, 173

D

Dalrymple, William, I., 443; II., 49, 71–73, 75, 77, 102, 110, 155
Dana, Francis, II., 306; III., 418; IV., 178, 230, 233, 234, 271
Dana, Richard, I., 1, 6, 8, 321, 397; II., 11, 18, 163
Danbrook, John, II., 159
Darby, Richard, II., 168
Dartmouth, Earl of, 2nd., I., 34, 35, 61, 97, 112; II., 10, 342, 343, 345, 389, 393, 395, 398; III., 20–22, 43, 49, 53, 59, 70, 76, 86, 103, 187; IV., 148
Dartmouth, Earl of, I., 26, 39, 56, 61, 248; II., 10
Dashwood, Samuel, IV., 297, 307
Davis, Aaron, Jr., II., 374
Davis, Caleb, IV., 253, 273
Dawson, III., 37
Deane, Silas, III., 114, 125, IV., 14, 40, 47, 48, 69–72, 97, 100, 108, 111–113, 115, 116, 118, 119, 131, 134, 135, 141, 157, 183
Deane, Simeon, IV., 21, 24, 40
Deane, The, IV., 151
Dearborn, III., 311
De Berdt, Dennys, I., 58, 61, 81, 89, 97, 99, 104, 111, 114, 132, 134, 153, 177, 187, 212, 213, 226, 232, 241, 248, 377, 397, 446; II., 66; IV., 114
Dedham, Mass., III., 214, 217, 221, 239
Delaware, III., 282

Delaware River, III., 372, 382, 383
d'Estaing, IV., 60, 80, 81, 89
"Determinatus," I., **236**; II., **4**
Devenson, I., 104
Dexter, Samuel, I., 106, 153, 184;
    III., 221, 222
Dick, Charles, III., **193**, 225
Dickinson, John, III., **13**, 14,
    104, 124, 158
Dickson, II., 94, 124
Dinwiddie Co., Va., III., 178
Dorchester, Mass., III., 109
Dorr, Harbottle, II., 35, 256, 276
Dove, John, III., 143
Dudley, Joseph, I., 126, 138
Dugan, IV., 254, 255
Dummer, Jeremy, II., 444, 445
Dunkirk, IV., 116
Dunmore, Lord, III., 319,
Dunmore, The, III., 192
Duxbury, Mass., III., 32, 33

E

"E. A.," I., **316**
Eagle, The, IV., 59
East Chester, N. Y., III., 316
East India Company, III., 61,
    63, 67, 69, 74, 76, 78, 79, 104, 110
Eden, William, IV., **25**
Edes & Gill, I., 201, 203, 208,
    241, 249, 251, 255, 282, 306,
    322, 336, 386, 396, 445; II.,
    35, 172, 176, 186, 193, 204, 212,
    222, 237, 246, 250, 256, 268,
    276, 281, 287, 293, 297, 313,
    322, 329, 332, 374; III., 130,
    234; IV., 250, 255
Edinburgh, IV., 101, 112, 118
Edward II., II., 439
Edward III., I, 154
Egg Harbor, III., 397
Eliot, John, I., 219; III., 306
Eliot, IV., 65
Elizabeth, II., 405
Elizabethtown, N.J., III., 323, 378
Ellery, William, III., 327, 331
Ellis, I., 47, 55
England, I., 27, 29, 30, 32,
    35, 36, 40, 44–46, 48, 49, 52–
    54, 59, 64–66, 69, 93, 136,
    142, 144, 155, 186, 192, 213,
    218, 270, 271, 283, 302, 317,
    324, 355, 377, 435; II., 53, 59,
    68, 179, 182, 206, 207, 222, 224,
    235, 239, 242, 246, 250, 254,

256, 257, 279, 288, 308, 325,
    326, 330, 355, 356, 358, 364,
    405–409, 412, 414, 416–418,
    420–422, 424, 434–441, 443,
    444, 446, 448–451, 453, 454;
    III., 57, 89, 91, 102, 104,
    125, 137, 145, 156, 159, 162,
    171, 172, 221, 228, 229, 232,
    241, 262, 263, 275, 279, 318,
    333, 369; IV., 24, 26, 77, 96,
    115, 116, 130, 135, 230, 243,
    250, 268, 275, 295, 312, 339,
    342
Erving, John, Jr., I., 8
Essex county, Va., III., 191, 200,
    201
Etombe, IV., 269, 315
Eugene, Prince, III., 296
Eustis, William, II., 350
Eyre, II., 236

F

Falkland Islands, II., 276
Falmouth, The, III., 74
Falmouth, Me., IV., 160, 162, 163
Faneuil Hall, I., 8, 13, 71, 89;
    III., 3, 70, 74, 287
Farmington, Conn., III., 148, 153
Fellows, John, IV., 166, **192**, 194,
    195, 196
Field, II., 110, 119
Fleet, T. & J., I., 254; II., 43, 374
Florida, IV., 128
Folger, Abishai, I., 312, 313, 316
Fort Chambly, III., 232, 233, 240,
    310
Fort Hill, I., 59
Fort Independence, IV., 17
Fort Lee, III., 322
Fort Pitt, III., 345
Fort Pownal, I., 214
Fort Randolph, III., 345
Fort Stanwix, IV., 313
Fort Washington, III., 322, 350
Fosdick, Nathaniel, II., 147
Foster, John, III., 194
Framingham, Mass., III., 35
France, I., 33; II., 288, 289; III.,
    275, 334, 343, 363, 367, 400;
    IV., 1, 4, 8, 10, 21, 22, 36, 40,
    48, 51, 69, 72, 79, 89, 95, 99,
    100, 106, 117–119, 127, 128,
    130, 157, 186, 187, 197, 202,
    230, 244, 278, 279, 289, 315,
    319, 357, 368, 372, 374

Francis, Ebenezer, III., 392
Franklin, Benjamin, I., 397; II., 10, 46, 59, 163, 177, 305, 345; III., 37, 48, 85, 102, 321, 363; IV., 7, 24, 40, 70, 72, 79, 89, 118, 183, 374, 375
Frazier, General, III., 274
Frederick county, Md., III., 202, 203
Frederick Town, Md., III., 203
Freeman, Enoch, IV., 160
Freeman, Samuel, III., 400; IV., 160, 162
Frost, John, IV., 161
Frost, II., 130
Fuller, Abraham, II., 19
Fyrman, Moor, III., 224

G

Gadsden, Christopher, I., 108; III., 141, 143; IV., 285
Gage, Thomas, I., 334, 336, 337, 364, 372, 373, 396, 398, 406, 422, 428, 432, 433, 438, 442, 444; II., 49, 77, 238, 239, 241, 397; III., 108, 138, 142, 159, 163, 170, 171, 194, 196, 205, 223, 275, 278
Gaine, Hugh, I., 324
Galloway, Joseph, III., 369
Gardiner, IV., 75, 76
Gardner, Henry, III., 373
Gardnerstown, Mass., III., 34
Gascogne, II., 440
Gaspée, The, II., 389
Gatchel, Samuel, III., 150, 151
Gates, Horatio, III., 291, 296, 311, 327, 331, 336, 338, 340, 341, 344, 386, 388, 389, 401, 403, 405, 406, 411, 413; IV., 10, 80, 110, 153, 158, 159, 161, 163, 207, 262, 263, 284
Gay, Fisher, III., 148, 153
George II., I., 155
George III., I., 26, 162, 184, 241, 349, 354, 368; II., 149; III., 45, 234
Georgia, I., 188; II., 337; III., 185, 233, 283, 302, 384; IV., 41, 234, 235, 330, 405
Germaine, George, IV., 232
Germantown, Pa., IV., 2
Germany, III., 332; IV., 127
Gerrish, Joseph, I., 106
Gerry, Elbridge, II., 339, 340, 346, 348, 380, 387; III., 82, 105, 119, 130, 218, 226, 229, 246, 267, 313, 322, 327, 331, 347, 418; IV., 7, 8, 11, 13, 142, 146, 167, 168, 169, 171, 192, 223, 227, 285, 292, 298, 300, 312, 324, 330, 405
Gilbert, Joseph, III., 152
Gill, Moses, III., 223, 225; IV., 142
Gillon, Commodore, IV., 145
Gilman, Peter, I., 188
Gerard, IV., 47, 48, 67, 110
Glover, John, III., 316
Goddard, William, III., 80, 81, 82, 93
Godfrey, George, II., 171; IV., 159, 160
Goochland county, Va., III., 177
Gordon, William, II., 333, 348; IV., 264, 320, 336, 337
Gorges, Ferdinando, II., 443
Gorham, Nathaniel, IV., 145
Grafton, Duke of, III., 263
Graham, Macaulay, IV., 314
Gray, Harrison, I., 12; II., 130, 296, 297
Gray, Samuel, II., 77, 87, 88, 109, 118, 121
Gray, Thomas, I., 7, 71
Gray, IV., 75, 76
Great Britain, I., 2–4, 5, 8, 9, 20, 24, 25, 28, 29–32, 35, 38–41, 43, 46–49, 51, 55, 62, 63, 67, 68, 69, 70, 72, 74, 91, 100, 103, 114, 132, 135, 141, 142, 145, 148, 150, 155–157, 159, 165, 169, 170, 174, 183, 186, 193–198, 213, 217, 218, 230, 231, 242, 243, 263, 270, 271, 273, 283, 287–289, 304, 337, 339, 343, 344, 351, 356, 357, 361, 366, 372, 373, 387, 388, 390, 393, 411, 441, 444, 446, 447; II., 4, 7, 48, 50, 52–55, 57, 61, 68, 101, 135, 137, 166, 167, 182, 201–203, 205–207, 220, 232, 234, 236, 242, 257, 260–262, 267, 289, 291, 299, 305, 309, 311, 313, 319–321, 324, 356, 357, 359, 362–369, 395, 398, 401, 402, 426, 444, 453; III., 10, 13, 38, 47, 63–66, 68, 86, 89, 90, 100, 101, 110, 111, 113, 115, 120, 121, 124, 126, 128, 129, 131, 138, 142,

Great Britain—(*Continued*)
143, 162, 171, 183-186, 190,
198, 209, 211, 212, 232, 234,
239, 241, 257, 261-266, 275,
276, 280, 324, 328, 332, 338,
340, 354, 361, 371, 384; IV.,
23, 30, 38, 54, 72, 84, 89, 90,
96, 127, 128, 133, 138, 147-
149, 165, 254, 261, 289, 296,
303, 305, 311, 313, 315, 322,
364, 391
Green, Joseph, I., 1, 8
Greene, Nathanael, III., 318, 327,
331, **370**
Greenleaf, Joseph, III., 219
Greenleaf, Stephen, II., 17
Greenleaf, William, II., 18
Greenleaf, IV., 24, 65
Greenwood, Thomas, II., 16,
130, 140
Grenville, George, I., 110, 284;
II., 202; III., 55
Gridley, John, II., 145
Gridley, Scarborough, IV., 293,
303
Gridley, I., 381-383
Griffith, Willard, IV., 405
Grobouval, IV., 14
Grotius, Hugo, II., 410, 437
Guinard, IV., 197
Gustavus Vasa, IV., 256, 257

H

Hadley, Mass., I., 208, 209; IV., 6
Haley & Hopkins, II., 9
Halifax, N. S., I., 59, 236, 237,
336, 363, 432, 443; II., 104,
114, 241, 242; III., 275, 279;
IV., 98, 186, 313, 402
Hall, James, II., 134; III., 72, 74
Hall, Stephen, II., 65, 133
Hall, Chaplain, II., 73, 74, 76
Hall, S. & E., II., 387
Hallowell, Benjamin, Jr., I., 60,
315, 407
Hampden, John, II., 222
Hampshire county, Mass., IV.,
152, 153, 193, 196
Hampton, Va., III., 253; IV., 218
Hancock, John, I., 73, 99, 130,
153, 241, 245, 246, 314, 321,
342, 346, 355, 371, 410; II.,
7, **9**, 11, 18, 19, 65, 168, 296,
297, 385; III., 23, 24, 36, 37,
63, 85, 104, 190, 199, 201, 210,

215, 279, 329, 374; IV., 41,
49, 54, 60, 167, 168, 171, 210,
211, 246, 247, 316, 354
Hancock county, Mass., IV., 405
Hancock, The, IV., 41
Hanover county, Va., III., 224
Hanson, Jonathan, III., **203**
Hardwick, Mass., I., 211
Harrison, Benjamin, III., 336
Hartford, Conn., III., 121, 218
Harvard College, II., 50, 64, 76
Hatch, Crowell, III., 192, 193
Hatfield, Mass., I., 209; III., 41-
43
Havana, IV., 165
Haverhill, Mass., I., 206, 207
Hawes, Benjamin, IV., **151**
Hawley, Joseph, I., 114, 153,
184, 342, 371; II., 430; III., **52,**
58, 238, 277, **294,** 347
Hayward, Thomas, III., 336, 359
Heath, William, III., 63, 67, 85,
227, 316, 350, **407,** 408; IV.,
178, 262, **264,** 330
Helyer, Joseph, II., 131, 161
Henrico county, Va., III., 175
Henry III., I., 16
Henry VIII., II., 182
Henry, Patrick, III., 224, 390;
IV., 337
Henshaw, Joshua, I., 12, 397;
III., 223, 364; IV., 24
Hersey, Joshua, II., 171
Hewes, Samuel, III., **384**
Hewet, II., 236
Hewet, George, IV., 155
Higginson, Stephen, IV., 278,
287, 298
Highlands, IV., 192, 193, 195
Hiller, Joseph, *see* Helyer.
Hillsborough, Earl of, I., 152,
153, **219,** 230, 234, 276, 304,
334, 336, 339, 353, 366, 385,
398, 406, 407, 415, 418, 428,
429, 431-433, 438, 441, 442,
445; II., 72, 74, 75, 141, 209,
212-214, 216, 223, 229, 233,
235, 238-240, 244, 245, 247,
275, 305, 342, 345; III., 19,
20, 23
Hillsborough, N. C., IV., 207
Hinckley, Ebenezer, II., 131, **145**
Hingham, Mass., III., 260
Hoar, Oliver, III., 14
Holker, IV., 40

Holland, IV., 8, 79, 89, 120, 200, 275, 290
Holten, Stephen, IV., 146, 287
Hood, Samuel, I., 396, 398, 435, 442, 444; II., 241
Hooker, Richard, II., 261, 317, 452
Hooper, Stephen, III., 224
Hopkins, Stephen, II., 389; III., 116
Horn, Captain, III., 253
Howard, Martin, I., 302
Howe, Richard, III., 297, 302, 312, 320, 321, 329, 344, 369; IV., **25**, 28, 80
Howe, Robert, IV., 192, 193, **194, 196**
Howe, William, III., 248, 249, 279, 295, 296, 312, 320, 324, 329, 330, 342–345, 348, 361, 363, 370–372, 376, 377, 382, 385, 386, 410, 411; IV., 21, 25
Hudson River, III., 274, 277, 278, 322, 330, 376, 398; IV., 15, 16; *see* North River
Hulton, Henry, I., 316
Hume, David, II., 189, 325
Humphrey, III., 261
Hunt, Captain, III., 198
Hunter, William, II., 99, 122, 124
Hunterdon county, N. J., III., 224
Huntington, Jedediah, III., 134
Hurd, John, I., 109
Hutchinson, Thomas, I., 13, 60, 101, 115, 246, 354, 377, 380; II., 23, 46, 58, 60, 135, 167, 185, 191, 233, 235, 237, 245, 246, 248, 254, 264–266, 276, 281, 294, 312, 316, 322, 327, 340, 343, 418, 420, 431, 446; III., 22, 38, 40, 44, 47, 48, 51, 52, 76, 79, 93, 94, 99, 108, 112, 121, 124, 171, 184, 199, 288; IV., 43, 55
Hutton, Henry, *see* Hulton.

I

"Impartialist, An," I., **380**
Independence, I., 38, 135; III., 25, 265, 281, 295, 297, 299, 301; IV., 4, 285, 357
Ingersoll, David, Jr. II., 168
Ipswich, Mass., II., 237
Ireland, I., 363; II., 262, 263; III., 115, 274, 332

Italy, IV., 408
Izard, Ralph, IV., 114, 280

J

Jackson, Henry, IV., 159–161, **162**, 164
Jackson, Jonathan, IV., 290, 291
Jackson, Joseph, I., 397
Jackson, Richard, I., 81, 179
Jamaica, I., 158; III., 186
James, Colonel, III., 199
James I., I., 66, 150, 163; II., 238, 405
James II., I., 138, 140, 158, 317; II., 189, 448, 449
James River county, Va., III., 191, 192, 224
Jarvis, Charles, IV., 410
Jarvis, Leonard, IV., 327, 330
Jay, John, IV., 98, 145
Jefferson, Thomas, III., 224; IV., **408, 411**
Jeffries, David, I., 219; III., 189
Jeffries, John, I., 218
John, II., 356, 435, 437
Johnson, Mary, IV., 118, 134
Johnstone, George, IV., **25, 46**, 97
"Jonathan Philanthrop," III., 197
Jones, John Paul, IV., 144, 320
Jones, Noble W., III., **139**
Jones, William, I., 139, 158
Judiciary, I., 3, 9, 20, 26, 46, 80, 129, 144, 155, 172, 193; II., 33, 52, 235, 237, 340, 343, 347, 369; III., 4, 49, 50, 80, 85, 97
"Junius Americanus," II., 57, 264, 274, 330; III., 38

K

Keith, Israel, IV., 330
Kennett, I., 324
Kent, Benjamin, I., 321, 397; III., **303**
Kilroi, Matthew, II., 86–88, 120, 122, 147, 158
King, Rufus, IV., 320
King, Samuel, III., 165
King William county, Va., III., 225
Kings Bridge, N. Y., III., 297, 316

Knox, Henry, II., 129, 133, 137; III., 227
Knox, William, IV., 157

L

La Fayette, III., 413; IV., 61, 81, 82, 187, **197**, 199, 259
Lake Champlain, III., 330, 332
Lambertville, N. J., *see* Coryell's Ferry.
Lancaster, Pa., II., 330
Lancaster county, Va., III., 224
Landais, Peter, IV., 44, 60, 144, 145, 278, 318, 319, 320
Langdon, John, III., **401**
Langdon, Woodbury, IV., 167, 405
Languedoc, The, IV., 47
Laurens, Henry, III., **418**; IV., 10, 26, 54, 95, 98, 99, 105, 108, 177, 200, 281
Laurens, John, IV., 177, 178, 230, 233, 260
"Layman, A," I., **322**; II., 176, 186, 187, 193–197
Leach, IV., 16, 17
Lee, Arthur, II., 59, 61, 66, **164**, **189**, **230**, **245**, **264**, **274**, **310** **342**, **379**; III., **18**, **36**, **37**, **39**, **40**, **44**, **48**, **70**, **73**, **77**, **78**, **97**, **117**, **169**, **179**, **194**, **339**, 367, **382**, **412**; IV., **14**, 40, 68, 69, 70, 71, 72, 73, **82**, 89, 97, 100, 101, 105, 106, 108, 111, 114, **115**, 118–120, 130, 131, 134–137, 140, 141, **155**, 178, 183, 207, 209, 211, 216, 217, 227, 233, 239, 241, 245, **275**, **277**, **281**, 326
Lee, Charles, III., 301, 316, 342, 343
Lee, Francis L., IV., **19**, 216, 326
Lee, George, IV., 241
Lee, Jeremiah, III., 202
Lee, Jonathan, III., 200
Lee, Richard Henry, III., **25**, **136**, **205**, **296**, 313, 321, 336, 340, 359, **376**, **386**, **389**, 413; IV., **1**, **21**, 82, 101, 102, **215**, **239**, 278, **308**, 312, 314, **318**, **323**, **326**, **329**, 332, **333**, **335**, 406
Lee, William, IV., 114, 241
Leffingwell, Christopher, III., 134
Leigh, II., 130

Leighton, Captain, III., 205, 209
Leonard, Colonel, III., 391
Lexington, Mass., III., 109, 355, 356, 384; IV., 262
Liberty, The, I., 398
Lincoln, Benjamin, III., 316; IV., 181, **282**
Lincoln county, Mass., IV., 163
Lindsay, Lord, IV., 97
Littleton, Mass., III., **14**, 15
Liverpool, I., 304; IV., 155
Livingston, Peter V., III., **164**
Livingston, Philip, III., 72
Livingston, Robert R., III., 336; IV., 261
Livingston, Walter, III., 306, 308
Lloyd, Robert, I., 188
Locke, John, I., 251; II., 210, 224, 257, 259, 263, 298, 300, 316, 317, 326, 352, 356, 357, 452
London, I., 34, 37, 56, 58, 134, 153, 179, 237, 244, 260, 261, 280, 286, 293, 304, 334, 369, 395, 397; II., 10, 14, 18, 56, 69, 111, 112, 136, 189, 206, 207, 209, 231, 234, 236, 242, 244, 267, 274, 306, 312, 347, 411, 419; III., 38, 54, 61, 71, 73–76, 92, 93, 112, 118–120, 196, 240, 277, 278, 302, 306, 332; IV., 100, 114, 291, 390
Long, Colonel, III., 391
Louis XI., II., 333
Louisburg, I., 32, 42, 181
Lovell, James, III., 248, 249, 255, 320, 352; IV., 13, **16**, **142**, **143**, **144**, 146, 155, **167**, **169**, 171, **180**, **183**, 227, 250
Lovell, Solomon, IV., **158**, 159, **160**, 161–164
Lovett [Lovell, James], IV., 155
Lowell, John, IV., 183, **203**, **272**, **274**, 300
Lucas, Charles, II., **163**
Lunenburgh, Mass., IV., 145
Luzerne, IV., 165
Lyde, Nathaniel B., I., 113; IV., 340
Lydia, The, II., 13
Lynch, Thomas, III., 159
Lynde, Benjamin, I., 101; II., 77, 135, 265
Lynn, Mass., II., **426**; III., 109

M

McCauley, William, III., 146
McDougall, Alexander, III., 316; IV., 261, **271**
McKean, Thomas, IV., **260, 262,** 405
McNeil, Hector, IV., 42, 43, 53, 57, 64
Machias, Me., IV., 282, 284
Mackay, I., 341
Madrid, IV., 89
Magna Charta, *see* Statutes.
Malcomb, I., 94
Malden, Mass., III., 261; IV., 50
Mamaroneck, N. Y., III., 317
Manchester, Eng., I., 66
Manigault, Peter, I., 188
Manley, John, IV., 41, 42, 45, 53, 57, 59, 60, 63, 64
Marblehead, Mass., I., 206; II., 347, 348; III., **80,** 83, 84, **94,** 95–97, 106, 108, **120,** 130, **150,** 151; IV., 270
Marbois, François, IV., 165
Marchant, Henry, II., **306**
Marion, Francis, IV., 207
Marlborough, Duke of, III., 296
Marshall, Thomas, II., 125–127
Marshfield, Mass., III., 196
Mary, I., 154, 163, 317
Mary, The, III., 143
Maryland, I., 188; III., 105, 139, 254, 282, 297, 358, 409; IV., 173, 207
Mason, George, IV., 326
Mason, Jonathan, I., 26, 34
Massachusetts, I., 13, 23, 71, 74, 83, 97–101, 104, 114, 115, 123, 130, 134, 152, 162, 166, 169, 173, 179, 180, 184, 189, 193, 219, 229, 354, 356, 358, 359, 365–368, 371; II., 19, 46, 57, 61, 168, 171, 177, 256, 276, 416, 417, 438, 451; III., 45, 62, 80, 85, 129, 156, 160, 161, 185, 197, 211, 214, 219, 225, 232, 240, 242, 255, 257, 271, 290–292, 306, 316, 325–337, 343, 346, 351, 359, 361, 373, 391, 392, 395, 404, 406, 407, 418; IV., 94, 95, 98, 99, 103, 113, 126, 135, 137, 140, 146, 147, 158, 159, 168, 172, 173, 182, 193, 194, 196, 199, 200, 202, 204, 205, 210, 217, 226, 228, 231, 233, 247, 253, 327, 339, 345, 363, 366, 369, 375, 382, 383, 386, 391, 396–399, 407
Massachusetts, Charter, I., 2, 8, 17, 19, 23, 27–29, 64, 70, 117–123, 125, 126, 128, 161, 163, 182, 191, 241; II., 1, 21, 29, 32, 33, 54, 67, 73–75, 169, 172, 178, 181, 223, 233, 260, 263, 277, 291, 303, 322, 327, 341, 358, 360, 362, 363, 420, 444; III., 56, 60; IV., 229
Massachusetts, Committee of Correspondence, III., 62, 85
Massachusetts, Constitution, IV. 187, 211, 219, 233, 250, 273, 274, 339, 354, 363, 370, 374, 386
Massachusetts, Constitutional Convention, IV., 177, 180, 183, 188
Massachusetts Council, III., **335,** 336
Massachusetts General Court, I., 1, 7, 10, 235, 346; II., 9, 25, 26, 27, 33, 64
Massachusetts, Governor, I., 13, **74, 83, 229,** 235, **342, 346, 371;** II., **168, 171, 327, 331, 401, 428, 431;** III., 3
Massachusetts, House of Representatives, I., 13, 23, 74, 83, 114, 130, 134, 152, 162, 167, 169, 173, 180, 184, 189, 193, 229, 342, 346, 349, 354, 371, 444–446; II., 19, 46, 61, 168, 171, 177, 327, 331, 401, 428, 431; III., 3, 45, 80, 129
Massachusetts, Lieutenant-Governor, II., **7, 19, 61**
"Massachutensis," III., 197
Mather, Samuel, III., **316**
Matlack, Timothy, IV., **75**
Mauduit, Jasper, I., **130,** 179
Maverick, Samuel, II., 77, 108, 118
Maxwell, Hugh, III., 378
Mears, Sampson, III., 191
Medford, Mass., I., 206
Meigs, Return J., III., 311
Mein, John, I., 378, 379
Melville, Thomas, IV., 405
Mendon, Mass., I., 210
Mercer, Hugh, III., 297, 353
Mermaid, The, IV., 66

Middle Brook, N. J., III., 375, 376, 378
Middlesex county, Eng., II., 209
Middlesex Resolves, III., 154
Mifflin, Thomas, III., 72, 219, 272, 291, 292, 297, 317, 319, 327, 329
Mighill, Thomas, III., **17**
Miller, Charles, III., 147; IV., 170
Mills & Hicks, II., 45
Millstone, III., 375, 377
Minchen, Lieut., II., 94
Mitchelson, David, II., 123
Moffatt, Thomas, I., 302
Mohawk Indians, III., **211**
Molineux, William, II., 18, 263; III., 1
Monmouth, N. J., IV., 79
Montesquieu, Charles, II., 303, 316, 322
Montgomery, Hugh, II., 158, 159, 160, 161
Montgomery, Richard, III., 267
Montreal, III., 182, 290, 310; IV., 265
Montresor, I., 442
Morgan, John, III., 345, 346
Morris, General, III., 270
Morris, Gouverneur, IV., 261
Morris, Robert, IV., 47
Morristown, N. J., III., 370
Morton, Elijah, III., **41**
Moses, Isaac, III., 191, 201
Moulton, Perez, III., 109, **293;** IV., 186
Moylan, Stephen, III., 319
"Mucius Scaevola," II., 276, 277, 278, 294
Murray, II., 145
Murray, Justice, I., 385; II., 16

N

Nantasket, Mass., III., 199
Nantes, III., 363; IV., 155
Nantucket, Mass., I., 312, 316
Nantucket Bank, IV., 279, 405
Navy Board, IV., **152, 154, 166**
Neal, Daniel, II., 419, 420
Nero, I., 96, 109
Nettleham, Baronet of, *see* Bernard, Francis
Neufville, John, II., 64
Newark, N. J., III., 323
Newburyport, Mass., III., 80, 113, 224

Newcastle county, Del., III., 189, 223
New England, I., 26–28, 32, 34, 40–42, 44, 47, 49–51, 53, 65, 71, 139; II., 226, 236, 395, 419, 420, 443, 449; III., 82, 260, 272, 275, 277, 283, 286, 289, 294, 295, 297, 325, 329–332, 334, 341, 345, 349, 350, 355, 366, 382, 383, 390, 391, 396, 397, 399, 401–403, 407, 412; IV., 67, 86, 87, 96, 97, 124, 153, 154, 259, 412
New Hampshire, I., 188; II., 64, 284, 297; III., 232, 233, 243, 258, 311, 331, 367, 373; IV., 155, 167, 202, 203, 205
New Haven, Conn., III., 343; IV., 6
New Jersey, I., 188; III., 108, 109, 283, 295, 297, 298, 302, 318, 323, 325, 328, 330, 334, 341, 344, 350, 361, 362, 376, 382–385, 387
Newport, R. I., I., 316; III., 80, 93, 121; IV., 81, 90, 98, 250
Newton, Mass., III., 109
New York, I., 57, 109, 111, 147, 304, 329, 330, 442, 443; II., 10, 65, 114, 166, 180, 193, 197, 221, 222, 228, 329, 365, 369; III., 26, 72, 79, 80, 82, 93, 107–109, 119, 120, 131, 164–166, 191, 196, 198, 201, 214, 218, 241, 248, 252, 269, 270, 274, 275, 277–279, 283, 295, 297, 300–302, 306, 308–310, 312, 318, 319, 326, 330, 336, 337, 345, 361, 362, 369, 378, 382, 385, 396, 399; IV., 9, 47, 54, 66, 80, 81, 90, 98, 99, 101, 102, 105, 108, 110, 125, 150, 178, 179, 203, 204, 219, 234, 250, 261, 264, 313, 330
Niles, Hezekiah, I., 58; III., 52
Noailles, de, IV., 233, 268, 271
Norfolk, Va., III., 174, 253, 284
Normandy, II., 440
North, Joseph, III., **34**
North, Lord, I., 301; III., 21, 61, 137, 141, 151, 171, 179
North River, III., 318; IV., 192
Northampton, Mass., I., 209, 210; III., 52, 294

Northampton county, Va., II., 236
North Carolina, II., 192; III., 26, 233, 274, 281, 284, 323, 384; IV., 41, 207, 218
Norwich, Conn., III., **134,** 135; IV., 60
Nova Scotia, I., 33, 181; III., 185; IV., 90, 128, 149, 282, 284
Noyes, Nathaniel, IV., 297
Nye, Joseph, III., **181**

O

Oliver, Andrew, I., 59, 101; II., 135, 264; III., 44, 47, 48, 184
Oliver, Peter, I., 101; II., 77; III., 51, 80, 98
Olivier, Laurens, IV., 10
Olney, IV., 44
Onondaga Indians, IV., 29
Orne, Azor, III., 94, 105; IV., 230
Osgood, Maj., III., 269
Otis, James, I., 1, 7, 12, 13, 71, 96, 106, 109, 114, 153, 184, 241, 321, 342, 346, 355, 371, 380–386, 397, 417; II., 9, 296, 342, 370; III., **1,** 22, 24, 37, **242**
Otis, James (of Barnstable), I., 355
Otis, Samuel A., IV., 7, **122,** 243, 244

P

Paca, William, IV., 173
Paine, Robert Treat, III., 175, 176, 313, 374; IV., 6, 260
Paine, Thomas, IV., **412**
Palfrey, William, I., 379; II., 9, 100; IV., 268
Palmer, Mass., IV., 24
Palmer, Joseph, III., **271**
Palmes, Richard, II., 138, 147, 158–161
Paris, IV., 3, 15
Parker, William, II., 126, 127, 134
Parks, III., 288
Parliament, Acts of, I., 2, 8, 15–17, 24, 29, 30, 35, 39, 44, 56, 57, 62, 74, 91, 112, 113, 134, 136, 138, 141, 146, 147, 155, 165, 171, 181, 184, 185, 191, 220, 221, 243, 249, 269, 284, 285, 375, 386, 387; II., 47, 52, 53, 178, 180, 181, 201, 229, 232, 262, 299, 313, 355, 367, 390, 417, 451; III., 50, 67,

106, 107, 109, 117, 136, 141, 170, 183, 185, 262; IV., 27
Paxton, Charles, I., 316, 401–403, 406
Payne, Edward, II., 127–129, 133
Peekskill, N. Y., III., 270, 375, 391
Pemberton, Samuel, II., 10, 163
Pendleton, Edmund, III., 159
Pennsylvania, III., 297, 309, 323–325, 328–330, 334, 337, 382; IV., 261, 373
Penobscot, IV., 152, 154, 159–163, 235
Perkins, James, III., 191, 201
Philadelphia, Pa., II., 241; III., 68, 79, 82, 108, **109,** 131, 134, 169, 173, 186, 196, 214, 309, 311, 312, 319, 327, 329, 331, 343, 348, 355, 356, 361, 377, 383; IV., 5, 54, 55, 97, **129,** 144, 155, 168, 170, 185, 263, 269, 278–280, 284, 301
"Philalethes," IV., 118
"Philanthrop," II., 121, 125, 148–152, 162, 329, 330
"Philanthrop, Jun.," II., 329
Phillips, William, II., 18; III., 63, 85, 134, 135, 411
Phillips, Capt., II., 71
Phips, William, I., 126
Pickering, John, Jr., II., 19; III., **78**
Pierpont, Robert, I., 321
Pitt, William, I., 82, 332; II., 301, 347
Pitts, John, III., 220, **255, 300, 359, 385;** IV., **147,** 173, 241
Pittsfield, Mass., III., 182
Plymouth, Mass., I., **71,** 162; II., 349, **394;** III., 33, **71,** 113; IV., 125, 170
Pole, de la, II., 235
Pope, Alexander, IV., 260
"Populus," I., **378**
Port Egmont, II., 168
Porter, Elisha, IV., 6
Portsmouth, N. H., III., 80, 93, **106,** 109, 121, 259, 373, 401; IV., 155, 162–164
Portsmouth, Va., III., 174; IV., 218
Portugal, I., 32, 63; III., 367
Powell, Jeremiah, IV., **93,** 152

Pownall, Thomas, I., 127, 396; II., 46, 196; III., 172; IV., 238
Prescott, William, III., 227
Preston, Thomas, II., 14–18, 35, 59, 77–79, 81, 89, 91, 93, 103, 112, 126, 130, 136, 137, 139, 140, 146–148, 154–161; III. 99, 199,
Princeton, N. J., III., 324, 377
Privy Council, I., 99, 354
"Probus," II., 43, 44, 70
Proctor, Colonel, III., 394
Providence, R. I., II., 389, 396; III., 80, 93, 109, 121, 215, 253, 254, 364; IV., 159, 161
Providence, The, IV., 150, 164
Prussia, IV., 10, 127
Puffendorf, Samuel, II., 437
"Puritan," I., **201, 203, 208**
Purviance, Robert, III., 223, 224, 353
Purviance, Samuel, III., **202,** 203, 204, 223, 224, 333, 352
Putnam, Israel, III., 316, 327, 329
Pym, William, I., 58

Q

Quebec, I., 59; II., 395; III., **182,** 185–187, 267, 311, 332; IV., 277
Queen of France, The, IV., 44 120, 150, 164, 166
Quibbletown, N. J., III., 378
Quincy, Josiah, III., 14, 156

R

Raleigh, Walter, II., 405
Randolph, Edward, I., 72; II., 206, 248, 418, 419
Randolph, Peyton, I., 188; III., 109, 224
Randolph, Richard, III., **175**
Ranger, The, IV., 150, 164
Raritan River, N. J., III., 375, 377
Read, George, III., 14, **189,** 223
Reed, Jonathan, III., 14
Reed, I., 446
Representation, I., 4, 5, 17, 24, 25, 30, 46, 68, 151, 158, 165, 175, 178, 182, 186, 191, 198, 282; II., 261
Resistance, The, IV., 44, 66
Revenge, The, IV., 144

Revere, Paul, III., 72, 108, 122 125, 156, 163, 172, 248, **393**
Rhode Island, I., 188, 302, 316; II., 284, 297, 306, 389, 390, 394, 395, 397, 398, 400; III., 27, 60, 109, 117, 326, 330, 331, 345, 382, 396, 398; IV., 54, 60, 61, 62, 64, 80, 151, 153, **174,** 175, 202
Richard II., II., 30
Richardson, Ebenezer, I., 96; II., 60
Richmond, Ezra, I., 184
Richmond, Duke of, II., 10
Rights of the Colonists, The, II., 350
Ritchie, Archibald, III., 200
Rivington, James, IV., 246, 259, 260
Roberdeau, Daniel, III., 418; IV., 12
Robinson, Col., I., 372
Robinson, John, I., 316, 380, 381, 382, 383, 384, 385, 386, 424; II., 11, 16
Rochambeau, John B. D., IV., 202, 406,
Rockingham, Marquis of, I., 152, **169;** II., 141
Rodney, Caesar, I., 58
Rogers, Robert, III., 317
Rogers, Theophilus, III., 134
Romane, IV., 1
Romanet, IV., 14
Rome, II., 41, 207, 251, 255; III., 163, 179; IV., 29
Romney, The, I., 236, 409, 422; II., 240, 241, 243
Rotch, Francis, III., 72, 75
Rowe, John, I., 8, 12
Rowley, Mass., III., 17
Roxbury, Mass., I., 424; II., 340, 349; III., **69,** 74, 109, 222, 227
Ruddock, John, I., 1, 8, 73
Ruggles, Timothy, II., 171
Russell, Lord, IV., 73
Russell, Nathaniel, II., 157
Russia, III., 330, 332, 367; IV., 127, 233
Rutland, Mass., III., 16

S

Sackville, George, III., 370
Salem, Mass., I., 206; II., 23, 342, 347; III., 78, 80, 106, 108, 143, 151, 164; IV., 143, 165, 202

Salisbury, Conn., III., 357, 358
Sally, The, III., 191, 201
Saltonstal, Dudley, IV., 154
Sanderman, Robert, III., 173
Sandis, Edwin, II., 436
Sandwich, Mass., III., 72, 181
Sandy Hook, N. J., IV., 47
Santee River, IV., 207
Saratoga, N. Y., IV., 164
Saunders, Thomas, I., 106
Savage, Samuel P., III., 277;
  IV., **49, 61, 67, 86, 92,** 123
Savage, William, III., 200
Savannah, Ga., III., 139, 140
Savit, Aaron, III., 14
Sayre, Stephen, II., **56, 66, 134,**
  164
Schuyler, Philip, III., 228, 296,
  308, 330, 335, 336, 387, 388,
  390, 391, 395, 396, 398, 401–
  404, 407; IV., 261
Scollay, John, III., 73, **285, 365,**
  IV., 170, **236**
Scollay, Miss, III., 364; IV., 170
Scotland, II., 53
Scott, Captain, III., 73
Scott, John M., IV., **179**
Seabury, Samuel, I., 322–331
Searle, James, IV., 199
Selkrig, James, II., 99, 122, 123,
  124
Seneca Indians, IV., 29
Sessions, Darius, II., **389, 395,**
  401, **427**
Shattuck, William, III., 225
Sheafe, Edward, I., 71, 114, 153
Shelburne, Earl of, I., 104, **152,**
  166, 214, 332, 357; II., 347;
  III., 103, 119; IV., 100, 106,
  130, 136
Shelburne, Mass., I., 316
Shepherd, James, IV., 207
Sherman, Roger, III., **404;** IV.,
  74
"Shippen," I., **297**
Shirley, William, I., 126, 127;
  III., 172
Shute, Samuel, I., 127
Simpson, Josiah, II., 131
Sinapunxint, III., 405, 407
"Sincerus," III., 261
Skeensborough, III., 310
Skene, Philip, III., 249
Skinner, Cortland, I., 188
Smith, III., 267

Smith, John, I., **39, 48, 56**
Smith, Samuel, III., 155
Snider, II., 60
Snow Bird, The, III., 253
Society of the Bill of Rights, III.,
  18, 22
Somerset Court House, N. J.,
  III., 372, 375, 377
Somerset county, Md., III., 360
Sourland Hills, III., 375, 377
South Carolina, I., 108, 188;
  III., 26, 142, 143, 151, 164,
  198, 233, 281, 302, 319, 323,
  345, 384, 410; IV., 113, 126,
  207, 234, 235, 285, 296, 300,
  405
Spain, I., 32, 63; II., 244, 288,
  289, 395; III., 254, 334, 337,
  343, 367, 400; IV., 89, 119,
  165
Sparhawk, Nathan, I., 106; III., 16
Sparta, III., 163
Spencer, Earl of, II., 439
Spencer, Joseph, III., 331
Spottsylvania county, Va., III.,
  193, 194
Springfield, Mass., III., 294; IV.,
  165, 205
St. Asaph's, Bishop of, III., 45
St. Clair, Arthur, III., 390, 392,
  396, 398, 401, 402, 404
St. Eustatia, III., 190, 191, 201,
  216, 350
St. John, III., 241, 310
St. Lawrence River, III., 275,
  278, 279
St. Vincent, III., 264
Staten Island, N. Y., III., 297
Statutes:
  "Magna Charta," I., 16, 19, 20,
    24, 28, 30, 65, 288, 289; II.,
    53, 324, 326, 355, 420, 421,
    435; III., 262
  "Molasses Act," I., 31, 62, 391
  "Stamp Act," I., 30, 31, 35,
    43, 44, 52, 56, 69, 73, 136, 138,
    200, 203, 244, 356
  "Boston Port Act," III., 106,
    107, 109, 111, 116, 117, 119,
    120, 124, 136, 141, 151, 160,
    169, 170, 174, 175, 178, 181,
    187, 190, 192, 193, 204, 210,
    225, 284
  "Quebec Act," III., 187
  25 Edw. III., II., 390

Statutes—(*Continued*)
25 Hen. VIII., c. 21, II., 182
1 Jas. I., I., 46, 55
2 Wm. & Mary, c. 18, II., 355
7 & 8 Wm. & Mary, II., 443
13 Geo. II., I., 24, 65
13 Geo. II., c. 7, I., 141, 155; II., 358
14 Geo. II., c. 37, II., 451
4 Geo. III., c., 15, I., 136; II., 52
6 Geo. III., c. 12, I., 136
7 Geo. III., c. 41, I., 146
7 Geo. III., c. 46, I., 136; II., 53, 181
7 Geo. III., c. 59, I., 147; and see II., 362, 366, 367, 417; III., 4, 5, 142, 160, 170, 195; IV., 27
Stedman, Ebenezer, II., 392
Stephens, Major, III., 391
Stephenson, IV., 40
Sterling, Lord, III., 316
Steuben, Baron, IV., 7, 10, **39**
Steven, General, III., 390
Stewart, Walter, III., 335, **336**, 338, **357**
Stillwater, N. Y., III., 405
Stockton, Richard, III., 298
Stone, Josiah, III., **35**
Stone River, IV., 235
Storer, Ebenezer, II., 18
Story, I., 60
Story, William, II., 237, 245, 246
Stoughton, William, II., 446
Strafford, Earl of, II., 235
Stringer, Samuel, III., 345
Suffolk county, Mass., II., 8; IV., 158
Suffolk Resolves, III., 156, 158
Sullivan, James, III., **257**
Sullivan, John, III., 372, 377; IV., 60, 80
Sumner, Captain, II., 19
Sumner, Increase, IV., 404
Sweden, II., 373; III., 275; IV., 257
Sydney, Algernon, IV., 73
Symmes, Captain, III., 38

T

"T. Z.," I., **282**
Tabb, Jonathan, III., **178**
Taxation, I., 3–5, 8–10, 15, 16,
24, 25, 30, 32, 39–42, 44, 57
68, 69, 136, 138, 139, 142,
157–159, 165, 175, 178, 184,
186 221, 243, 282, 375, 387,
389; II., 47, 178, 180, 235, 300,
315, 360, 363; III., 16, 54, 68,
129; IV., 23
Taylor, Colonel, I., 126
Temple, John, I., 316; IV., 54, 55, 56, 95, 96, 99–104, 106, 108–110
Thacher, Oxenbridge, I., 1
Thacher, Peter, III., 412; IV., **50**
Thaxter, John, IV., 271
Thayer, Captain, II., 19
Thomson, Charles, III., **122**, **133**
Thornton, George, III., **193**, 225
Ticonderoga, N. Y., III., 310, 330, 332, 358, 390, 391, 395, 397, 400, 402, 404, 407; IV., 17, 164
Timothy, Peter, II., **64**; III., **147**
Tobey, Captain, III., 181
Tompkins, Captain, III., 175, 176, 191
"Tory, A.," II., **62**
Townshend, Charles, I., 260
Trade, Regulation of, I., 3, 4, 31, 42, 43, 62, 63, 114, 142, 159, 193–195, 217, 303, 378, 379, 393–395; II., 4, 58, 62, 65, 275, 313, 323, 361, 366; III., 68, 126, 131, 138, 145; IV., 7
Trecothick, Barlow, I., 397
Trecothick & Apthorp, II., 306
Trenton, N. J., III., 344, 383
Tresilian, Robert, II., 31, 32
Trowbridge, Edmund, I., 101; II., 77; III., 50, 51, 98
Trumbull, Jonathan, III., 336, **357**, 358; IV., **15**, 60, **74**, **120**, **152**, 154, 165, 192, 194, 195
Trumbull, Jonathan, Jr., III., 307; IV., 74, 287, 290
Trumbull, Joseph, III., **306**, 417
Tryon, William, II., 197; III., 275, 278
Tudor, Owen, I., 279
Tullius, II., 437
Turner, Charles, III., 45
Tuscarora Indians, IV., 29
Tyler, Royall, I., 1, 12
Tyng, William, I., 239

U

Union Club, III., **164**

United States, Constitution, IV., 324, 326, 331, 333, 335, 345, 357, 389, 400
United States *v.* Wong Kim Ark, II., 439
Upshaw, Jonathan, III., **200**

V

Valentine Hill, III., 316
"Valerius Poplicola," II., **256, 332**
Van Dam, Isaac, III., **190,** 201
Vandyke, Nicholas, III., 189
Varick, Richard, III., 391
Vattel, Emmerich, II., 258, 323, 325, 326, 356; III., 266
Veazey, Jonathan, III., 204
Vermont, IV., 180, 183, 193, 196, 203, 204, 264, 265
Versailles, IV., 79, 89, 190, 233
"Vindex," I., **255, 264, 269, 272;** II., **1, 77, 83, 89, 98, 102, 110, 122, 124, 135, 142, 153, 329, 374;** IV., **188**
Virginia, I., 188; II., 193, 205, 236, 405, 406, 408, 409; III., 20, 21, 24, 26, 109, 139, 174–178, 192, 205, 209, 274, 278, 282, 299, 319, 323, 384; IV., 6, 7, 215, 281, 326

W

Wadsworth, John, III., **32**
Walker, Thomas, IV., 10
Walpole, Robert, II., 232
Ward, Artemas, IV., 227, 249
Ward, III., 384
Warren, James, III., **92, 111, 219, 232, 243, 250, 254, 268, 288, 299, 300,** 306, **321, 322, 329, 337, 340,** 342, **346, 350, 355, 360, 373, 375, 379, 395, 398, 406;** IV., **41, 45, 52, 58, 68, 72, 75, 88,** 97, **113, 123, 139,** 170, 187, 199, **207, 212, 221, 242**
Warren, John, IV., 169
Warren, Joseph, I., 397; II., 10, 11, 163, 342, 350, 370, 394; III., 25, 63, 77, **156, 157,** 196, 199, 220, 353; IV., 171, 236
Warren, Joseph, Jr., IV., 169, 172
Warren, The, IV., 150, 154
Washington, Charles, III., **193,** 225
Washington, George, III., 218, 219, 248, 249, 254, **290, 326,**
330, 331, 334, 338, 342, 344, 375, 377, 383, 385, 397, 398, 399, 402, 411; IV., 10, 83, 140, **150, 165,** 191–195, 202, 204, 246, 265, 293, 301, 314, 336, 337, 402
Washington, Jonathan A., III., **210**
Waterhouse, S., IV., 143
Waters, III., 227
Watertown, Mass., III., 225, 226, 238, 268, 269, 272, 293, 312, 355, 356
Watkins, Benjamin, III., **176**
Watson, III., 92–94
Weare, Meshech, IV., **155**
Webb, Colonel, IV., 9
Webster, Noah, IV., **303**
Wellington, Roger, III., 152
Wells, Andrew Elton, II., **337;** III., **146,** 216
Wells, Colonel, III., 391
Wells, Elizabeth, III., 214; IV., 223
Wells, Samuel, I., 7, 12
Wells, Samuel, III., 216, 319
Wells, Samuel A., I., 153, 342; II., 14, 56, 64, 66
Wells, Thomas, IV., 56, **223**
Wendel, Oliver, III., 106
Wentworth, Benning, I., 328, 329, 330
Wentworth, John, III., 106
West, Zebulon, I., 188
West Florida, III., 140
West Indies, I., 59; III., 115, 120, 254; IV., 81, 89, 179, 231, 296
Westerly, R. I., III., 121
Westfield, N. J., III., 378
Westminster, I., 17, 58, 237; II., 53, 209
Westmoreland county, Va., III., 210; IV., 241
West Point, N. Y., IV., 192, 193, 196
Wethersfield, Conn., III., 149
Weymouth, Mass., III., 33, 34, 260
Whately, Thomas, III., 171
Whipple, William, III., 311, 327, 331, 336, 359, 373, 375, 403
Whitcomb, John, III., 391
White Plains, N. Y., III., 316
Whitfield, George, IV., 237
Whitmarsh, Ezra, III., **33**

Whittemore, Lieutenant, III., 310
Wilkes, John, II., **100**; III., 23, 36
Wilkinson, II., 145, 147
Willard, Joseph, IV., 270
William III., I., 154, 163, 317; II., 73, 363, 448–450; III., 160
Williams, Colonel, III., 406
Williams, Ezekiel, III., **149**
Williams, Israel, III., 148, 149, 153
Williams, John, I., 244
Williams, Josiah, II., **69**
Williams, II., 161
Williams, IV., 270
Williamsburg, Va., III., 224
Williamson, Hugh, III., 76, 97
Wilson, James, III., 225
Wilson, Captain, I., 212, 213
Winthrop, John, IV., **101, 121**
Witherspoon, John, III., 298
Wood, Captain, III., 102, 103

Wood, III., 145
Wood, Joseph, II., 13
Woodbridge, N. J., III., 323
Wooster, David, III., 331
Worcester, Mass., I., 210; III., **50,** 132, 215, 218, 356
Worcester county, Md., III., 360
Wrentham, Mass., IV., 151
Wylly, Alexander, I., 188
Wythe, George, III., 260

Y

Yancey, IV., 285
York county, Me., IV., 161, 163
York, Me., I., 207
York, Pa., IV., 24, 48, 129
Young, Thomas, III., **162**
Young, II., 374, 376, 377, 378, 386

Z

Zwingli, Ulrich, II., 250

CORRIGENDA.

Page 155, line 28, Lovett (as in the text used) *should read* Lovell.

Page 205, line 10, *for* punctural *read* punctual.

Page 273, line 22, Lord *should read* Lovell, *and the first foot-note should accordingly be omitted.*

Page xv., 8th entry, *for* 360 *read* 361.